Simon Frith

D0376103

Performing
On the Value of Popular Music
Rites

Harvard University Press Cambridge, Massachusetts

This book is for Gill.

First Harvard University Press paperback edition, 1998

Library of Congress Cataloging-in-Publication Data

Frith, Simon.
Performing rites : on the value of popular music / Simon Frith.
p.   cm.
Includes bibliographical references and index.
ISBN 0-674-66195-8 (cloth)
ISBN 0-674-66196-6 (pbk.)
1. Music and society.   2. Popular music—History and criticism.
3. Music—Philosophy and aesthetics.   I. Title.
ML3795.F738   1996
781.64′117—dc20   96-1121

Contents

....

Acknowledgments

The arguments in this book started as a course on the aesthetics of popular music at McGill University in Montreal in 1987. I'm grateful to my students for their help and tolerance, to the Graduate Program in Communications for inviting me to Canada, and to Will Straw and Sylvie Roux for all the talk, love, and music. I further developed my ideas (and took the opportunity to bury myself in a wonderful library) while a Senior Fellow at the Society for the Humanities, Cornell University, in 1991. I'm grateful to Jonathan Culler and Martin Hatch for this opportunity; to the students in my course on "The Good and Bad in Popular Culture"; to my fellow followers of pop fashion, Alex Doty, Karal Ann Marling, Rachel Bowlby, Jane Feuer, Nöel Carroll, and Sally Banes; and to Aggie Sirrine, Mary Ahl, and Linda Allen for making our time in the A. D. White House such fun. The first draft of the book was written while I was the visiting Bonnier Professor of Journalism at the University of Stockholm in 1994. My thanks to Peter Dahlgren and Mark Cormerford for their hospitality, to Marianne and Philippa Scheffold for a room of my own (in a house full of friendship), and to Johan Fornäs, Hillevi Ganetz, and Roger and Goral Wallis for sounds, food, and argument.

My graduate students at the John Logie Baird Centre since 1989 will, I hope, recognize how much they've contributed to my understanding of popular music, and I'm very grateful also to my colleagues John Caughie (for his unflagging enthusiasm for our work) and Sandra Kemp (for making me think properly about performance). None of this would be possible without the support of Margaret Philips, who, among other things, keeps us from taking ourselves too seriously.

In writing this I have become increasingly aware of my dependence on the work of IASPM (the International Association for the Study of Popular Music) and *Popular Music*. I'm proud to have been closely associated with both, and I hope that my intellectual debts to my fellow scholars are evident in what follows.

Many of my ideas on the value of popular music were first floated in my Britbeat column in the *Village Voice*, and I'm grateful to my editors there—Doug Simmons, Joe Levy, and Robert Christgau—for giving them a clearer shape. I've also learned much from my role as chair of the Mercury Music Prize—thanks to my fellow judges for the disputes, and to David Wilkinson, Robert Chandler, and Samm Gibson for the support. My editor at Harvard University Press, Lindsay Waters, has been more patient than even an academic author could expect; I'm grateful for his faith that there was a book here somewhere, and to Bruce Phillips at Oxford University Press for his graceful agreement.

As ever, my thoughts on music (and much else) have been much stimulated and challenged by my friends Jon Savage, Greil Marcus, and Gill Frith, and I am particularly in debt to a friend I've never met, Frank Kogan, for a correspondence that has made me, again and again, stop and rethink. Finally, Deborah Cameron and Wendy Wolf read my original manuscript with as sharp and critical eyes as I could wish—if the book now works it is thanks to their advice; if it doesn't it is due to my obstinacy.

Some of the material here first appeared in article form: "What Is Good Music," *Canadian University Music Review* 10(2), 1990; "The Good, the Bad, and the Indifferent: Defending Popular Culture from the Populists," *diacritics* 21(4), 1991; "Adam Smith and Music," *New Formations* 18, 1992; "Representatives of the People: Voices of Authority in Popular Music," *Mediterranean Music Cultures and Their Ramifications* (Madrid: Sociedad Española de Musicología, 1994); "What Is Bad Music?" *Musiken år 2002* 11 (Stockholm: Kungl. Musikaliska Akademien, 1994); "The Body Electric," *Critical Quarterly* 37(3), 1995; "Introduction: Performance Matters," *New Formations* 27, 1995; "Music and Identity," in Stuart Hall and Paul du Gay, eds., *Questions in Cultural Identity* (London: Sage, 1996).

Music Talk

The Value Problem in Cultural Studies

I used never to weep at Great Art, at Couperin or Kirkegaard, maintaining it was too multidimensional for the specific of tears. I wept at the rapid associative revelations of a Piaf, or at Lana Turner's soapy dilemmas. Crying was caused hence by entertainment, not masterworks.

Today tears dictate my first judgment of any works, their levels be damned. What counts is to be kinetically moved. And who says Edith and Lana aren't art—or, if they are, that Kierkegaard is more so?

Ned Rorem[1]

There is no way possible that Poison can EVER be on top. Them little underdeveloped chromoshoes don't got cock big enough to fuck an ant. So all you fucking whores out there who praise the ground Poison walks on are in shit. METALLICA RULES and that will never change.

Letter from LaDonna to *Metal Mania*, May 1990[2]

It was my third night in Stockholm, a very cold February night, and I'd gone to have supper with old friends, people I see maybe every two years, usually at conferences. There was one other guest, the professor in the department in which I was a visiting scholar, a man I hadn't met before. A few years older than I am, I'd guess; just as Johan Fornäs and Hillevi Ganetz are a few years younger. We talked, we ate, and about halfway through the main course, Johan said, "Let me play it to you!" and jumped over to the CD player.

The rest of the evening was driven by the dialectic of liking things. We ate, we talked, and at least some of the time (this wasn't an obsessive boys' night in, rock critics pouring over the runes) we argued about music. As hosts, Johan and Hillevi had the advantage—they could illustrate their claims

3

(why someone could or couldn't sing; why the Flesh Quartet were Sweden's most amusing band; why Eva Dahlgren's latest album was more interesting than it first sounded). I could only respond—"Yeah, that's really good"; "No, I don't like that at all"—and write down titles, and ask occasionally, "Have you heard . . .? I must tape it for you."

A mundane and enjoyable evening, in short, not unlike Sunday evening suppers happening all over this and many other cities; and if the conversations elsewhere weren't necessarily about music they would almost certainly have been, at some point, about books or films or TV programs, about footballers or models or magazines. Such conversations are the common currency of friendship, and the essence of popular culture. We may have been a group of intellectuals, used to talking, to arguing publicly for our prejudices, but similar talk can be heard every day in bars and on buses, on football terraces and in school yards, as people wait at the hairdresser or take lunch in the office cafeteria, and have conversations about last night's TV, Take That's hit record, the new Clint Eastwood film, the latest headline in the *Sun*.

Part of the pleasure of popular culture is talking about it; part of its meaning is this talk, talk which is run though with value judgments. To be engaged with popular culture is to be discriminating, whether judging the merits of a football team's backs or an afternoon soap's plots. "Good" and "bad" or their vernacular versions ("brilliant," "crap") are the most frequent terms in everyday cultural conversation. I will be saying much more about this later, but to return to that Stockholm evening for a moment, two further features of our talk need noting. First, though all of us knew well enough that what was at issue was personal taste, subjective response, we also believed, passionately at times, that we were describing something objectively *in the music*, if only other people could hear it. Value arguments, in other words, aren't simply rituals of "I like/you like" (which would quickly become tedious, even in *Metal Mania*); they are based in reason, evidence, persuasion. Every music fan knows that moment of frustration when one can only sit the person down and say (or, rather, shout) despairingly, "But just listen to her! Isn't she fantastic!"

But if value judgments in popular culture make their own claims to objectivity (to being rooted, that is, in the quality of objects), their subjectivity can't be denied either—not, however, by banal reference to people having their own (essentially irrational) likes and dislikes, but because such judgments are taken to tell us something about the person making them. I was struck that evening in Sweden by how little the professor contributed to the talk about music (he talked engagingly about everything else), not, I think, because he was uninterested (I discovered later that he was a great jazz fan, a gifted amateur jazz pianist), nor because he didn't have things to say, but because he didn't really know me: he could not yet judge how an argument about music might affect the evening's good will.

In his pioneering sociological study of literary taste, Levin Schücking comments on the importance of books for the shifts in courtship rituals in late nineteenth century Germany: "Here, in reading together, the opportunity was gained of securing from the other's judgement of men and things an insight into thoughts and feelings; an insight likely to become the first bond between kindred souls."[3] And nowadays listening to music, watching television, and going to movies together serve similar functions. We assume that we can get to know someone through their tastes (eyeing someone's book and record shelves the first time we visit them, waiting nervously to see what a date says as we come out of a movie or a concert). Cultural judgments, in other words, aren't just subjective, they are self-revealing, and to become another person, to fake ourselves for whatever reason, means having to pretend to like things in which we find nothing valuable at all—a problem, as Pierre Bourdieu points out, for people attempting to *buy* cultural capital, and a secret shame, as Frank Kogan suggests, for those of us who have ever tried to impress new friends.

The point is not that we want friends or lovers just like us; but we do need to know that conversation, argument, is possible. In the pop world this is most obvious to musicians, who have to get along well enough to play together, who have to balance the creative/destructive effects of shared and different tastes, and who conduct the delicate business of coming together (and falling apart) almost entirely through stated pop judgments:

> Me and Graham thought that King was terrible but The Three Johns were great; we go down the pub and Malc and Chris thought King was great and hated The Three Johns—that said it all really so we split up.

> We were into bands like Bryan Adams and King, whilst Clint and Ad were into The Three Johns and The Shop Assistants. It was just no good.[4]

As Pat Kane (from Hue and Cry) concludes:

> Everybody has a theory of pop—not least those who make it. Even the least self-conscious of artists can be jolted into an extended analysis of "what's good about rock'n'roll," if you trade the wrong reference with them. There is a real evaluative disdain when two musicians react opposingly to the same source. "How can you

love/hate Van Morrison/Lou Reed/Springsteen/Stevie Wonder/ Kraftwerk? These people are/are not 'great popular music.' How can you say otherwise?" I have suffered (and inflicted) the worst aesthetic hauteur, as my opponent and I push each other to our fundamentalist positions. You are a rocker, I am a soulboy; you find solace in raw-throated guitar release, I am consoled by the bubbling symmetry of a Muscle Shoals rhythm section. Different planets, Kiddo.[5]

For fans, whose musical values don't matter so much, or, rather, matter in different ways, with different consequences, trading pop judgments is a way to "flirt and fight." As Frank Kogan suggests, this means that for the pop listener (if not for the pop player) the stability of our judgments matters less than their constant deployment: as pop fans we continually change our minds about what is good or bad, relevant or irrelevant, "awesome" or "trivial" (our judgment in part determined by what happens to a sound in the marketplace, how successful it becomes, what other listeners it involves), but we never cease to believe that such distinctions are necessary "social pressure points, gathering spots for a brawl over how we use our terms. If our comparisons stood still, how could we have our brawl?"[6]

As I was leaving that supper party I got involved in a dispute about the Pet Shop Boys, which delayed me in the hall for another twenty minutes. "But *you* like disco!" said Hillevi, in mock dismissal, as I left. I got back to my room and put on *Very.*

It *is* a good record. What makes the Pet Shop Boys special is their sense of musical space. Using what is, in fact, a rather limited repertory of sounds (a thin lead voice; the most superficial resources of the digital synthesizer—supporting noise tends to be buried deep in the mix), the Pets conjure up a remarkable variety of soundscapes—the dance floor obviously, but also shops and cars and flats and dreams; on "To Speak is a Sin," for example, the discreet bar setting is prepared with the care of a high-class set designer and lighting cameraman.

One reason for the effectiveness of the Pets' approach to songs as scenes is that the duo realized from the start that computerized instruments freed sounds from a performance context. (Other electronic groups have, of course, come to the same conclusion—Kraftwerk and Yello most obviously. In this, as in their disco tastes, the Pets are continentally European; other British electro duos, Blancmange and Tears for Fears and even Erasure, have never quite shaken off a sense of being boy boffins in their bedrooms.) Most other forms of rock and pop bear the traces of their construction (of their ideal, imagined, construction, that is to say). Even on record a concerto means a concert hall, a chamber piece a drawing room, an opera an opera house; just as jazz means a jazz club, a big band a dance hall, a rock band a pub back-room or stadium. But because electronic sounds aren't produced like this, even in pop fantasy, they tend to be as much associated with musical consumption as musical production, consumption that isn't confined either to the disco or dance club (as later rave, house, and acid musics are) or to the living room, but describes, rather, the way in which all-around sounds are absorbed (like rap) into daily urban life. (And so in their "live" shows the Pet Shop Boys have had to go to great trouble, hiring filmmakers and stage designers, to put on musical events that don't feel like pop concerts at all.)

The Pets' musical appeal is rooted in this sense of mobile space, in the use of sounds which as both texture and hook surprise us by their very familiarity. But this sonic reassurance is overlaid with (or, perhaps, makes possible) an unusual pop sensibility: the Pet Shop Boys, unlike most rock groups, seem to be listening to their own numbers, to be picking up their own references and ambiguities. This means that their music is always funny (a surprisingly unusual quality in pop), most obviously here in the camp utopianism of their version of Village People's "Go West": Neil Tennant's effete voice sets off the chorus of butch baritones, whom I can't help hearing as a shipful of Russian sailors from a 1920s Soviet film. But there's also a profoundly regretful undertow to the Pets' ironies, a regret permanently lodged in the rhythmic hesitations of Chris Lowe's keyboard lines, in Tennant's flat tones. This means that Pet songs, for all their simple pop forms, are run through with emotional tension. "One in a Million" is thus a straight-forward breaking-up song—if you've got to go, you've got to go—but with a chilling threat: only "one in a million men can change the way you feel," how sure are you that you'll find another one besides me? "Young Offender," an older man's love song to a younger one, leaves one confused as to which lover is, in the end, more physically, emotionally, and aesthetically vulnerable: "who will give who the bigger surprise?" "Dreaming of the Queen" shifts from the cheeky, silly image of "you and Her and I," joined at tea by Lady Di, to a sober sense of the romantic landscape of AIDS, as the Queen says (troubled mother), "I'm aghast, love never seems to last," and Di replies (worldly wise) that "there are no more lovers left alive."

Now this is to read images into the lyrics that may not be there (always a pleasure of pop), but the underlying, troubled feelings are there—in the sighing quality of the Pets' pop voice, in the brittle elegance of their arrangements. It's as if the Pet Shop Boys are both quite detached from their music—one is aware of the sheer craftiness of their songs—and completely implicated by it: they suggest less that they have been touched by the banality of love than by the banality of love songs; they seem to understand the fear as well as the joy of sex (fear and joy which always lie in the *anticipation* of the physical moment); they capture the anxiety of fun. Their gayness is less significant here (at least for a heterosexual fan) than their emotional fluency; it's as if the spaces they occupy are actually frozen moments in time, the moments just before and just after emotion (which is why this is disco music with an intensely intellectual appeal), the moments which the best pop music has always defined (nothing else can stop time like this). Listen to any Pet Shop Boys track and you know that they too have had their life reduced to a single catch in the voice, a single melodic phrase (here, for me, the opening of "Liberation") that must be played again and again. They know that in this sort of music it is such surface noise that resonates most deeply in our lives.

In writing about the Pet Shop Boys this way (wearing my rock critic's hat) I'm not actually saying much that I haven't already said to friends, Pet lovers and haters alike. Note the knowledge I'm assuming, about the Pets' own history and sexuality, about disco music, about other electronic sounds. Pop judgment is a double process: our critical task, as fans, is first to get people to listen to the right things (hence all these references to other groups and sounds), and only then to persuade them to like them. Our everyday arguments about music are concentrated on the first process: getting people to listen the right way. Only when we can accept that someone is hearing what we're hearing but just doesn't value it will we cede to subjective taste and agree that there's no point to further argument. Popular cultural arguments, in other words, are not about likes and dislikes as such, but about ways of listening, about ways of hearing, about ways of being.

The importance of value judgment for popular culture thus seems obvious, but it has been quite neglected in academic cultural studies. I will examine some of the reasons why in this chapter, but I should begin by confessing my own failure in this respect. I may have spent the last twenty years writing pop and rock criticism, judging records for a living, but I have tended to keep such arguments (plunging assertively into fan talk at the bar and in the record store) out of my academic work. I am well aware, to put this another way, of the reasons why value questions are difficult to raise in the cultural studies classroom, journal, and textbook. A couple of weeks after that supper party, for example, I argued in a graduate seminar that academics had a duty to make (rather than evade) value judgments when teaching popular culture. Not to say that Charles Dickens was better than Barbara Cartland (which I certainly believe) seemed to me to be not only dishonest and/or condescending to one's students, but also to evade an important analytic problem, how judgment works in all cultural spheres. Hillevi Ganetz, with whom I'd been arguing about the Pet Shop Boys just a few nights earlier, in a conversation in which we'd flung around "good" and "bad" words with ready abandon, strongly disagreed, saying that such a statement of personal preference had no sanctioned place in the classroom; it begged too many questions—"better" for whom or for what?

In the subsequent seminar discussion what became clear to me was that the issue wasn't really value but authority: the question was not whether Barbara Cartland (or the Pet Shop Boys) are any good or not, but who has the authority to say so. Now in everyday terms this isn't necessarily a problem—one could define popular culture as that cultural sector in which all participants claim the authority to pass judgment; no one needs to be licensed by study or qualification to speak "authoritatively." In practice, though, there clearly are people—loosely defined as "fans"—who do claim precisely that their superior knowledge, experience, and commitment give their judgments a particular weight: this is how both rock critics and season ticket holders to football games claim a special attention. There is such a thing, in other words, as popular cultural capital, which is one reason why fans are so annoyed by critics, not just for having different opinions but for having public sanction to state them.

Pierre Bourdieu's argument in *Distinction* is that the accumulation of cultural knowledge and experience—through education, as part of one's upbringing—enhances the richness and pleasure of the reading of cultural texts, not least because of the pleasure of displaying one's superior enjoyment and discrimination. His interest, though, is in the creation of a taste hierarchy in terms of high and low: the possession of cultural capital, he suggests, is what defines high culture in the first place. My point is that a similar use of accumulated knowledge and discriminatory skill is apparent in low cultural forms, and has the same hierarchical effect. Low culture, that is to say, generates its own capital—most obviously, perhaps, in those forms (such as dance club cultures) which are organized around exclusiveness, but equally significantly for the fans (precisely those people who have invested time and money in the accumulation of knowledge) of even the most inclusive forms—sports or soap operas, say. Such fans certainly do claim, with good justification, to have a richer experience of their particular pleasure than "ordinary" or "passive" consumers, and this is one reason why it is problematic to take fans as ordinary consumers, as models for popular cultural "resistance" (a concept to which I will return).[7]

But if there are forms of popular cultural authority—represented by fans, determined by institutions (critics, deejays, and A&R departments, for example, all explicitly engage in popular musical discrimination)[8]—these are not easy to exercise in the classroom, where everyday questions of the good and the bad are entangled with academic concepts of the high and the low.

In his book *Origins of Popular Style,* the musicologist Peter Van Der Merwe suggests that "reviewing the popular music of the twentieth century as a whole, most people would probably agree that some of it is excellent, some unbearable and most of it very indifferent. What the good, bad and indifferent share is a musical language."[9] Most people probably would agree with this; disagreement would be about which records and songs and performers were good, which bad, which indifferent. But, as Van der Merwe points out, aesthetic arguments are possible only when they take place within a shared critical discourse, when they rest on an agreement as to what "good" and "bad" music mean—the argument, that is to say, is not about the labels but about what should be so labeled.

Take, for example, the following confident statements. "Rock music," writes rightist cultural critic Allan Bloom in *The Closing of the American Mind,* "has one appeal only, a barbaric appeal, to sexual desire—not love, not *eros,* but sexual desire undeveloped and untutored . . . these are [its] three great lyrical themes: sex, hate and a smarmy, hypocritical version of brotherly love."[10] "The rock critic," writes leftist cultural critic Mark Crispin Miller in the *New York Review of Books,* "struggles to interpret something that requires no interpretation . . . tries to appraise and explicate a music whose artists and listeners are anti-intellectual and usually stoned, and whose producers want more than anything to own several cars."[11] Both writers seem remarkably assured that they know what rock means to its listeners and that the meaning of what they heard (I'm assuming, perhaps wrongly, that both men did listen to rock before holding forth about it) was transparent.

Compare now a different voice. At one point in *The Shoe,* Gordon Legge's fine novel about being a pop fan in Scotland in the 1980s, the central character asks,

> How could people get so worked up about relatives and cars when there were records? Records cut so much deeper. For him *Astral Weeks, Closer,* and *For Your Pleasure* (the three best LPs of all time, [he] said. No contest . . .) articulated the mundanity, despair and joy of existence . . . [He] said his records were the most important things in his life—more important than Celtic [football club] easily . . . It's just that football was easier to talk about for five hours down at the pub on a Saturday night.[12]

Legge's point, with which any pop fan must agree, is that the exercise of taste and aesthetic discrimination is as important in popular as in high culture but is more difficult to talk about. No, that should read: but is more difficult to talk about in terms that are recognized as aesthetic and discriminatory by high cultural authorities. This means that the glib, professional talkers, the Blooms and Millers (and I could multiply examples of such confident statements about the meaning of pop culture from both left and right) have the voices that are heard in the pulpit, the lectern, and the upmarket journal.

This remains the case even after the rise of cultural studies as an academic concern. Contemporary popular culture may now be a familiar topic on the curriculum, but in being constituted as a fit object for study it has become an oddly bloodless affair—the aesthetics of the popular continues to be at best neglected and at worst dismissed. One obvious reason for neglect is that cultural studies emerged from disciplines in which questions of taste and judgment were already kept well away from issues of academic analysis and assessment. Sociologists, anthropologists, and social and cultural historians have always been wary of proclaiming the activities they study as good or bad (such judgments are not their business); perhaps more surprisingly, "evaluation," as Barbara Herrnstein Smith suggests, was also long ago apparently "exiled" from literary criticism.[13]

As I've learned since becoming a professor of English, Smith is clearly right about this (the effects are most dramatic in the literature department–derived subject of film studies, in which students have to be taught in their first week that whether they think a particular film is any good or not is quite irrelevant to its proper analysis), but I wonder whether "exile" is quite the right metaphor here. "Deep entry" may be the more appropriate term, in honor of those Trotskyites whose infiltration of the Labour Party was so disguised that they could never do anything that might reveal that they were not, in fact, just like any other Labour Party members. So values are there in literary criticism, but they must never ever show themselves (or they will, indeed, be "exiled," or, in Labour speak, expelled). This is possible because of the underlying assumption in literary studies that every text studied in a course is valuable, by definition: what is English literature as an academic discipline if not the study of valuable literature? This assumption becomes clear at unexpected (unexpected by me, anyway) moments of staffroom conflict. We can't teach a course in *contemporary* literature, I'm told, we don't yet know which authors and titles are any good.[14] We can't offer a degree course in creative writing, I'm warned, we wouldn't know how to assess it—this from the only group of people in the country who make a full-time living from literary criticism.

It's not so much evaluation that has been exiled from literary criticism, then (and this is Herrnstein Smith's real point), as discussion of evaluation; value, to put this another way, is taken for granted (and is certainly not an issue open to student dispute in the classroom even if it is, as Deborah Cameron put it to me, "the very stuff of their corridor conversation"). Professors of cultural studies can't, one would think, make the same assumption that the underlying value of what they teach is proved by the fact that they teach it, although, even after little more than a decade, it's already surprisingly easy to point to a popular cultural canon, a selection of films, TV shows, ads, stars, performers, genres, sites, and events which are valued primarily for their richness as a subject of academic argument. In film studies, for example, most film teachers do now assume, as I think literature teachers do, that they teach "good films" even if, unlike literature teachers, they can't refer to quite the same general high cultural extra-academic agreement on this.[15] And while cultural studies lecturers themselves may not be deluded that a Barbara Cartland novel or Madonna video, a *Sun* front page or Kleenex ad is aesthetically valuable in itself (as against being effective or semiotically interesting or "good of its kind"), they rarely encourage classroom discussion about what, in this context, "aesthetically valuable in itself" might mean.

Culture as an academic object, in short, is different from culture as a popular activity, a process, and the value terms which inform the latter are, it seems, irrelevant to the analysis of the former. To give a simple example: when Judith Williamson, one of Britain's finest academic cultural theorists, became film critic for the *New Statesman* she immediately faced an insoluble problem. Her (academically derived) approach to films as texts meant treating them, discussing them, as finished, structured objects; readers, however, wanted reasons for watching (or missing) a movie *which didn't give away the plot!*[16]

In universities, then, just as in high schools (and however many pop icons are now pinned up on classroom walls) there is still a split between what Frank Kogan describes as the discourse of the classroom (with its focus on a subject matter) and the discourse of the hallway (with its focus on oneself and one's opinions about a subject matter and one's opinions about other people's opinions about a subject matter and one's opinions about other people).[17]

One consequence is what Joke Hermes calls "the fallacy of meaningfulness," the academic assumption that popular cultural goods must signify something (her research on women's magazines suggested that many of their readers actually valued them for their insignificance, because they were "easy to put down.")[18] Popular culture, to put this point another way, has as much to do with sociability, and how we talk about texts, as with interpretation, and how we read them. In Kogan's terms, in the hallway the question is not what does it mean but what can I do with it; and what I can do with it is what it means—interpretation is a matter of argument, of understanding wrought from social activity.

In the classroom, meanwhile (and despite first impressions), academic approaches to popular culture still derive from the mass cultural critiques of the 1930s and 1940s, and particularly from the Marxist critique of contemporary popular culture in terms of the production and circulation of commodities. For the Frankfurt School, analyzing the organization of mass production, on the one hand, and the psychology of mass consumption, on the other, commercial popular culture was worthless aesthetically, and Adorno and Horkheimer developed a number of concepts (such as standardization and repetition) to show why this must be so. In creating markets for their goods, cultural entrepreneurs developed manipulative sales methods that ensnared consumers in self-delusion, in the continual pursuit of false (and easily satisfied, easily dissatisfied) desire. "If one seeks to find out who 'likes' a commercial piece, one cannot avoid the suspicion that liking and disliking are inappropriate to the situation, even if the person questioned clothes his reactions in those words. The familiarity of the piece is a surrogate for the quality ascribed to it. To like it is almost the same thing as to recognize it." [19]

In broad terms, the analytic response to Frankfurt pessimism has been to accept the organizational account of mass cultural production, to ignore the complexities of Adorno's aesthetic theory, and to look for the redeeming features of commodity culture in the act of consumption. The task, beginning with American liberal sociologists in the 1950s (inspired by the émigré scholar Paul Lazersfeld, who opted to stay in the United States), was to find forms of mass consumption that were not "passive" and types of mass consumers who were not stupefied, to provide a sociology of watching and reading and listening. If it is through consumption that contemporary culture is lived, then it is in the process of consumption that contemporary cultural value must be located.

In the cultural studies tradition with which I am most familiar, British subcultural theory, this reworking of Frankfurt theory took on the particular form of identifying certain social groups with what we might call "positive mass consumption" (which became—and remains—the pithiest current definition of "popular"—as against mass—culture). The value of cultural goods could therefore be equated with the value of the groups consuming them—youth, the working class, women.

The Value Problem in Cultural Studies 13

I want to make two points about this argument (which I have used myself in analyzing rock and roll). First, it remains a highly politicized approach to popular cultural value (this is the key Frankfurt inheritance), whether explicitly, as in the British use of terms like "resistance" and "empowerment," or implicitly, as in the American celebration of opinion leaders and taste publics in the name of a pluralist democracy. The importance of popular culture, in other words, is rooted here in its ideological effects; other ways of valuing a song or film or story, by reference to beauty, craft, or spectacle, are notable for their absence. Cultural value is being assessed according to measures of true and false consciousness; aesthetic issues, the politics of excitement, say, or grace, are subordinated to the necessities of interpretation, to the call for "demystification."

This is a way to solve the authority problem that lies at the heart of the difficulty of discussing cultural values in the classroom. The teacher now has the authority to explain why Madonna videos or *Aliens 2* matter—not by saying whether they're any good or not, but by assessing their ideological implications, which are, paradoxically (this approach began with the importance of what consumers *do*) all there in the text, for the academic analyst (like any good literary critic) to uncover. The 1990s thus saw a boom in the academic Madonna business—the books! the articles! the conferences! the courses! Scouring compulsively through all this material, I couldn't tell whether Madonna was a good singer (as well as a skilled media operative); whether she was an engaging dancer (as well as a semiotic tease); whether I'd actually want to play her records and videos as well as read about them.

In the classroom, then, when a popular text (a TV show or a shopping mall, a Madonna video or a Nirvana CD) is read positively, what's at issue is not its immediate qualities or effects, but the opportunities it offers for further interpretation, for a reading, for a reading *against the grain*. And from this perspective even the judgment that something—a Jeffrey Archer novel, an Andrew Lloyd Webber musical—is "bad" is really a political rather than an aesthetic assessment, a comment on markets, not form.

As cultural studies has established itself as an academic subject, particularly in the United States, there have been obvious signs that it has been "depoliticized," that the original, radical thrust of the Birmingham School in Britain, which was explicitly Marxist and developed cultural studies as a critique of conventional academic subjects like literature, history, and sociology, has been blunted. What was once an argument about cultural class, race and gender conflict, has been translated into a kind of celebratory political pluralism. But if this is depoliticization, it is so in a more complex way than it first appears. After all, John Fiske, who is usually held up as the villain in this narrative, still provides a radical, class-based account of American popular culture (his "populism" is quite different from the cheerful train-spotting version developed over the years at Bowling Green), and the academic rise of cultural studies has meant less a declining interest in cultural politics than its diffusion across a much wider media site—it sometimes seems that for Fiske every act of popular consumption is thereby "resistant."

From the value perspective, then, the problem of populist cultural studies is less its politics than its sociology, its assumption that the "popular" is defined by the market. The populist position is that whatever our (class-bound) personal tastes and values may be, we have to accept that sales figures, box office returns, and record charts tell us what "the people" want. It's only a residual academic elitism that leads us to celebrate the radical or avant-garde; if *The Price is Right* is more popular than *Twin Peaks*, for example, then it must be, culturally, more important. We, as intellectuals, may think *Hill Street Blues* or Martin Scorsese is good; but "the people" clearly use quite different value criteria—they choose *Blind Date* and Stephen Spielberg.

This equation of popular culture with market choice is problematic. It means that "popularity," by default, is consumption as measured by sales figures and market indicators—Nielsen ratings, the music charts, box office returns, best-seller lists, circulation statistics, and so on (figures that in turn become the regulators of popular cultural history). Even if such figures were accurate (which is doubtful), they provide no evidence as to why such goods are chosen by their consumers nor whether they are actually enjoyed or valued by them (it is a common enough experience to go to a blockbuster film, watch a high-rated TV program, read a best-selling book, or buy a chart record that turns out to be quite uninteresting). The elision between what sells and what is popular (the assumption that what sells is therefore "valuable") is obvious in Fiske's account of "popular discrimination," for example. He stresses rightly the inability of mass culture industries to predict or manipulate popular taste (as indicated by the vast number of "failed" records, films, TV shows, magazines, and so forth) but does not question the assumption that a market failure is by definition unpopular or that a market success has by definition a popular audience.[20] In accounts of popular music, at least, this is to ignore the significant unpopularity of certain stars (Meat Loaf, say, or Bryan Adams) and the popular influence of such market failures as Velvet Underground or Joy Division or Neil Young. If nothing else, consumer research among pop fans immediately reveals the intensity with which musics and musicians are loathed as well as loved, and to argue, like Dave Harker, that we need to rethink existing cultural accounts of the 1960s because the soundtrack of *The Sound of Music* topped the British album charts for more weeks than the Beatles, and of the 1970s because punk records sold far less than Elton John LPs, seems to me perverse.[21] Are market choices (as measured somewhat inaccurately by the culture industries' own research devices) really all we mean by "the popular"?

The analytical effect, at any rate, is contempt for the consumers supposedly being celebrated, for their varying tastes and interests. The populist assumption is that all best-selling goods and services are somehow the same in their empowering value (as they are in terms of exchange value); the populist suggestion is that we can somehow equate romance reading and *Star Trek* viewing, Madonna and metal fans, shoppers and surfers. The aesthetic discrimination essential to cultural consumption, and the considered judgments it involves—to buy the new Madonna record or not, to choose Janet Jackson instead—are ignored.

It is hard to avoid the conclusion that the more celebratory the populist study, the more patronizing its tone, an effect, I think, of the explicit populist determination to deny (or reverse) the usual high/low cultural hierarchy. If one strand of the mass cultural critique was an indictment of low culture from the perspective of high art (as was certainly the case for Adorno), then to assert the value of the popular is also, necessarily, to query the superiority of high culture. Most populist writers, though, draw the wrong conclusion from this; what needs challenging is not the notion of the superior, but the claim that it is the exclusive property of the "high."

To deny the significance of value judgments in popular culture (to ignore popular taste hierarchies) is also hypocritical. How often, I wonder, do populist cultural theorists celebrate popular cultural forms which they themselves soon find boring? How are their own feelings for the good and the bad coded into their own analyses? If, in my own cultural practice, I prefer Dickens to Barbara Cartland, Meat Loaf to U2, shouldn't I be prepared to argue the case for my values? Shouldn't I *want* other people to read Dickens rather than Cartland, to listen to Meat Loaf rather than U2? Shouldn't I be able to persuade them with classroom as well as hallway arguments? The problem is, precisely, how to do this, but to gloss over the continuous exercise of taste by the pop cultural audience is, in effect, to do their discriminating for them, while refusing to engage in the arguments which produce cultural values in the first place. This is, in the end, to reduce people to a faceless mass or market every bit as effectively as the mass cultural theorists against whom the populists are supposedly arguing.

This book is about taking popular discrimination seriously. It starts from two assumptions. The first is that the essence of popular cultural practice is making judgments and assessing differences. I'm not just thinking here of the marketing use of endless hit parades and best-seller lists but also of the ubiquitous use of competitions in the popular arts—talent contests, battles of the bands, and so forth—in which judgments, distinctions, and choices have to be publicly justified: to examine the question of value in popular culture is to examine the terms of such justifications. Take this description of music making in turn-of-the-century New Orleans:

> In the frequent "bucking contests" that took place between bands, it was the crowds of onlookers that decided when one band had fallen noticeably behind the other in quality. When that happened the people watching would crowd around the victorious musicians cheering and encouraging them to go on. The process by which the audiences determined which band was superior intrigued [Sidney] Bechet. He concluded it had to do with the fact that the audience was more than an audience, it was also participating: "how it was they could tell—that was the music too. It was what they had of the music inside themselves." It was always the people who made the decision. "You was always being judged."[22]

And half a century later Brian Jackson sat in the audience of a brass band contest in Yorkshire. Each band had to play the "test piece," which was therefore heard over and over again throughout the day: "There were a large variety of interpretations, and each of the twenty-two performances was argued out aloud as 'very musical' or 'bit pedestrian' or 'too much of a sameness.'"[23]

My second assumption is that there is no reason to believe a priori that such judgments work differently in different cultural spheres. There are obvious differences between operas and soap operas, between classical and country music, but the fact that the objects of judgment are different doesn't mean that the processes of judgment are. As Richard Shusterman has argued, the general distinctions usually drawn between high and low art don't stand up to close philosophical scrutiny. He examines, for instance, the suggestion that the pleasures of popular art are not "real" but fleeting, "that transience entails spuriousness, that gratifications are unreal and fraudulent if they later leave us hungry for more"—an argument that could equally well be applied to high art. And he goes on to ask if it is really possible, in practice, to differentiate high, intellectual aesthetic appreciation from low, sensuous bodily response; or to distinguish between a high engagement with real life and a low escape from it; or to make a clear contrast between high art's complex structures and low art's formless simplicity.[24]

For Shusterman the point is that low culture can be treated as if it were high culture—his analysis of Stetasonic's 1988 track, "Talkin' All That Jazz," is therefore designed to reveal its complexity, its philosophical content, its artistic self-consciousness, its creativity and form. This is a familiar strategy in rock criticism: one way of ascribing popular cultural value is to show that a successful record is, in fact, art. But Shusterman's strategy is subtler in that he wants to value low culture's "low" values too. Here he examines the old distinction (used, in different ways, by both Adorno and Fiske) between the "autonomy" of high art (which exists only for "artistic reasons," its value an effect, therefore, of its form) and the "function" of low art, which exists to serve some end (commercial, hedonistic) and is valued accordingly, by reference not to its internal features but to its *use*. Fiske accepts the distinction between form and function, but redefines it as a contrast between measures of quality and aesthetics, on the one hand, and measures of relevance and productivity, on the other.[25] High cultural audiences thus assume the value of an art object is contained within it; low cultural audiences assume that the value of an art object lies in what it can do for them.[26]

I'm not sure that this distinction can be sustained sociologically (as a statement of what audiences expect and do); I'll come back to this in the next chapter. In any case, Shusterman is not convinced that it can be maintained philosophically. He suggests, for example, that rap "not only insists on uniting the aesthetic and the cognitive; it equally stresses that practical functionality can form part of artistic meaning and value."[27] Rap's consciousness raising function lies in its aesthetic form, in other words, and vice versa.

Shusterman's suggestion that the aesthetic and the functional are inextricable from each other in the way we respond to and make sense of popular art is a kind of reverse echo of Pierre Bourdieu's point that the aesthetic interpretation of high art is, in fact, functional: it enables aesthetes to display their social superiority. My position is that it is not only the bourgeoisie who use aesthetic criteria for functional ends. If social relations are constituted in cultural practice, then our sense of identity and difference is established *in the processes of discrimination*. And this is as important for popular as for bourgeois cultural activity, important at both the most intimate levels of sociability (an aspect of the way in which friendships are formed and courtship organized), and at the most anonymous levels of market choice (in the way in which the fashion and advertising industries seek to place us socially by translating individual judgments of what we like and dislike into sales patterns). These relationships between aesthetic judgments and the formation of social groups are obviously crucial to popular cultural practice, to genres and cults and subcultures.

I want to end this chapter with a bolder assertion. As a matter of analytic strategy I believe that we should begin from the principle that there is no difference between high and low culture, and then see how, nevertheless, such a difference has become a social fact (the result of specific historical and social and institutional practices). This seems to me a more fruitful strategy than either taking the high/low difference for granted (whether from the elitist perspective of an Allan Bloom or the populist perspective of a John Fiske) or seeking to prove that it is spurious (as with Shusterman). Rather, I would argue, at least as a starting premise, that in responding to high and low art forms, in assessing them, finding them beautiful or moving or repulsive, people are employing the same evaluative principles. The differences lie in the objects at issue (what is culturally interesting to us is socially structured), in the discourses in which judgments are cast, and in the circumstances in which they are made.

It is arguable, for example, that there are a number of aesthetic/functional axes around which all cultural judgments work: believability (and its complex relations with both realism and fantasy); coherence (whether in terms of form or morality—and with a great variety of ways in which cause is taken to relate to effect); familiarity (and the constant problem of the new, the novel); usefulness—whether at the most material level (is that painting the right size, shape, and color for this space on this wall in this room?) or at the most spiritual (does this experience *uplift* me, make me a better person?).

What I'm suggesting here is that people bring similar questions to high and low art, that their pleasures and satisfactions are rooted in similar analytic issues, similar ways of relating what they see or hear to how they think and feel. The differences between high and low emerge because these questions are embedded in different historical and material circumstances, and are therefore framed differently, and because the answers are related to different social situations, different patterns of sociability, different social needs.

I remain enough of a sociologist, in short, to agree with Bourdieu that the interesting question is how to relate cultural judgments to material conditions (by reference to specific experiences, discourses, skills, and knowledge). And I remain enough of a Marxist to be wary of answers to this question which are static, undialectical, which suggest that the way things are is the way they have to be. The old leftist anxiety about the inadequacy of popular culture reflected an assessment of the *thinness* of the experiences which commercial art seemed to offer: this was a theme in Raymond Williams's work, for example, and was a central point in Richard Hoggart's *Uses of Literacy*.[28] But such arguments are as much about the thinness of people's everyday experience as about popular songs and magazines and films as such, and those contemporary novelists who best understand today's popular culture, Gordon Legge, say, or Bobbie Ann Mason, make clear that things like shopping malls and *NME* and top 40 music and reruns of *M.A.S.H.* matter so much because people's lives are otherwise tedious and desperate and sad.

In the end, then, the populist cultural studies line that popular consumer culture serves people's needs, and that by denigrating it we therefore denigrate those needs and thus the people themselves, misses the point. The issue is whether people's lives are adequate for human needs, for human potential. The political argument, in other words, concerns culture as reconciliation versus culture as transformation.[29] And this is the context in which the concept of "resistance" is so slippery. How should we distinguish between the ways in which people use culture to "escape," to engage in pleasures that allow them a temporary respite from the oppressive relations of daily life (a functional use of working class leisure that the bourgeoisie have always encouraged), and those uses of culture which are "empowering," which bring people together to change things?

This is partly an empirical and historical question—one would need to examine the role of popular culture in revolutionary as well as routine situations—and one can assume that what's at stake is not a simple matter of either/or: "resistance" shifts its meaning with circumstance. But it's also a question about where oppositional values come from, and how people come to believe, imaginatively, in something more than resistance. Culture as transformation, in other words, must challenge experience, must be difficult, must be *unpopular.* There are, in short, political as well as sociological and aesthetic reasons for challenging populism. The problem is how to do this while appreciating the popular, taking it seriously on its own terms. And I know this is where my own tastes will inform everything that follows, my own tastes, that is, for the *unpopular popular,* my own belief that the "difficult" appeals through the traces it carries of another world in which it would be "easy." The utopian impulse, the *negation* of everyday life, the aesthetic impulse that Adorno recognized in high art, must be part of low art too.

The Sociological Response

If a man has a big voice without knowing in the least how to use it, without having the most elementary ideas of the art of singing; if he produces a sound violently he is applauded violently for the *sonority* of this note.

If a woman possesses only an exceptional vocal range, when she produces, *a propos* or not, a *sol* or lower *fa* more like the dying moan of a sick person than a musical sound, or a high *fa* as agreeable as the yelp of a little dog when you step on his paw, that is enough for the whole hall to resound with acclamations.

. . . But, you will say, will anyone be bold enough to say that the public does not applaud, and very warmly, the great artists, masters of every resource of dramatic song, endowed with sensitivity, intelligence, virtuosity, and that rare faculty called inspiration? No; doubtless the public applauds *them* also. The public at that time resembles those sharks that follow a ship and which men fish for; it swallows everything—the piece of fat and the harpoon.

Hector Berlioz[1]

In *Contingencies of Value,* her book about high cultural evaluation, Barbara Herrnstein Smith suggests that "what we are doing in making an explicit judgment of a literary work is (a) articulating an estimate of how well that work will serve certain implicitly defined functions (b) for a specific implicitly defined audience (c) who are conceived of as experiencing the work under certain implicitly defined conditions."[2] This could equally well describe what's going on in the judgment of pop songs or TV shows, shopping centers or newscasters, and it suggests a sociology of aesthetic discrimination: to understand cultural value judgments we must look at the social contexts in which they are made, at the social reasons why some aspects of a sound or spectacle are valued over others; we must understand the appropriate times and places in which to voice such judgments, to argue them.

I'll return to the social settings of evaluation in Chapter 3. First I want to examine another aspect of Herrnstein Smith's argument: that value judgments also have a discursive context. They must be put into words, and in any fruitful aesthetic argument there must be agreement about what these words mean, however excited the disagreement about their application. In this chapter, then, I want to explore the discursive context of the aesthetics of popular music. And to introduce the discussion I will describe four examples of moments when discourses about music have clashed, when argument has indeed collapsed, when accounts of the "good" and "bad" in music have gone past each other to ridiculous or outraged effect.

My first example comes from the autobiography of John Culshaw, for many years head of the classical division of Decca Records. His autobiography is instructive in general terms because it takes it for granted that classical records are produced commercially. The tension between judgments of commercial value and judgments of musical value was thus ever-present in Culshaw's work. The nicest example concerns the original recording of Benjamin Britten's *War Requiem*. Culshaw was convinced of both its musical and its commercial worth—the *Requiem* was being given its first performance as part of the celebrations surrounding the rebuilding of Coventry Cathedral; its launch would be accompanied by a mass of radio, television, and press publicity. Unfortunately, Britten was not, historically, a best seller, and Decca's bosses were not convinced that any new classical music sold particularly well—its place in the Decca catalogue was a matter of prestige rather than profit. Culshaw therefore lost the internal argument about how many copies of the *War Requiem* to press; its run was the same as for previous Britten works.

As it turned out the pressing (which covered the North American as well as the European market) was far too small; the *War Requiem* sold out in a week. Culshaw had to wait several months for more copies (Decca's pressing plants were fully booked up with pop product), by which time the sales impetus had been lost. Furious, he confronted the man who had made the original pressing decision. The latter apologized and explained: "Daren't take the risk old boy. First thing of Britten's that's ever sold at all. Do you think you could talk him into writing another *Requiem* that would sell as well? We wouldn't make the same mistake twice."[3]

Culshaw tells this story to get a laugh, but it wouldn't be particularly funny if told about a pop composer—one only has to think of the industry kudos as well as huge sales that Virgin got for coming up with Mike Oldfield's *Tubular Bells 2* and Meat Loaf's *Bat Out of Hell II,* follow-up versions of supposedly "unique" rock compositions. In Decca's pop division, then, this was a perfectly reasonable comment—"Write another! We know how to sell it now!"—and what Culshaw is describing is an unbridgeable gap between commonsense assertions about the meaning of the *War Requiem* as product and as art. To put this another way, when an increasing tension between creative and sales processes began to be experienced within record companies' pop divisions too, toward the end of the 1960s, it was a sign that art discourses were beginning to be applied to "commercial" sounds.

My second anecdote comes from the biography of the novelist Radclyffe Hall, who also wrote pop lyrics. Her biographer quotes a correspondence she had in 1918 with William Davey, the chairman of Chappell and Company, then Britain's largest music publishers. Hall complained that she had received no royalties for her lyrics for "The Blind Ploughman," a song which had "swept the country." Davey replied as follows:

> I yield to no-one in my admiration of your words to "The Blind Ploughman." They are a big contributing factor to the success of the song. Unfortunately, we cannot afford to pay royalties to lyric writers. One or two other publishers may, but if we were to once introduce the principle, there would be no end to it. Many lyrics are merely a repetition of the same words in a different order and almost always with the same ideas. Hardly any of them, frankly, are worth a royalty, although once in a while they may be. It is difficult to differentiate, however. What I do feel is that you are quite entitled to have an extra payment for these particular words and I have much pleasure in enclosing you from Messrs Chappell a cheque for 20 guineas.[4]

This letter is interesting in a number of ways, not least for its revelation that Chappell was, apparently, routinely breaking the law—the Copyright Act of 1911 included lyricists in musical copyright regulations even though the music publishers had campaigned against this. In broad terms, though, the publisher's differentiation between the appropriate rewards for routine pop production and for individual craft skill did (and still does) have legal support. It is illuminating, for example, to follow plagiarism cases through the British courts since 1911. What criteria have judges established for proof of musical "originality"? From the start they took it for granted that anybody with even a modicum of musical skill could write a pop song, that there were only a limited number of note combinations that could be arranged to make a popular tune. To prove plagiarism, then, it was not enough to show that two songs were the same; one had to prove that the person who "stole" your song had heard it before they wrote their own. Otherwise evidence that two pieces of pop music were identical simply reflected the fact that all pop composers were constrained by the same pop formulas.

The arguments here concern the role of individual authorship in establishing the value of a piece of music; the discursive clash reflects quite different accounts of what's meant by lyrical "creativity." I've always found, for instance, that students, deeply implicated in the romantic mythology of rock, are genuinely shocked by Sheila Davis's *The Craft of Lyric Writing*, the most intelligent and entertaining of all the "how to write a pop song" books. They seem to be shocked less by the baldness with which she lays out lyrical formulas than by the fact that so many of her formulaic examples come from canonical rock texts, texts which precisely stand for individual expressivity. What she implies, in short, is not just that Morrissey could write another "Heaven Knows I'm Miserable Now," but that anyone who had read her book could do it for him.[5]

The third argument I want to describe occurred a few years ago at an event I organized in Birmingham. We arranged for a young, local group who were booked to play in a city center hall that evening to come along at two o'clock in the afternoon. The sound crew (hired by the concert promoter) arrived early too, and carried out the soundcheck—setting up the amplification equipment, measuring the hall's acoustics, miking up the musicians—in public. The audience (a surprising number of whom were local musicians) sat in a circle around the mixing desk while the mixers explained, sound by sound, what they were doing.

When everyone was wired up and leveled off, the band ran through a complete song. As it finished somebody in the audience asked them to do it again "with the vocal mixed up because we couldn't really hear the voice." The engineers adjusted their levels, the band played the song again, and the audience agreed that they sounded much better. The mixers were asked the obvious question: "Why didn't you mix it like that the first time?" They replied, "because she [the band's lead singer] can't sing." And suddenly there was a raging argument between mixers and musicians about what constituted a "good sound." The mixers were categorical: musicians do not understand good sound. They're egomaniacal, concerned only to hear themselves; they have no sense at all of what is going on in acoustic space. Audience pleasure depends on sound "experts," professionals who are "detached." The musicians were equally categorical: all sound mixers are deaf; this is one of the reasons they become sound mixers. Instead of listening to music they simply look at lights and knobs and dials, adjusting them not by reference to musical effects but according to the rules of pseudo-scientific acoustic theory (the theory they'd been expounding all afternoon). The musicians felt more strongly than I'd realized that as public performers they were powerless (particularly when starting out), that sounds were imposed on them by engineers in the studio and on stage alike; and the afternoon collapsed into shouted abuse and walkouts.

The argument here was about professionalism, but it also involved conflicting accounts of the relationship between music and sound quality, as does my final example of value clash, the critical debate around the introduction of compact discs. CDs were first promoted, like previous technological innovations in sound recording, in terms of "fidelity." The sales pitch was that a digitally stored sound was more "faithful" to the sound and dynamics of the original (as if "live") performance than an analog recording could ever be. CDs' detractors, meanwhile, argued that digital sound storage was actually "unfaithful" to those musical forms (like rock 'n' roll) which were essentially "impure."

This argument didn't last long—partly because, in the end, CDs' appeal was their convenience and not their sound quality, and partly because rock critics soon discovered that CDs actually enhance the presence of the roughest of studio sounds. But what interests me here is less the technological evaluation of sound than the implicit disagreement about what it means to listen to a record. I was reminded of the earlier (and, to me, much more irrational) debate about the introduction of the vinyl LP. In the late 1940s Compton Mackenzie, founding editor of the British classical music magazine *The Gramophone*, argued against LPs, not simply because he resented having to replace an entire record collection, but also because of the LP's threat to what he considered to be a superior listening experience. The collector of 78 recordings had to be an "active" listener, had to use her imagination to hear the sound that was buried in the 78's bumps and crackles, had to keep jumping up to change the record, which could never be, then, background music. By contrast, Mackenzie suspected (accurately enough), LP listeners would be essentially passive, able to put their feet up, their thoughts aside, not needing to work at listening at all.[6] The same sorts of anxieties, I think, underlay rock critics' initial suspicions of CDs (and pop videos); we also believed that an "active" relationship between listener and record was being threatened by a new technology.

Such critical suspicions draw attention to a recurring discursive clash in twentieth-century popular music, in which nature is pitted against artifice, "true" music ("live" music) against "false" (studio or electronically manufactured) sounds. The most interesting reflections on the impossibility of this argument I've come across are gathered in a 1966 issue of *High Fidelity*, to accompany a polemical article by Glenn Gould. One point Gould wanted to establish (as part of his championing of recorded over live performance) was that whatever their public claims, record companies had inevitably to fake live music. Classical record producers, at least, had to persuade people that they were having the ideal—concert hall—experience of their music, in the restricted acoustic space of their homes.[7]

I've been describing examples here of musical arguments which broke down, whether in farce (as with the *War Requiem*), in retreat (as with Chappell's payment of Radclyffe Hall's royalties), in violence (as at the sound mixing seminar), or in deception (as with new sound technologies). They broke down not because of disagreement about the value of particular pieces of music, but because of disagreement about what it meant to "value" music in the first place. What I want to suggest, in other words, is that to understand what's at stake in arguments about musical value, we have to begin with the discourses which give the value terms their meaning. Musical disputes are not about music "in itself" but about how to place it, what it is about the music that is to be assessed. After all, we can only hear music as valuable when we know what to listen to and how to listen for it. Our reception of music, our expectations from it, are not inherent in the music itself—which is one reason why so much musicological analysis of popular music misses the point: its object of study, the discursive text it constructs, is not the text to which anyone else listens.

The question then becomes, what do people hear? What are the possibilities? I want eventually to suggest that these days music is heard through three overlapping and contradictory grids, grids mapped by what I call the art discourse, the folk discourse, and the pop discourse. But like all discursive practices, these are the effects of specific historical situations; they have to be rooted, that is to say, in the cultural landscape established by industrial capitalism in the nineteenth century and, in particular, by the high/low cultural constructs that we came across in Chapter 1. These constructs, after all, are implicated in the very idea of making aesthetic judgments, being discriminating, exercising taste, in the first place. So before coming back to art and folk and pop, I want to say something about the construction of the more general discourses of the high and the low. And I have a secondary purpose in choosing this approach: cultural historians have produced some of the most subtle (and best informed) analyses of popular culture, and yet their work remains oddly distanced from (and ignored by) cultural studies, a subject with, it seems, a cavalierly postmodern attitude to the past.

Peter Van Der Merwe argues that in nineteenth-century Europe musical categorizations revolved around three axes: musical literacy, social class, and aesthetic status. Aesthetic judgments, that is to say, rested on criteria that were both musical and social. On the one hand, this meant that the high/low distinction only came into play in what might be called a common musical field. Music hall was low culture in a way that folk music was not, because music hall could be seen as an impoverished or banal use of a musical language also employed by "serious" composers.[8] (The same distinction is apparent today in the different attitude of the classical music world to Western pop and to so-called "world musics," and in the academic distinction between music studied by musicologists and music studied by ethnomusicologists.) On the other hand, this meant that as the class structure got more complicated (particularly with the rise of a new sort of middle class), so did musical judgments, the ways in which high/low boundaries were defined.

One could put this another way: the high/low cultural boundary was partly defined by the choices made by people (composers, performers, listeners) within a shared musical context. It was only through such choices (the serious over the frivolous, the idealistic over the commercial) that the social significance of the judgment could be made clear. If such choice wasn't possible, if the different musics were simply, well, different (like different folk musics), then musical taste revealed nothing about one's aesthetic facilities at all (just as the habit of listening to one sort of religious music rather than another would be an effect of one's religious beliefs and not one's musical tastes). Dave Russell makes clear the resulting confusions of class, aesthetic, and musical differences in his history of popular music in England at the end of the nineteenth century. He quotes, for example, from the Reverend Haweis's *Music and Morals:* "Music is not to our lower orders a deep-rooted need, a means of expressing the pent-up and oppressive emotions of the heart, but merely a noisy appendage to low pastimes." And from the *Yorkshire Orchestra:*

Our bandsmen are all mechanics; some of them, no doubt fine specimens of humanity—rough, hard-working, honest fellows— deserving our highest admiration as mechanics, *but lacking the refinement of feeling or the ability to become efficient musicians.* The greatest delight many of them have is to wear a grand military uniform, so that they may parade in the streets at night, followed by a large crowd (usually composed of all the tag-rag and bobtail of the town) when "bang" goes the big drum, immediately followed by a terrific crash of nasty, coarse, brassy sounds, enough to terrify into fits our little ones, who are frequently awoke out of the first sleep by these noisy, thoughtless, brassy men.[9]

This has something of the same disdain as Mark Crispin Miller's view of rock musicians and fans quoted in Chapter 1, but it suggests the recurring anxiety of those who originally made such high/low distinctions that they were, in fact, spurious. As Van Der Merwe points out, the very effort that went into distinguishing classical music from parlor songs reflected a furtive pleasure in the latter (just as musicians frequently crossed the boundaries, whether as professionals, taking paid work where they could find it, or as amateurs, piano players and choral singers, shifting in and out of the classical and the popular repertoires).[10]

One aspect of this, as cultural historians have shown in entertaining detail, is the amount of work that had to go into the production of "high culture" as something special in the first place. William Weber, for example, suggests that in the eighteenth century there was little distinction between high and popular music (distinctions were only made in terms of musical literacy: some music needed performers and listeners with specific forms of musical training). But in the early nineteenth century, under the influence of Romanticism, with its concepts of "genius" on the one hand, and "the folk" on the other, German classical music came to be seen as high art, while other forms of composed music (Italian opera, for example) or virtuoso performances (soon to be embodied in Liszt) were seen as "popular." Such differences were institutionalized within what we would now think of as the classical music world: the "popular" music public going for novelty, stars, salons, and benefit shows; the "art" music public going to orchestral and chamber music concerts which put the emphasis on a musical canon, on composers and compositions (with choral music left to lower middle class amateur choirs).[11]

In other words, the nineteenth-century mapping of musical taste in Europe was bound up with shifting identities within the middle class. From the 1830s a high-status, affluent "popular" classical music public came to dominate musical institutions, and to merge with upper-class audiences, to adopt "art" musical values. Weber notes two aspects of this process in particular: first, the importance of music for middle-class family life, and for the social and courtship rituals that now began to integrate the bourgeoisie into landed capitalist families; and second, the increasing power of the professional musician in this marketplace (as performer, teacher, promoter, and publisher)—amateur musicians (the upper-class model) were displaced, and a new sort of musical "magnate" appeared. What we now recognize as the classical music world marked, in short, a simultaneous economic and aesthetic movement: "high culture" was commercialized and professionalized, but popular middle-class culture was infused with the ideal of transcendence. New boundaries now had to be drawn within the "popular": amateur music making was increasingly a lower middle class affair (as reflected in the history of the piano); entertaining music (music in cafés and dance halls and parks) was increasingly seen as "vulgar."[12]

Lawrence Levine has traced the same developments (under German influence) in the even more complicated musical class structure of the United States, showing how the cultural flexibility of eighteenth-century America gave way to the uplifting aesthetic ideology of the mid-nineteenth. "A concert given in Baltimore on September 12, 1796, attests to the prevalence of a musical ethos quite divergent from the one we have come to know, an ethos that thought it quite proper to follow a Haydn overture with the song 'And All For My Pretty Brunette,' and a Bach overture with the song, 'Oh, None Can Love Like an Irish Man.'"[13]

The development of a new musical ethos meant first promoting the concept of "a sacralized art," an "art that makes no compromises with the 'temporal' world, an art that remains spiritually pure and never becomes secondary to the performer or to the audience, an art that is uncompromising in its devotion to cultural perfection"—the words are taken from *Dwight's Journal of Music*—and then marking off this sort of cultural experience from all others.

> Thus by the early decades of this century the changes that had either begun or gained velocity in the last third of the nineteenth century were in place: the masterworks of the classical composers were to be performed in their entirety by highly trained musicians on programs free from the contamination of lesser works or lesser genres, free from the distractions of the mundane; audiences were to approach the masters and their works with proper respect and proper seriousness, for aesthetic and spiritual elevation rather than mere entertainment was the goal.[14]

And Paul Di Maggio has shown how this aesthetic argument was fed into the development of a class-conscious American bourgeoisie: the distinction between high and popular culture, he writes, emerged in the second half of the nineteenth century "out of the efforts of urban elites to build organizational forms that, first, isolated high culture and, second, differentiated it from popular culture." His examples are the Boston Symphony Orchestra (which sloughed off the Boston Pops) and the Boston Museum of Fine Arts. What became high art rituals, connoisseurship and so on, were, then, an aspect of bourgeois "distinction" which combined social, aesthetic, and ethical superiority: if art had become the experience of the transcendent and the ineffable, then it was also the exclusive property of "those with the status to claim that their experience is the purest, the most authentic."[15]

The problem, though, was to make this distinction stick, to hold on to high art as an exclusive property, particularly when it was, in fact, being made and consumed as a commodity in a marketplace. "The art must not be degraded," complained a columnist in London's *Music World* in 1845 in response to an announcement of cheap concerts. "To play the finest music to an audience which has been admitted at a shilling apiece is what I can never give consent to."[16]

And despite such calls to control taste by price, in England, at least, by the end of the nineteenth century "something very close to a mass musical culture had emerged—a sharing of common taste across a broad social range."

> Through the people's concert, the concert-hall, the music-hall, the choral contest, the brass band performance and other routes, Handel, Wagner and Donizetti to name but three, were known to many 'ordinary people': vaguely by some, intimately and expertly by a significant minority.[17]

This is not to deny that there was, by the end of the nineteenth century, a "Great Musical Schism" between classical and parlor music, but, rather, that the differences could not be easily mapped onto the class structure. Just as professional musicians of the time moved easily between opera and music hall pit bands, between winter seasons in symphony orchestras and summer seasons in pier shows, so listeners from all social spheres could be fans of Wagner and Vesta Tilley, choral music and comedy turns. Dave Russell describes concert bills in the late nineteenth century which match Levine's examples from late eighteenth century America, suggesting that the musical ethos had not, perhaps, changed as much as the aesthetic argument suggested: "A popular concert in Bradford in 1871 featured the music hall star The Great Vance, Miss Newbould, a local soprano, and the Halifax Glee and Madrigal Society; in 1897 visitors to the Bournemouth Winter Gardens could have heard the municipal orchestra follow Mendelssohn's *Ruy Blas* with a medley of Albert Chevalier's coster songs."[18] And Katherine Preston's study of professional musicians in Washington, D.C. at the end of the century suggests that the high/low distinction was really a matter of occasion. Orchestras which were available for anything from a family picnic to the opening of a new shop, from a steam trip to a fashion show, reserved their "elevated" music for elevated events. "At dances, for parades, in the theater, at athletic events, at private parties, and on excursion boats," the musicians played popular songs and dances, melodies from musical theater and operetta; at university commencements and official ceremonies they switched to classical, European sounds.[19]

"Highbrow and lowbrow lived in the same world," as Van Der Merwe puts it, and "quite often they were the same person." A fact that turn-of-the-century entrepreneurs were quick to exploit. In its 1934 obituary of Edward Elgar, the *Times* remembered what a "rage" his first (1904) symphony had been: "For some time the regular orchestras of London could not play it often enough, special concerts were arranged for it, [and] enterprising commercialists even engaged orchestras to play it in their lounges and palm courts as an attraction to their winter sales of underwear."[20]

To trace the social meaning of high and low culture, then, it is not enough to point to the aesthetic ideology of the urban bourgeoisie; we also need to look at the effects of mass cultural production, which marked out the emergence of bourgeois culture and worked on it (just as it marked out and worked on the urban proletariat). The "transcendent" meaning of classical music, for example, was both exploited and denied by its use in the new movie houses, just as it has been since by radio and record and television companies, as the background sound of advertisements and airplanes and shopping malls. And the mass cultural notion of stardom, combining a Romantic belief in genius with a promise to make it individually available as commodity (and merchandise) derives as much from the packaging of "high" artists as from the hype of the low. Levine describes, for example, how "three of the most popular European visitors to the United States in the first half of the nineteenth century—the Viennese ballerina Fanny Elssler, the Norwegian violinist Ole Bull, and the Swedish soprano Jenny Lind," were able "to assume a place in a cultural lexicon that cut through class and income." This wasn't just a matter of repertoire; it also meant that their names could be exploited in the most crass ways without it, apparently, demeaning their art. During her American tour in 1840–1842, "shops peddled Fanny Elssler brand boots, garters, stockings, corsets, parasols, cigars, shoe polish, shaving soap and champagne."[21]

Merchandising in the name of Jenny Lind (whose first American tour was masterminded by P. T. Barnum) was even more extensive, and it is certainly arguable that it was with "classical" rather than "pop" musicians that the music business came to understand the possibilities of mass marketing: if Elssler and Lind set the pattern for touring and merchandising, Caruso showed what it could mean to be a recording star and Toscanini what money could be made out of a radio station/record company tie-up (just as Pavarotti became a force for the spread of CDs and global multimedia exploitation). The case of Jenny Lind is particularly instructive because Barnum was so explicit about his use of her purity, her "transcendence" ("art in its sanctity," as Hans Christian Anderson described her voice) in his sales strategy:

> From a Swedish artist, [he] acquired a romanticized portrait of Jenny Lind for fifty dollars. He had it reproduced in newspapers and periodicals and handbills. He hired an English journalist who had heard Jenny Lind sing, and instructed him to grind out weekly news stories stressing her chastity, charity and European triumphs. These stories were released to the Press under a London dateline. Barnum encouraged publishers to bring out biographical pamphlets on his vocalist. Monthly magazines devoted completely to her were put on sale.

Barnum's strategy was triumphant. The *New York Tribune*'s music critic duly described how he and the enraptured first-night audience watched "the divine songstress, with that perfect bearing, that air of all dignity and sweetness, blending a childlike simplicity and half-trembling womanly modesty with the beautiful confidence of Genius and serene wisdom of Art, address herself to song." What Barnum was selling was the classical ideal.[22]

Three lessons can be learned, I think, from mass cultural history. First, if high culture is defined too simply as bourgeois culture, then it becomes an equally over-simple reflex to equate mass culture with the working class. In fact mass culture (if we define it as the culture made possible by technological change, by the use of the means of mass cultural production) has always been a form of middle-class culture, characterized by middlebrow concerns, marked by highbrow traces. As Janice Radway has shown in her studies of the Book of the Month Club, the rise of a mass culture at the beginning of this century actually meant a blurring of the distinctions between high and low, art and commerce, the sacred and the profane.[23] This was, indeed, a point made by Max Horkheimer and Theodor Adorno in *Dialectic of Enlightenment,* where they note that the culture industry compromises the vulgar and the absurd as much as it does the serious and the difficult: "The culture industry is corrupt not because it is a sinful Babylon, but because it is a cathedral dedicated to elevated pleasure . . . The fusion of culture and entertainment that is taking place today leads not only to a deprivation of culture, but inevitably to an intellectualisation of amusement."[24]

The implications of this for musical tastes are examined in detail in

Joseph Horowitz's *Understanding Toscanini,* an illuminating case study of what, following Dwight Macdonald, he calls midcult, "high culture diluted for mass sales and consumption."[25] Here we see how that mode of rapt, superior musical appreciation so laboriously constructed by Theodore Thomas and his followers in the nineteenth century was adapted to new media (record companies and the radio) and a new audience (the advertiser-friendly middle class). Radio, notes Horowitz, "feasted on great music"—and he's talking about commercial radio, American radio, not the BBC.

> Radio offered the Metropolitan Opera and the NBC Symphony on Saturdays, the New York Philharmonic and "The Ford Hour" on Sundays. As of 1939, these four well-known longhair broadcasts were said to reach more than 10 million families a week . . . and the weekday schedule might include more than a dozen live broadcasts of hinterlands orchestras, and studio recitals. Moreover, when the radio was off, the phonograph was on . . . RCA Victor's sales rose 600% between 1933 and 1938, with symphonic, not popular, releases leading the way.[26]

As Horowitz argues, what this "commercialization" of classical music involved was not simply an exercise in transforming something transcendent into something commonplace, nor was it an entirely cynical exercise in using "great music" as a source of prestige (just as obvious in the drive of every American town of reasonable size to have its own civic orchestra). There was also an idealism here: "to partake in great music's exclusivity was made a democratic privilege." The selling of classical music on radio and record was mediated by "musical appreciation," by instruction about how you, as an "ordinary" person, should listen to and therefore come to appreciate extraordinary music. And such an educational strategy was an aspect of the classical record market from the beginning (in Britain, for example, EMI funded *The Gramophone,* and ran classes for shop assistants, so that they could in turn educate record shoppers). Music appreciation followed the Great Books model of literary appreciation, and the record industry certainly looked to book publishing for guidance to records' market potential. In particular, pop music's appeal was taken to be unstable (especially after the collapse of record sales at the end of the 1920s); people had to be persuaded to build a "library" of recordings, to treat music-on-record as something to treasure and keep. Horowitz quotes *The Victor Book of the Symphony,* published by RCA in 1934: "The importance to music of modern methods of reproducing sounds is parallel to that of the printing press to literature, philosophy and the whole sum of the world's knowledge."[27]

Horowitz suggests that we should not overstate the aesthetic impact of midcult. If a minority of the new audience "purposely used music appreciation to enhance their social esteem and social rank," an equal minority undoubtedly "moved from music appreciation to understanding, fortified by 'active listening' and praxis." And for the majority of listeners what mattered "was the excitement of newfound experience, of an unsuspected passion whose rituals included record collecting, radio listening, and starting or supporting a first-class symphony orchestra." In other words, "adapting mass culture to the high cultural world" (or the reverse) meant, above all, developing new forms of sociability, and what is most striking is how much this depended on clubs and societies—the gramophone society, the book club, the film society, the rhythm club (the label in Britain for "jazz appreciation societies," which met in the 1930s and 1940s to listen to and discuss jazz records).[28] Paradoxically, in short, the rise of "mass culture" meant new forms of social activity, new ways of using aesthetic experience to define social identity.

My second historical point follows from this: if one effect of mass culture was to "discipline" the nineteenth-century urban "unrespectable," another, equally important, was to loosen up the nineteenth-century urban (or suburban) respectable. There is, by now, much illuminating historical work on the former process. In *Rudeness and Civility,* for example, John F. Kassan shows clearly how the rise of consumer culture, the "orderly spectacle," meant the decline of a participatory, communal leisure culture in American working-class neighborhoods, a move from "enthusiasm" to "disciplined spectatorship."[29]

But the other side of this story is the selling of "safe" ways for middle-class city dwellers (and the respectable working class) to enjoy the proletarian pleasures of noisy public behavior. Kathy Peiss, for example, suggests that the rise of mass culture (the cinema is a good instance) meant developing those aspects of working-class leisure that the middle class found attractive and shedding those things of which they disapproved. Mass culture meant "Polite Vaudeville," "regulated pleasure," for all classes; it was organized, in particular, around "hetero-sociability" and a new valorization of youth. Her example is Coney Island:

> Steeplechase incorporated into its notion of mass entertainment cultural patterns derived from working class amusements, street life and popular entertainment. Like them, the park encouraged familiarity between strangers, permitted a free-and-easy sexuality, and structured heterosocial interaction. This culture was not adopted

wholesale, but was transformed and controlled, reducing the threatening nature of sexual contact by removing it from the street, workplace and saloon. Within the amusement park, familiarity between women and men could be acceptable if tightly structured and made harmless through laughter. At Steeplechase, sexuality was constructed in terms of titillation, voyeurism, exhibitionism and a stress on a couple and romance.[30]

From this historical perspective, popular culture describes the process in which class and other group values and conflicts are *mediated* (rather than directly expressed), which is one reason why popular commodities (heavy metal music, say, or splatter movies, or the tabloid press) can be and often are simultaneously "transgressive" (of "respectable" values) and reactionary.

My third point follows: if mass culture is defined not against middle-class culture, against art, but as a way of processing it, then the crucial high/low conflict is not that between social classes but that produced by the commercial process itself at all levels of cultural expression, in pop as well as classical music, in sport as well as literature. High/low thus describes the emergence of consumer elites or cults, on the one hand (the bohemian versus the conformist), and the tension between artists and their audiences (the modernist and avant-gardist versus the orthodox and the mainstream), on the other. I'll come back to the value terms of these conflicts in Chapter 3; here I just want to reiterate a point well made by Geoffrey Nowell-Smith, who notes that because of the culture industries' inability to control taste themselves (for all their efforts), they have to rely on other "taste-forming machines" (or what in this chapter I'm calling discursive practices). It is for this reason that "traditional criteria of what is good and what is not" continue to be influential, and that "the culture industry can often be happier with art—or what passes for art—than with items of acknowledged junk culture like game shows and pop singles."

> The conservative critique of the culture industry—and some "left" critique as well—has focused on the way it has marginalized art and displaced it with commercial pap. This critique seems to me misplaced. Living art may well be marginal, thriving only in the interstices of society untouched by the culture industry. But what has replaced it in the mainstream is not just the novelty of popular culture. All too often the replacement for living art is dead art.[31]

This is the context in which I want to turn now to a more orderly, sociological approach to contemporary aesthetic discourse. My arguments are derived from two sociological models: Howard S. Becker's account of "art worlds" and Pierre Bourdieu's concept of "cultural capital."[32] Becker suggests that to understand art objects and people's response to them we have to understand the institutional and discursive processes (the art world) in which they are constructed as art objects, as works to which a particular sort of aesthetic response is socially appropriate. Bourdieu uses the concept of cultural capital to relate cultural values to social structural variables (social class variables in his case), to questions of power and hierarchy that Becker puts to one side. The reason different people engage with different art worlds has to do with the amount (and type) of cultural capital they possess. For Bourdieu, in other words, the aesthetic response can only be understood by reference to the social organization of taste which patterns people's lifestyle, morality, and habitus. Putting Becker and Bourdieu together (and extrapolating somewhat from what they actually say), I want to suggest that, in very broad terms, music is valued according to three types of discursive practice (related to Becker's three sorts of art worlds, to Bourdieu's three kinds of taste groups).[33]

The first art world I want to describe, the first taste group, is what I will call (although it is not an altogether satisfactory term) the bourgeois world (or what Bourdieu calls dominant culture). In terms of my argument in this book, the bourgeois art world is the world of classical (or art) music, the world of nineteenth-century high culture (and twentieth-century midcult) which I have already described.

The organizing institution of bourgeois musical discourse is, as Bourdieu argues, the academy, by which I mean the music departments of universities, conservatories, the whole panoply of formal arrangements and practices in which classical music in its various forms is taught and handed down the generations. Central to this world is the teacher/pupil relationship, the belief that musicians must serve an apprenticeship, must progress through fixed stages (like the Associated Board's instrumental grades in Britain) before they are "qualified" to play. (I'm always struck by the way in which concert program notes describe soloists in terms of their teachers, as if establishing a sort of *provenance* for their talent; jazz musicians, by contrast, are described by reference to whom they have previously played with.) As in the similarly academic fine art world, to compose or play without having the right credentials, without having had one's talent "passed on," so to speak, is to be labeled "primitive" or "naive." Kyle Gann suggests that in the United States the operative distinction for composers is thus that between the amateur and the professional. In Morton Feldman's words, "In music, when you do something new, something original, you're an amateur," while the professional composer

> writes a piece occasionally. It is played occasionally . . . His pieces are well made. He is not without talent. The reviews aren't bad. A few awards—a Guggenheim, an Arts and Letters, a Fulbright—this is the official musical life of America. You can't buck the system, especially if it works. And this system does work . . . These men are their own audience. They are their own fame. Yet they have created a climate that has brought the musical activity of an entire nation down to a college level.[34]

As Feldman (who sees himself as working in the unprofessional, "icono-clastic," passed-over-in-one's-lifetime tradition of Charles Ives and Edgard Varèse) makes clear here, the bourgeois music world faces a constant tension between its firm sense of musical tradition (which has to be preserved, documented, refined, and elaborated) and its equally firm belief in the value of creativity and the importance of the new and the original. And I would make a further point here, with specific reference to composition. The ideology is that the composer is answerable only to herself; she does not compose for an audience; she is, in this respect, free of the crowd-pleasing pressures that afflict the "hack." In practice, though, the "professional" composer (the composer, that is, whose living is composition) has to please an audience—teachers, grant givers, concert programmers, specialist record companies—which is in many respects more tightly in control of the "acceptable composition" than the so-called mass public. Truth-to-self, in other words, depends on others' approval until (just as in the pop world) one reaches a sufficient level of success (in terms of both esteem and earnings) to be "autonomous."[35]

The best account I know of these tensions is Henry Kingsbury's sensitive and revealing study of a music conservatory. The problem for the music student, suggests Kingsbury, is focused on the concept of "talent." Talent is something that students possess, it is talked about as something real, but it can only be recognized by someone else, by a teacher, and the paradox of music education is its underlying assumption that only the "talented" few can be taught what is in the end unteachable (because it is, in fact, a quality of the student). On the one hand, this confirms the importance of the teacher/pupil relationship—musical apprenticeship as a process of recognition by someone with the authority to recognize (and be recognized); on the other hand, it means that from the students' point of view their "talent" is never actually in their possession at all: it exists only in its validation by others. And this comes to the heart of the problem of tradition versus creation, or, in Kingsbury's terms, between playing music and playing notes, between technical skill (the ability to play the notes "correctly") and musical skill, the ability—the talent—to do what? To be recognized as talented! The problem (and a cause of great stress and paranoia at music schools) is that while talent is assigned and described individually, it only exists in the making of music as a social event; in Kingsbury's words, "musical meaning is social meaning."[36]

As we'll see in the next chapter, this makes for profound value conflicts between performers and audiences even as the applause for the performance rings out, but for the moment it is enough to say that the role of the academy is not simply to produce performers and to nurture "talent," but also to institutionalize a familiar way of thinking about music: as the creation of composing geniuses, embodied in sacred scores (texts guarded religiously by music scholars), faithfully but feelingly articulated by gifted performers to reverential audiences guided by enlightened critics.[37]

In terms of consumption too, then, the bourgeois art world depends on scholarship, on the accumulation of the knowledge of musical history and the compositional process without which score and performance cannot be understood. As Aaron Copland put it in a 1936–37 music appreciation course (later published as *What to Listen for in Music*),

> No composer believes that there are any short cuts to the better appreciation of music . . . It is very important for all of us to become more alive to music on its sheerly musical plane . . . The intelligent listener must be prepared to increase his awareness of the musical material and what happens to it . . . Above all he must, in order to follow the composer's thought, know something of the principles of musical form.[38]

The scholarly skills developed in university music departments—archive skills, reading skills, interpretive skills—are, then, just like those developed by art historians or literary critics. Their purpose is the same: to establish the canon, to come up with a coherent, linear historico-aesthetic narrative.[39] But to sustain the classical music world such academic skills must make their way out of the university to the general bourgeois public, which depends for its knowledge on a set of semi-academic institutions and practices—liner notes, music journals, newspaper critics, concert programmers, and classical music radio stations—which bridge the gap between high music scholarship and everyday domestic music listening.[40]

While laymen and women can thus gain access to the classical world, it remains strictly hierarchical. There is a clear distinction, that is, between the composer of a work and its performers, between performers and their audience; and the central bourgeois music event, the concert, offers (in its ideal) a transcendent experience, something special, something apart from the everyday world. As Thomas Russell put it in his best-selling 1942 book on the London Philharmonic Orchestra, "To leave a concert hall after a vital experience and fight for a seat in a bus or a train, to jostle for a place in a crowded café, surrounded by people *not blessed with the same experience* is to become aware of an anti-climax."[41]

The seriousness of the classical concert is both made possible by and registered in a series of performing conventions. Lawrence Levine has shown how sternly the nineteenth-century American audience had to be taught these conventions, taught to listen silently and respectfully, taught that the highest musical experience was, well, religious; in the twentieth century these listening conventions have been coded into the building and organization of concert halls themselves. In an illuminating comparison of musical performance in London's Royal Festival Hall and in a New Orleans jazz café, Christopher Jackman shows the elaborate extent to which audiences are now prepared for a spiritual experience in a classical venue, with its strict separation of bodily needs (toilets, bars, and cloakrooms) from musical uplift (No Drinks to be Taken into the Auditorium), and its careful use of staging and lighting to mark out the boundaries of the musical moment. In the jazz café the musicians employ a very different set of performing conventions (negotiating with the waitresses, for example, a balance between letting customers listen and hassling them for orders), and the difficulty of responding properly to a rock show in a concert hall is familiar: in Britain, at least, there is a ceaseless skirmish between the dancers in the aisles and the patrolling security staff.[42]

To summarize, then, bourgeois or what I shall now call the art music discourse is organized around a particular notion of musical scholarship, a particular concept of musical talent, and a particular sort of musical event, in which music's essential value is its provision of a transcendent experience that is, on the one hand, ineffable and uplifting but, on the other, only available to those with the right sort of knowledge, the right sorts of interpretive skills. Only the right people with the right training can, in short, experience the real meaning of "great" music.

The second source of evaluative musical discourse is what I'll term the folk music world (roughly speaking, what Bourdieu means by popular culture). The starting argument here is that the value of music has to be understood in terms of cultural necessity—ideally, there is no separation of art and life. The appreciation of music is therefore tied up with an appreciation of its social function. Many of the terms and arguments of this discourse are familiar from ethnomusicological studies of non-Western, non-capitalist cultures, but the point I want to make here is that the terms of folk culture are sustained in the ways in which people talk about popular music in the West too. How, then, is folk discourse sustained in societies in which folk music is, according to its own anti-modernist ideology, impossible?

The most sustained sociological answer to this question can be found in Niall MacKinnon's *The British Folk Scene*, a study which reveals two problems in particular. First, the folk values of the natural, the spontaneous, and the immediate are, in fact, only realized through a kind of subterfuge. The folk world, in MacKinnon's words, depends on "an elaborate construction of informality," an informality which operates as a form of "constraint" on performers and audiences alike. He describes folk's subtle performing conventions—the way stages are set and lit and amplified, the rules of when audiences should talk and when they should keep silent, the obligation on performers to "shrink from overtly stylised presentations of self," to avoid elaborate stage movements.[43] Second, such folk conventions only work because of their difference from the perceived rules of commercial pop. What's involved in folk performance, as MacKinnon puts it, is "a very conscious destroying and destruction of glamour."[44]

Now it's easy enough to be cynical about folk discourse, which seems to rest on an essential self-deception—that which is worked hard for is presented as coming naturally, that which is commodified is presented as communal. But this is not to say that folk ideology isn't (perhaps for just this reason) rhetorically very persuasive, and there are two further reasons for this. First, the folk world, like the classical world, in preserving its ideals puts a central emphasis on tradition. It has its own archives and archivists, its own scholars and scholarly magazines, its own instructive use of liner notes ("the record as teaching device").[45] The emphasis, though, is less on history and the accumulation of knowledge than on "purity" and the correct (traditional) way of doing things. Folk music is thus evaluated (and condemned—Dylan going electric) according to concepts of unchanging musical "truth."

Second, the folk world is organized around a set of performing rituals, not the rituals of bourgeois transcendence but nonetheless rituals that mark off the musical experience from everyday life. Folk discourse, in other words, can only be understood as a critique of quotidian commerce. Robert Cantwell describes how the 1950s folk revival in the United States drew on a vision of "the old Free America": "The revival made the romantic claim of folk culture—oral, immediate, traditional, idiomatic, communal, a culture of characters, of rights, obligations, and beliefs, against a centrist, specialist, impersonal technocratic culture, a culture of types, functions, jobs and goals."[46]

The most developed and important folk rituals are therefore the club and the festival. MacKinnon remembers his first—conversion—experience of the folk club: "People sang. They sang to each other, without a stage, without amplification, with no special clothes, and with no special flourish which said 'we are performers.'" And he goes on to describe how folk clubs attempt to minimize the distance between performer and audience, to provide a "different form of socialising in which active musical performance and participation [are] integrated."[47]

The folk festival describes a time (usually a weekend) and a space (usually outdoors) within which folk values—the integration of art and life—can be lived (and this is a form which is therefore used—for folk ends—by other musical genres, by rock, soul, and rave). Hence the strict festival conventions: the famous performer must come and have a drink with the audience in the tent after the show, and, often enough, take part in workshops; anyone in the audience must be able to stand up somewhere on the site—in a "club room"—and perform herself, informally; there is a constant attempt to deny the actual (commercial) separation of folk stars and folk fans. Folk festivals are more likely to be organized around a large number of small stages than one big spectacle; there is, as MacKinnon puts it, no "back room" for folk performers, no place to prepare themselves. Bruce Jackson describes how the Newport Folk Festival was remade in 1967–68: there was an increased emphasis on education sessions and workshops, a decreased use of microphones and stars, as the organizers sought to reestablish the gathering as a folk rather than a pop event. And Georgina Boyes notes how at the same time in Britain folk festivals offered "folk club members the chance to live the Revival lifestyle for days at a time."[48] In short, the folk festival seeks to solve the problem of musical "authenticity"; it offers the experience of the folk ideal, the experience of collective, participatory music making, the chance to judge music by its direct contribution to sociability.

The third source of musical discourse is the commercial music world (what Bourdieu would call majority culture), which I won't describe in detail here since I've dealt with it extensively elsewhere.[49] Its values are created by and organized around the music industry, around the means and possibilities of turning sounds into commodities—musical value and monetary value are therefore equated, and the sales charts become the measure and symbol of "good" pop music. The commercial music world is also organized around particular sorts of musical events—events (such as promotional concerts and discos) which offer a kind of routinized transcendence, which sell "fun." Fun is an escape from the daily grind (which is what makes it pleasurable) but is, on the other hand, integrated with its rhythms—the rhythms of work and play, production and consumption.

The tripartite structure I've suggested here of bourgeois, folk, and commercial music worlds, of high art, folk art, and pop art, is familiar enough, and one can readily observe the discourses in operation. Wilfrid Mellers's rock musicologies, for example, describe performers who start out as "folk" musicians, get absorbed into the "pop" process, and then emerge as "artists."[50] And in *Sound Effects* I suggested that in trying to distinguish the practices of rock from those of "commercial" pop, rock's '60s ideologists were obliged to draw on both folk values and art values.[51] Even more dramatically, the jazz critic Ernest Borneman suggests that

> every cycle of civilisation re-enacts the Fall of Man in every generation and on every level of experience. Awareness wrecks the naive innocence of a folk culture and divides it, like Cain and Abel, into embodiments of an ever widening conflict between the eclectic upper-class culture of the few and the epigonic cliché culture of the vast masses who have lost the innocence of a naive folk art without gaining the awareness of a fully developed aesthetic.[52]

In the end, then, what is involved here is not the creation and maintenance of three distinct, autonomous music worlds but, rather, the play of three historically evolving discourses across a single field—hence the sorts of disputes with which I began this chapter.[53] For musicians and listeners in the bourgeois, folk, and commercial music worlds alike, value judgments reflect a path being traced with some difficulty through the confusing noise of competing discourses. If, for example, the standard line of rock 'n' roll history is that an authentic (that is, folk) sound is continually corrupted by commerce, it could equally well be argued that what the history actually reveals is a commercial musical form continually being recuperated in the name of art and subculture.[54] In the folk world, similarly, the terms "authentic" and "artificial" are used to describe the same musical processes. Thus bluegrass, a musical form whose invention can be dated fairly precisely, stands now (in the annual summer season of bluegrass festivals) not just for the North American folk tradition but for the North American mountain and country traditions too.[55]

Art music makers also know well enough that their livelihoods depend on commercial logic, that art and commercial values have to be reconciled in practice if kept apart in rhetoric. This was the symbolic importance of Toscanini (and, indeed, of the development of the conductor as star), and one can still hear the argument at work on North American classical music radio stations: listen to the deejays imply in their reverent tones of voice that what is on offer is still a transcendent experience even if it is now punctuated by advertisements for insurance. As classical music becomes a ubiquitous part of the commercial soundscape—as the background hum of upmarket offices, shops, and telephones on hold—we are, in George Steiner's words, enveloped by "A Muzak of the sublime."[56]

But value discourses don't themselves work autonomously either: their terms were developed in relationship to each other; each discourse represents a response to the shared problems of music making in an industrial capitalist society; each can be traced back, therefore, to the late eighteenth century; and each can be found in the ways all sorts of musics have made sense of themselves in the twentieth century, whether in the Romantic mythology of rock or in the spiritual ambitions of the brass band movement, with its "sincere attempt to apprehend the good, the beautiful and the true," to help "mankind on an upward journey."[57]

It seems unduly restrictive, in short, to treat the classical, folk, and pop music worlds (as most analysts have) as if they were distinct objects of study; it is more fruitful, as Ruth Finnegan has argued, to treat them comparatively, tracing contrasting solutions to shared problems.[58] How are the different musics learned and taught, for example? How is skill defined? How are the lines drawn between the "amateur" and the "professional"? I'll return to these and other contextual questions in Chapter 3, but I can make the point here that a comparative sociology reveals far less clear distinctions between music worlds than their discursive values imply. And one of the most striking aspects of popular music history is that musics may anyway change their discursive meaning, may cross apparently firm cultural boundaries. As Ernest Borneman once argued, "All standards of musical criticism are abstractions from a previously developed and digested practice of music. Theory limps: it is always a step behind practice. A new music requires a new aesthetic rationalisation."[59]

And it first of all needs to be heard as a "new music." I've discussed elsewhere the ways in which pop was rethought as art in the 1960s and 1970s, so I'll focus here on the case of jazz.[60] Examining its initial reception in Britain, Howard Rye notes that one question critics had to answer (and to begin with answered quite differently) was to what extent this African-American music was continuous with what was already familiar from the nineteenth century—minstrelsy and Negro spirituals: "The inconsistency of responses underlies the absence of any established critical standards." But the issue, at least to begin with, wasn't so much the absence of standards as a confusion

The Sociological Response

about which ones to apply. Thus Joe Jordon's Syncopated Orchestra, which made a brief British tour after appearing in a London revue, *Push and Go,* in 1905, was firmly placed in the perceived nineteenth-century black musical tradition:

> Jordon's Syncopated Orchestra at Newcastle's Empire Theatre are unquestionably one of the smartest combinations since minstrelsy was in its prime. They, numbering ten, present an entertainment anything but antiquated, and . . . sing and dance in a manner that entirely drives away dull care and compels one to be joyful.[61]

The Southern Syncopated Orchestra (which included Sydney Bechet) was described in rather different critical terms when it played in London fourteen years later, in 1919:

> This negro folk music is quite an art-music of its own and is of course best when interpreted by those who truly love and understand the spirit of it as these thirty-six players do. There is richness of melody, diablerie, merriment and some pathos interwoven, but the unique entertainment is one music lovers should not miss as it serves to demonstrate how very far from its original sources nine-tenths of the ragtime we get howled at us has strayed.

While in the words of another critic, "Mr Sydney Bechet's extemporised clarinette solo"—which was also impressing Ernest Ansermet—"compels admiration, so true is his ear and so rhythmical and vital his conception."[62]

The confusion over quite what to hear in this music—minstrelsy, folk culture, art, craft?—continued in Britain until the end of the 1920s, when *Melody Maker*'s critics changed the way they wrote about it—and therefore, presumably, the way they heard it—in the space of a few months.[63] Ron Welburn has examined the parallel discursive shift in American jazz criticism. In brief, in the 1920s, critics (music critics rather than jazz critics then) focused on "symphonic jazz" and ignored improvised ensembles. The early critics, that is to say, were interested in the ways in which jazz's "nonintellectual" elements (rhythm, showmanship) were being used by "serious" composers (like Stravinsky or George Gershwin) in "complex" musical structures; by the 1930s symphonic jazz was rarely treated sympathetically by either music or, now, jazz critics.[64]

There were two elements in this shift. First, it began to be argued (by Roger Pryor Dodge in *The Dancing Times* in 1929, for example) that jazz was not a folk music but an art music. It was already "composed"; its "nonintellectual" elements were therefore already being used to maximum artistic effect. Symphonic jazz was thus an arrogant nonsense. As Borneman, writing nearly twenty years later (when jazz's critical criteria were well established) puts it:

> There is no such thing as "symphonic jazz." By our standards, "symphonic" jazz is a term of abuse and not of praise. Bix Beiderbecke's little piano pieces which have been compared to Debussy would therefore tend to make us doubt rather than confirm his value as a jazz musician. Gershwin's *Rhapsody in Blue, American in Paris, Concerto in F*, etc., may be admired for any amount of reasons but certainly not for "raising jazz to the level of symphonic music." Jazz has a function in its own right: any attempt at "raising" it can only result in lowering it to the level of a musical hybrid.[65]

When this sort of argument was first made, in the late 1920s, it was still assumed that jazz was a "primitive" art; its musical values were primitive musical values. The best jazz was the most "low down" jazz; it was best played by black jazz musicians and, in Dodge's words, by "those lower members of the white race who have not yet lost their feeling for the primitive." Jazz, in short, had to be understood as "a musical form produced by the primitive innate musical instinct of the negro," and the task of jazz critics was, in the words of B. H. Haggin in 1930, to oppose "arty refinement."[66]

And there was clearly a racial shift here: whereas before it was critically obvious that white jazz was better than black jazz because of its refinement, now the same musical description led to the opposite judgment: black jazz was better than white jazz because of its lack of refinement. But the argument had barely reached this position when critics had to make sense of Duke Ellington. Now what was recognized was a kind of appropriate refinement, a development and elaboration of the "nonintellectual" elements of jazz in ways which could not be understood as either "primitive" or "arty." And it was in making sense of Ellington, suggests Welburn, that jazz criticism developed its basic form, the record review, and a discourse which depended on formal and musical (not functional and sociological) analysis. Welburn cites the case of Robert D. Darrell, who wrote the first detailed praise of Ellington (as against Gershwin) in the *Phonograph Monthly Review* in 1927: "Duke Ellington's music, with its multi-thematic and improvisatory characteristics, provided Darrell a means of shaping and refining the language specifically of the record review and in general the evaluative tenets of jazz criticism."[67]

The sociological point, to conclude, is that we're dealing here with different sorts of music, whether jazz or rap, folk or rock, which are all, in one way or another, handling the issues thrown up by their commodification. (If we wanted to look at musics with really different sociological bases, we'd need to examine those with quite other functions than market exchange—religious music, for example, or military music, which cannot be discussed in art/folk/pop terms.) Whether we are looking at a composition student in a conservatory, a session player on a cruise ship, or a would-be rapper in the Bronx, we're looking at musicians faced with the same problems in deciding whether their music is any good or not. The issues concerned—the position of the artist in the marketplace, the relations of class and community, the tensions between technology and tradition, the shaping of race and nation, the distinction of the public and the private—are not confined to any one social group, to any one musical practice. Whether they become pressing or not depends on circumstances, not ideology. And it is to those circumstances that I will now turn.

Common Sense and the Language of Criticism

If he [the critic] studies music as an aspect of cultural anthropology he is not allowed to judge its value with the current standards of his own civilisation; faced with, say, the boat-songs of seventeenth century Dahomey, he is not in a position to say that song A is "better" than song B, or that singer X is "better" than singer Y. Similarly, on approaching a native American pattern of culture such as the jazz idiom and its tradition, it would be inadequate to say that "St Louis Blues" is a better piece of music than "Pistol Packin' Mama," or that Louis Armstrong is a better trumpeter than Clyde McCoy; instead, we will want to know how and why "St Louis Blues" and "Pistol Packin' Mama" came to exist, what function they perform in the American social pattern and, finally, why Armstrong is considered by our own musicians and critics as a better musician than McCoy.

Ernest Borneman[1]

Every trained pop musician and working pop critic would agree that Jimi Hendrix is a better, and a greater guitarist than Eddie Van Halen; that Frank Sinatra is a better singer than Eddie Fisher.

Jim Miller[2]

In Chapter 1 I suggested that value judgments are the common currency of popular culture. Anyone who's any sort of pop fan is used to the arguments involved—that's a good song, a good tune, a good sound, a good beat—but such judgments have been of surprisingly little interest to cultural theorists. What's going on when these remarks are made? What's being described? What's being inferred? What's the point of making this judgment of this record in these terms at this moment?

Recent theorists of popular meaning have tended to start from the quantitative measures of market research; these are taken to reveal, in themselves, a map of popular taste, an account of popular values (so that when *Billboard* alters its methods of compiling its charts, it's as if American music preferences have changed overnight). But even if they were accurate such measures wouldn't tell us why people chose to tune into a program, go to a movie, buy a CD, nor whether they enjoyed them, nor, indeed, what "enjoyment" might mean. A measurement of popularity, in short, is not a measurement of value.

Market researchers do use qualitative measures too, of course. Cultural producers are always keen to answer the missing questions—why people bought something, whether they enjoyed it, whether they'd buy it again—and television researchers have thus developed the Appreciation Index, and film researchers the use of response cards at previews. The problem with these methods is that their value terms are almost always determined by the researchers, not the respondents. "Appreciation" is indicated by checking boxes which may not describe how people usually think at all, a problem that market researchers then try to solve with focus groups, discussions driven by audience rather than research discourse. But focus groups are not the usual settings in which judgments are made either; they don't tell us much about the everyday process of appreciation, the pleasures of popular discrimination itself.

I haven't got any solutions to these methodological problems. There is some secondary evidence of how people like and rate things in the media themselves, in readers' letters (published and unpublished), in calls to television stations and in requests to radio programs, but these are self-selected samples of viewers and listeners with particularly strong feelings—and a reason for wanting to make them public.[3] This is a problem too with cultural studies' recent interest in self-declared fans, people who are certainly well enough organized to express their views—and, indeed, organize fan clubs in order to do so—but whose terms of judgment are, for just that reason, likely to be a bit peculiar (even if we accept, with the Vermorels, that this peculiarity is just an extreme and obsessive version of what we all do and feel anyway).[4]

I want to start this chapter, then, from a different source of popular criticism, from audience comments on films and film tastes gathered by the British research organization Mass-Observation in the 1930s and 1940s. Mass-Observation was itself a peculiar organization, founded by an anthropologist, a poet, and a filmmaker with two impulses: first, to document "ordinary" British life, to describe, from an anthropological standpoint, British mores, customs, and rituals as they were articulated in the everyday; second, to reveal the oddities, the *unconscious* foundation of British habits.

The methodological basis of its work was therefore to be a mixture of observation ("mass observers" were themselves "ordinary" members of the public, and the line between "observing" and spying or voyeurism was not always clear) and self-observation, through people's use of diaries and questionnaires.[5]

Mass-Observation certainly didn't solve the research problems of sampling or question-begging, but its data do seem to reflect the everyday more than other market research, to give a sense, that is, of how the different things in people's lives fit together. And Mass-Observation also did take for granted people's ability to account for their own actions; the observers were not much interested in the hidden "effects" of the media on people, in how the cinema, say, was changing the patterns of people's lives, their moral values, sense of reality, and so forth, without their knowing it.[6]

The Mass-Observation cinema surveys were designed to discover, like other sorts of research, why people went to the cinema and what sorts of films they enjoyed, but Mass-Observation was also interested in cinema-going as a ritual in itself, and observers were instructed to go to cinemas and take notes of behavior, of those aspects of the occasion that didn't have anything directly to do with the film. They were told to note when people laughed or talked, shouted out remarks or fell silent, to describe all the incidents that formed a night out.[7]

The evidence I want to look at comes from questionnaires handed out and comments elicited (with promises of free tickets) through newspaper advertisements. In 1938 cinema-goers in Bolton were asked to explain their preferences between British and American films; in 1943 a more widely distributed questionnaire asked people to name the best films they had seen in the previous year, and to explain their choices. For my purposes this evidence is interesting because it focuses on specific value judgments and asks people to account for them—the results are less useful, that is, as a measure of British cinema audience taste in 1938–1943 than as a source of evaluative discourse.[8]

It is clear, to begin with, that films were judged in terms of *technique, skill, and craft*. The question for viewers was whether something was done well (acting, most obviously), and there were also recurrent references to cinematic detail, to care (with scenery), and so on. Second, there were recurring evaluations in terms of the *expense* involved, by reference to production values. Cheapness (or tackiness) is a term of abuse, and there is clearly a tendency to value the *spectacular* (which, of course, has a long history in popular theater and melodrama).

These first two clusters of judgment revolve around what people perceived as having gone into the picture, which was well enough understood as an industrial product, a commodity depending for its success on both capital investment and box office returns. Audiences expected that their role as consumers would be taken seriously, and American films were constantly rated more highly than British ones for just this reason: they took moviegoers more seriously in terms of trouble taken (and costs run up). Hollywood has always been aware of this attitude, of course; boasting about how much money a film has cost is a routine part of the marketing process.

A third kind of evaluation referred to films' *truth-to-life*, their believability. This was usually stated in terms of characters (can I identify with them?) and was seen as an issue of both form and content. Judgments refer to conventions of realism (is an actor sincere? was an actress's response authentic? was the story well shaped? did it make sense?) and to experience—the viewer's life is compared to life on the screen, and vice versa.

Fourth, respondents referred to films' ability to *take-one-out-of-oneself*, to give them a quality of experience measured by the intensity of feeling. Judgments of this sort covered thrills and excitement, laughter and surprise (respondents noted that such experiences were quite likely to be matters of moments, found in visual gimmicks and stunt-laden scenes). The point is that entertainment should meet the promise of being different from the everyday.

There are obvious contradictions between the third and fourth criteria here, but these seem to be built into popular film values themselves. It's not that some people want to see films that are true to life and other people films that are different from the everyday; nor even that the same person wants to see one sort of film one day, the other the next. Rather, people want both sorts of qualities simultaneously, and this was evident in the fifth kind of value criterion: the positive evaluation of films in terms of *the range of experiences* offered: a good laugh and a good cry, realism and spectacle, truth and fantasy.

Finally, and again in apparent contrast to this, what is striking in these responses is the significance of *genre distinctions*, the use of genre markers to shape expectations about what kinds of pleasure a film may offer. The recurring negative evaluation only makes sense in these terms: people constantly referred to their *disappointment* in a film—it didn't live up to its promises, it wasn't what I was expecting. Such a judgment reflects people's easy familiarity with genre conventions, but also how they rate films by reference to other films, in terms of their knowledge of stars and directors and studios, of marketing strategies and trailers and billboards. And there is obviously a kind of popular cultural capital at play here too—we can draw a distinction between film fans and ordinary moviegoers, between expert and casual viewers (a distinction taken for granted in people's responses to the questionnaires).

There is a further point to make about this: in assessing their cinematic experience, people brought with them both a knowledge of the cinema and what it could do, and a knowledge of culture and what it could do. This is partly reflected in the way in which films are judged by reference to other cultural forms, to adapted books and quoted paintings. But it is also reflected in a more diffuse sense of the high and the low which runs through these questionnaire answers and which people applied to the films they saw. In everyday terms most of us distinguish between easy and hard listening, between light and heavy reading, between entertaining and serious viewing, and in the Mass-Observation surveys the cinema is thought to be primarily about entertainment and escape, and not usually, therefore, to offer "real" aesthetic experience, though some particularly good "art films" may be "demanding" in the right sort of way. There is, in short, a sense of indulgence (and even guilt) running through even the positive evaluations of films in these surveys (particularly by middle-class viewers), and the food metaphor is recurrent: cream cakes versus something good for you.

Which leads me to the final evaluative theme, the argument that a film should have a *moral*, should teach one something (especially if it hasn't been entertaining!), but also, and I think that's the significance of this term here, should have a *meaning*. The pursuit of a moral (a point, a closure) is, in academic cultural studies, seen as naive if not reactionary; it ensures that commercial popular culture, whatever the supposed content, remains orderly. On the other hand, in pursuit of such order, a popular reading often has to pursue what Jonathan Culler once called (with reference to the story of the Three Little Pigs) "improper questions," just as in their concern for the real, popular readers or viewers or listeners are often in pursuit of improper detail, of gossip, of anecdotal truth.[9]

The compulsion to explain the inexplicable, a recurring theme of popular narrative, has the effect of making the remarkable banal and thus, literally, even more remarkable. This is not a political impulse (politics starts from the material conditions in which people live, not with the cultural strategies that make those conditions livable), but it does generate a certain critical momentum, and much of what I've said here about popular values in moviegoing could, I think, be repeated for popular uses of music. Pop records too are assessed in terms of technique and skill and craft, with reference to things, details, done well. Pop records too are evaluated in terms of expense and spectacle, in terms of what has gone into their production, although of course in rock, to a greater extent than in film, there is also the counter-value of cheapness, the small scale, the "independent," which relates, in turn, to how music is judged as believable, true-to-life, sincere. And music is judged too in terms of its ability to take one out of oneself, to offer intense experiences, an overwhelming mood; and by reference to the range of experiences it offers, to genre expectations, to cultural hierarchy.

I'll come back to these points; in particular to the question of how such criteria can be applied to music, which does not appear to have a "content" quite like film or fiction. But before discussing how people talk about music, I want to say something more about the context of judgment. In the end, after all, even the Mass-Observation material is really only evidence of how people thought about film when thinking about it for the purposes of a survey. And what still concerns me are the social circumstances in which people make musical judgments in everyday life, in the usual processes of popular cultural activity.

In music making and listening practice, three social groups are of particular importance (though this obviously doesn't exhaust the musical world). First are the *musicians*.[10]

Of everyone involved in the popular music world, musicians most routinely use value judgments, and use them to effect. Musicians have to make a series of decisions—should I play this note, use this take, hire this musician, change the melody here, the order of the set there, shorten my solo, change the key; and these decisions rest on a constant process of evaluation—that's the wrong chord, the wrong tempo, the wrong sound, the wrong mix—and a constant process of encouragement: that's *good*, leave it! Such decisions are both individual, a reflection of one's own talent (musical talent describes, among other things, the ability to make the right decisions about what's good), and social—only other people, other musicians, can legitimate your decisions. And on the whole my own interviews with rock musicians confirm Borneman's account of jazz musicians' "critical standard,"

> which tends to accept jazz as a trade, a skill and an enjoyable activity. This is a purely pragmatic standard: good is what the good musicians play. Commercial success, instrumental skill, professional acclaim are accepted as self-evident proofs of good musicianship. There is no theory, no intellectual speculation, no nostalgia for the "good old days."[11]

In their study of musicians' experience of stress, Wills and Cooper found that the "prime concern of the popular musician is that he will not be able to play to the best of his ability." Stress is therefore associated with fears that instruments and equipment won't work properly, that rehearsals were inadequate, that one might be too tired or ill to keep up (musicians are notorious hypochondriacs). The basic point is that for the musician, the highest stress factors are those that impinge directly upon *performance*.[12]

At the core of musicians' value judgments, then, are the values on which successful performances depend: values concerning collaboration, the ability to play with other people; the values of trust, reliability, a certain sort of professionalism—even the most anti-professional punk band needs its members to turn up at rehearsals or gigs, to be in a fit state to take to the stage. This is the context in which skill and technique become valued not as abstract qualities but by reference to what must be done in a particular musical genre, what fellow players can take for granted (classically trained musicians routinely report how difficult they first found it to play in rock bands; their supposedly superior technical skills were irrelevant to the music they now wanted to play; and the skills they really needed, for improvisation, were only rudimentary). Similarly, as part of this collaborative work, musicians are expected to have a certain basic knowledge of their instrument and of technology—they need to be able to change a string, tune a drum, program a sampler.

The second cluster of musicians' values emerges from the experience of performance itself, and what interests me most here is how this leads, inevitably it seems, to a sense of alienation from the audience which becomes, in turn, a kind of contempt for it.[13] This is, in one sense, a sociological response: what is work for the musician is play for the audience; the very rhythm of their lives is different, in terms of day and night, let alone status and attention.[14] But what's more significant here is that the bases of musical appreciation are also different, a necessary consequence of the power relation involved: on the one hand, musicians learn to read and manipulate audiences, to please them with tricks and devices that they, the musicians, despise; on the other hand, the musicians experience rejection by audiences, often of the things with which they are most pleased. As Art Hodes puts it neatly, "They don't always applaud what knocks me out; they applaud what knocks them out."[15] And in the words of a New York club date musician, "I can show you a dozen different bands where the musicians are terrible. I mean, they can play, but not well. But, they know when to play a certain song—when to do a rock set, when to do a cha-cha, and get the people riled up so they have a good time. Musicianship plays only a 50 percent role—the rest is knowing how to control the people."[16]

Performance inevitably comes to feel like a compromise, a compromise which is blamed on the audience.[17] But musicians are also, in my experience, surprisingly quick to accuse each other of "prostituting" themselves, whether by following the whims of an employer, an audience, or a market. Earl Van Dyke, for example, notes that for Motown studio musicians in the 1960s, "Jazz was our first love. The reason why we worked at night was to take out all our musical frustrations from playing all that shit during the day in the studio."[18] The implicit assumption is that the most valuable noise is made without reference to anything but "the needs of the music."[19]

In this respect, I don't think there is any great divergence between the basic outlooks of musicians across different music worlds and genres (even if different musics have different "needs"). This relates to the point I made at the end of Chapter 2: musicians of all sorts face similar problems; the sociological question is how different musical values emerge in their solution. I'll consider four such problems here, the first of which is *learning*.

In all music worlds, learning music means learning to play a musical instrument; and in all music worlds, as far as I can tell, a distinction is made between being able to play an instrument, technically, and being able to "feel" it emotionally or instinctively—something which, by definition, cannot be taught. For popular musicians two issues arise here. One is the problem of voice. Singers, it seems, have a "natural" instrument, not simply in the fact that learning to sing for popular performance is not as obviously a technical problem as learning to play guitar or saxophone, but also because the voice is taken to define individuality directly—trying to play guitar just like Hendrix or Clapton is an honorable way into rock music-making; trying to sound just like Lou Reed or Poly Styrene would be thought silly. (Just as club date musicians strive to reproduce, as accurately as possible, the instrumental sound of, say, a Bruce Springsteen track, but would not pretend to put on Bruce's "voice.")

On the one hand, then, singers are not really musicians—their apprenticeship is different. Until 1979 they were not even eligible to join the American Federation of Musicians; as George Seltzer explains, "Before then, a singer with a band applied for AFM membership as a tambourine or cocktail drum player, a real farce."[20] On the other hand, in most pop groups the voice is central to the collective sound, to its popular appeal, and it is taken for granted that the singer will be the star, the center of public attention. The problematic relationship of singer and band feeds into disputes about creativity, as I'll discuss below.

But first I need to make another point about music learning: it is important that we dispose of the myth of the "untrained" pop performer. Pop musicians may be "unschooled" (although, as Rob Walser suggests, rather more have had formal music lessons than one might suppose), but they are not "unlearned," even if this is primarily a matter of learning by doing. And learning in all pop genres is a matter of imitation: the "master" is available in the grooves, and nearly every musician to whom I've spoken has rueful stories of teenage years spent listening to sounds on records and then trying to reproduce them, over and over and over again. As The Who's John Entwistle recalls, "I didn't know it was James Jamerson. I just called him the guy who played bass for Motown, but along with every other bassist in England, I was trying to learn what he was doing."[21]

Such imitation becomes, paradoxically, the source of individual creativity: without the master there to tell you what to do (as in the conservatory) it's up to the would-be musicians to put together what's heard and what's done, to come up with their own way of doing things (which, given the disparities of home and studio sound technology, is likely to be quite novel). At the same time, though, this means that in most popular music genres music-making emerges from obsessive music listening; a certain sort of "fandom" is thus built into the process—which is why when bands come together and fall apart, they do so (as we've seen) in the name of their various musical models, by reference to their record collections.

The second shared problem I want to examine is *rehearsing*. This is the moment when learning becomes social, when other people's judgments come into consideration, when musicians have to move from "messing around" to taking things seriously, from playing to playing together. It indicates, as Konstantin Economou argues, a new kind of "musical awareness," an awareness that takes into account an audience:

> The notion of musical awareness can be said to relate to a notion of socialization into a way of living, and thinking, like a "producer" of music, of making a transition from listener to creator. The production of your own [music] is an important step also in another sense. It highlights the fact that the music you make as a band [will] become more "public," and . . . subject to evaluation by others.[22]

On the one hand, then, musicians have to shift from a personal to a social value system: from trying to sound, to one's own satisfaction, like a record, to trying to sound right for the band, to everyone else's agreement. On the other hand, they have to face the brute fact that "talent" is unequally distributed: you can't always play what you want, but *she* can! The central sociological peculiarity of the popular music world, in short, is that it involves primarily music made by small groups: popular music-making is a small group experience.[23]

I'll come back to the general implications of this, but one aspect that needs special attention from a value perspective is *the audition*. Auditions are useful settings in which to observe musical judgments at work because they are here made explicit: musicians are being judged, discussed, against each other. In the pop world everyone has always been clear that this is not an entirely "musical" judgement. While certain sorts of abilities to do certain sorts of things are obviously a requirement, so is the right sort of person: someone who fits into a band's image and ethos and ambition, someone whose playing suggests a shared world view.[24]

It is sometimes assumed that this distinguishes pop from classical auditions, but, as we've seen, musical "talent" is a problematic concept everywhere, and one only has to look at the systematic exclusion of women from symphony orchestras until fairly recently to wonder what else was at issue besides musicality. Appearance, in particular, is an issue for all public performers. MacLeod notes the increasing importance of appearing young in the club date world, quoting a guitarist (in his early thirties): "Audiences like to *look* at a band . . . and they want to take it from what they see . . . they want it to reflect. People want to look at something and get a feeling of youth and vigour. That's what entertainment is all about."[25] And there are certainly areas of classical music performance too where how one looks is significant, just because the player (as in a rock or pop group) is going to be performing in highly visible circumstances. These days, opera singers, instrumental soloists, and conductors are chosen (by orchestras, record companies, and concert promoters) on the basis of a definition of talent that has as much to do with marketing as musical possibilities.[26]

Which brings me, finally, to the issue of *creativity*. None of my friends who have been through music school has ever been able to explain to me how or when the would-be classical musician decides between composing and interpreting other people's work, or whether the decision marks any sense of "failure." The art music world seems to occupy a position somewhere between the art college, on the one hand (where all students are expected to create their own work) and the literature department, on the other (where studying English literature is not held to mean writing it, even if it is assumed that good writing depends on good reading). In the art music world there is, in short, a paradoxical relationship between performer and contemporary composer: the former is more likely to make a living from music, is unlikely, in fact, to have any interest in contemporary composition, and yet in discursive terms the composer is the genius on whom the whole edifice rests.[27]

For most popular musicians the highest goal these days is obviously "creativity." Since the Beatles British rock bands, for example, have been expected to write their own material; in the United States "cover bands" are taken to be, by definition, inferior to their sources; Frederickson and Rooney have even argued that session players, playing to employer order, become, in effect, "non-persons."[28]

But there are complications to this ideology. If everyone is agreed that creativity (or originality) is a Good Thing, there is often bitter disagreement among musicians as to what musical creativity (or originality) *is*. One aspect of the resulting dispute is the tricky relationship in most pop genres of the "new" to the "formulaic." Another reflects the sociology of pop as a small group activity, and the resulting problems of individualism (which is when pop's own version of the composer versus the performer comes in, particularly when the songwriter is, as is often the case, the singer, the non-musician).[29] These issues are most clearly expressed, perhaps, in *negative* judgments.

For musicians, bad music seems to fall into two broad categories. First, *incompetent* music, music that is badly played, that reflects inadequate skill, technique, and so forth (the magazine of the British Musicians' Union has over the years carried articles and correspondence attacking, successively, rock 'n' roll, disco, punk, and rave music on just these grounds). But even here there's a confusion of a technical "objective" judgment—one can point to a player getting behind the beat, having erratic pitch, only being able to play two notes on the bass guitar—with an ideological, subjective one. The reason given for musicians' incompetence is either that they are *untutored* (which may mean, among other things, that they have "bad habits," that they are simply unable to do certain things because they haven't been taught how to) or that they are *unprofessional* (they're unwilling to learn proper techniques). If the former argument implies that bad musicians want to play differently but can't, the latter implies that there are pop genres in which "bad musicianship"—erratic pitch, wrong notes—is actually welcomed.

This argument spills over into a second sort of musician conception of bad music, that it is *self-indulgent*. I've often heard this criticism (not only from musicians, of course), and it seems to conflate at least three different sorts of description:

> *selfishness:* bad musicians forget that "good music" is a collective
> practice, and use performance to show off their own virtuosity
> or character, to dominate the microphone or sound mix, to play
> too long or too loudly. Such musicians don't properly offset their

musical colleagues, and the resulting music is "unbalanced" (this, as we've seen, is the sound mixers' view).

emptiness: bad musicians indulge in form at the expense of content, make music that "has nothing to say" but says it elaborately anyway. Their music is not made for any good reason but merely as a display of technical ability; such musicians play something only to show that they can. This is a common critique of "session musician music."

incomprehensibility: bad musicians play in a completely introverted way, for self-satisfaction or for therapeutic reasons, as a matter of private obsession. Their music is not communicative; it does not acknowledge or address an audience. This is the workaday musician critique of "arty" music, of the "new" jazz, for example, and of avant-garde rock.

As these arguments make clear, for most musicians, "creativity" cannot be judged in abstraction; it has to be defined in terms of music's perceived social and communicative functions. And there is a further complication here. In pop terms "originality" can be understood both as a kind of free-floating expressive individuality and as a market distinction, a selling point.[30] Popular musicians may, then, be trapped as well as freed by their "originality" (if it becomes just a moment of fashion), and in this world it is not even assumed that they will improve with age (as with jazz and classical performers). Does anyone—the Stones themselves?—believe that the Rolling Stones are a *better* band now than they were thirty years ago?

But I want to end this discussion on a different note, with the suggestion that when musicians talk about good and bad music they reveal an aesthetic as strongly rooted in ethical values and a sense of responsibility (to each other, to ideal listeners) as in technical values, the ability to make sounds that other people can't. Hence their use of the terms *right* and *wrong*.

John Miller Chernoff has written an eloquent account of what it means to be an African musician:

His musical creativity directly dramatizes his mind as it is balanced on the understanding that his individuality, like the rhythms that he plays, can only be seen in relationship. In the distinctive style of the expression which he must bring forward in the fulfilment of his complex social role, the personality of the musician becomes important in the sense that the quality and maturity of his aesthetic contribution either limits or expands the realization of a general concern, determining whether the people present constitute a community.[31]

Compare the more mundanely expressed thoughts of a Yorkshire brass bandsman:

> Well, what always inspired me is that you have twenty-four men sweating and straining away, and for nothing. They don't get any money out of it. It's just to *make music better*. It's a movement . . . And if you're on your holidays, just find out where there's a band playing and go around and you've got friends. Lots of community spirit.[32]

A different sort of community, but the same belief that it is something *made sense of in music-making*. I'm reminded of how much of the local music described in Ruth Finnegan's *The Hidden Musicians* is made for charity, not just to raise money but also, again, to articulate a community (or, in the Milton Keynes context, many different communities). Popular musicians, who are on the whole unromantic about themselves and what they do, have a surprisingly moral attitude to what "music" should ideally be.

The case is very different for the second significant group to exercise judgment in the everyday pop process, the *producers*. I'm using this term loosely, to describe the broad range of people whose concern is to turn music and musicians into profitable commodities, and to draw attention to the recording studio as the place where the most interesting and influential musical value judgments are made.[33] But the studio is, in fact, only one site for the long chain of decisions which make up "the production of culture," as musicians lay down demo tracks (deciding on their best songs, their best versions, their best takes); as A&R departments determine which, if any, of the accumulated demos are any good, which need following up, which group or musician or song has any "potential"; as groups are signed and groomed and new decisions are made about song and image, about recording and the recording process, about releases and promotion; as the records go off to deejays and critics, to promoters and retailers, who in turn decide whether this group, this music, is worth playing or reviewing or booking or stocking; as consumers tune in, turn up, and make their own market choices.[34]

The point I want to make about this process is that at each stage, presumably, something—an act, a song, a record—has been judged positively; otherwise it wouldn't be passed along the line. And yet there is also a considerable dropout rate: the percentage of tracks or performances that are eventually rated positively by the public is tiny. The biggest fallout occurs at the beginning of the process (very few demos actually result in recording contracts) and at the end (fewer than one in ten releases command much of an audience). Two things follow. First, record companies spend a considerable amount of time producing "failures," and yet there are very few studies of these failures—the "public verdict" is allowed a retrospective authority. But, *at the time,* people in those record companies were making enthusiastic judgments. On what basis? How on earth, I used to wonder as a record reviewer, did *anyone* come to release this? Second, it's easy to use this model to set up a clash of art and commerce cast in terms of musicians versus the business (and one can see why from the musicians' point of view, as their demos are rejected, their releases "not properly promoted," the stress line falls like this).

There are a number of ways, however, in which this description doesn't work. To begin with, the musicians' relationship with a record company in the production of their sound is as much collaborative as combative, and, indeed, at least one aspect of A&R judgment concerns a group's collaborative potential, its professionalism. Both parties, in other words, expect art and commerce to be intertwined.[35] It is clear, moreover, that producers have a *more* romantic ideology of creativity (and creative success) than musicians; just as in the conservatory, the key term is "talent" (the key task its exploitation). And while company personnel know how exploitation works, talent remains mysterious, especially when the public fails to hear it. Record companies, or, at least, record company executives can, in fact, be surprisingly obstinate in sticking with their belief in a talent that hasn't yet been "recognized," and their value judgments are shot through with Romantic terminology—the musician as genius, music as ineffable, the musical experience as overwhelming. At the core of this, of course, is the problem I've already mentioned, the double articulation of originality, as the source of both art and profit (a double articulation defined by the copyright laws on which music as business depends).[36]

My second general point about industry values is that all producers' judgments rest, as Hennion argues, on an imputed audience. Each decision, at each step of the way (and this includes the musicians' original preparation of their demo) means a judgment both about the "quality" of the music and about its likely market. Sometimes these can be separated—in genre terms, for example: many demos are rejected because A&R teams decide that there is no market for "that kind of music." But often they are impossible to disentangle, they are part of the same evaluative process, and this means that the audience too is romanticized, its tastes and choices also treated as mysterious. There is a touching faith in the industry in anyone who can claim to read the audience, to be in tune with public taste (the usual measure of which is a previous success); such people carry a special authority in in-house arguments: they have a "good ear," and it takes many failures to offset the original success.[37]

But then record companies don't just produce cultural commodities and lay them out in the marketplace. They also try to persuade people to buy them, and this means telling the potential consumer why the product is valuable. The product, to put this another way, is laid out for us so as to *invite* assessment. The record company works to define the evaluative grounds, thus ensuring that we make the right judgment.

The problem for the record industry is that its best means of communication with its consumers are mediated: sounds reach us through radio, film, and television; stars reach us via newspapers, magazines, and video. And media people judge music according to their own criteria. Does it suit my playlist? My demographic? A skilled record company marketing department is, therefore, skilled in its handling of a complex of value frames, in its role in ongoing value arguments. I came to learn as a rock critic that press handouts weren't just designed to sell a sound to me, but also to persuade me to write about a record or artist in the right way, in the right discursive frame. Take, for example, Chrysalis's 1990 pitch for Child's Play:

> Good playing, solid songwriting, hard work and perseverance. Remember when these were the qualities that set apart a band destined for the big time? In a highly competitive market, these are still the elements that decide who will be in for the long haul—the kind of band that *earns* their success by winning over their fans' hearts as well as ears. That personal connection has been the key element in the success of Chrysalis recording artist Child's Play, whose powerful debut album is titled *Rat Race.*
>
> Drummer/vocalist John Allen pegs his band's music as "blue-collar rock" and that seems an apt description for their versatile sound. Child's Play's identity is not based on a specific musical idea, but rather on an attitude towards life and the struggle it involves. This is a band who have seen tough times and dry spells, and they reflect their deep-seeded determination with an aggressive hybrid of blues, metal, punk and good old rock and roll. Child's Play are more familiar with jeans and sweat than hairspray and eyeliner, and followers in their hometown of Baltimore, Maryland know they can count on the band to understand and even share their daily concerns.
>
> "We have a lot of songs that are 'pay your dues' or 'times are tough'

sort of ideas," Allen relates. "We all come from working-class backgrounds, so we've got the stories and inspiration to write songs about trying to get ahead. Our fans relate to our down-to-earth attitude. We write and sing about real-life stuff; the relationships that middle-class people go through."[38]

And this is what BMG had to say about Raging Slab, the same year:

The band's first single, "Don't Dog Me," is a perfect representation of their classic hard rock style. Over a matched guitar lick, lead singer/songwriter/guitarist Greg Strempka howls the title as heavy white-boy-blues riffs not heard since the early '70s boil out of the speakers . . . From the dynamic melodicism of "Geronimo" to the aching balladry of "When Love Comes Loose" and ending up with the bruising double kickbass wallop of "Dig A Hole," the album is diverse. "We've been called Lynyrd Skynyrd meets Metallica," explains Greg, "which is not as unlikely or ridiculous as it first sounds. There's a great diversity in the band. We're capable of doing a lot of styles, but most of the time we do them all at once."[39]

What interests me here is less what these blurbs say—how they put the groups concerned into a story—but why they do so. My final point about producers, then, is this. They too mediate between performers and audiences. To put this another way: once rock and pop (or classical) performers are embroiled in the sales process they cease to have unmediated access to their listeners (even live performance is staged in the terms of a sales narrative). This situation is usually treated negatively: producers are seen to "interfere" in the proper communication of musician and audience. But this is not necessarily the case: they may, in fact, make that communication possible. At the very least (to come to the *consumer*, the third major player in the pop world), the musician is protected to an extent from having to answer the producer's obsessive question: "But what does the listener want?"

Academics have been no more successful in answering this question than market researchers, but they have confirmed two general principles as relevant to any answer: first, that what listeners want is determined by who they are; second, that what they want is an effect of the nature of "wanting." The first principle implies a connection between people's social and aesthetic values; the second suggests that aesthetic theory must be related to an account of fantasy. The first argument has been developed most systematically in terms of "homology," music interpreted as a coded expression of the social aims and values of the people to whom it appeals.[40] Fantasy-based theories focus, instead, on why a particular piece of music is appropriate for a certain kind of pleasure, on how it meets psychological needs.[41]

These arguments have been developed primarily in the study of youth music, and there is an obvious tendency to divide them up along gender lines: the appeal of boys' music explained by boys' social lives; the appeal of girls' music explained by their private fantasies. But the best academic accounts of youth music consumption show that these approaches must be combined to make sense.[42] If consumers (of all ages) value music for the function it fills, then that "function" must be defined both socially and psychologically.[43]

Given this, the question becomes how consumers' attitudes to music relate to musicians' values (compare, for example, Donna Weinstein's consumer-led analysis of heavy metal with Robert Walser's performer-led account),[44] which is to return to the issue of professional musicians' apparent contempt for their audiences (whatever their communal ideals). In exploring the musician/listener value gap now from the listener's side I want to begin from an argument about high cultural musicology.

In his stimulating exploration of the reason why what musicologists say about music appears to bear no relationship to how ordinary people hear it, Nicholas Cook argues that the problem is not the difference between two sorts of listeners, but between two sorts of music. He generalizes, that is to say, from a point Kathryn Bailey makes about a work by Webern: it consists of "two quite different pieces—a visual, intellectual piece and an aural, immediate piece, one for the analyst and another for the listener."[45] But what Cook goes on to suggest is that there is a similar difference between the music a composer writes (and a performer plays) and the music a listener hears: "What makes a musician is not that he knows how to play one instrument or another, or that he knows how to read music: it is that he is able to grasp musical structure in a manner appropriate for musical production—the most obvious (though of course by no means the only) example of such production being performance."[46]

And musicologists seek to "grasp" music this way too—in a manner appropriate for musical production, rather than for musical listening. (A similar point could be made about literary theorists since New Criticism; the descriptions of how a text works make much better sense to someone trying to write a poem than they do to someone reading it—a point of which T. S. Eliot, at least, was well aware.) As Cook puts it, "notes simply do not exist for the listener"; they hear sounds. And he concludes that a musical culture "is a tradition of imagining sound as music. Its basic identity lies in its mechanism for constituting sounds as intentional objects, from the level of a single note to that of a complete work. This means that the ubiquitous discrepancies between the manner in which musicians conceive music and that in which listeners experience it are endemic to musical culture. Indeed, they define it."[47]

In the pop music world it was obvious from the start that the object the musicologist defined was not the object the pop fan heard. But when William Mann's and Wilfrid Mellers' and Deryck Cooke's elaborately technical analyses of the Beatles were mockingly quoted (by musicologists and pop fans alike), it was never quite clear whom the laugh was against: the Beatles for being too simple to carry the weight of such words? Or the critics for so misunderstanding pop pleasures?[48]

What Cook suggests is that musicologists in fact misunderstand all listeners' pleasures; and what was really at issue in the 1960s was the nature of pop composition: did the Beatles really *write* like this, in Aeolian clusters and so forth? The orthodox musicological view of the time was bluntly stated by Sir Jack Westrup, in an editorial for *Music and Letters* in 1968:

> The world of pop is largely a featureless desert. It is hardly surprising that the life of a "pop" song is so short. This is not simply because most of the performers have unlovely and insignificant voices, which would be inaudible without the aid of a microphone. The reason lies rather in the appalling poverty of melodic invention, which is not relieved by a persistent rhythm or even by harmonic ingenuities which serious critics mistakenly attribute to the singers instead of the expert musicians who write the "backing."[49]

Only the arranger, the "expert" musician, did something that felt to Westrup like real composition; only the arranger organized notes on a page. And twenty-five years later Robert Walser can write an entirely convincing musicological analysis of heavy metal not because pop musicians now compose like classical musicians (though the processes are rather more similar than Westrup realized) but because Walser (himself a guitarist) knows how the rock composition process works, can "grasp" (in Cook's words) rock's "musical structure in a manner appropriate for musical production."[50] The question remains, though: does a technical understanding of what metal musicians do explain what metal audiences hear? Is what sounds right to the music's makers what sounds good to the music's listeners?

Enter the critic. In high cultural history, when at the beginning of the nineteenth century good music became autonomous, something conceived for its own sake, irrespective of audience response, then the critic became necessary as an expert, as someone who could explain the music to the public, teach it how to listen. The musician/listener gap was taken for granted and the critic was by definition on the artist's side, championing the new and the difficult. As a large-scale commodity culture emerged at the beginning of this century, though, the mediation role became equally significant the other way around: the mass audience had to be interpreted to producers, and the critic became the ideal consumer too.

Or at least, some critics did, because what really happened was a split, which helped define modernism, between writers on the side of the artist and writers on the side of the audience, and different discursive values emerged accordingly. For the former, as Levin Schücking notes of theater reviewers, the critical observation that "the play succeeded with the public" became a standard line in the scathing review, as German theater critics sought to ally themselves with experimental playwrights (and the future) against audiences (and the past).[51]

"The crowd liked them" remains a standard line in a scathing review.[52] Andrew Porter's 1990 *New Yorker* notice of the Met's *Ballo in Maschera*, for example, one of the most scathing reviews I've ever read (Porter begins by calling the production "a disgusting exhibition," "an obscenity," and "a circus"), suggests sarcastically that perhaps director Piero Faggioni "meant to mock and satirize the opera in question, the whole idea of opera, the Met, and a Met audience uncaring about music and easily pleased . . . If his aim was to make fun of *Ballo*, he missed the mark with the first-night audience. The show was acclaimed."[53]

Built into such criticism is a suspicion of popularity itself—in Schoenberg's words, "If it is art it is not for all, and if it is for all it is not art"—and, in particular, of the effects of the pursuit of popularity.[54] Such suspicion is equally common among critics writing about music that is, supposedly, commercial to begin with. Here is Ernest Borneman, for example, on the plight of jazz in the late 1930s, faced with "the opulence of the new music industry that had arisen phoenix-like out of the ashes of the depression":

> So much money was invested in each "hit tune" that the investors could no longer permit it to be submerged in the contrapuntal intricacies of old-time jazz; thus harmonisation replaced counterpoint, arrangement replaced improvisation, and Tin Pan Alley tunes replaced folk tunes. So much money had at the same time been invested in each band that the band manager could no longer afford to let the musicians play as they liked. In the old days the musicians could take occasional busmen's holidays to play the music as they thought music should be played; they still made enough money to earn a living. But now they had to make money for a whole dragon's

tail of hangers-on and go-betweens—managers, bookers, agents, pluggers, publicity men, girl singers and front men. To pay for these vast new overheads, the music had to be tailored to a much wider public than jazz had ever been able to attract. This process of making jazz intelligible to the moron was based on a simple recipe: Mix the phrasing of New Orleans jazz with the arrangement and orchestration of sweet jazz and the result will be swing music. The logic of the process was based on the assumption that the common denominator of all audiences is the lowest intelligence prevailing among them.[55]

Compare this to Ira Robbins, one-time editor of *Trouser Press* and long-time champion of "independent" American music, writing forty-five years later about the crisis facing the rock scene at the end of the 1980s:

Goals that were once considered standard—innovation, artistic effort, motivation beyond the pursuit of the market share—are no longer prized, and the mute, ignorant acquiescence of a generation raised on a steady diet of garbage rubber stamps the worst and the cheesiest, encouraging the record industry to search out and exploit ever inferior artists whose marketing skills increasingly outweigh their ability (or even interest) in making original (or even cleverly derivative) music. Singers who can't sing, bands who can't play, producers who do all the work and trivialize the artist, classic records borrowed wholesale, soundalike songwriting factories, superstars totally beholden to technology for their creations, Oz-like pop icons who hide behind a carefully groomed image—it all adds up to a total abandonment of the creative autonomy that once was the hallmark of the rock era.[56]

In short, the themes that haunted modernist writers and critics at the beginning of the century (their "high" cultural concern to be true to their art, to disdain mere entertainment, to resist market forces; their longing for a "sensitive minority" readership, for what Ezra Pound called "a party of intelligence") still haunt popular music.[57] What needs stressing, though, is that it is not just critics who hold these views, but also the readership for whom they write (and which they help define): music magazines like *Melody Maker* or *Rolling Stone* in the late '60s and early '70s, like *New Musical Express* in the mid to late '70s, like *Spin* in the '80s, were aimed at consumers who equally defined themselves against the "mainstream" of commercial taste, wherever that might lie. (And this goes back to a point I made in Chapter 2:

the most interesting aesthetic distinctions aren't those between the high and the low, but those between the select and the mainstream, the radical and the conservative.)[58]

For most rock critics, then (this was certainly my experience), the issue in the end isn't so much representing music to the public (the public to the musician) as creating a knowing community, orchestrating a collusion between selected musicians and an equally select part of the public—select in its superiority to the ordinary, undiscriminating pop consumer. The critic is, in this respect, a fan (most rock writers start on fanzines; most are, indeed, collectors), with a mission to preserve a perceived quality of sound, to save musicians from themselves, to define the ideal musical experience for listeners to measure themselves against. Ernest Borneman suggests that the jazz collector

> tends to identify enjoyment of this or that musician's style, or pleasure in listening to records from this or that period of jazz, with evidence of the musician's or the style's objective value. Collectors are impetuous, emotional, rarely interested in any music but jazz alone. The degree of musical illiteracy among them is astonishing to the academic critic . . . They attack the current name bands as "commercial" and consider all musicians inferior to their chosen idol.[59]

And even if, as critics, rock fans (and collectors) have to suggest some sort of "balance" in their opinions, the language of music criticism still depends on the confusion of the subjective and objective, on the championing not so much of music as of a way of listening to music. Roland Barthes famously remarked that music critics are obsessed with adjectives.[60] Henry Kingsbury notes their strange habit of imbuing notes with personality.[61] My favorite example of this is Norman Lebrecht's description of Harrison Birtwistle's music: "It is a totally personal sound—tough, gritty, even violent; and at the same time shy, warm and slyly humorous."[62] Such descriptive terms, designed to capture in words what the music sounds like, are also always implicitly theoretical, referring to a general account of how music works. In this there is no difference between the classical and the pop critic. Compare Lebrecht on Birtwistle, just quoted, and Robert Sandall on Lou Reed's *Magic and Loss:* "the deep reverberation of Mike Wasserman's slithery bass, the spry twang/cosmic howl of the guitars and the booming spaces around Michael Blair's drums."[63] In both cases the adjectives turn description into interpretation and are effective only to the extent that we are prepared to agree that, yes, this is how musical sounds mean.

In general, pop criticism uses adjectives to two ends: to relate the music to its possible uses ("Plaintive Malian folk-blues ballads for single voice and lonesome guitar. Fragile, delicately strummed, soothing and sorrowful. Good for a self-indulgent sulk in the small hours") and to place it generically ("Impressively trashy and abrasive punk'n'roll with chainsaw guitars, a jittery Cramps-style breakneck approach and angry Iggy vocals recorded over the CB, possibly. Looks like we got ourselves a convoy").[64]

In either case the purpose is consumer guidance, and the reviewer draws on conventional assumptions about what different sorts of music, different sorts of sound, are good for. Which is where the knowingness, the collusion of critic and reader, comes in. Such reviews are incomprehensible to anyone who is not already informed in the right way. Criticism, in other words, is not just producing a version of the music for the reader but also a version of the listener for the music. Take this quote (from a review of Teenage Fan Club's *Bandwagonesque*): "'December' is a fey, honey-dripping exercise in Chiltonese, 'Guiding Star' is the Jesus and Mary Chain attempting to write a No. 1 single for the Christmas of 1974, 'Star Sign' degenerates, after a glassy, ominous intro, into lily-livered Byrds-by-rote anaemia."[65]

I think these descriptions are, indeed, elegant and pithy ways of saying just what these tracks sound like, but they encode in a few words an extraordinary number of references to both pop history and pop motivation. Rock criticism, in short, makes arguments about audiences as well as about sounds, about the ways in which music works as a social event. This is most obvious, of course, in concert reviews, for ideological reasons neatly summarized by Geoffrey Himes: "Live performances have always been the most intense, most revealing experiences in pop music. That's where you can tell if an artist can really sing, really make you dance, really deliver an unfaked emotion or epiphany to a breathing audience."[66] The argument here hinges on the word "really," and it is a very peculiar argument: the suggestion that if an artist can make you dance on record she's not really making you dance is capped by the implication that record and radio listeners aren't really breathing!

If high critics tend to see the audience as accountable to the artist, rock critics are equally concerned to make the artist accountable to the audience. In the former case the critics' authority, the reason why anyone should take any notice of them, rests on their technical and historical knowledge of the music at issue, their academic credentials. In the latter case the critics' authority rests on their knowledge of the audience and its needs and values and this, in turn, rests on who the critic is. The self thus becomes a key part of rock critics' argument, a key term in their evaluative vocabulary; what's at issue is how the music engages them emotionally, and audiences are found wanting not just as philistines—refusing to listen to difficult and demanding sounds—but also as dull, unable to be moved by them.

Rock criticism is driven by the need to differentiate: music is good because it is different, different from the run of "mainstream" pop, different in the special intensity of feelings it brings about. It follows that most judgments of music are simultaneously explanations of music: the judgment is the explanation, the explanation is the judgment. Musical descriptions are routinely couched, for example, in sociological terms: "bad music" is so assessed by reference to a "bad" system of production or to "bad" social effects; critical evaluation works by reference to social institutions or social behavior for which the music simply acts as a sign.

I can clarify this by going through the most common critical arguments about musical production. There are two familiar positions. The first is that music is judged in the context of or by reference to a critique of mass production. Bad music is "standardized" or "formula" music. Good music is implicitly "original" or "autonomous," and the explanation built into the judgment depends on the familiar Marxist/Romantic distinction between serial production, production to commercial order, to meet a market, and artistic creativity, production determined only by individual intention, by formal and technical rules and possibilities.

Among other things, this means that "formula" or "standard" production that is not capitalist is not, in this discursive context, usually judged bad: the fact that all disco numbers in the late 1970s "sounded the same" is a mark of unhealthy (commercial) formulaic production; the fact that all folk songs collected in east Norfolk in the late 1870s sounded the same is a sign of their (healthy) roots in a collective, oral history. More generally, we could say that such "formula criticism" tends to be genre-centric: minor variations in teeny-bop music (the fact that the stars have different vocal registers, say) are taken to be quite insignificant; minor variations in rural blues guitar phrasings are taken to be of great aesthetic importance.

A second sort of criticism, which refers to production but without a Marxist edge, equates bad music with imitative music—again, the implicit contrast is with "original" or, perhaps, "individual" sounds; a record or artist is dismissed for sounding just like someone else (or, not least, for sounding just like their own earlier records or songs). The critical assumption is that this reflects a cynical or pathetic production decision; it is not just an accident or coincidence.

There are many variations on this sort of argument. The most interesting is the distinction between "the cover version" and "the version." The cover version is almost always heard as bad—this is now the usual attitude to the white pop versions of black songs and records in the 1950s, for example: Pat Boone's "Tutti Frutti" is probably the nearest thing to a consensual bad record in popular music history, a track that is both exploitative and feeble. (One aspect of learning to be a rock fan in the 1960s was, in fact, learning to prefer originals to covers. And this was, as I recall, something that did have to be learned: nearly all the records I had bought in the late 1950s had been cover versions.) The fact that Pat Boone's "personal stamp" was put on Little Richard's music is clearly a bad thing.

"Version," by contrast, refers to a situation in which the "copy" is taken to improve on the original, to render it "bad" by revealing what it could have been. Here, reversing the previous argument, black covers of white originals are routinely valued positively (Ray Charles singing "I Can't Stop Loving You"), and rock arrangers are taken to make pop songs more interesting (Vanilla Fudge's "You Keep Me Hanging On," Phil Collins' "You Can't Hurry Love"). The fact that Ray Charles puts his personal stamp on Don Gibson's song is obviously a good thing. Imitation, in short, is as much an ideological as a musical matter; the critical response depends on an account of who is imitating whom and for what attributed reason.

Musical judgments referring to production processes obviously depend on particular sorts of knowledge. To condemn a record as imitative, we must know (or know about) the "original"; to describe a song as "standardized" means that we have heard (or heard of) other songs of a similar type. Such knowledge may be more or less extensive, more or less valid; judgments in this respect often rest on what one might call hypothetical knowledge, on unexamined assumptions about record company, studio, and marketing decisions. Listeners read from a record how they think it must have been produced, and then condemn it (or not) accordingly. Hence the familiar enough experience (to which people are loath to admit) that we need to know who a record is by before we can evaluate it. But whatever knowledge we might need in order thus to label music good or bad, we are still, in the end, referring to the something "in the music" that led us down this discursive path in the first place. And the recurring musical judgment here seems to be in terms of excessive familiarity: a piece of music is bad because it uses musical clichés; because its development is easily predictable; because nothing happens.[67]

Critical musical judgments, in short, are almost always entangled with social explanations of why the music is good or bad, and much of our day-to-day argument about music is conducted in just this way: aesthetic judgments are tangled up with ethical judgments. One could argue further, though, that what's involved here is not an explanation of good or bad music as such (though that is how such judgments are presented) but a justification for using the labels "good" and "bad" in the first place, labels which are, in fact, assertions of personal taste and depend on a different system of musical meaning altogether.

Consumers' everyday judgments (as against critics' "considered" views) tend to take place in noisy situations, in free-wheeling conversations about musical meaning and value, and their terms and judgments are inevitably less consistent, less coherent, and less self-conscious than I have so far implied. In conversational criticism we certainly use terms which draw on articulated discourses, which deploy assumptions about art and folk and pop, which refer to the ways in which musicians speak and critics write; but we also, equally certainly, confuse them. Three everyday terms seem particularly significant here.

First, *authenticity*. This clearly relates to questions of production but not to a thought-through theory; "inauthentic," that is to say, is a term that can be applied evaluatively even within genres which are, in production terms, "inauthentic" by definition—fans can distinguish between authentic and in-authentic Eurodisco, and what is being described by implication is not how something was actually produced but a more inchoate feature of the music itself, a perceived quality of sincerity and commitment. It's as if people expect music to mean what it says, however cynical that meaning, and music can be heard as being "false" to its own premises. How do people hear music in such an ethical way? What is it about a record that makes us say, "I just don't believe it!" (my reaction to Paul Simon's *Graceland*, for example)? This is obviously related somehow to the ways in which we judge people's sincerity generally; it is a human as well as a musical judgment. And it also reflects our extra-musical beliefs—what I already knew about Paul Simon obviously had an effect on how I heard his music (and new knowledge—new music—might mean I changed my mind).

Second, *taste*. The question here concerns the musically appropriate. On the one hand, this is a functional question, whether narrowly (is the music right for this dance floor, this party, this film?) or broadly (is the music right for this situation—the Trammps' "Disco Inferno" for a gay funeral? Whitney Houston's "I Will Always Love You" for everyone else's?). Answers depend on one's assumptions about music's place or function in the artistic or social situations concerned. On the other hand, this is an ethical question about the suitability of popular music (as a form of entertainment) to deal with certain issues—disease and death, for example—and, in particular, to deal with them in an "entertaining" way (hence the common negative response to country music "maudlin" songs, to pop and rock commentaries on social and political affairs—Phil Collins on the homeless; Bono on Bosnia). Judgment, in short, rests less on what this particular music is than on an argument about what music in general should be. (And we can have quite contradictory responses to a song or record, disapproving of our own enjoyment!)

Third, *stupidity*. This is a very common term in popular discourse that is not often (or at least not in quite this way) articulated by professional critics. And it is an interesting term because it is not only applied to words or lyrics—people can and do find tunes and arrangements and sounds stupid too. What is meant here? Clearly the analogy is with the way we call a statement (or the person making the statement) stupid, a suggestion not just that their account of the world is wrong, but that it is also somehow demeaning, that it demeans us through our involvement, however unwilling, in the collusive act of listening (to someone making, say, a racist or sexist remark). Stupid music in this (non-academic) context is offensive because it seems to deny what we're capable of, humanly, rationally, ethically, aesthetically.

And that brings me to the essence of everyday musical value. I'm happy to concede that musical assessment is, as they say, a matter of taste, that it involves a judgment which depends on the particular (changing, irrational) social and psychological circumstances of the person making it. On the other hand, whatever the individual bases of our judgments, once made we do seek to justify them, to explain them, and my concern in this chapter has been to describe the discursive languages that are available to us, and to point out some of their problems. But the questions I want to stress now, the issues that I will focus on in the rest of this book, are different.

First, it is clear that we need concepts of good and bad music even if we know full well that we won't be able to agree on how the labels should be applied. The marking off of some tracks and genres and artists as "good" and others as "bad" seems to be a necessary part of popular music pleasure and use; it is a way in which we establish our place in various music worlds and use music as a source of identity. And "good" and "bad" are key words because they suggest that aesthetic and ethical judgments are tied together: not to like a record is not just a matter of taste; it is also a matter of morality.

Second, even though, as a sociologist, I've translated this evaluative process into a use of language, a matter of discourse, what's really at issue is feeling. In the end, "bad music" describes an emotional rather than an ideological judgment. We don't like a record; we then seek to account for that dislike (we don't, on the whole, arm ourselves with a grid of ideological consistency through which everything must pass before we feel it). Feelings, particularly feelings of like or dislike—for music, for people—are often surprising, contradictory, and disruptive; they go against what we're supposed to feel, what we'd like to feel. The important point here is not that critical judgment is always a process of justification (and not really explanation), but that the feelings it describes are real (and not just discursive).

When we label something as "bad music," then, it is because it is music that upsets or offends us, that we don't want to listen to. *Please* play something else! Do I *have* to listen to this? It grates, hurts, bores; it's ugly, it's painful; it's driving me *mad!* As Howard Becker once wrote, the problem for a sociologist of culture is that "people do not experience their aesthetic beliefs as merely arbitrary and conventional; they feel that they are natural, proper and moral."[68] And the word I would emphasize here is "feel." Nobody needs to be told what is good or bad music—you know it the moment you hear it.

Half a century after Mass-Observation investigated popular film values, the Music in Daily Life Project in Buffalo, New York, set out to ask equally ordinary people, "What is music about for you?"[69] The replies echo the themes of the moviegoers. Truth to life: "I like music by people who seem to have a grip on life, and they're not just selling themselves out or being superficial." "People hearing those songs know that they're real things, that really happened, not just someone sitting down and trying to write a hit." The significance of genre: "Rock is wild, violent, and everything I don't want to hear . . . Rock music is a cultural [*sic*] I don't care for." "It [country music] doesn't have too much relevance in my life."[70]

But what is most striking about the accumulated voices of people talking about music is the sense that music matters not just because it is (like film) a powerful force for taking one out of oneself, but also because it can take one deep inside. On the one hand, "Well, it is a . . . I suppose, a kind of tonic or medication of sorts. It enables me to feel better usually, even if it is a small piece or sad piece. I feel some sort of relief when I'm listening to music. I can be transported or get out of myself or my immediate surroundings and . . . take a journey on the melody." On the other hand, "It brings out feelings you didn't even know you had." "It gives me the same kind of happiness that being angry gives me. A kind of fierce feeling." "Without music, I would die . . . I just wouldn't be. I wouldn't have a personality . . . It just fills up every muscle and vein in my body." "Like it's either, um, music's gotta, it's gotta like . . . hit you a certain way like it's gotta . . . give you some kind of feeling like either if you're in a depressed mood, you want to be, you know, it helps you to be depressed."[71]

The problem, of course, is to explain how it does this, and the other recurring point here, one on which to end this chapter, is that musical talk is both necessary and useless:

A: I just think this is great . . . I don't know why I like it so much. And some of them I've listened to so many times that I sing along. (laughs) Like "Here Comes Jesus" in German.

Q: But why is it so great?

A: I don't know.

Q: Well, you have to tell me.

A: It's hard to explain . . . it's all feelings and emotions . . .

Q: You gotta tell me why, though.

A: I don't know why. (annoyed) Just like you don't know why your music is a particular way . . . even if I tried to tell you a million reasons, you know, like it reminds me of home or because of the key . . . even if I say all these things . . . (she stops and gasps as a new part of the piece starts, an oboe solo) Now this part is *sad*. (listens for a while)

Q: Why is this part sadder than the other part?

A: (glares) I'm getting annoyed.

Q: Why?

A: Because the fact is it *is* sad. It evokes certain feelings. It has and it probably always will. Why? Well I don't know why. I could talk about the notes or the voice or the oboe.

Q: Well, go ahead then.

A: But I feel no . . . I mean I feel somewhat of a . . . maybe I just want to enjoy it, I don't want to explain it. I don't want to start describing "what" and "why." I just like it and like to hear it . . . like to be moved by it. I feel no *need* to explain it . . . Maybe it's programmed into my genes so that a G-sharp really knocks me out.

Q: Okay, okay . . .

A: . . . It's not a scientific experiment. And I'm glad because I don't want to know . . . I don't want to know. I don't care.[72]

Genre Rules

4

The little child is permitted to
label its drawing "This is a
cow—this is a horse" and so
on. This protects the child. It
saves it from the sorrow and
wrong of hearing its cows and
its horses criticized as kanga-
roos and work-benches.

Mark Twain[1]

**When we obtain a theory of genres we
will then be able to see that every genre
has its own specific objective laws which
no artist can ignore without peril.**

Georg Lukács[2]

There was a program on a college radio station in Ithaca when I was
living there in early 1991 which described itself as "Pure American folk from
singers who defy labels," and this self-contradictory statement can stand as
the motto for this chapter, in which I will examine the role of labels in popular
music and consider the seemingly inescapable use of generic categories in the
organization of popular culture. These are so much a part of our everyday
lives that we hardly notice their necessity—in the way bookshop shelves are
laid out (novels distributed between romance, mystery, science fiction, horror,
popular fiction, contemporary fiction, classics, and so on); in the way TV
program guides classify the evening's entertainment (sitcom, game show, talk
show, crime series, documentary); in the ways films are advertised and videos
shelved (comedy, Western, horror, musical, adventure, adult); in the way
magazines are laid out at newsagents (women's, children's, hobby, general
interest, fashion, computers, music). Such labels are only noticeable, in fact,
when we want a book or video or magazine *that doesn't fit* and suddenly don't
know where to find it.

In this chapter I will argue that such labeling lies, in practice, at the heart
of pop value judgments. I'll start (as with the examples already cited) with
the use of genre categories to *organize the sales process*.

Genre distinctions are central to how record company A&R departments
work. The first thing asked about any demo tape or potential signing is what

75

sort of music is it, and the importance of this question is that it integrates an inquiry about the music (what does it sound like) with an inquiry about the market (who will buy it). The underlying record company problem, in other words, how to turn music into a commodity, is solved in generic terms. Genre is a way of defining music in its market or, alternatively, the market in its music. (Exactly the same could be said of the way publishers handle manuscripts and book ideas, film companies scripts, and television companies program proposals.)

Whatever decision is made generically (and this may mean serious argument, may involve composite or "crossover" markets, and thus may not be straightforward at all) will have a determining influence on everything that happens to the performer or record thereafter. A record company will, for example, immediately look at the spread of its acts. (Does it need something or something else of this sort? Will the new signing compete with or complement existing talent?) And once signed, once labeled, musicians will thereafter be expected to act and play and look in certain ways; decisions about recording sessions, promotional photos, record jackets, press interviews, video styles, and so on, will all be taken with genre rules in mind. The marketing and packaging policies, in other words, that begin the moment an act is signed are themselves determined by genre theories, by accounts of how markets work and what people with tastes for music *like this* want from it.

Initially, then, to understand how a genre label works—why these particular musical characteristics have been put together in this particular way—is to understand a reading of the market. In 1907, for example, the American music publisher Jerome H. Remick offered songs for sale under the following labels: ballad, cowboy song, novelty, Irish comic, coon song, Indian love song, waltz song, topical song, sentimental ballad, march song, and march ballad. In the same period E. M. Wickes, in his book *Advice to Songwriters,* distinguished between the ballad and the novelty song: the former included "the Semi-high-class, March, Rustic, Irish, Descriptive, and Mother"; the latter "Flirting, Juvenile, Philosophical, Comic, Irish, Production, Stage, Suggestive, and Ragtime."[3] As Nicholas Tawa points out, musical labels in Tin Pan Alley at this time sometimes referred "to subject or emotional content and sometimes to the basic music meter," sometimes to lyrical themes, sometimes to musical forms. The logic of labeling depends on what the label is for: publishing catalogues were written for amateur and professional singers who needed songs appropriate for their particular style or repertoire; advice manuals were written for would-be songwriters with different musical skills and linguistic facilities.

If the music industry has always used labeling procedures, then, they have never necessarily been clear or consistent. Genre maps change according to who they're for. And there is a further complication. The point of music labels is, in part, to make coherent the way in which different music media divide the market—record companies, radio stations, music magazines, and concert promoters can only benefit from an agreed definition of, say, heavy metal. But this doesn't always work smoothly, if only because different media by necessity map their consumers in different ways. Record retailers, for example, don't always organize their stock in the same way as record companies organize their releases (indeed, for reasons I'll come back to, retailers are likely to anticipate record companies in labeling new markets and redrawing old genre distinctions). Sometimes this has to do with immediate consumer demand (most stores have a category, "TV advertised," to cater for the market that results from such promotion regardless of the musical category involved). Sometimes it has to do with material conditions: how one organizes the racks depends on how many racks one has. And sometimes it reflects the fact that people shop in ways that are not easy to classify generically: my favorite sections in British record shops used to be those labeled "male vocal" and "female vocal," which were, in effect, residual light pop categories (all those singers who couldn't be filed under rock, soul, jazz, or nostalgia). Why in this category, unlike any other, was the musician's gender taken to be significant?

Record shopping is instructive in this context for many reasons. A committed music fan will soon find, for example, that she's interested in sounds that seem to fit into several categories at once, and that different shops therefore shelve the same record under different labels.[4] Or one can follow the emergence of new shelving labels—world music (which may or may not include reggae); rave (which may or may not include American imports). It's as if a silent conversation is going on between the consumer, who knows roughly what she wants, and the shopkeeper, who is laboriously working out the pattern of shifting demands. What's certain is that I, like most other consumers, would feel quite lost to go to the store one day and find the labels gone—just a floor of CDs, arranged alphabetically. This happens sometimes, of course, in the bargain-bin special offer sales, and while I approve in principle of the resulting serendipity, I mutter to myself all the time that it would have been much easier if somebody had sorted out these cut-outs before dropping them in a heap.

In terms of later embarrassment, record stores have the advantage that no one can remember how they once organized genre categories (rock 'n' roll as "novelty") or placed particular acts (Bob Marley as "folk"). And so the best evidence (except, possibly, *Billboard*'s chart terms) of how music business labels so often seem to miss the point can be found in the history of the Grammy Awards. In 1958, for example, the main pop categories were plain: record of the year; album of the year; song of the year; vocal—female; vocal—male; orchestra; dance band; vocal group or chorus (there were separate slots for country and rhythm & blues performers). In 1959 new titles included Performance by a Top 40 Artist and Folk Performance. In 1960 the Top 40 award became Pop Singles Artist; in 1961 there was, for the first time, an award for Rock and Roll Recording (which was won by "Let's Twist Again"). In 1964 the Beatles won the Grammy for Vocal Group of the Year; Petula Clark made the winning Rock and Roll Recording. By 1965 the latter category was labeled Contemporary (Rock and Roll); this became Contemporary Pop in 1968, Pop in 1971, and Pop, Rock, and Folk in 1974. In 1979 it was split between Pop (male and female vocal, group, instrumental) and Rock (male and female vocal, group, instrumental). One would, indeed, get a strange notion of popular music history from Grammy categories (and winners) alone. Soul Gospel appears from 1969, Ethnic or Traditional (including blues and "pure" folk) from 1970, disco (for one year only) in 1979. A Video award was made (rather more promptly) from 1981; the decade also saw, eventually, awards for metal, hard rock, and rap.[5]

I've always felt that the Grammies give one a good sense of how the American music industry would like to see the market even as, reluctantly and tardily, it has to adapt to the way the market really is. And the oddity of the Grammies lies in their subsequent air of fantasy: no one in any individual record company could afford to be so stupid about public tastes, but collectively and anonymously record companies can still show how they'd like things to be.

Back in the real world, the problem, at least for the record industry in the United States, is radio. Out of promotional necessity record companies must constantly adapt their product not to consumer taste as such, but to consumer taste as understood and organized by radio stations. From a British perspective just the names for U.S. radio formats seem exotic: Adult Contemporary (full service, gold-intensive, lite, music-intensive, adult alternative), AOR (album oriented rock), Beautiful Music, Big Band, CHR (Contemporary Hit Radio), classical, country, easy listening radio, gold (gold—classic rock), gospel, Hispanic, jazz, Music of Your Life, New Age, nostalgia, Quiet Storm, Urban Contemporary.[6]

The thinking behind such labels is captured in a *USA Today* story about the emergence at the beginning of the 1990s of so-called "adult Top 40," "hot adult contemporary," or "mix" stations, playing "top singles with grown-up appeal."

> "Standard Top 40 has gotten so extreme that mothers and daughters don't like the same music anymore," says Guy Zapoleon, national program director for the 12-station Nationwide Communications.
>
> Lots of stations are going with Mom, sacrificing the kids to rival stations. It's a money decision. In the radio business, the 25–55 age group is called the "money demographic" . . .
>
> Stations move into the adult Top 40 format from two directions. Some are former adult contemporary stations that now mix in many current releases with their soft fare from the past couple of decades for a "hotter" sound. Others are former standard Top 40 stations that have deleted the jarring extremes of teen-aimed tunes.
>
> Zapoleon says similar formats have sprung up in other eras when pop music has become fragmented, but were abandoned when superstar innovators with across-the-board appeal reunited listeners.[7]

The peculiarity of generic definitions in music radio terms is that programmers are using the sounds to put together an audience (or market or demographic) for delivery to advertisers. Sometimes the radio definition of this market-by-taste coincides with the record industry's (as with country music, for example); often it does not. Record companies can never be sure how radio programmers will classify a new sound (or whether that classification will make sense to record buyers). Genre labeling, in this context, becomes both slippery and powerful (given radio's control of the pop soundscape). It's as if radio programmers can create a territory by mapping it. And record companies can't find their way to market without that map; they don't even know where they may be going.[8]

The problem of radio-driven definitions of music is raised equally acutely (and more hilariously) when the state gets involved: both Canada and Britain, for example, have generic definitions built into broadcasting legislation. Canadian legislators took an interest in pop genres for two reasons. First, in a compromise between public service and commercial broadcasting principles, it was determined that while entrepreneurs could bid for licenses to run advertising-funded radio stations, the local population still had the right to a diversity of programming principles, to a range of different musics. Local licenses, then, are granted under principles of *balance:* would-be licensees have to declare (and stick to) a programming policy; the licensers have to ensure that each radio locality has the right mix of pop and rock and jazz and classical and country. To do this such categories have to be defined: when does the music on a so-called country station playlist, for example, cease to be "country"?

Second, for reasons of national cultural policy, broadcasters in Canada are subject to a content law: a percentage of the music played must be "Canadian" (written by Canadians, performed by Canadians, produced by Canadians, or some combination thereof). The difficulty here is that some musical genres have more Canadian material available than others; it didn't make sense to make the same Canadian content demands on, say, classical and country stations, or on rock and folk and jazz. To apply different quota regulations to different stations according to different genres meant, again, giving such generic definitions legal clout.

Canadian radio law thus defines music radio under the following headings:

> Category 6: *Music–General*
> Live or recorded entertainment music, extending from the advent of mass-produced recordings to the latest hits as defined in charts of recognized trade publications, including popular songs and compositions which fall under the headings "pop," "country-and-western," "rhythm and blues," "rock," "easy listening," "middle-of-the-road," "beautiful music," "mood," and "mainly for dancing"; popularized arrangements of classical music, jazz or authentic folksongs, music written in a folk idiom by present-day artists; songs of protest and political and social comment, humorous and satirical songs, chansonniers and chansonnettes, English music hall and North American vaudeville, individual excerpts from works for the musical stage, non-religious Christmas songs, popular music for films and television, and international pop songs; popularizations of folk idioms, such as Latin American, Hawaiian and Calypso, and the popular music of Canada's various ethnic cultures, other than authentic traditional folk music; for greater particularity, this category includes the following five subcategories:
>
> Subcategory 61: *General Popular*
> This subcategory includes all musical selections that fall within the terms of the general description for category 6 but are not included in subcategories 65, 66, 67, 68.
>
> Subcategory 65: *Rock and Rock-Oriented*
> This subcategory includes rock and roll, rhythm-and-blues, rock, country-rock, folk-rock, jazz-rock, and pop-rock, where the music is

characterized by a strong beat, the use of blues forms, and the presence of rock instruments such as electric guitar, electric bass, electric organ, or electric piano.

Subcategory 66: *Country and Country-Oriented*

This subcategory includes simple, guitar-accompanied "country," back country or "western" songs; orchestrated, citified or "town and country" songs, including those in a Nashville and country-pop styles; old-time fiddle music, breakdowns, hoedowns, jigs and reels other than those in subcategories 67 or 77; bluegrass music, and country yodelling.

Subcategory 67: *Folk-Oriented*

This subcategory includes music in a folk style composed by the troubadours and chansonniers of our time, popular arrangements of authentic folksongs, and popularization of folk idioms.

Subcategory 68: *Jazz-Oriented*

Music sung or played in a popular style by performers with a jazz background, including the work of the jazz-influenced dance bands, "cocktail" jazz and jazz improvisation when presented against a popularized orchestral background, but not including jazz-rock falling under subcategory 65.[9]

Several things are striking about the genre definitions here. First, because what is at issue is, supposedly, content (not market), the approach is basically musicological; rock, for example, is defined in terms of what it sounds like (beat, form, and instrumentation) rather by reference to who might listen to it. Second, even within such "objective" measures there are, nevertheless, ideological implications, as indicated by the use of the terms "authentic" and "popularized" with reference to folk and classical music. Such descriptive terms are not purely musical. Third, the boundaries between the various subcategories are, inevitably, imprecise, and an interesting question emerges: can a record be played on more than one sort of station? Does it thereby change its meaning?[10] Fourth, how can musical tastes ever change in this system? Can the legislators' "objective" account of musical meaning really be written over the much more fluid, "subjective" approach of radio listeners?

This question was posed in an even starker (and more ludicrous) manner in the British parliament. Here the legislative problem was both simpler and more difficult: how to distinguish between "rock" and "pop." The question also emerged from radio policy, and from a muddled compromise between public service principles and market forces. The 1980s Conservative government had decided to license three national commercial radio stations (previously, commercial operators had only been licensed to broadcast locally). Rather than just license the three highest bidders, though, the Tories too retained a belief in "balance." One station was to be talk, and one was to be "other than pop." More particularly, the first wavelength to be released, the only one of the three with FM access, was to be non-pop. The Thatcher government, which combined belief in the market with a strong sense of the state's right to enforce moral standards, had always been wary of simply opening up the airwaves to more "pop and prattle" (a phrase used by the minister then in charge of broadcasting policy, Douglas Hurd). What was involved here, in other words, wasn't just a matter of choice—listeners could already choose nationally from the BBC's Radio 1 (pop/rock), 2 (easy listening), 3 (classical), and 4 (talk)—but also a matter of value.

This became clear when the bidders for the station began to declare themselves. One of the most powerful was Rock FM, a consortium put together by Britain's leading rock promoter, Harvey Goldsmith, and the publishing company EMAP (publishers of Britain's leading rock magazine, Q). From their perspective rock was clearly "other than pop"; it meant "album-based music for adults" rather than "instant, singles-based music aimed at teenagers."[11]

This was not at all what the government had intended, and it hastily introduced an amendment to the Broadcasting Act. "Pop music" was now defined to include all kinds of music "characterised by a strong rhythmic element and a reliance on electronic amplification for their performance."[12] The amendment was introduced in the House of Lords, and the flavor of the resulting debate is captured in the following exchange. Earl Ferrars, for the government:

> It has been argued that rock music is not the same thing as pop music. I do not know whether it is or not. But I do know that it would be an odd result—and not, I am sure, what your Lordships intended—if a rock music or similar application were able to win the licence for the non-pop service . . . The somewhat intricate style of the amendment was thought appropriate because the parliamentary draughtsman thought that my definition of "pop," which was thump, thump, thump, would not be parliamentary or statutorily adequate.

The Viscount of Falkland, speaking on behalf of the record industry:

> Pop music, as it is understood by the music industry in this country and in the United States, now has a clear definition. There is a clear

understanding that pop music as such is music which is recorded in single versions mainly for a teenage market and which forms part of what is generally known as the Top of the Pops table. It is generally accepted that pop music is a single which is part of a market-based table or chart of 40. That may be even more esoteric to your Lordships, but that is the fact of the matter. It is well known that in this country there are other forms of music which have been grouped by the Government, or those who are helping to draw up the legislation, with those singles in the charts that I have described. That includes rock music to which the noble Earl referred . . . Noble Lords may wonder about the kind of music to which I refer. I shall simply mention two names. In this country there is an artist, who is I believe very popular with the Royal Family, called Phil Collins. He is an extremely successful rock artist and something of a film actor. His albums come within the term "rock." They are extremely successful and popular. In the United States there is a recording artist called Bruce Springsteen, known popularly as The Boss, who is a world-renowned artist in this kind of music. Sales of his records continue to boom. Rock goes into other areas, some of which are perhaps more limited in appeal. However, there is a world of difference between pop music and rock music and indeed many other forms of music which have the same thump, thump element. [Earl Ferrars: Thump, thump, thump, my Lords.] My Lords, I apologise; a thump, thump, thump element. That includes a great deal of ethnic music such as music of West Indian origin.[13]

The terms of this debate are clear. The British government (like the Canadian government) sought to define rock musicologically, in terms of form (thump, thump, thump); the industry (and Rock FM) sought to define it sociologically (by reference to its market) and ideologically (by describing its market function).[14] The problem with the sociological argument, as Earl Ferrars pointed out in the House of Lords, was that it didn't stand up to close analysis: both Phil Collins and Bruce Springsteen had released singles that were included in the "Top of the Pops Table." The British popular music world doesn't fall into neat pop and rock divisions, musically or sociologically; it is more logical to treat it as a market unity. And where the industry argument was powerful—with respect to ideology (Bruce Springsteen fans just know they're different from Kylie Minogue fans)—it made no legislative sense: how could one safely define music in terms of attitude? As the American critic Barry Walters puts it (commenting on *Rolling Stone*'s list of "The

100 Best Singles of the Last Twenty-Five Years"), "Since the form pop music takes is more consistent than any other commercial art, quality is most often a matter of style, which eludes objective appraisal. The meaning, the ultimate value, of pop emerges out of the meeting between music and listener, an interaction that changes over time."[15]

Bruce Springsteen's music has, after all, already been recuperated as nostalgia (it's the classic radio accompaniment to ads for classic jeans and classic beer) and will, inevitably, become "lite," "gold," and "easy listening" in the years to come. If nothing else, then, the Lords pop/rock debate did make clear that generic labeling involves a complex interplay between musical, marketing, and ideological forces. This is obvious in the other sectors of the music business in which labels are essential: the music press, which is designed to appeal to pop fans generally but also to forge them into a newly committed—ideological—readership; and clubs and club nights, which use music labels in their flyers and posters (Techno-Rave-Acid-Jungle) to attract a particular sort of crowd and thus to ensure a particular sort of evening.[16]

Readers and clubbers (unlike radio listeners) thus become an important part of the labeling process—a new genre is recognized by a new audience. The key ideological moment each year for music papers is the readers' poll, which serves as a public display of the magazine's success in forging a community out of its disparate consumers, a process which is particularly important (not least in maintaining advertising revenue) when a magazine changes its generic base (whether in response to reader interest or not). The British folk magazine *Southern Rag* redefined its brief in the mid-1980s, for instance, to include "roots" music (which referred less to musical form than to the spirit in which it was played—local, live, cheap rock and roll of all kinds) and ethnic sounds (the same spirit reflected in music from the Third World). The shift had more to do with what was happening on the live folk circuit (who was being booked into pubs and clubs; what folk musicians themselves found interesting and relevant) than with any obvious sense of reader dissatisfaction (or falling circulation). In changing its name to *Folk Roots,* in other words, in redefining "folk," the magazine was making a pitch for a *new* sort of reader who was thought to be out there. Publicity material now carried the endorsement of the *NME,* a rock paper: "*Folk Roots* is both modern, yet steeped in tradition; it has a historical importance, yet it is always hunting for the sounds of the future . . . *Folk Roots* does not have its finger in its ear, it has its finger on the pulse."[17]

Folk Roots went on to play a key role (alongside a handful of radio and club deejays and concert promoters) in defining—and putting together the market for—"world music," a genre label (in the United States the term was "world beat") which emerged from a 1987 meeting with eleven independent record labels:

> Whilst not all of these labels are devoted exclusively to World Music, they have united to bring recognition to the many diverse forms of music as yet unclassifiable in Western terms. Trying to reach a definition of "WORLD MUSIC" provoked much lengthy discussion and finally it was agreed that it means practically any music that isn't at present catered for by its own category, e.g.: Reggae, jazz, blues, folk. Perhaps the common factor unifying all these WORLD MUSIC labels is the passionate commitment of all the individuals to the music itself.

The object was to improve the music's sales situation: "The term WORLD MUSIC will be used to make it easier to find that Malian Kora record, the music of Bulgaria, Zairean soukous or Indian Ghazals—the new WORLD MUSIC section will be the first place to look in the local record shop."[18] But what was equally significant (hence *Folk Roots'* role) was the perception of the potential world music market as people drawn from the rock and folk audiences, people, that is, with a particular set of musical attitudes, needs, and expectations. Not all the music made in the world, after all, got to be "world music."[19]

I want to make two general points about this. First, in using genre labels to make the marketing process more efficient, record companies are assuming that there is a manageable relationship between musical label and consumer taste. This rests, in turn, on a set of assumptions about who these consumers are, in terms of age, gender, ethnicity, disposable income, leisure habits, and so forth. In broad market research terms, such assumptions are usually efficient enough. Record companies aren't stupid about the decisions they make as to how to package and market musicians—where to advertise world music or heavy metal records, say, or in which magazines and TV shows to place a would-be indie star or teen idol.

Nevertheless, what is going on here is an idealization, the creation of a *fantasy* consumer (the sort of fantasy consumer being invoked by the press releases I quoted in Chapter 3) and, in this, the industry follows tastes rather than forming them. (I can't think of an example of a musical genre created by a marketing machine, rather than given a hasty definition, like "world music," after its loose characteristics had already emerged through new consumer alliances.) As fantasies, then, genres describe not just who listeners are, but also what this music means to them. In deciding to label a music or a musician in a particular way, record companies are saying something about both what people like and why they like it; the musical label acts as a condensed sociological and ideological argument.[20]

The second general point follows from this: although we are ostensibly dealing here with sound qualities, it may be difficult to say what different acts or records in a genre have in common *musically*. This is obvious, for example, in the case of "indie" music. Such a label refers both to a means of production (music produced on an independent rather than a major label) and to an attitude, supposedly embodied in the music, in its listeners, and, perhaps most important, in the relationship between them.[21] It can therefore lead, in turn, to intricate (and fiercely debated) judgments as to whether a band "sells out," changes the meaning of its music, by appealing to a wider audience.[22]

It is difficult to explain how such arguments about genre boundaries work to people uninvolved with the genre in the first place, people ignorant, that is to say, of a basic (if unstated) agreement within a genre about what their music is *for*. To take another British example, "student music" (as record companies realize) must fit student life, fit the student rhythm of collective indulgence and lonely regret, boorishness and angst, and also draw on shared teen memories and the sense of exclusiveness that being a student (at least in Britain) still entails. Take this list of albums, for instance: *The Wall* (Pink Floyd), *The Joshua Tree* (U2), *Brothers in Arms* (Dire Straits), *Bat Out of Hell* (Meat Loaf), *The Queen is Dead* (The Smiths), *Love Over Gold* (Dire Straits), *Graceland* (Paul Simon), *Steve McQueen* (Prefab Sprout), *Sgt. Pepper's Lonely Hearts Club Band* (The Beatles), *Dream of the Blue Turtles* (Sting). At first sight (on first hearing) it would make little sense generically, and yet as "The Nescafe Student All Time Favourite Albums, 1988" it is explicable in terms of both range of sounds covered and the odd mix of the "classic" and the ephemeral (I doubt if students five years later had even heard the Prefab Sprout or Sting LPs).[23]

Similarly, "women's music," a sales label used in both Britain and the United States, is a category which jams together very disparate sounds. *WRPM* (Women's Revolutions Per Minute), the British women's music catalogue, is laid out in familiar ways (feminist/politics; spoken; classical; blues and jazz; folk and country; world/roots music; gospel; for young people; rock/pop/soul; humor—only "healing and ritual" is a category unlikely to be found in other general catalogues), and if the common denominator is that the music is made by women, the catalogue still excludes many different types of female performers. "Women's music" thus seems to describe something *brought* to a sound, whether that sound is "US synthesizer politico-pop" (Sue Fink), "theatrical brilliance and original anti-racist humour backed with disco music" (Frank Chickens), "soft rock and silky ballads" (Deidre McCalla), or "very sexy rock music" (Tret Fure). And if there are social tendencies here (the music is quite likely to be feminist, to be lesbian, to be independently produced, to be live or acoustic), none of these factors is determinate. Caroline Hutton describes *WRPM*'s principles as follows: "This catalogue is part of the process of change in our lives. The music, I hope, will touch you. It can heal, inspire, energise and give great pleasure to us all. Many of the lyrics will say a lot more about the world and our experiences than 'I love you baby.'"[24]

"Women's music," in short, is defined ideologically, and, more to the point here, it is defined *against* other ways of music-making. Like "indie," it is a category that only makes sense as an argument about "mainstream music" as well as about women; it describes what is not included—male-dominated music of all sorts. In fact, the logic of the label seems obvious enough, even (perhaps especially) to those people who don't much like "women's music" anyway.[25]

I'll come back to genres as ideologies shortly. First, a few words on the second way in which genre labels work in popular music evaluation: as a way of organizing *the playing process.*

Perhaps because of their lack of formal or academic music education, popular musicians are accustomed to using generic labels as a basic shorthand for particular sounds (or riffs or beats). This is obvious in the way in which musicians talk to each other in rehearsal or in the recording studio, in the instructions given to players or engineers about their musical and sound decisions. The basis of session players' reputations, for example, often rests on their ability to respond to such shorthand without explanation being needed. And one of the services that sampling devices and "sound banks" currently offer is precisely such generically labeled sounds, on demand, over the phone line.

In musical terms, the words used here are difficult to understand unless one already knows their meaning (a technically skilled but generically ignorant musician would not be able to understand requests to "give it some funk!"; to "try a reggae bass!"; to "hit that Phil Collins hi-hat!"; to "fall into the Stock-Aitken-Waterman groove!"). Genre discourse depends, in other words, on a certain sort of shared musical knowledge and experience (think, for example, of the use of musical labels in the ads published by groups seeking a new member, or on the "musician wanted" cards pinned up in musical instrument stores). What is obvious from this language is that for musicians too, genre labels describe musical skills and ideological attitudes simultaneously.[26]

This is even more obvious in the third use of genre labels, as a way of organizing *the listening process.* In Chapter 3 I suggested that rock critics rarely describe music in formal language, but almost always through comparison: new sound X is described by reference to already known sound Y. Done well, this is an elegant and economical form of descriptive shorthand (a good critic could be defined as one who can make such comparisons both original and telling), and genre labeling is, from this critical perspective, an *implied* comparison (or set of comparisons)—generic labels are, in fact, among the critic's most essential tools.[27]

Deejays have probably been even more effective than journalists in defining new genres, "discovering" new markets (if only because they put their arguments to practical test, on the dance floor), though often all they are doing is routinizing terms taken from club chatter, and, in practice, it is virtually impossible to say where a new term (house, rave, rap, grunge) first came from. Genre origins remain a matter of elaborate and unresolvable debate. Or, to put this more sensibly, the genre labeling process is better understood as something collusive than as something invented individually, as the result of a loose *agreement* among musicians and fans, writers and disc jockeys. It is in fanzines, for example, that sounds are most systematically lined up with attitudes (musicians with audiences) and genres most earnestly argued about ideologically (and related to ways of life).[28]

Focal ideological figures and their programs, clubs, and magazines play, then, something of the same role in the formation of popular genre-consciousness as galleries in the formation of new movements in the fine arts. A new "genre world," that is to say, is first constructed and then articulated through a complex interplay of musicians, listeners, and mediating ideologues, and this process is much more confused than the marketing process that follows, as the wider industry begins to make sense of the new sounds and markets and to exploit both genre worlds and genre discourses in the orderly routines of mass marketing.[29] The issue then becomes how to draw genre boundaries. Genres initially flourish on a sense of exclusivity; they are as much (if not more) concerned to keep people out as in. The industry aim is to retain the promise of exclusivity, the hint of generic secrets, while making them available to everyone. It sometimes seems, indeed, as if a genre is only clearly defined (its secret revealed) at the moment when it ceases to exist, when it can no longer be exclusive. Fanzines, that is to say, are surprisingly often *launched* on the premise that the music they are celebrating no longer really exists.[30]

In looking at the various ways in which genre labels are used to organize music making, music listening, and music selling, I have been circling around the same point: popular music genres are constructed—and must be understood—*within* a commercial/cultural process; they are not the result of detached academic analyses or formal musicological histories.[31] For people who *live* in genres there are continuous questions to be answered about new acts and releases: does this fit my playlist, my roster, my review pages, my collection? And the answers are inevitably reached by measuring the new music against a notion of the real thing: is this really jazz or punk or disco or New Age? Authenticity is a necessary critical value—one listens to the music for clues to something else, to what makes the genre at issue valuable as a genre in the first place. The musical judgment is necessarily a social judgment: does this music understand the genre, is it true to it? For people who *study* genre, the questions are retrospective: how were these decisions made, what was it about these records that caused them to be labeled the same way, what do they have in common? The answers are much more formal: blues or punk or progressive rock are described in terms of the musical language they deploy; records are excluded from the definitions because they don't fit technically—have the wrong structure, beat, or orchestration.

The problem of these different approaches is apparent in the writing of genre histories, which matter both because what happens to genres over time is a crucial part of their meaning and because genre self-consciousness derives in the first place from an account (usually mythical) of its own past.[32] The crunch comes when the academic account is written over the mythical one—by *the collector*—and the history of the genre is rewritten in terms of a new purism. Now the critical question (most familiar, I suppose, in folk music) becomes what might be called formal authenticity: does this singer or song obey the genre's musicological rules?[33]

I'll come back to the issue of genre rules and their authority. Before that I need to refer to one of the few pieces of empirical research on the history of genres in everyday life, Ruth Finnegan's *The Hidden Musicians*. Musical labels are the key to Finnegan's map of "music-making in an English town," and I want to draw attention to two of her arguments in particular. First, Finnegan shows that to have a musical interest, a genre taste, is to engage in the set of relationships which give meaning to that taste. An individual's liking for punk or opera, for country music or progressive rock, whether as performer or audience, is a commitment to a taste community, the taste community, in fact, which defines what I earlier called a genre's "ideal consumer."[34]

Second, Finnegan, doing her social scientific duty, tries to relate the resulting genre ideologies to social characteristics, to class, age, gender, ethnicity, and so forth. Her question becomes: do social identities and needs map onto musical identities and needs? does a homological approach to musical values make empirical sense? Her answer is, perhaps surprisingly, no! While it was apparent, for example, that each new teenage generation had its own music (punk at the time of Finnegan's research), it was also clear that thereafter the enjoyment of such music was not confined to its own generation: old youth musics (rock 'n' roll, progressive rock, heavy metal, glam rock) were played by the people who had grown up on them *and* by musicians from subsequent generations (the rock 'n' roll scene thus included musicians of any age from 20 to 55). Ironically, the only music world whose members shared social class characteristics, the folk world (which was essentially middle class), was also the only music world with a clear class ideology: it defined itself as working class.[35]

Finnegan concludes that in relating music and society, we should reverse the usual sociological approach. Rather than looking for people's material conditions in their aesthetic and hedonistic activity, we should look at how their particular love and use of music inform their social situations. She suggests, for example, a distinction between musical activities that are continuous with people's other social ties (this is often how people come to be in choirs or amateur operatic societies, for example, and can explain tastes—running in the family—in country music or rock 'n' roll), and musical activities that are used by people to mark themselves off from their families or community (as with the middle-class punk or the orchestra member from a non-musical family). One can distinguish, similarly, between the degrees of ritual a musical life involves: the annual operetta or weekly folk night matter to their participants in different ways than the occasional participation in a disco or pub singalong. The use of music, in other words, can vary as to how important it is in defining one's social identity, how significant it is in determining one's friendships, how special it is in forming one's sense of self. The question of musical value is, as I suggested in Chapter 1, inevitably tied up with questions of sociability. And the significant social differences may be less those between genres than between degrees of commitment (or types of commitment) to them.[36]

What does seem clear is that it is through its generic organization that music offers people, even so-called passive at-home listeners, access to a social world, a part in some sort of social narrative, offers them what Finnegan calls "social pathways." In aesthetic terms, musical sounds, ideologies, and activities, musical texts and their implied contexts, cannot be separated. The pleasures popular music offers us, the values it carries (and I include classical music as popular here), have to be related to the stories it tells about us in our genre identities. Or, to put this the other way around, genre analysis must be, by aesthetic necessity, narrative analysis. It must refer to an implied community, to an implied romance, to an implied plot. In examining how the elements of popular music work (the sound, the lyric, the voice, the beat) we always have to take account of their genre coding: popular musical pleasures can only be understood as genre pleasures; and genre pleasures can only be understood as socially structured.

To conclude this chapter, then, I want to return to the question of genre rules, and the pioneering work of Franco Fabbri. Fabbri argues that a musical genre is a set of musical events (real or possible) whose course is governed by a definite set of socially accepted rules, and suggests that these rules can be grouped under five headings.[37]

First, *formal and technical rules.* These are the rules of musical form (to be classified as punk or country, a piece of music has to have certain aural characteristics)which include playing conventions—what skills the musicians must have; what instruments are used, how they are played, whether they are amplified or acoustic; rhythmic rules; melodic rules; the studio sound quality; the relation of voice to instruments (whether there's a voice at all); the relationship of words to music; and so forth. Such rules can be very loose (anything can be "rocked") or very tight (as in Canada's legal definition of authentic country music). But just as turning noise into "music" means knowing how to organize the sounds we hear in particular (conventionalized) ways, so to hear music generically (hearing this as punk, this as hard core; this as acid, this as techno) means organizing the sounds according to formal rules.

Second, *semiotic rules.* These are essentially rules of communication, how music works as *rhetoric;* such rules refer to the ways in which "meaning" is conveyed (referential meaning, emotional meaning, poetic meaning, imperative meaning, metalinguistic meaning, phatic meaning: Roman Jakobson's communicative functions). How is "truth" or "sincerity" indicated musically? How do we know what music is "about"? Consider, for example, how different genres (opera, folk, rock, punk) read singers: as the protagonists of their songs? As revealing themselves? Rules here, in other words, concern musical expressivity and emotion; they determine the significance of the lyrics— different genres, for example, having quite different conventions of lyrical realism: soul versus country, the singer/songwriter versus the disco diva. Rules here also concern issues like intertextuality (to what extent does the music refer to other music?) and the ways in which a genre presents itself as "aesthetic," "emotional," or "physical." Part of what is involved here is the placing of performer and audience in relationship to each other, the degrees of intimacy and distance. Such rules have practical effects. As Ola Stockfelt argues (quoting from Fabbri), "adequate listening" depends upon them: "The distance between musician and audience, between spectator and spectator, the overall dimension of [musical] events are often fundamental elements to the definition of a genre . . . often 'how you are seated' says more about the music that will be performed than a poster does."[38]

In short, as Fabbri admits, it is difficult to distinguish semiotic rules from the next category, *behavioral rules*, which cover performance rituals in a widely defined sense. These are gestural rules, then; they determine the ways in which musical skill and technique, on the one hand, and musical personality, on the other, are displayed—compare a Bruce Springsteen and a Kraftwerk concert, for example, or Erasure and the Mekons. Behavioral rules apply to audiences as well: an audience for the Cocteau Twins behaves differently from an audience for Nirvana. Lawrence Levine has a nice example of the misunderstandings that result when an audience behaves "wrongly":

> Ethel Waters, who began her career in 1917, did not sing before a northern white audience until the 1920s, and the sharp difference in audience reactions confused her and led her to conclude that she had been rebuffed when in fact she had scored a great success. "You know we took the flop of our lives just now," she told her partner, Earl Dancer. "Those people out front applauded us only because they wanted to be polite. Nobody stomped as they always do in coloured theatres when I finish my act. Nobody screamed or jumped up and down. Nobody howled with joy."[39]

Behavioral rules also concern offstage performance, behavior in interviews, packaged performance, the artist in videos and press photographs. Fabbri notes, for example, how different types of singers in Italy appear (or are packaged) differently on television:

> Traditional and sophisticated singers are in their element on television; their gestures are no different from those of the presenters . . . The pop singer is in his element too, but tends to overdo the smiles and raised eyebrows which reveal his underlying anxiety to please. The rock singer and the *cantautore* are uncomfortable on television: the former because television is too bourgeois, and is too small for his exaggerated gestures, and the latter because it is too stupid. Anyway, the *cantautore* must always give the impression of being uncomfortable in front of his audience, because privacy is his "true" dimension. In either case nervous tics are acceptable . . . The political singer hardly ever appears on television, and the gestures associated with him are those of the participant in a political meeting.[40]

Rules of conversation and etiquette apply here, guiding the meetings between performers and journalists, performers and concert organizers, performers and fans.[41] As Fabbri notes, the apparent spontaneity of offstage rituals is exposed by the laughter that breaks out when rules are broken—one of the pleasures of *Smash Hits*, the British teen pop magazine, is the way it insistently breaks behavioral rules, asking "serious" rock stars intimate teen-pop questions: what's in your handbag, what did you eat for breakfast, who do you fantasize about in bed? Behavioral rules apply to audiences off stage too: there are "appropriate" ways to listen to a record, to respond to it. And such rules are not just random, as it were; they reflect what performers (and listeners) are meant to be and thus how their "realness" as stars and communities is indicated.

The fourth category consists of *social and ideological rules*. These cover the social image of the musician regardless of reality (a heavy metal or hard core musician has to be "outrageous" socially in a way that a folk or classical musician does not), but also refer to the nature of the musical community and its relationship to the wider world. These are the rules concerning the ethnic or gender divisions of labor, for example, and, in general, reflect what the music is meant to stand for as a social force, its account of an ideal world as well as of the real one.

Finally, there are *commercial and juridical rules*. These refer to the means of production of a music genre, to questions of ownership, copyright, financial reward, and so on; they determine how musical events come into being, as well as the relations of musics to record companies and the recording process, and records to live concerts and the promotion process.

The problem of such a schematic overview (as Fabbri emphasizes) is that it implies a static picture of genres with clearly defined boundaries, whereas, in fact, genres are constantly changing—as an effect of what's happening in neighboring genres, as a result of musical contradictions, in response to technological and demographic change.[42] Fabbri notes too that the relative importance of the different sorts of rules varies from genre to genre. The "ideological" rules of punk, for example, were more important than those of Euro-disco, and Helfried Zrzavy has argued persuasively that the defining feature of New Age was less how it sounded than how it looked: it was "ultimately, the cohesion in the aesthetics of New Age cover art that established the genre's unmistakeable identity" as "a primarily visual musical genre."[43]

The final point to make here, though, is that one way in which genres work in day-to-day terms is in a deliberate process of rule testing and bending. As Charles Hamm has argued, popular musicians "work within a tradition that allows and even demands flexibility and creativity in shaping a piece. Genre is not determined by the form or style of a text itself but by the audience's perception of its style and meaning, defined most importantly at the moment of performance. Performers can thus shape, reinforce or even change genre."[44] It is out of such "transgressive" performances that genre histories are written: old genres "fail" when their rules and rituals come to seem silly and restrictive; new genres are born as the transgressions become systematic. The value question here is a particularly interesting one: how do people recognize a good example of a genre? As music that follows the rules so effectively that it is heard to *exemplify* them? Or as music that draws attention to the way in which a genre works by *exposing* the unstable basis of its rules? This is another version of a recurring question in popular cultural studies: how should we relate the pleasures of novelty and repetition? The answer will, of course, depend on the genre involved, but there is one general point to make: as we saw in the Mass-Observation surveys, the importance of all popular genres is that they set up expectations, and disappointment is likely *both* when they are not met *and* when they are met all too predictably.[45]

The value of Fabbri's approach here is that it clarifies how genre rules integrate musical and ideological factors, and why *performance* must be treated as central to the aesthetics of popular music. I could reorganize Fabbri's argument by dividing his rules more neatly into sound conventions (what you hear), performing conventions (what you see), packaging conventions (how a type of music is sold), and embodied values (the music's ideology). But this would be to break the connections (if only for analytic reasons) that Fabbri was concerned to emphasize. The particular way in which a guitarist gets a guitar note, for example (whether George Benson or Jimi Hendrix, Mark Knopfler or Johnny Marr, Derek Bailey or Bert Jansch) is at once a musical decision and a gestural one: it is the integration of sound and behavior in performance that gives the note its "meaning."[46] And if nothing else this makes it impossible to root explanations of popular music in consumption. It is not enough to assert that commodities only become culturally valuable when they are made "meaningful" by consumers: they can only be consumed because they are *already* meaningful, because musicians, producers, and consumers are already ensnared in a web of genre expectation.

To summarize my argument so far:

We can only begin to make sense of the aesthetics of popular music when we understand, first, the language in which value judgments are articulated and expressed and, second, the social situations in which they are appropriate. Value language is itself shaped by historical and social circumstance; and in the West, at least, how people think about popular music is an effect of the nineteenth-century industrialization of culture, and the use of music as a commodity. These historical developments put into play a set of assumptions about the "high" and the "low" and a way of making sense of cultural experience through the mutually defining discourses of art, folk, and commerce. We still live within these discourses, and it is impossible to understand what it means to value music without reference to the *ideological* baggage we carry around with us.

We can only make sense of musical value judgments, moreover, if we understand the circumstances in which they are made—and what they are made for. I have divided these circumstances up in orthodox sociological fashion: the processes of music making, selling, and consuming; but the general point (what these circumstances have in common) is that value judgments only make sense as part of an argument, and arguments are always *social* events.

Finally, in the world of popular music, ideological and social discourses are invariably put together *generically*. It is genre rules which determine how musical forms are taken to convey meaning and value, which determine the aptness of different sorts of judgment, which determine the competence of different people to make assessments. It is through genres that we experience music and musical relations, that we bring together the aesthetic and the ethical.

With these broad sociological assertions in mind, I will turn now to the music.

Part II

On Music Itself

Where Do Sounds Come From?

The practice of making music with two or more simultaneous sounds is perhaps one of the great testimonies to the human struggle against boredom.

Richard Norton[1]

When [Georges] Auric composed the score for Jean Cocteau's film, *The Blood of a Poet,* he produced what is commonly known as love music for the love scenes, game music for game scenes, funeral music for funeral scenes. Cocteau had the bright idea of replacing the love music with the funeral, game music with the love, funeral with game.

Ned Rorem[2]

Musical evaluation as I've discussed it so far seems inevitably to mean thinking backwards: first the experience, the music; then the judgment, the account of the music. Even everyday criticism frames the music discursively *after the event,* as it were. The question I want to ask now is this: what was the event? And the question concerns cognition as well as evaluation: we have to recognize something as something (noise as music; music as genre) before we know what to do with it, how to assess it.[3] How does this cognitive process work? Even if we adopt Herrnstein Smith's account of evaluation at its most functional—so that the question "is it good?" really means "is it good *for* something or somebody?"—there is still the question of what the "it" is. And this leads us to the familiar question of philosophical aesthetics: is music, as music, meaningless? If so, where do the musical meanings coded into musical descriptions, conversations, genre distinctions, and critical assessments come from? How do people move from something they hear (a tone or a beat, an instrument or vocal quality) to some understanding of what it is "about"?

There are a variety of answers to this question, but we must begin by distinguishing music from noise. Music is an ordered pattern of sounds in the midst of a vast range of more or less disorderly aurality. Music is marked out as different from noise; as our sense of noise changes, so does our sense of music. In the twentieth century there has been not only a significant increase in the sheer quantity of noise, but also a shift in our underlying sense of silence: technology provides us with a permanent hum, a continued sonic presence. What does it mean to his music, as Philip Tagg once asked, that Mozart never heard a steam engine, a car, an aeroplane, a power drill, a ventilator, air conditioning, a refrigerator, a police siren, the central heating boiler, or the mains buzz; what does it mean for our listening to Mozart's music that we rarely hear the sound of horses' hooves on cobbles, a wood fire, the rustle of layers of petticoats? Is such noise entirely irrelevant to the meaning of his music?[4]

One of the effects of twentieth-century technology has certainly been to blur the boundaries between noise and music, as music, including (perhaps especially) classical music, has become part of the soundscape as "background noise," as a sound against which other sounds (such as conversation) are foregrounded (rather than vice versa).[5] The point here is simply that the meaning of music *as sound* depends, in the first place, on the quality of concentration with which it is attended. Music becomes music by being heard as such by the listener; it follows that to make music is not just to put sounds together in an organized way but also to ensure that these sounds *make their mark.*

An alternative way of relating musical meaning to non-musical sounds is in terms of imitation. At least some music "means" what it sounds like. It imitates nature; it works onomatopoeically. This can be a simple enough process. Gillian Anderson cites C. Roy Carter's 1926 manual, *Theatre Organist's Secrets,* in which he describes "how to imitate the following effects on the organ":

> The Snore, Laughter, Yell or Scream, The Kiss, R. R. Train, Aeroplane, Thunder and Rain Storm, Steam Whistle, Policeman's or Other Shrill Whistle, Prize-Fight Gong, Dog Bark, Dog Yelp, Cat Meow, Lion Roar, Cow's Moo, Rooster Crow, Pig Grunt, Cuckoo, Bag Pipes, Music Box, Banjo, Hand Organ, Accordion-Harmonic, Telegraph-Typewriter.[6]

Is what is being described here music (as opposed to a noise being made by a musical instrument)? Once imitation becomes a formal *organization* of noise, then the imitation is, by necessity, impressionistic. The music doesn't sound exactly like the real noise but gives an impression of it, whether the sea (Debussy's *La Mer*) or the Morse code of ticker tape (the TV news jingle). And once we're talking impressions we're talking conventions, agreements to hear certain musical combinations (particular instruments, textures, rhythms, melodies) as sounding "like" what they claim to represent. Storms as depicted by Wagner, the Doors, Vangelis, and Kate Bush sound no more like each other (or the real thing) than "onomatopoeic" sounds for animal noises (moo, woof, miaow) sound the same in different European languages.

Philip Tagg provides an entertaining example of the conventional (rather than imitative) way in which people hear music as "sounding like" nature:

> In at least twenty different seminars or courses during which *The Virginian* was under discussion, music students facing the question, "what's happening here?" after hearing only the first two bars almost unanimously responded "horses" or "riding" but were rarely able to give any unequivocal answers to the questions "where are the horses in these two bars?" or "how can you hear all those horses here?" This is not simply because the musical semiosis of horse hooves goes little beyond knocking coconut shells along the lines of the Monty Python gag at the opening of the *Holy Grail* movie. Or, to reverse the problem, unless you are watching a sped-up video of some novel trick taught to a show horse at the Spanish Riding School in Vienna, no horse actually puts its hooves to the ground in time with the initial *Virginian* rhythms . . . So if people hear horses after one or two bars, where are they in the music?[7]

Tagg's argument is that there is not a direct connection between real horse noise and musical horse noise. Rather, this interpretation is derived from a chain of the "representational" meanings of "musemes" (the basic musical elements that people actually hear, which may be instrumental sounds, melodic phrases, kinds of beat, or whatever). The *Virginian* theme thus combines a fandango rhythm (which moviegoers have learned to associate with Spanish/Mexican/Western America) and rimshots (which are associated with country and western dancing, with poor rural whites). "Fandango" plus "rednecks" equals "cowboys"; this is now a settled convention of Western film scoring, though it was presumably once learned—settled—by composers and audiences alike. We always hear these sounds together; we always thus hear "horses." In short, as Tagg puts it, "horses" in music follow not the iconic logic of *anaphones*, musical sounds "painting" natural sounds directly, but an indexical logic: musical sounds, as a matter of convention, *standing for* natural sounds. And the question is how such sonic conventions are established.[8]

The psychologist's answer is that there is a biologically necessary relationship between sounds and human responses to them, so that the meaning of the music *is* the response: "sleepy music," a lullaby, for example, is music which sends one to sleep; that is what this music—this sort of tune, this instrumental quality, this rhythm—means. If the response is the meaning, what triggers that response is physiology: the music makes us feel or do something directly. The baby doesn't interpret the song as a lullaby and therefore feel sleepy; the song just puts her to sleep. Not surprisingly, such biological claims have tended to focus primarily on the rhythmic quality of music, on the supposed effects of a regular beat on repeated body movements—on the heartbeat, the pulse, the gyrating hip, on sexual and nervous "agitation." It is by now a deeply rooted commonsense assumption that a funk beat necessarily *means* sex.

The problem with such arguments (I'll come back to sex and rhythm in Chapter 6) is their level of generality. From an ethnomusicological perspective, that is to say, there is no obvious relationship between human experience and musical sounds, between what we all feel as humans and how we express and evoke those feelings as members of particular societies. As Philip Tagg argues, the fact that all peoples make music doesn't mean that they all make the same music, any more than the fact that all peoples speak means that they speak the same language. In his illuminating study of musical accounts of death, Tagg shows that the "appropriate" sound of grief varies widely and can only be explained ideologically, in terms of social attitudes. In fact, as Tagg makes clear, there are very few universally understood aspects of musical expression, and these establish no more than extremely general types of bio-acoustic connections between musical structure and the human body and its acoustic and temporo-spatial surroundings. All evaluative and affective musical symbols are culturally specific.[9]

It may be true, in short, that in all cultures sounds must be louder the bigger the space they have to fill, that the human capacity to hold a breath or note is biologically determined, that more or less energetic noise (in terms of both tempo and volume) is necessarily associated with more or less energetic social activity—"nobody," as Tagg puts it, "yells jerky lullabies at breakneck speed," just as "nobody uses *legato* phrasing and soft or rounded timbres for hunting or war situations." But to turn such "bio-acoustic" facts into musical principles requires "rhythmic, metric, timbric, tonal, melodic, instrumental or harmonic *organisation*. Such *musical* organisation requires some kind of *social* organisation and cultural context before it can be created, understood or otherwise invested with meaning."[10] In other words, the biological approach to the meaning of music does not take us very far.

If music is meaningful in emotional terms it is therefore largely as an effect of cultural rather than psychological conditions. Enter musicologists, who have long argued that to understand music is to interpret stylistic codes, not to respond to physiological triggers. Take Susan McClary's ground-breaking project of a feminist musicology, for example.[11] One of McClary's concerns is to examine sexuality (a human universal) in classical music, and one of her crucial arguments is that the sexual meaning of music is necessarily metaphorical, that it necessarily reflects changing gender ideologies and changing compositional conventions. She notes the German encyclopedia definition of the sonata form: "Two basic principles are expressed in each of these two main themes; the thrusting, active masculine principle and the passive feminine principle." The first (masculine) theme is aggressive, has "thrust"; the second (feminine) theme is softer, has "give." To listen to a symphony is to listen to the masculine theme "quash" the feminine theme in a moment of triumphant "climax."[12]

This tells us as much about nineteenth-century sexual as musical discourse, and it raises a key musicological question: if music is encoded this way, is that code a necessary part now of that music's meaning? McClary shows quite convincingly how "the celebration of [male] sexual desire, which culminates in a violent ejaculation, becomes virtually a convention of nineteenth-century symphonic music," and what's at issue here is not biological necessity but cultural understanding. If, as McClary shows, the sexual meaning of a Beethoven symphony is an effect of a musical style, then to miss this meaning is to misread the code, but the question is whether to appreciate music is to understand it. Can we enjoy a piece of music without knowing what it means? Does such pleasure involve grasping that meaning— Beethoven's sexual aggression—*without knowing it?*

McClary argues that

> the principal innovation of tonality is its ability to instill in the
> listener an intense desire for a given event: the final tonic cadence.
> It organized time by creating an artificial need (in the real world,
> there is no reason one should crave, for instance, the pitch E; yet by
> making it the withheld object of musical desire, a good piece of tonal
> music can within ten seconds dictate even one's breathing). Further,
> tonal procedures strive to postpone gratification of that need until
> finally delivering the payoff—its violent release of pent-up ten-
> sions—in what is technically called the "climax," which is quite
> clearly to be experienced as metaphorical ejaculation.[13]

This is, I think, to raise two issues: on the one hand there is an argument about *musical structure* (to hear a piece of music as music is to hear sounds ordered in a particular way); on the other hand there is an argument about musical appreciation, about what we might call the listener's *interpretive freedom*.[14]

The first argument is that the structure of the music evokes feelings in listeners which are then given emotional and/or metaphorical interpretations. It is the music itself that sets up our sense of "tension," "incompletion," "dissatisfaction," and so forth, that conveys a sense of liveliness or languor, movement or rest. Such terms refer to our feelings on hearing the music (relate them to our usual narratives of emotion), but we are actually describing something caused by the experience of the sounds themselves, by our response to what is happening structurally.

The most eloquent general statement of this view can be found in Leonard Bernstein's Harvard lectures:

> That's one of the questions I'm most frequently asked by nonmusicians: why is the minor "sad" and the major "glad"? Isn't this proof of the "affective" theory of musical expression? The answer is no; whatever darkness, or sadness, or passion you feel when you hear music in the minor mode is perfectly explainable in purely phonological terms . . . this so-called "affective" phenomenon of the minor mode is not an extrinsic metaphorical operation at all; it is intrinsic to music, and its meaning is a purely musical one.[15]

Bernstein is making this argument in the context of a discussion of music as a communicative activity. His question is *how* does music communicate (which is, for him, a prior question to what it does), and his starting assumption is that it must "mean" the same thing to composer, performer, and listener, otherwise communication would be impossible. In investigating this problem Bernstein draws on linguistics, on Chomskyan linguistics, in particular, on a theory of what makes communication *possible*: an underlying human capacity to grasp the "deep structure" of the communicative process. Bernstein thus argues that the musical effects he is describing happen (at this "deep" level) whether or not we understand how they are caused. Chopin's *Prelude No. 4 must* make me feel "unsatisfied" (a feeling of which I give my own emotional interpretation) whether or not I understand Bernstein's technical analysis of why it must (which I don't). The effect is not the result of any particular process of musical education or socialization—we don't have to be *taught* to hear Chopin as sad—though we are talking about cultural rather than biological norms here. People from different musical cultures would, at least, have to learn to hear Chopin's preludes as music. Bernstein's point is that in doing so, in learning how to make sense of Western harmonic forms, they would also necessarily learn to hear the fourth prelude as sad music.

Bernstein's argument here is one taken for granted by film scorers, who are, among all popular music composers, perhaps the most concerned to use music to communicate particular feelings to a great range of people (to people with a great range of musical knowledge and experience). In his study of Bernard Herrmann's music, Graham Bruce therefore makes exactly the same point as Bernstein about the relationship of structure and feeling:

> Percy Scholes, speaking of the effect of the seventh chord in certain works by J. S. Bach, suggests that "All the mere triads gave a feeling of satisfaction in themselves; they were *Concords.* This 'chord of the seventh' gives a feeling of restlessness; the ear is dissatisfied until it has passed to the next chord and the seventh itself (C) has moved to the note below (B). This chord of the seventh, then, is a Discord— not necessarily, observe, a chord of harsh effect, but a chord that demands following in a certain way, i.e. 'Resolution.'"
>
> It is just this feeling of "restlessness" and "dissatisfaction," that Herrmann exploits as a means of creating musical suspense.[16]

Nöel Carroll has characterized such use of music in film as "modifying music—the music modifies the movie."

> Modifying music is one of the major uses of music in popular movies. It may be used to embellish individual scenes and sequences, or it may be integrated into leitmotif systems. Structurally, modifying music involves the use of movie elements—photography, narrative, dialogue and synchronized sound—as *indicators* that fix the reference of a shot, scene or sequence. The associated musical elements are *modifiers* which attribute expressive qualities to the referent, thereby characterizing it emotively as, for example, dreamy or jaunty.

More particularly,

> If adding music to the movie enhances one's expressive control over the action, it is also the case that the imagery intensifies the impact of the music by particularizing its affective resonance. The unnerving, shrieking strings in *Psycho* are cruel, painful, and murderous when matched with Norman Bates' descending knife. Here, the reference afforded by the movie elements serves to individuate the

emotive content of the music in the way that narrative and panto-mime do in ballet, and as words do in a popular song or opera.[17]

Carroll's is one of the more helpful analyses of film music, and I will return to it, but the points I want to stress here are, first, that he describes the working assumptions of both film scorers and film viewers (we do all understand the conventions) and, second, that he can therefore assume that certain musical elements do have, in themselves, predictable emotional effects. In his words, "modifying music, given *the almost direct expressive impact of music,* assures that the *untutored* spectators of the mass movie audience will have access to the desired expressive quality and, in turn, will see the given scene under its aegis."[18] Carroll is here, like Leonard Bernstein, drawing on an argument about the structure of classical music: "that the Prelude to *Tristan and Isolde* is expressive of yearning or that the 'Great Gate at Kiev' from *Pictures at an Exhibition* is expressive of majesty are part of the *incontestable* data of aesthetic theorizing."[19]

It is clear that musicological accounts of Western art music, musicological theories of classical musical codes, are essential for studies of popular music too. Take, for example, the film scorers' use of twelve-tone techniques, which are by now rather more familiar to cinema than concert hall audiences. The aspects of twelve-tone music that the classical public doesn't like—the lack of tonality which makes such dissonant music "difficult," "ugly," and "pointless"—are precisely those aspects which can be used by film scorers to their own ends, "for moments of tangled texture and stress." Fred Karlin and Rayburn Wright cite, as an example, Jerry Goldsmith's music for the scene in *The Omen* in which Mrs Baylock, the evil nanny, fights Gregory Peck:

> The music has the sound of twelve-tone procedures without being a strict application of the system . . . Bar 10 is a typical twelve-tone procedure. All 12 tones derived from the intervals of the original bass ostinato are heard without duplications. Much of the rest of the cue is constructed in the same way. To get the full impact of these relationships listen to the closing Ave Satani cue to hear the original ostinato and then listen to the fight with Mrs. Baylock.
>   Whether used in technical strictness or not, the sense of twelve-tone lines and their resulting "harmonies" adds bite and tension to a film score when this quality is desired.[20]

The importance of such technical analysis for our understanding of how film music works is incontestable, but there are hints here of the problem with the structural approach to musical meaning: how free are listeners to make their own interpretation of what they hear? Karlin and Wright talk about film scorers' use of "the *sense* of twelve-tone lines," and this "sense" of twelve-tone as dissonant and tangled can only be derived from its relationship to the norms of tonality. Its meaning lies in aural contrast: it is an effect of musical expectations derived not simply from the structural imperatives of this or that piece, but also from a cultural or social sound experience, from a cultural or social listening position.

In her discussion of Janika Vandervelde's *Genesis II*, Susan McClary notes both that the composer had a clear sense of her piece (it opens "with what Vandervelde intends as a musical image of childbirth: the pulsation of a fetal heartbeat, the intensifying strains of labor, and the sudden emergence into a fresh and calm new world") and that different listeners hear Vandervelde's contrasting piano and string parts (representing women's and men's time) quite differently (in part because of their own position as men or women):

> There are listeners who quickly tire of the "minimalistic" clockwork [piano] and who identify more with the string parts when they break away. I know people who hear the clockwork as mechanistic, or as a beautiful yet inanimate mineral formation, against which the strings become the specifically human voice. Others (and here I must count myself) are attracted to or identify with the gentle ebb and flow of the cyclic clockwork and are unnerved by the violence wreaked upon it by the impulsive self-expressive strings.[21]

It is not accidental that McClary is describing here "new music," musical meanings which are not yet fixed. It's not so much that listeners disagree about the meanings of the musical elements of Vandervelde's piece as that they read its overall *argument* differently, place different weights on the relations between the elements. In his polemical attack on music criticism, Hans Keller writes:

> I have, in fact, always listened as uncritically as possible, especially to begin with, at the very moment when, in view of something new, the critic is expected to employ his critical capacities to the utmost. But at the outset, one has to discover what the artist has to say or is trying to say; how can we judge how he is saying it if we don't know what it is?[22]

My question is: how does such "discovery" work? For a pop fan the oddest aspect of new art music is the role of the program note of the author's intentions, a necessary part, it seems, of the listening experience. I'll quote two examples:

Mebasi for chamber orchestra.

Last fall, when I first heard the music of the Bibayak Pygmies of West Africa, I was immediately struck by their fascination with very gradual voice leading and polyrhythms—techniques which have recently fascinated me, also. "Mebasi" is their word for a festival vocal game in which singers compete with one another in long, modulated cries. I've borrowed the spirit of the game, as well as some of the music, to make a miniature chamber concerto featuring each instrument in competitive solos. Besides contesting one another, the musicians also engage a variety of sharp-edged, polyrhythmic pulses. Finally, the music self-destructs as a solo trombone hurls its African theme against hammer blows which gradually become unhinged— while composing, I imagined the unsynchronized gears and springs of a robot falling apart.[23]

Charmonium for harpsichord and chamber orchestra.

In the colorful language of elementary-particle physics, "charmonium" refers to the family of bound states of the charm quark and its antiparticle. As a musical title, then, it is deceptive: not only does the root "charm" in "charmonium" imply no aesthetic qualities or magic, but the cognate relationship to the Latin "harmonia" and its derivatives is strictly false.

Chordal fanfares of short repeated cells alternate with solo episodes in which "improvisatory" figures are spun out against a backdrop of converging or diverging chromatic lines moving at independent speeds. The resulting contrasts of rhythm and perceived *tempi* put me in mind of the paths of elementary particles as photographed in bubble- and streamer-chamber experiments, with some tracing great sweeping arcs while others whirl in tight spirals or dart mercurially; hence the title.[24]

Three points can immediately be made about such wordy approaches to musical meaning. First, they draw to our attention the fact that virtually all instrumental music has some sort of associated verbal description, even if only in its title. It may therefore be difficult to disentangle the way we interpret the meaning of a piece of music from the way we interpret its title. This is, perhaps, most intriguing for jazz, in which titles (*A Love Supreme, Sketches of Spain,* "Misterioso") work like labels to supply interpretive information, an indication of how to listen.

Second, though, it is not at all obvious that we can only *enjoy* a piece of music if we understand it according to the program note. Is a piece of music meaningless if we don't know what, in the words of the composer, it is about?

Which leads to a third question: not *does* our listening experience bear any relationship to an author's account of the music, but *can* it? To put this more strongly: is "interpretation" necessary for musical enjoyment? What does "misinterpretation" mean? Nicholas Cook notes that misinterpretations (or "false" labels) are not uncommon in classical music history. For example, the standard nineteenth-century interpretation of Beethoven's "Les Adieux" sonata was that it was about the parting and reunion of two lovers; now (as the result of proper historical data) we know that it concerned Archduke Rudolph's departure from and return to his dukedom. Did this "wrong" reading matter? What changed when the "correct" meaning was found: the music? The way people heard the music? Or simply the way they wrote about it?[25]

Arguments about musical meaning depend on shared understandings of musical codes (otherwise there would be nothing to argue about), and there can be no doubt that Western music listeners in the late twentieth century do take for granted a series of relationships between what they hear and what they feel. As Leonard Meyer has elegantly argued, this is what we mean by musical "acculturation."[26] We may not all have attended music schools, but we have all been to the movies; we may not be able to tell the difference between a major and a minor chord, but we do know when a piece turns sad. Musicologists can rightly claim, in short, to be able to relate the structural qualities of a certain sort of music to the emotional effects it has on its listeners; or, to approach this the other way around, we can examine instrumental music which is labeled as sad or angry or happy and find that such labels match specific structural qualities.[27] Such feelings *are* caused by the musical elements themselves, but through a process of conventional association.

From a sociological perspective, then, music listening can only occur in music cultures. To hear combinations of sounds as music, it is necessary to know something about the conventional meanings of agreed musical elements.[28] One obvious aspect of this is the way music quotes music—composers may evoke church bells or a marching band, folk music or popular tunes.[29] As Christopher Ballantine notes, such quotation isn't only a matter of using sounds for their "semantic connotations." By putting the quoted music in a new context, the composer can also indicate an attitude toward those connotations, through homage, celebration, pastiche, irony, and so on.[30] Quotation has been equally common in popular music, in the use of other genre clichés, for example, and is now essential to the use of sampling and the construction of music as montage.[31]

Further clues to everyday musical interpretation can be found in song lyrics. As Keir Keightley notes, because in practice song words are usually written after the music, this, ironically, "makes them a source of insight into common conventions of *musical* meaning."[32] I'll come back to this in Chapter 8. I want to focus here on film music—partly because it is a form which depends, for economic reasons, on quotation, and partly because film music enables us to *see* how musical/emotional coding works (a coding heavily dependent on the conventions of Western art music).

Film music is an oddly neglected area of popular music studies (and has been of even less interest to film scholars). I say "oddly," because if we include under the label the soundtracks of commercials on television, then it is arguable that this is the most significant form of contemporary popular music; or at least, of the popular understanding and interpretation of instrumental music. Perhaps for both these reasons—its neglect and its importance—it has also brought forth some of the most interesting and subtle academic accounts of how music works.[33]

The starting point for any study of the meaning of film music is that it depends on a relation of sound and drama. The cinema draws on both popular and art traditions—on vaudeville, melodrama, the circus, and pantomime, on one hand; on opera and ballet, on the other—and in very general terms I would suggest that in the former, popular forms, the music *accompanies* the action, is used to describe the action aurally, to identify characters, to "coax" extra emotion from the audience, and so forth.[34] In the latter, art forms, the music *produces* the action: in their different ways opera and ballet interpret the music, put sound into action.

Film music uses both strategies and, in doing so, raises intriguing questions about the relation of sound and image in the making of cinematic meaning. There's a common exercise in the teaching of film music composition in which a silent film image is shown: a woman walking down some stairs. As either a narrative or an emotional image this doesn't really mean anything (or rather, perhaps, can mean everything). Show the same clip with music, and according to the nature of the music the image takes on different meanings: play "suspense" music and we immediately know something is going to happen; melodramatic music and we know that something has already happened; within these frames the music can also indicate whether what's going to happen will be fearful or joyful (a killer or a lover at the bottom of the stairs) or indeed (as in a Herrmann score) both; whether what has happened is a matter of joy or grief (a mother living or dying).

What we hear can, then, be a more powerful source of meaning than what we see. In this exercise, it seems, the music is more meaningful than the photography; it provides us with the clues to the character and situation that allow us to read them. If the exercise were to be reversed, if the same piece of music were shown accompanying scenes of laughter or tears, violence or lovemaking, we would still be more likely to change our reading of the scene than of the music; if the music for a happy scene is violent or suspenseful, for example, then we assume that this scene won't last, that something else is going on.

The argument here is a commonplace in film music theory, which follows Robert Bresson's edict that "a sound always evokes an image but never the reverse," and Schopenhauer's that "suitable music played to any scene, action, event, or surrounding seems to disclose to us its most secret meaning, and appears as the most accurate and distinct commentary upon it."[35] But the question begged here is what Schopenhauer means by "suitable." Gillian Anderson quotes a 1922 manual for cinema organists which spelled out the possible pitfalls in this regard:

> If you are playing pictures, do so intelligently. To give you an idea of how easily a wrong number can be chosen for a scene, a man and a woman were shown on the screen in each other's embrace. The organist began playing a silly love song, only to find that the couple were brother and sister. Here is another example: during the last war an army of soldiers were shown marching in the distance. Immediately the organist began playing "Three Cheers for the Red, White and Blue." Naturally the audience rose to their feet only to find that they were greeting an army of German soldiers instead. The audience seeing their mistake gradually slipped into their seats but the organist tore madly though the number not noticing the difference. I once heard in a prominent theatre in one of the eastern cities, an organist play "I Am Always Chasing Rainbows" when Salome was chasing John the Baptist in the picture. There is no logical reason for anyone playing a drinking song such as "How Dry I Am" on an echo or cathedral chimes. Yet you hear it done and many other things equally as ridiculous. Persons of good taste would not be seen in a bathing suit at a church wedding, yet players do just as absurd things in the fitting of pictures.[36]

The application of music to image can be "absurd" as well as "suitable," then. The domination of image by sound in the making of meaning may not be straightforward, may even seem ridiculous. The problem with that scoring exercise is that it is an exercise; in practice films have other sources of narrative meaning, whether immediate (what we *see* happen next) or in terms of expectation (about this star, this genre). Two points follow from this. First, the systematic use of certain sorts of music in films can change the meaning of that music: fairground music has been used in enough suspense or horror films, for example, that these sounds, which once presumably connoted happiness and play, now make one feel uneasy (just as it is difficult now for filmmakers to have a ringing telephone portend good rather than bad news, a relaxing rather than a disturbing conversation). Or, to cite a different sort of example: thanks to its use in Kenneth Anger's *Scorpio Rising* and David Lynch's *Blue Velvet,* that once rather bland and innocuous Bobby Vinton ballad now has a perverse erotic charge.

Second, to return to Nöel Carroll's argument about "modifying music," both sound and image are necessary for meaning making because they have different roles: the music gives us "vague" emotions (suspense, joy, fear, anger); the images provide us with the occasion for these feelings, their causes and thus their specific shape. As Carroll puts it, music is expressive of "emotive qualities but ones that are inexplicit, ambiguous and broad." To become explicit emotion must refer to something; the broad feeling must be focused on the relevant object on the screen or in the narrative.[37] Even in the case of the woman walking down the stairs, while the music may indicate to us roughly what we should feel about the situation (and, by projection, what she may also feel), it is, nevertheless, the visual image (and our visual imagination) that gives us the source for these diffuse feelings, and thus allows us to give them a precise shape. (And if the argument here is about film images it could equally well be applied to dancing bodies in ballet, and to the voices and words of pop songs: it is the extra-musical information which enables us to hear the music as *specifically* meaningful.)

One issue that is relevant here is the relationship of film and opera. One can obviously make a simple contrast in terms of power (though there are exceptions on both sides): in opera the composer is a more significant figure in determining the nature and meaning of the narrative than the librettist or the director; in film the director (and scriptwriter) are more significant in determining the nature and meaning of the narrative than the composer. There is, in consequence, a different relationship between sound and image, between the use of sound to bring out the meaning of what's seen (film), and of image to bring out the meaning of what's heard (opera).[38]

Despite these differences, film composers certainly draw on opera writing conventions, in at least two important respects. The first is the way in which musical meaning is constructed as structurally *internal* to a work. In film as in opera, for example, a musical sign may be attributed to a character, and this is what the sign (whether it is a fully developed leitmotif or simply the use of a particular instrument) means. And, in a more complicated process, an equation can be made (in film and opera alike) between narrative structure and musical structure, such that the musicological notions of tension, thrust, climax, dissatisfaction, and so forth are given a narrative translation through the stage or film plot: the "climax" of the music will come at the moment of triumph or death.

Second, musical meaning in film, as in opera, may be constructed symbolically; the musical element (whether instrument, melody, key, or harmonic principle) is used to stand for or symbolize an aspect of the plot (good or evil, male or female, class, ethnicity, character, culture or nature) in a way that is *not* necessarily coherent in terms of the soundtrack's overall musical structure.[39]

The difference between film and opera, then, is not that they use different devices, but that they organize them differently. In opera musical logic is supreme (though the great operas are precisely the ones in which musical and narrative logic, structural and symbolic meanings are integrated, as in Wagner); in films, narrative logic is supreme (though the great film scores are the ones in which musical and narrative logic, structural and symbolic meanings are integrated, as for Bernard Herrmann). Herrmann, in fact, deliberately changed his approach to musical structure so that his commitment to musical coherence might survive the demands of film narrative. As Graham Bruce puts it,

> An even more radical challenge to the late nineteenth-century romantic style of Korngold and his colleagues was Herrmann's rejection of melody. Herrmann argued that, since the symmetrical span of a melody required a certain space to unfold, continual use of melody would require that a purely musical logic would prevail, the piece being governed by the predetermined shape of the melody rather than by the movements of the film narrative. Herrmann sought a more flexible unit, one which could interact fully with the filmic articulation. This he found in the short phrase, the brief musical module consisting of one or two measures, or sometimes as few as two notes. The possibilities which such flexible musical units offer for interaction with dialogue, narration, actor movement, cam-

era movement, and editing are evident . . . [in] *The Magnificent Ambersons.*[40]

Or, as Herrmann put it himself, "a composer's first job is to get inside the drama. If he can't do that he shouldn't be writing the music at all."[41]

In short, from the scorer's perspective, the "meaning" of the music in a film is clearly a "musical meaning," derives from the organization of a musical structure, is an effect of the relations between notes, but now a "correct" reading is grounded not in a musical knowledge of that structure (in a study of the score) but in the accompanying organization on screen of the dramatic narrative. And, at the same time (which is what makes film scoring so interesting a challenge to musicians), our understanding of that dramatic narrative is determined by what we hear—is an effect of the musical process. This double process—meaning given by the *mutuality* of musical structure and dramatic narrative—is, as Nicholas Cook argues, perhaps most obvious (because, by necessity, most condensed) in television commercials. Cook describes the closing sequence of a commercial for the Prudential Building Society:

> The tempo gets slower and slower; the harmony outlines a classic II-V-I progression, and the melody rises towards the upper tonic cadencing an octave higher than it began. As I mentioned, the final phrase is the only one that is not arch-shaped, and its ascent to the upper tonic coincides with the appearance of the Prudential logo on the screen. In this way, a purely musical process is being used not just to highlight the product name, but to assert what is really the fundamental message of the commercial—a message that is not spoken (and indeed cannot quite be spoken), but to which everything in the commercial seems to lead with the force of inevitability: *Prudential is the [re]solution of all your problems.*

And Cook goes on to argue that in commercials generally, "Music transfers its own attributes to the story line and to the product, it creates coherence, making connections that are not there in the words or pictures; it even engenders meanings of its own. But it does all this, so to speak, silently."[42] Cook's point (following Claudia Gorbman) is that music doesn't simply bring meaning to images from the outside, as it were (through its semantic connotations); music, in its internal organization, acts to interpret what we see: *it allows meaning to happen.*

So far (starting from the opera analogy) I have been describing this process in structural terms, in terms of concepts like "coherence," which imply an *orderly* relationship between film score and film script. In sound practice, of course, most films (unlike most TV commercials) are much messier, much more *disorderly*. Michel Chion thus asks:

> What do sounds do when put together with a film image? They dispose themselves in relation to the frame and its content. Some are embraced as synchronous and onscreen, others wander at the surface and on the edges as offscreen. And still others position themselves clearly outside the diegesis, in an imaginary orchestra pit (non-diegetic music), or on a sort of balcony, the place of voiceovers. In short, we classify sounds in relation to what we see in the image, and this classification is constantly subject to revision, depending on changes in what we see. Thus we can define most cinema as "a place of images, plus sounds," with sound being "that which seeks its place."[43]

The "place" of music in film is usually defined functionally. Aaron Copland, for example, describes five broad functions: "creating atmosphere, underlining the psychological states of characters, providing background filler, building a sense of continuity, sustaining tension and then rounding it off with a sense of closure."[44] Bernard Herrmann explained that the music in a film could seek out or intensify the "inner thoughts" of a character; invest a scene with terror, grandeur, gaiety, or mystery; propel a scene forward or slow it down; lift dialogue into the realm of poetry; and act as "the communicating link between the screen and the audience, reaching out and *enveloping* all."[45] Michel Chion suggests that in the cinema, music "fits" or "enfolds" a scene like clothes "fit" or "enfold" a body.[46]

This last is a nice image, with its implication that film music (like clothes) both conceals the plot (the body) and expresses and reveals it; that the meaning of the music (like the meaning of clothes) has as much to do with the meaning of other musics (other clothes) as it has to do with the particular shape of this story (this body); that the shape of the narrative is, in fact, determined by the shape of its implied score (just as the nude in art is shaped by its implied clothes)[47]—this is particularly obvious in terms of genre (think, for example, how Ennio Morricone's fragmented scores for Sergio Leone's westerns determine how these stories must be told). In short, what the clothes metaphor makes clear is that film music has to be read semiotically, as part of a musical "fashion system," as well as by reference to the immediate clothing needs of this particular story.

Such an approach to film music, through its codes, is by now well developed; here I just want to summarize those themes that are relevant for popular music analysis, those codes that are used by popular musicians and composers whether they are writing for films or not.[48]

The first set of codes, *emotional codes*, concern the ways in which music is taken to signify feeling. The arguments here reflect the continuing influence of the compositional conventions of classical music on film scoring, and it is, in fact, difficult now to disentangle film and classical musical/emotional meanings. There are historical reasons for this, reflecting the way in which music was used in the "silent" film era. On the one hand, cinematic music was then live music, and the orchestral musicians employed, primarily classically trained, took their cues from the classical repertoire. Gillian Anderson has documented, for example, the astonishing range of orchestral overtures that were played at the beginning of each of the four daily film showings at the Rialto in New York between 1918 and 1921, and even in small, local cinemas the theater organist often prepared the audience for the show using similar works.[49] As a musical experience, early cinema was more like a popular classical concert than the burlesque or vaudeville from which its story conventions came.

On the other hand, classical music also became the root source for the music accompanying the pictures themselves. Classical music was, from early in American cinema history, used as "mood" or "modifying" music. Max Winkler recalls how, working for the orchestral music publisher Carl Fischer in the early 1910s, he found himself serving an increasing number of film exhibitors and theater managers, looking for suitable scores for their pianists and organists so as to prevent films from being shown with inappropriate or incoherent accompanying sounds. Interestingly enough, the problem was conceived as the poor fit between the popular tunes favored by the jobbing professional pianists employed in the smaller theaters and the "serious" emotions and situations being projected on the screen—"unsuitability," as we've already seen, combined an aesthetic and an ethical judgment. As the cinema began to take itself more seriously narratively, in other words, and sought to attract a better class of customer with proper stories and moral dramas (moving away from the earlier emphasis on novelty, voyeurism, and spectacle), so it began to take the musical accompaniment more seriously too. Winkler understood the situation in commercial terms:

One day after I had gone home from work I could not fall asleep. The hundreds and thousands of titles, the mountains of music that Fischer's had stored and catalogued kept going through my mind. There was music, surely to fit *any* given situation in *any* picture. If we could only think of a way to let all these orchestra leaders and pianists and organists know what we had! If we could use our knowledge and experience not when it was too late, but much earlier, before they ever had to sit down and play, we would be able to sell them music not by the ton but by the train-load![50]

Winkler thus invented the "cue sheet." He saw films before release and roughly scored them; theater managers bought from him a musical guide to each silent film they showed, a scene-by-scene breakdown suggesting the most appropriate accompanying music—which they could then, of course, also buy.

The question was where such music would come from. Initially Winkler thought in terms of original compositions. Unfortunately,

Every scene, situation, character, action, emotion, every nationality, emergency, wind storm, rain storm and brain storm, every dancer, vamp, cowboy, thief and gigolo, eskimo and zulu, emperor and street walker, colibri and elephant—plus every printed title that flickered in the faces of the five-cent to twenty-five-cent audiences—had to be expressed in music, and we soon realized that our catalog of so-called Dramatic and Incidental Music was quite insufficient to furnish the simply colossal amounts of music needed by an ever-expanding industry . . .

In desperation we turned to crime. We began to dismember the great masters. We began to murder the works of Beethoven, Mozart, Grieg, J. S. Bach, Verdi, Bizet, Tchaikovsky and Wagner—everything that wasn't protected by copyright from our pilfering.

The immortal chorales of J. S. Bach became an "Adagio Lamentoso for sad scenes." Extracts from great symphonies and operas were hacked down to emerge again as "Sinister Misterioso" by Beethoven, or "Weird Moderato" by Tchaikovsky. Wagner's and Mendelssohn's wedding marches were used for marriages, fights between husbands and wives, and divorce scenes: we just had them played out of tune, a treatment known in the profession as "souring up the aisle." If they were to be used for happy endings we jazzed them up mercilessly. Finales from famous overtures, with "William Tell" and "Orpheus" the favorites, became gallops. Meyerbeer's "Coronation March" was slowed down to a majestic pomposo to give proper background to the inhabitants of Sing Sing's deathhouse. The "Blue Danube" was watered down to a minuet by a cruel change in tempo. Delibes' "Pizzicato Polka" made an excellent accompaniment to a sneaky night scene by counting "one-two" between each pizzicato. Any piece using a trombone prominently would infallibly announce the home-coming of a drunk; no other instrument could hiccup with such virtuosity.[51]

Winkler's initiative meant that when "talking" pictures arrived, when integrated film scores were required, it was composers adept at using these nineteenth-century European bourgeois musical conventions who were seen as best fitted for the task. The emotional codes of nineteenth-century symphonic music, the particular sentimental use of tonal structures and harmonic rules, familiar in rough-and-ready form in the accompaniment of silent films, now became, more subtly because carefully composed for each movie, the norm of talkies too. And just as the earlier use of these conventions (rather than those of popular American entertainment) was a gesture at the emotional importance of what was being enacted on screen, so the use of classical music conventions in talkies reflected the belief that its "transcendent" and "universal" qualities could give the scenes it "enveloped" a *general* meaning. Everybody—working-class, middle-class, and upper-class characters, audiences in America and Europe—could kiss to this music; too obviously popular or vernacular musical forms would limit a scene, would be too indicative of divisive national and social identities.[52]

Within film music's emotional codes we need to distinguish two functions. First, there is music designed to tell the *audience* how to feel. Here we find most obviously the accepted rhetoric of symphonic music and the use of general mood musical signs. Music here can imply, among other things, the right audience attitude toward the film and toward their own feelings about the film (it can be used, that is, both ironically and intertextually; Bernard Herrmann used to quote from his own previous scores). In general terms, this use of music is *culturally determined:* it draws on what is assumed to be the audience's shared understanding of particular musical devices. The shift in film scoring in the 1970s and 1980s toward the use of marketable title cuts and youth-oriented scores (which brought to an end a composing career like Herrmann's) was not simply a matter of demographics or marketing. It also reflected, I think, a generational change in what was heard as the basic language of the emotions. For the rock generation popular music was as capable of expressing "serious" emotion as classical music; Jennifer Warnes and Joe Cocker as expressive of romantic intensity as ersatz Mendelssohn; John Barry as expressive of dramatic tension as ersatz Wagner.

The second function of emotional codes in film music is to tell us what the *characters in the film* are feeling. Here we find the most obvious use of operatic devices, leitmotifs, and so on, and here the codes are, in a sense, *composer determined*. The score itself, as I have already discussed, provides the context in which we read the significance of certain melodic or instrumental figures.

In the end, though, the most interesting (and powerful) aspect of film music is that it integrates these cultural and composer codes, dissolves the distinctions between "how I feel" and "how they feel." As in music generally, in interpreting film sounds emotionally we are, in effect, interpreting our own feelings on hearing them, and the effect is, as Herrmann suggested, "enveloping." Sartre, the philosopher of egoism, has given perhaps the best description of the cinema as a musical experience:

Above all, I liked the incurable muteness of my heroes. But no, they weren't mute, since they knew how to make themselves understood. We communicated by means of music; it was the sound of their inner life. Persecuted innocence did better than merely show or speak of suffering; it permeated me with its pain by means of the melody that issued from it. I would read the conversation, but I heard the hope and bitterness; I would perceive by ear the proud grief that remains silent. I was compromised; the young widow who wept on the screen was not I, and yet she and I had only one soul; Chopin's funeral march; no more was needed for tears to wet my eyes. I felt I was a prophet without being able to foresee anything; even before the traitor betrayed, his crime entered me; when all seemed peaceful in the castle, sinister chords exposed the murderer's presence. How happy were those cowboys, those musketeers, those detectives; their future was there, in that premonitory music, and governed the present . . . the virgin's desperate struggle against her abductor, the hero's gallop across the plain, the interlacing of all those images, of all those speeds, and, beneath it all, the demonic movement of the "Race to the Abysss," an orchestral selection taken from the *Damnation of Faust* and adapted for the piano, all this was one and the same: it was Destiny . . . What joy when the last knife stroke coincided with the last chord! I was utterly content, I had found the world in which I wanted to live, I touched the absolute. What an uneasy feeling when the lights went on; I had been wracked with love for the characters and they had disappeared, carrying their world with them. I had felt their victory in my bones; yet it was theirs and not mine. In the street I found myself superfluous.[53]

Nöel Carroll explains the same experience in cooler terms:

> In contrast to our encounters in everyday life, movie events have an unaccustomed intelligibility and lucidity; movies, that is, are so much more legible than life . . . Unlike our quotidian experience of events, the music constantly alerts us to the feeling with which we see. Where in life the affect that goes with an observation is so often unknown, in movies, we not only have some affect but also the appropriate affect tied to virtually everything we see, through modifying music . . . Reciprocally, the focusing function of the movie indicators renders the emotive content of the music more and more explicit, enhancing their clarity in yet another way.[54]

In short, through the use of emotional codes, film music has taught us how to see, while film images have taught us how to hear.

This leads me to the second semiotic dimension of film music, the *cultural code*. This is the use of music to tell us where we are; to reveal as economically as possible (so we can get on with the story) the basic social and cultural facts of the images we're seeing: place and time (geography and history), social setting (sociology and political economy). The most efficient means of musical shorthand is the use of generic conventions, whether these are indicated by melodic structures or by rhythmic rules or, most simply, by instrumentation (the quickest way of indicating, for example, that a film is set in China or Scotland, in Nashville or Paris). Such references may be crude (bagpipes, an accordion) or subtle—as in the indication of a moment in social experience by precise pop quotation (famously in *The Big Chill*, for example). Leith Stevens comments in these terms on his score for *The Wild One:*

> The characters of the play are young people, full of tensions, for the most part inarticulate about their problems, and, though exhibition-istic, still confused and wandering.
>
> These characteristics suggested the use of progressive jazz or bop (call it what you will) as an important segment of the score. This music, with its complicated, nervous searching quality, seemed best suited to complement these characters. This is the first score, to the writer's knowledge, to use contemporary jazz in actual scoring of scenes.[55]

This is obviously an area where questions of musical authenticity arise. Miklós Rózsa contrasts film and opera composing in terms of "realism":

The orientalism in *Aida, Samson and Delilah,* or *Queen of Sheba* is only used as color, and they are full-blooded romantic operas mirroring the style of the period of their creation with no attempt whatsoever to represent the true style of the period of their action. But the motion picture is different. It is realist and factual. It not only tries to capture the spirit of bygone eras but also tries to make believe that it projects before the eyes of the spectator the real thing.

On the other hand, having been assigned the score for *Quo Vadis,* and having researched the sounds, instruments, and composing conventions in Rome in the year 64 A.D. ("there is absolutely no record of any music of the classical times of Roman history"), Rózsa realized that "as the music for *Quo Vadis* was intended for dramatic use and as entertainment for the lay public, one had to avoid the pitfall of producing only musicological oddities instead of music with a universal, emotional appeal." At the same time, "the archaic sound had to be created with our modern instruments." In short, Rózsa had to *imply* archaism, through the use of familiar musical and instrumental conventions; "realism" in music, as generally, is a matter of representational conventions.[56]

The same issues are involved in the use of all the other devices of socio-musical representation—representations of race and class, gender and nation. Kathryn Kalinak describes the musical conventions developed in Hollywood to depict female sexuality:

> Certain types of instrumentation, melody, harmony and rhythm came to denote certain types of women. These musical stereotypes helped to determine the audience's response to and evaluation of female characters, and like signposts, directed the audience towards the "correct" estimation of a woman's character . . . The fallen woman was characterized by a nucleus of musical practices which carried indecent implications through an association with so-called decadent musical forms such as jazz, the blues, honky-tonk, and ragtime. Instrumentally the fallen woman was characterized by a predominance of orchestral colors associated with popular jazz such as saxophones and muted horns; harmonically, by the inclusion of unusual harmonies, chromaticism and dissonance; rhythmically, by the use of dotted rhythms and syncopation; and structurally, by the use of portamento and blue notes.
>
> The virtuous wife and mother, on the other hand, was characterized by musical practices with strong positive associations. Her

instrumentation was orchestral, with the violins usually carrying the melody; the harmonies were lush, based on late nineteenth century models; the rhythms were even and lyrical; and the melodies often had an upward movement, or included upward leaps in the melodic pattern.[57]

Here, clearly, Hollywood taught us how to hear musical signs, through moral plots, even as it drew on our commonsense readings of sound settings.

Finally, film scorers may employ *dramatic codes,* use music for its narrative effect, to propel the action forward or hold it back. The music is neither telling us where we are nor what to feel about this, but, rather, helps us to place ourselves in the *unfolding* of the story. Film music, for example, can indicate how quickly time is passing, can suggest a spatial perspective, can tell us how close we are to the action.[58] One of the most interesting findings from Philip Tagg's listening tests is the extent to which people hear instrumental music "narratively" rather than "emotionally"; music is understood both in terms of specific physical movements (by boat or train, for instance) and by reference to a vaguer, narrative movement (toward a meeting, away from a confrontation).[59]

While such listening is clearly an effect of years of going to the cinema, it does not depend on specific cinematic images; and this is true of our understanding of film music's emotional and cultural codes too. Rather, such codes are free-floating; they inform *all* our music listening. We hear music in the cinema as if we were hearing it "in reality" (the film scorer's starting assumption), but we also hear music "in reality" as if we were in the cinema. Writing about cinematic sound realism more generally, Michel Chion asks: "If we are watching a war film or a storm at sea, what idea did most of us actually have of sounds of war or the high seas before hearing the sounds in the films?"[60]

And the same point could be made about music: if we are watching a melodrama or a suspense sequence, what idea did most of us actually have of the emotional meaning of this chord sequence, this tangle of strings, before hearing the sounds in the films? We are left with a wonderfully circular process: scorers bring sounds *to* films, for their everyday semantic connotations, from their roots in Western art music and musicology; listeners take musical meanings *from* films, from the cinemas in which we've learned what emotions and cultures and stories sound like.

Rhythm: Race, Sex, and the Body

Great variety and quick transitions from one measure or tone to another are contrary to the genius of the beautiful in music. Such transitions often excite mirth, or other sudden and tumultuous passions; but not that sinking, that melting, that languor, which is the characteristical effect of the beautiful, as it regards every sense.

Edmund Burke[1]

The Red Hot Chili Peppers are putting the three most important letters back into FUNK, taking the piss out of the idiots who forgot what it was for in the first place and are being censored left, right and centre because of it.

"From our viewpoint it's impossible to ignore the correlation between music and sex because, being so incredibly rhythmic as it is, it's very deeply correlated to sex and the rhythm of sex, and the rhythm of your heart pounding and intercourse motions and just the way it makes you feel when you hear it. We try to make our music give you an erection."

Melody Maker[2]

Everyone seems agreed, the music's lovers and loathers alike, that rock and roll means sex; everyone assumes that this meaning comes with the beat. I don't, and in this chapter I suggest that if rock does sometimes mean sex it is for sociological, not musicological reasons. (And besides, as the Red Hot Chili Peppers' casual male chauvinism makes clear, in this context sex is an essentially sociological sort of thing, anyway.) Deliberately misreading the Chili's point, then, I will start this chapter with the concept of *fun*.

"Fun" can only be defined against something else, in contrast to the "serious" and the "respectable," and in musical discourses the opposition of "serious" and "fun" sounds (the aesthetic versus the hedonistic) involves both a moral-cum-artistic judgment and a distinction between a mental and a physical response. In classical music criticism, "fun" thus describes concerts which are not the real thing—benefit or charity shows, the Last Night of the Proms; the critical tone is a kind of forced, condescending bonhomie: "it was just a bit of fun!" In pop criticism "art" and "fun" define each other in a running dialectic—if 1970s progressive rockers dismissed first Motown and then disco as "only" entertainment, 1980s progressive popsters saw off rock's pretensions with the tee-shirt slogan "Fuck Art, Let's Dance!"[3]

As I noted in Chapter 2, the equation of the serious with the mind and fun with the body was an aspect of the way in which high culture was established in Europe and the United States in the nineteenth century. John Kassan quotes Mark Twain's description of the audience "at the shrine of St. Wagner" in Bayreuth:

> Absolute attention and petrified retention to the end of an act of the attitude assumed at the beginning of it. You detect no movement in the solid mass of heads and shoulders. You seem to sit with the dead in the gloom of a tomb. You know that they are being stirred to their profoundest depths; that there are times when they want to rise and wave handkerchiefs and shout their approbation, and times when tears are running down their faces, and it would be a relief to free their pent emotions in sobs or screams; yet you hear not one utterance till the curtain swings together and the closing strains have slowly faded out and died.[4]

Twain then watched the audience burst into "thunderous applause." Other observers, more ideologically correct Wagnerians, claimed that even after the performance there was just intense silence. Such complete physical control—or mental transportation?—did not become a classical concert convention (orchestras would be dismayed to get *no* applause at the end of a show), but the denial of any bodily response *while* the music plays is now taken for granted. A good classical performance is therefore measured by the stillness it commands, by the intensity of the audience's mental concentration, by the lack of any physical distraction, any coughs or shuffles. And it is equally important, as we have seen, to disguise the physical effort that goes into classical music-making—Wagner kept the orchestra hidden at Bayreuth, and "from early in his career ridiculed those who enjoyed '*looking* at the music instead of listening to it.'"[5]

A good rock concert, by contrast, is measured by the audience's physical response, by how quickly people get out of their seats, onto the dance floor, by how loudly they shout and scream. And rock performers are expected to revel in their own physicality too, to strain and sweat and collapse with tiredness. Rock stage clothes (like sports clothes) are designed to show the

Performing Rites

musician's body as instrumental (as well as sexual), and not for nothing does a performer like Bruce Springsteen end a show huddled with his band, as if he'd just won the Super Bowl. Rock acts conceal not the physical but the technological sources of their sounds; rock audiences remain uneasy about musical instruments that appear to require no effort to be played.

The key point here, though, is that the musical mind/body split does not just mark off classical from rock concert conventions; it also operates within the popular music domain. When rock (or jazz) acts move into seated concert halls, for example, it is often to register that the music is now "serious," should now be appreciated quietly. (I sometimes suspect that it is at such sit-down shows—for Leonard Cohen, say, or the Cure, or P. J. Harvey—that one best gets a sense of what the mid-nineteenth century battles over classical concert behavior were like, as the listening and the dancing sections of the crowd get equally annoyed with each other, and as the attendants struggle to keep *everyone* seated.) The underlying contrast here between listening with the mind and listening with the body is well captured by photography: the classical audience *rapt,* the rock audience *abandoned;* both sorts of listener oblivious to their neighbors, both with eyes shut and bodies open, but the classical listener obviously quite still, the rock listener held in the throes of movement.[6]

The question that interests me in this chapter, then, is how the musical mind/body split works. Why is some music heard as physical (fun), other music as cerebral (serious)? Is there nothing of the mind in the former? Nothing of the body in the latter? And in approaching these questions the first point to make is that just as "sin" is defined by the virtuous (or would-be virtuous), so fun (or music-for-the-body) is, in ideological practice, defined in contrast to serious music, music-for-the-mind. The Red Hot Chili Peppers' crude equation of musical pleasure, rhythm, and sex derives, in short, from a high cultural argument.

The musical equation of aesthetic/mind and hedonistic/ body is one effect of the mental/manual division of labor built into the Industrial Revolution, and into the consequent organization of education.[7] In the mid-nineteenth century this was mapped onto the original Romantic dichotomy between feeling and reason: feelings were now taken (as at Bayreuth) to be best expressed spiritually and mentally, in silent contemplation of great art or great music. Bodily responses became, by definition, mind-less. "The brain," wrote Frank Howes in the *British Journal of Aesthetics* in 1962, is associated with art music; "brainlessness" with pop. Popular music, agreed Peter Stadler, is music requiring "a minimum of brain activity."[8]

For Stadler, this isn't necessarily to devalue popular music, which (thanks to its rhythms) may well be sexy and humorous; jazz, in particular, he suggests, gives us direct access to bodily sensation; it is not a music that has to be interpreted, it is not a music *that has to be thought about.*[9] A decade later Raymond Durgnat celebrated rock in much the same way, as a music which in its use of rhythm was immediately, gloriously, sensual.[10]

The meaning of popular music is being explained here by intellectuals who value (or abhor) it because it offers them a different experience from art music. A telling example of such a celebration of otherness can be found in Guy Scarpetta's description of going with friends from the French art and music magazine *Art-Press* to see Johnny Halliday, the rock 'n' roll singer, perform in Nice. For these self-conscious intellectuals, the "flagrant" pleasure of the show began with the opportunity to slough off their class distinction, to identify with their generation, but what most struck these young men about this particular experience of "encanaillement" (or slumming) was the corporal presence of the music. Scarpetta heard in rock "une intensité organique, une force pulsionelle," saw in Halliday "une fantasmatique directement sexuelle." This was not something on offer from the essentially "conceptuel" Parisian avant-garde of the time—Halliday's performance was "fun," in short, because it stressed the physical pleasure of music in ways repressed elsewhere; for Scarpetta and his friends it articulated something otherwise forbidden.[11]

Two points emerge from this passage. First, it describes a musical experience which can only be understood in high cultural terms (it tells us nothing of what Halliday's low-class fans made of his music). The organization of high culture in terms of bourgeois respectability has meant, inevitably, the identification of low culture with the unrespectable (and obviously, in institutional terms, while high art took its nineteenth-century place in the secular temples of gallery, museum, and concert hall, low music continued to be associated with the bodily pleasures of the bar and the brothel).[12] By the beginning of this century, in other words, low music was both a real and a fantasy site for casting off bourgeois inhibitions.

The second point here concerns race. In 1922, forty years before Johnny Halliday's Nice concert, another French avant-garde intellectual, Darius Milhaud, was taken by a friend to a Harlem "which had not yet been discovered by the snobs and the aesthetes." As Bernard Gendron explains, "in a club in which 'they were the only white folks' he encountered a music that was 'absolutely different from anything [he] had ever heard before.'"

This surprising experience moved him from an exclusively formalist and experimentalist preoccupation with jazz to one tempered by a strong interest in its lyricism and primitivism. Such "authentic music," he was sure, had "its roots in the darkest corner of negro soul, the vestigial traces of Africa." It is in this "primitive African side," this "savage" "African character," "still profoundly anchored" in black North American music, "that we find the source of this formidable rhythmic, as well as of such expressive melodies, which are endowed with a lyricism which only oppressed races can produce."

Milhaud starkly contrasted the archaic lyricism of negro blues with the hyper-modernity, worldliness *(la mondanité)*, and mechanicalness, of white jazz.[13]

There is, indeed, a long history in Romanticism of defining black culture, specifically African culture, as the body, the other of the bourgeois mind. Such a contrast is derived from the Romantic opposition of nature and culture: the primitive or pre-civilized can thus be held up against the sophisticated or over-civilized—one strand of the Romantic argument was that primitive people were innocent people, uncorrupted by culture, still close to a human "essence."[14]

It's important to understand how this argument works, because it lies at the heart of claims about rock, rhythm, and sex. The logic here is *not* that African music (and African-derived musics) are more "physical," more "directly" sexual than European and European-derived musics. Rather, the argument is that because "the African" is more primitive, more "natural" than the European, then African music must be more directly in touch with the body, with unsymbolized and unmediated sensual states and expectations. And given that African musics are most obviously different from European musics in their uses of rhythm, then rhythm must be how the primitive, the sexual, is expressed. The cultural ideology produces the way of hearing the music, in short; it is not the music which gives rise to the ideology. Or, as Marianna Torgovnick puts it, "within Western culture, the idiom 'going primitive' is in fact congruent in many ways with the idiom 'getting physical.'"[15]

I can best illustrate this argument by quotation: the histories of both jazz and rock 'n' roll are littered with such racist readings. The Bloomsbury art critic Clive Bell, for example, complained in the *New Republic* in 1921 about the people "who sat drinking their cocktails and listening to nigger bands . . . Niggers can be admired artists without any gift more singular than high spirits: so why drag in the intellect?" For Bell, as D. L. LeMahieu notes, jazz represented a rebellion not only of "the lower instincts," but of "an inferior race" against European "civilization."[16]

In France after World War I, wrote the ethnographer Michel Leiris, a newly adult generation ("the generation that made Josephine Baker a star") colluded in "an abandonment to the animal joy of experiencing the influence of a modern rhythm . . . In jazz, too, came the first public appearances of *Negroes*, the manifestation and the myth of black Edens which were to lead me to Africa and, beyond Africa, to ethnography."[17] In the United States, as Lawrence Levine writes, "jazz was seen by many contemporaries as a cultural form independent of a number of the basic central beliefs of bourgeois society, free of its repressions, in rebellion against many of its grosser stereotypes. Jazz became associated with what [Aaron] Esman has called the 'vital libidinal impulses . . . precisely the id drives that the surperego of the bourgeois culture sought to repress.'" Young white musicians were attracted by jazz because it seemed to promise cultural as well as musical freedom; it gave them the opportunity "to be and express themselves, the sense of being *natural*."[18]

Ted Gioia has shown how these strands of white thought about black music—as instinctive, as free—became entangled in jazz criticism. The French intellectual ideology of the primitive, the myth of the noble savage, meant that jazz was heard as a "music charged with emotion but largely devoid of intellectual content," while the jazz musician was taken to be an "inarticulate and unsophisticated practitioner of an art which he himself scarcely understands." (As late as 1938 Winthrop Sergeant could write that "those who create [jazz] are the ones who know the least about its abstract structure. The Negro, like all folk musicians, expresses himself intuitively.") At the same time, young white musicians (and fans) had their own reasons for asserting that jazz was quite different from art music: "cerebral" became a term of jazz critical abuse ("energy" the contrasting term of praise). Robert O'Meally notes that John Hammond, for example, objected to Billie Holiday's work after "Strange Fruit" as "too arty." Holiday herself "felt that she had finally begun to discover herself as a singer."[19]

Gioia notes that the underlying body/mind split here—the supposed opposition of "inspired spontaneous creativity" and "cold intellectualism"— makes no sense of what jazz musicians do at all. *All* music-making is about the mind-in-the-body; the "immediacy" of improvisation no more makes unscored music "mindless" than the immediacy of talking makes unscripted speech somehow without thought. Whatever the differences between African- and European-derived musics, they cannot be explained in terms of African (or African-American) musicians' lack of formal training, their ignorance of technical issues, their simple "intuition" (any more than what European musicians do can really be described as non-physical).

The matrix of race, rhythm, and sex through which white critics and fans made ideological sense of jazz was just as important for the interpretation of rock 'n' roll. As Charles Shaar Murray writes in his illuminating study of Jimi Hendrix:

> The "cultural dowry" Jimi Hendrix brought with him into the pop market-place included not only his immense talent and the years of experience acquired in a particularly hard school of show business, but the accumulated weight of the fantasies and mythologies constructed around black music and black people by whites, hipsters and reactionaries alike. Both shared one common article of faith: that black people represent the personification of the untrammelled id—intrinsically wild, sensual, dangerous, "untamed" in every sense of the word.[20]

And Linda Martin and Kerry Seagrove's study of "the opposition to rock 'n' roll" shows how appalled 1950s observers automatically equated the rhythm of rock 'n' roll with savagery of various sorts, whether they were moralists like the Bishop of Woolwich ("the hypnotic rhythm and wild gestures in [*Rock Around the Clock*] had a maddening effect on a rhythm-loving age group"), high musicians like Sir Malcolm Sergeant ("nothing more than an exhibition of primitive tom-tom thumping . . . rock 'n' roll has been played in the jungle for centuries") or Herbert von Karajan ("strange things happen in the bloodstream when a musical resonance coincides with the beat of the human pulse"), or psychologists like Dr. Francis J. Braceland, director of the Institute of Living, who explained that rock 'n' roll was both "cannibalistic and tribalistic." The various strands of the argument were brought together in an editorial in the academic *Music Journal* in February 1958. Adolescents were, it seemed, "definitely influenced in their lawlessness by this throwback to jungle rhythms. Either it actually stirs them to orgies of sex and violence (as its model did for the savages themselves), or they use it as an excuse for the removal of all inhibitions and the complete disregard of the conventions of decency."[21]

The academic witnesses who lined up against rock 'n' roll (historians and anthropologists, psychologists and music analysts) conflated a number of different arguments about rhythm and the primitive. "Experts Propose Study of 'Craze,'" ran a rock 'n' roll headline in the *New York Times* on February 23, 1957, "Liken It to Medieval Lunacy, 'Contagious Dance Furies' and Bite of Tarantula." A Dr. Joost A. M. Meerlo, Associate in Psychiatry at Columbia University, explained that, as in the late fourteenth century, there was now a "contagious epidemic of dance fury." He himself had observed young people moved by a juke box to dance themselves "more and more into a prehistoric rhythmic trance until it had gone far beyond all the accepted versions of human dancing."

> Why are rhythmical sounds and motions so especially contagious? A rhythmical call to the crowd easily foments mass ecstasy: "Duce! Duce! Duce!" The call repeats itself into the infinite and liberates the mind of all reasonable inhibitions . . . as in drug addiction, a thousand years of civilization fall away in a moment . . . Rock 'n' roll is a sign of depersonalization of the individual, of ecstatic veneration of mental decline and passivity. If we cannot stem the tide with its waves of rhythmic narcosis . . . we are preparing our own downfall in the midst of pandemic funeral dances. The dance craze is the infantile rage and outlet of our actual world.[22]

The primitive in music (rhythm), the primitive in social evolution (the medieval, the African), and the primitive in human development (the infantile) are thus reflections of each other. In the words of the psychoanalyst Heinz Kohut, "the rocking of disturbed children and of schizophrenics, and the ecstatic rites of primitive tribes" are thus equally examples of the "regressive" function of rhythm. From a psychoanalytic perspective, people's pleasure in music is clearly "a catharsis of primitive sexual tension under cover." Under cover, that is to say, of melody and harmony. "The weaker the aesthetic disguise of such rhythmic experiences," the less "artistic" the music.[23]

Eric Lott suggests that in the United States, at least, what may be at issue here in terms of racial ideology is not so much the infantile as "the state of arrested adolescence . . . to which dominant codes of masculinity aspire . . . These common white associations of black maleness with the onset of pubescent sexuality indicate that the assumption of dominant codes of masculinity in the United States was (and still is) partly negotiated through an imaginary black interlocutor."[24]

And if "black culture in the guise of an attractive masculinity" was "the stock in trade of the exchange so central to minstrelsy," it was equally essential for the use value of rock 'n' roll. As Bernard Gendron has argued, "the claim that rock and roll brought real sexuality to popular music is usually understood to be related to the claim that it brought real blackness," and from this perspective it certainly does seem "reasonable to place [Jerry Lee] Lewis's 'Whole Lotta Shakin' in the tradition of black-faced minstrelsy." "If 'Whole Lotta Shakin' was to succeed in advertising itself as *white-boy-wildly-sings-black*, it had to do so quickly and simply. The result had to be a coarsely outlined cartoon of what it means to sing black. That is, the result had to be a caricature."[25]

The racism endemic to rock 'n' roll, in other words, was not that white musicians stole from black culture but that they burlesqued it. The issue is not how "raw" and "earthy" and "authentic" African-American sounds were "diluted" or "whitened" for mass consumption, but the opposite process: how gospel and r&b and doo-wop were *blacked-up*. Thanks to rock 'n' roll, black performers now reached a white audience, but only if they met "the tests of 'blackness'—that they embody sensuality, spontaneity, and gritty soulfulness." [26] As Gendron writes:

> The black pioneers of rock and roll were also driven to produce caricatures of *singing-black*. Chuck Berry, Little Richard, and Ray Charles . . . quite radically changed their styles as their audience shifted from predominantly black to largely white. Though all three began their careers by singing the blues in a rather sedate manner (at least by rock and roll standards), they later accelerated their singing speed, resorted to raspy-voiced shrieks and cries, and dressed up their stage acts with manic piano-pounding or guitar acrobatics. According to rock and roll mythology, they went from singing less black (like Nat King Cole or the Mills Brothers) to singing more black. In my judgement it would be better to say that they adopted a more caricaturized version of singing black wildly, thus paving the way for soul music and the British invasion.[27]

The problem of rock and roll arguments about rhythm and sex (the arguments still made by bands like the Red Hot Chili Peppers) is not just their racist starting point, but also their confusion about what's meant by rhythm, by musical rhythm in particular. The assumption that a musical "beat" is equivalent to a bodily beat (the heartbeat, the pulse) doesn't stand up to much examination (why isn't musical regularity compared to mechanical repetition—neither metronomes nor clocks are thought to rouse their listeners to a frenzy).

There is equally little evidence that Western readings of African rhythmic patterns as "sexual" have anything at all to do with their actual use, musical or otherwise. As John Miller Chernoff points out, "African music and dance are not performed as an unrestrained emotional expression." They are, rather, ways of realizing aesthetic and ethical *structures*. "Ecstatic" is, in fact, the most inappropriate adjective to apply to African music: "The feelings the music brings may be exhilarating but not overpowering, intense but not frenzied. Ecstasy as we see it would imply for most Africans a separation from all that is good and beautiful, and generally, in fact, any such loss of control is viewed by them as tasteless, ridiculous, or even sinful."[28]

In her study of African oral poetry, Ruth Finnegan notes similarly that "*cultural* factors help to determine what is appreciated as 'rhythmic' in any given group or period: it is not purely physical." If some oral poetry is bound up with a regular physical action (as in a work song), nevertheless "the rhythmic movements are accepted by current convention rather than dictated by universal physiological or material requirements." As Maurice Halbwachs once put it, "Rhythm does not exist in nature; it, too, is a result of living in society."[29]

The point here seems so obvious that it's surprising that it still has to be made: musical rhythm is as much a mental as a physical matter; deciding *when* to play a note is as much a matter of thought as deciding *what* note to play (and, in practice, such decisions are anyway not separable).[30] In analyzing the differences between African and European musics, then, we can't start from a distinction between body and mind; that distinction, while now an important aspect of musical meaning, is ideological, not musicological.

What are the alternatives? One common analytic strategy is to rework the nature/culture metaphor in terms of the simple and the complex: African music is simple, European music is complex. There is an obvious evolutionary claim here: European music, it is implied, was once simple too—that's what we mean by "folk music." Thus, although this argument may not be biologically racist (blacks as "naturally" more rhythmic than whites), it remains historically racist: African cultures, it seems, haven't yet "advanced" to the European level. In short, the association of the rhythmic with the primitive is retained: simple music is music driven by rhythmic rules; music becomes "complex" when it is concerned with melodic and harmonic structure.

Lawrence Levine notes a particularly lucid statement of the combined musical and social assumptions of this attitude in a 1918 issue of the *New Orleans Times-Picayune*. There were, the paper suggested, "many mansions in the houses of the muses." There was the "great assembly hall of melody," where "most of us take our seats." There were the "inner sanctums of harmony" where a lesser number enjoyed "truly great music." Finally, there was, "down in the basement, a kind of servants' hall of rhythm. It is there we hear the hum of the Indian dance, the throb of the Oriental tambourines and kettledrums, the clatter of the clogs, the click of Slavic heels, the thumpty-tumpty of the negro banjo, and, in fact, the native dances of the world."[31]

The different pleasures offered by the musically "simple" and the musically "complex" are, then, still being related to differences between body and mind. Leonard Meyer suggests that "the differentia between art music and primitive music lies in speed of tendency gratification. The primitive seeks almost immediate gratification for his tendencies whether these be biological or musical." Meyer's definition of "primitive" here refers to music that is "dull syntactically" rather than to music "produced by non-literate peoples," but it is difficult not to read the familiar equation of musical, social, psychological, and racial infantility into an assertion like the following:

> One aspect of maturity both of the individual and of the culture within which a style arises consists then in the willingness to forego immediate, and perhaps lesser gratification. Understood generally, not with reference to any specific musical work, self-imposed tendency-inhibition and the willingness to bear uncertainty are indications of maturity. They are signs, that is, that the animal is becoming a man. And this, I take it, is not without relevance to considerations of value.[32]

Musicologists themselves have criticized the simple/complex, African/European distinction in two ways. Some accept Meyer's broad descriptive terms but reverse his evaluative conclusions—the spontaneous, human expression of African communities contrasts positively with the alienated rationalism of the European bourgeoisie; improvised musical creativity is valued over rule-bound musical interpretation, "jes' grew" over "The Wallflower Order."[33]

Others dismiss Meyer's position as ethnocentric. The argument here is that African music is just as complex as European music, but complex according to its own conventions. Andrew Chester, for example, contrasts the "extensional" form of Western musical construction—"theme and variations, counterpoint, tonality are all devices that build diachronically and synchronically outward from basic musical atoms"—with the "intensional" development of non-European music: "In this mode of construction the basic musical units (played/sung notes) are not combined through space and time as simple elements into complex structures. The simple entity is that constituted by the parameters of melody, harmony and beat, while the complex is built up by modulation of the basic notes, and by inflection of the basic beat."[34]

What's still taken for granted in these arguments—that African music's "simplicity" is a sign of its superiority; that African music is complex in-its-own-way—is that African and European musics do work and mean differently. And this assumption, as Philip Tagg has argued, is still rooted in ideology rather than musicology, still concerns not different musical principles as such, but different institutional uses of these principles.[35]

Further, sweeping comparisons of "African" and "European" musics are decidedly unhistorical. Ernest Borneman makes the point most clearly:

When I hear the enthusiast talking lightly of the "African roots" of jazz, I wonder invariably what part of Africa they are talking about. Africa is the largest of all continents. It has a greater variety of genetic and lingual groups than any comparable land mass. Negroes, generally considered the typical Africans, actually form a comparatively small part of the continent's population. Their music differs more profoundly from that of the Berbers in the North or the Bushmen in the South than the music of any two European nations ever differed from each other during the whole history of the European tradition. During the 325 years that have elapsed since the first Negroes reached America, African music has changed more deeply than our music between Palestrina and Schoenberg. And even within each lingually coherent group of African musics there is a complex gradation from folksong through dance music to the highly skilled and highly specialised activities of the professional dancers and musicians. These gradations are never stable over any length of time and within any single community: their patterns have altered so much over the last three hundred years that any parallel drawn between the present-day music of African and American Negroes is highly suspect in its applicability to the key period of the seventeenth century when American Negro music split off from its African roots.[36]

From an ethnomusicological point of view, then, an understanding of how rhythm works in African music has to begin with the question of how the music works in its particular historical and social contexts; it cannot be deduced from what it means to white listeners in quite different situations altogether.[37] And here two (related) arguments come into play, one concerning the *function* of music in African societies, the other having to do with *music-making practices*. Borneman, for instance, suggests:

What we do know with a fair degree of accuracy is the strictly functional nature of seventeenth century West-African music and the complete absence of "art music" in the European sense of the term. All West-African music from the Gold Coast to the Ivory Coast had a strict purpose in the cultural pattern of the community. Each type of song was used by one group within the community, and by that group alone, to exert an effect on another group or on the gods who controlled the affairs of the group . . . All social occasions had their distinct functional music . . . each forming a distinct pattern, but all of them united by a common quality: they could be danced as well as sung, and it was in their function as dance music that all these songs transcended the level of functionalism and were raised to the level of artistic integrity . . . Geoffrey Gorer in *Africa Dances* goes so far as to say that . . . "the West-African Negro is not so much the blackish man or the cannibal man or the primitive man as he is the man who expresses every emotion with rhythmical bodily movement."[38]

As Chernoff's 1970s studies make clear, what is being invoked here is not African nature but African society—"very few villagers can themselves play the drums . . . most 'drummers' rarely progress beyond the lesser drums," but "there is a special kind of sophistication to the ways that rhythms work in African music," there is a particular "sensibility," an "orientation to music and to life which defines the significant dimensions of excellence within the total configuration of a musical event."[39]

Music defined in these terms describes a form of *communication*. One aspect of this in some African cultures is the integration of verbal and physical means of expression. In Borneman's words, "language and music are not strictly divided." On the one hand, many African languages use what Europeans would regard as "sung" elements (variations of pitch, vibrato, and timing)—these elements are as essential to what an utterance means as the use of vowels and consonants; on the other hand, African musicians expect to "talk" instrumentally: African drummers, for example, vary the pitch, vibrato, and timing of their sounds just as skillfully as African singers. "It is high time," writes Borneman, "that the myth of African 'jungle rhythm' were put in perspective by the propagation of some concrete facts and data on the use of timbre in African music which is the invariable and inseparable complement of its rhythmical structure."[40]

The significance of rhythm for African music and culture, then, lies not in its simplicity and "directness" but in its flexibility and sophistication, not in its physical expressivity but in its communicative subtlety, its ability to make coherent *all* the movements of the body. As Richard Waterman once put it, "Essentially, this simply means that African music, with few exceptions, is to be regarded as music for the dance, although 'the dance' involved may be entirely a mental one."[41]

In his history of African-American culture and consciousness, Lawrence

Levine cites a study of schoolyard games in St. Louis in 1944 in which the researcher found that children were still singing and dancing to songs she remembered from the 1890s:

> Little Sally Water,
> Sitting in a saucer,
> Weeping and crying for someone to love her.
> Rise, Sally rise,
> Wipe off your eyes;
> Turn to the east,
> Turn to the west,
> Turn to the one that you love the best.

Young black children, however, sang their own version:

> Little Sally Walker,
> Sitting in a saucer,
> Weeping and crying for a nice young man.
> Rise, Sally, Rise;
> Wipe your weeping eyes.
> Put your hand on your hip,
> Let your backbone slip;
> Shake it to the east, O baby;
> Shake it to the west;
> Shake it to the one you love the best.

Not only the words but the gestures accompanying these play songs differed from those of the white children: "They have syncopated the rhythm, and they accompany the hand-clapping with a 'jazz' and 'swing' rhythm of the body." [42]

The point here is not that young black children were naturally more physical than white children, more "sexual" (though one can easily imagine disapproving white teachers and admiring white peers both thinking so), but that they were more rhythmically *articulate,* better able to bring together verbal and bodily expressive devices, bring them together, that is, under the name of "rhythm."

This is clearly an aspect of what is involved when white musicians learn to play black musics. Art Hodes remembers the process this way:

> Many times they'd ask me to play. I was kidded plenty. Someone would holler, "Play the blues, Art," and when I played they would laugh. Not mean, but they would laugh. That hurt but I couldn't blame them. I hadn't as yet learned the idiom. I was entranced by

their language but I hadn't learned to speak it. The next night I was there again, putting my nickels into that piano. That music did something to me. I can't explain. I had to hear it. That's one feeling that never left me. Jackson would say to me, "Art, I'll show you how to play the blues; just watch my hands." And I'd answer him, "No, don't teach me, just play." Because I knew I couldn't learn that way. I knew that I had to feel the blues myself and then they'd flow easily.[43]

It was not that Hodes had somehow to become black to play black, nor that the blues could only be expressive of a specifically racial experience, but rather that to "feel" the music he had to get *inside* it. And this is as true for listeners as players. How is this different for other sorts of musicians? The European, suggests Christopher Small, "tends to think of music primarily in terms of entities, which are composed by one person and performed to listeners by another." "Pieces" of music thus exist "over and above any possible performance of them . . . Composition and performance are separate activities, and the composer dominates the performer as the performer dominates the audience."

The African musician, on the other hand, thinks of music primarily as action, as process, in which all are able to participate. In so far as musical entities exist at all, they are regarded not as sacrosanct, but rather as material for the musicians, whose primary responsibility is to the listeners and to the occasion for which they have come together, to work on . . . Composition and performance are thus part of a single act which Europeans call improvisation but others call, simply, playing.[44]

Music, in other words, is defined by its performance, only exists *as it is performed*. This has profound aesthetic consequences. In general terms, it reflects

the idea that the arts, and especially that great performance art of music-dance-drama-masking-costume for which we lack a name, are vital means by which human identities and relationships are explored, affirmed and celebrated, and human societies criticized . . . [This idea] is not unique to Africa but it is without doubt there that it is most highly developed and best understood; it is the unique and precious contribution of Africans to human culture.[45]

More specifically, as Charles Keil has brilliantly argued, it means that we *can* distinguish between African and African-derived and European and European-derived musics aesthetically: not in terms of body and mind, the simple and the complex, or even the "intensional" and the "extensional" (though these terms come closer to what is at issue); rather, what's at stake is the difference between "embodied meaning" and "engendered feeling." The former term refers to the way in which the meaning of a piece of music is embodied "within" it, formally, structurally, and syntactically; the analytic assumption (this is the norm of Western musical aesthetics) is that it is in response to these embodied meanings that we, as listeners, "experience" music. Interpreting, feeling, and evaluating thus constitute a single process. But in musical cultures where the emphasis is on performance (not composition), there is "an on-going musical progress that can be subsumed under the general heading of 'engendered feeling.'" Obviously this distinction is not absolute (after all, European music is performed, African music has syntax; European music engenders feeling, African music embodies meaning), but there are, nonetheless, clear contrasts of aesthetic emphasis, differences in what is being referred to when music sounds "right."[46]

Alan Durant makes this point lucidly in a commentary on Pierre Boulez's disdain for improvisation. First, Boulez:

> Instrumentalists do not possess invention—otherwise they would be composers. There has been a lot of talk of "improvisation," but even taken in the best sense of the word it cannot replace invention. True invention entails reflections on problems that in principle have never been posed, or at least not in a manner which is readily apparent, and reflection upon the act of creation implies an obstacle to be overcome. Instrumentalists are not superhuman, and their response to the problem of invention is normally to manipulate what is stored in the memory. They recall what has already been played, in order to manipulate and transform it.

And this is Durant's comment:

> Boulez repeatedly implies that interest in music lies in posing and solving intellectual problems. But playing and listening to music are material activities, and also involve potential cross-fertilisation between intellectual, sensual and physical pleasures. For all its own unresolved conceptual difficulties, it has been a major accomplishment of improvised music that it has helped wrestle contemporary musical argument away from increasingly arid post-serialist debates over formal complexity and artistry into more direct consideration of issues of pleasure, which can come just as effectively from repe-

tition and simple contrast as from complex combination or trans-formation. The idea of taking pleasure as freely from repetition as from permutation and combination—which is fundamental to jazz, rock and most non-Western musics—challenges the *formalist* ideas of composers such as Berio and Boulez; and when these alternative ways of gaining pleasure then combine with pleasures of physical activity in *making* music, a challenge is also made to the distinction Boulez everywhere confidently assumes between categories of "in-strumentalists," "composers," and "audiences."[47]

In a "processual" aesthetic the decision of what (and when) is the "right" next note is a decision for which the musician has to take personal respon-sibility—but in a social setting. As Chernoff notes in his study of African drumming, "A rhythm which cuts and defines another rhythm must leave room for the other rhythm to be heard clearly, and *the African drummer concerns himself as much with the notes he does not play as with the accents he delivers.*"[48] African music may, then, be improvised, but it is not "made up on the spot, nor is it particularly loosely structured," and, as Keil suggests, from the musicians' point of view what matters most here is movement (not architecture), the perceived "vital drive" of what they are doing. Improvised music is, in this sense, a permanent *presence;* there's no time to wonder where it's going, where it has come from; the only thing to do is indicate where one is, now.

From this perspective, as Chernoff repeatedly emphasizes, "improvisa-tion" describes an ethical commitment to social participation rather than purely individual or "random" expression—"African music is improvised in the sense that a musician's responsibility extends from the music itself into *the movement of its social setting.*"[49] And listeners also have a responsibility—to engage with the music (rather than just to contemplate it), to follow the musicians' decisions as they are made, and to respond to them. On the one hand, this is because, as in any other communicative performance, the music's success, in rhetorical terms, depends on that response (and on the musicians' further response to it); on the other hand, it is because the combination of feeling, interpreting, and evaluating involved here depends on listeners en-tering into the *performing* process (rather than the compositional one). To put this another way, the only response that matters here is the first response: what we feel about the music is what it means; like the musicians, we don't have time to interpret the sounds first, and respond to them later. This comes back to Richard Waterman's point: the ideal way of listening to music is to dance to it, if only in one's head.[50] This is the only way, in Chernoff's words, "to mediate the rhythms actively," by engaging with the same vital drive as the musicians. Ron Brown, himself a Motown bassist, thus describes listening to James Jamerson:

> He had a unique ability to set your ear up in terms of listening to music. Like a rider on a horse, it would be like . . . he'd start you off at a nice galloping pace and race down the track; and all of a sudden, he'd take a right turn and throw you and you'd be out flying in space not knowing where you are. Then just before you touch the earth, he's right back there and you land in the saddle. You see, he had the ability to suggest to your ear where he wanted you to think that he was going . . . but then he wouldn't go there. But then somehow, he'd always manage to wind up back on his feet when beat one came around.[51]

One can imagine both technological and technical reasons why percussive skills might become central to a process-based musical aesthetic. In some societies the most complex musical instruments doubtless tend to be things that can be hit and plucked (rather than bowed or blown), while in all oral cultures musicians have to store their techniques and traditions in the body. Both playing and listening tend to deploy (and develop) an elaborate sense of rhythm, and the ability to make precise decisions about the timing of a note. Some African musicians are therefore certainly used to doing things that Western musicians are not—they hear complex polyphony in rule-bound, patterned terms; they maintain a complex rhythmic drive and structure without needing an external guiding force (a conductor or a metronome). A. M. Jones was startled to find that African musicians could "hear" time intervals as small as one twenty-fifth of a second: "When we Europeans imagine we are beating strict time, the African will merely smile at the 'roughness' of our beating."[52] Chernoff adds:

> I have a cousin who trained as a pianist to the point that she contemplated a professional career. During a discussion we had about African music, I asked her to beat a steady rhythm on a table top, and she of course did so quite well until I added the off-beats between her beats. She became so erratic in her beating, speeding up and slowing down, that she accused me, incorrectly, I would think, of deliberately syncopating my beats in an effort to confuse her. I replied that she should have been able to maintain her rhythm anyway. That such an apparently simple task should have presented her with such difficulties is an indication, particularly in view of her

specialization, that the Western and African orientations to rhythm are almost opposite.[53]

It should be obvious by now that the equation of rhythm and sex is a product of European high cultural ideology rather than of African popular musical practice. It is, in fact, the rhythm-focused experience of *music-in-the-process-of-production* that explains the appeal of African-American music and not its supposed "direct" sensuality. The body, that is to say, *is* engaged with this music in a way that it is not engaged with European musics, but in musical rather than sexual terms.

"In African music," writes Chernoff, "it is the listener or dancer who has to supply the beat: the listener must be *actively engaged* in making sense of the music; the music itself does not become the concentrated focus of an event, as at a concert."[54] John Blacking, who of all ethnomusicologists has argued this point most eloquently, concludes that rhythm describes not a sound but the *making* of a sound, the relationship with a "non-sound," the hand being lifted as well as the hand coming down on the drum skin.[55] If to describe either melody or harmony is immediately to move into an abstraction, the relationship of notes to each other in the imagination, to describe a rhythm is always to describe an action, to describe that which produces the sound (and, indeed, rhythmic description need not refer to *sounds* at all). Keil describes the jazz drummer's "attack" as "the type of contact the player makes with his instrument in the initial production of a note." What's at issue musicologically is the drummer's relationship to the musical pulse—"on top" or "laid back"—and the bass player's sonic mode of "plucking"—"chunky" or "stringy"; but such terms inevitably describe physical actions, the movements that create the sounds as much as the sounds themselves.[56]

What we mean by "feeling" in popular music (what Art Hodes meant by "feeling" the blues) is, then, a physical as much as a mental experience; "feeling" describes the way the body feels as it produces sounds, whether by hitting, plucking, or blowing things, or by singing (and, of course, even Western classical music involves physical feeling too—the first instruction in the middle-class piano lesson is to "relax," to "feel" the music). As John Blacking argued so persuasively, if grasping music means feeling it, then musical understanding is a bodily as well as a mental process (with which argument Stravinsky agreed, writing that "the sight of the gestures and movements of the various parts of the body producing the music is fundamentally necessary if it is to be grasped in all its fullness").[57]

People who play musical instruments, therefore, do hear music played on their instrument differently from the way people who don't play the instrument hear it—they listen with a felt, physical empathy. But my general point is that for the popular music audience the easiest way into the music is almost always rhythmically, through regular body movements (we can all participate in the music's percussive action, even if we have no instrumental skills at all). From this perspective, the difference between African- and European-based musics just describes the conventional requirements of different sorts of musical events: more participatory musics are more rhythmically complex (and harmonically simple); more contemplative musics are rhythmically simpler (and more harmonically complex).

It is in this context that one can begin to see clearly why "African" and "European" are somewhat arbitrary labels. The musical differences at issue (the focus on performative participation; the emphasis on structural cognition) are really differences between ideologies of *listening*. And, in the end, "structural cognition" is a peculiar approach to music even in Europe: it describes the high cultural ideal (but not necessarily normal listening practice) only of the last two hundred years or so.[58] In musical terms, which is the odder event: a classical music concert where we expect to see musicians bodily producing the music which we listen to thoughtfully, silent and still; or a club night at which we don't expect to see the musicians (or even the deejays) producing the sounds, but in which *our* physical movement is a necessary part of what it means to listen?

This is to reiterate that dance matters not just as a way of expressing music but as a way of listening to it, a way into the music *in its unfolding*— which is why dancing to music is both a way of losing oneself in it, physically, and a way of thinking about it, hearing it with a degree of concentration that is clearly not "brainless": "One who 'hears' the music 'understands' it with a dance, and the participation of the dancer is therefore the rhythmic interpretation which we have described as the aesthetic foundation of appreciation, the essential foothold on the music, so to speak."[59] In short, it is through rhythm, through decisions regarding when to move, at what pace, with what sort of regularity and repetition, that we most easily participate in a piece of music, if only by tapping our feet, clapping our hands, or just jigging our head up and down. And in terms of live performance this is certainly experienced both as *collective* participation, our movements tied in with those of other people, and as *musical* participation, our response (as in the classic African call-and-response tradition) a necessary part of the music in itself.[60]

Having said that, it is also true that *how* we enter music bodily and take pleasure in it is a matter of the discursive conventions and expectations we bring to it—"artless" movement (idiot dancing) involves as significant a statement about what music means as artful dance (like ballet).[61] And it is here, in what we bring *to* music rather than in what we find *in* it, that sexual suggestions lie. Dancing, after all, is, as Wendy Wolf put it to me, the socially sanctioned way of being physically *with* "someone you fancy." The sensual meaning of music, in other words, may be coded "in the rhythm," but how those codes are constructed, how rhythms are read, is a matter of cultural, not musical politics. Arguments about "sex" in music have always also been arguments about public behavior (and about the public which is so behaving).

The implicit suggestion about public and private music listening here is aesthetically misleading. Listening to classical music is taken to be a more private, "in the head" sort of experience than listening to heavy metal, head banging, even though empirically speaking the latter is probably a more private or at least individualized affair, whether the listener is using a walkman or has her ears shoved up against the speakers at a live show. In the same way, because sex is usually an intimate activity, "sexy" music (music to have sex by) is conventionally not, in fact, the rock 'n' roll that inspired teenagers to orgy in the 1950s or the Red Hot Chili Peppers to strip on stage today, but the yearning, lush balladry of Johnny Mathis and Luther Vandross, the Romantic porno-classical sounds of a Francis *"Emmanuelle"* Lai. (And it may reveal something of the poverty of the Chilis' sexual ideology that they associate good sex with a 4:4 beat.)

There's a familiar elision of categories in the usual rhythm/sex arguments: the mind is associated with individuality, the self; the body with the mass, the crowd, the public. African-American music is heard as more "bodily" because it is more collective (which does indeed make both historical and musical sense), but then descriptions of the music become confused with attitudes toward its collectivity. Music, to put this another way, is seen as "orderly" or "disorderly" by reference not to different types of audience participation but simply to different types of audience.[62]

The reason why rhythm is particularly significant for popular music is that a steady tempo and an interestingly patterned beat offer the easiest ways into a musical event; they enable listeners without instrumental expertise to respond "actively," to experience music as a bodily as well as a mental matter. This has nothing to do with going wild. Rather, a regular beat, some sense of order, is necessary for the participatory process which rhythm describes (we talk about the tempo being "strict" as a source of discipline). Rhythm, like dance, is always about bodily control (not the lack of it). Polyphony, for example, first came into European music, replacing the monody of plain chant, through peasant dances, which required mensuration and therefore made possible the rhythmic order on which polyphony depended. In Philip Tagg's words, "The more music is used in connection with bodily movements (dancing, working, marching, etc.) the *greater* the probability of regular tempo and periodicity."[63]

While different dance styles have different textures, different pulses and tempos, the most popular dance musics in the West during this century have used tightly repetitive rhythms and firmly fixed time signatures. "It is particularly difficult to dance to white rock music," concludes Chernoff, from his Africanist perspective, "because the main-beat emphasis is retained and the use of off-beat accentuation and multiple rhythms is restricted. There is no room inside the music for movement."[64]

This makes it all the more striking that the pleasures of rock music continue to be explained by intellectuals in terms of *jouissance*, the escape from structure, reason, form, and so forth. As should by now be obvious, what's involved in such assertions is not a musical (or empirical) judgment at all, but an ideological gesture, a deviant expression of respectable taste. So-called "hot" rhythms, that is to say, don't actually mean bodily abandon but signify it, signify it in a particular ideological context.

It may seem to follow from this that the erotics of pop has nothing to do with rhythm at all. But my argument is, rather, that it is an erotics of the orderly. The sexual charge of most pop music comes, in fact, from the tension between the (fluid) coding of the body in the voice (in the instrumental voice) and the (disciplined) coding of the body in the beat—hence the classic disco (and rave) sound of the soul diva mixed over electronic machines.[65]

In the end, music is "sexy" not because it makes us move, but because (through that movement) it makes us feel; makes us feel (like sex itself) intensely present. Rhythm, in short, is "sexual" in that it isn't just about the experience of the body but also (the two things are inseparable) about the experience of time.

Rhythm: Time, Sex, and the Mind

What else can one call these recordings of Holiday's? They lament, they celebrate, they philosophize, they cajole, seduce, satirize, protest, question, laugh, cry, shatter in vulnerability, or pose with stoic grace. And since they address aesthetic problems through the medium of improvisation, they propose to give the moment something it never has—order, which is the greatest contribution of jazz: it shows over and over that the present, the most anarchic region of experience, can be given perceivable form.

Stanley Crouch[1]

Music is movement, flow, time, and yet it is based on recurrence; all transmissible themes are potentially recurrent— the more so when transcribed; all music included in the sound continuum is repeatable; all melodies tend towards an end that may start a repeat . . . There can be a recurrence of motif, of theme and of combined intervals in a melody. Emotions and feelings from the past are re-evoked and moments recalled by and through music . . . music is nothing else but number and proportion (intervals, rhythm, timbres) and it is at the same time nothing else but lyricism, profusion and dream. It is all vitality, exuberance and sensuality and all analysis, precision and permanence.

Henri Lefebvre[2]

What all music offers us is a way of being present; what "music listening" means is the experience of "inner time." This, argues Alfred Schutz, is "the very form of existence of music"; it is what makes musical communication possible.

The flux of tones unrolling in inner time is an arrangement meaningful to both the composer and the beholder, because and in so far as it evokes in the stream of consciousness participating in it an interplay of recollections, retentions, protentions, and anticipations which interrelate the successive elements. To be sure, the sequence of tones occurs in the irreversible direction of inner time, in the direction, as it were, from the first bar to the last. But this irreversible flux is not irretrievable. The composer, by the specific means of his art, has arranged it in such a way that the consciousness of the beholder is led to refer what he actually hears to what he anticipates will follow and also to what he has just been hearing and what he has heard ever since this piece of music began. The hearer, therefore, listens to the ongoing flux of music, so to speak, not only in the direction from the first to the last bar but simultaneously in a reverse direction back to the first one.[3]

In terms of time, Schutz's point is this: our inner experience of time is not the same as the experience of real time. (And it can't be measured in the same ways—for a listener, as Schutz puts it, "it is not true that the time he lived through while listening to the slow movement was of 'equal length' with that which he dedicated to the fast one." Inner time is not so commensurable.) But for musical communication to work, different people's experiences of inner time (the composer's, the beholders') must match. They must live together, as it were, in a shared temporal continuum: "The beholder, thus, is united with the composer by a time dimension common to both, which is nothing other than a derived form of the vivid present shared by the partners in a genuine face-to-face relation such as prevails between speaker and listener."[4]

And whereas when reading "space-objects" we only need to reproduce a writer's thought processes in order to grasp her argument or meaning, in "time-objects" (such as music, dance, and poetry) understanding is *the same thing* as "the very polythetic constitutional process itself."[5] One cannot summarize or paraphrase a musical message, translate it into a different language. "And it will 'take as much time' to reconstitute the work in recollection as to experience it for the first time. In both cases I have to re-establish the quasi-simultaneity of my stream of consciousness with that of the composer."[6]

Schutz's final point is that in *playing* music together, musicians have to relate their inner time experience of the music to the physical actions which take place in "outer time" (the real time of the performance). The musicians' inner times must be shared and coordinated, whether by following each other's actions and expressions in a small group's performance, or by following a conductor or band leader—"his evocative gestures into which he translates the musical events going on in inner time, replace for each performer the immediate grasping of the expressive activities of all his co-performers."[7]

Schutz's account of musical communication is based on the model of the European chamber concert, and in applying it to popular music a number of questions arise. First, what are the communicative implications of *improvisation?* Chernoff suggests that "the most evident dynamic feature of African music is that the way the rhythms are established in relationship creates a *tension in time."* In a polyrhythmic music, that is, listeners (and performers) have to "resist the tendency to fuse the parts," while "the tension of the rhythms works to make time seem to speed up or slow down." In effect, "African music is *both slow and fast."* It doesn't have one inner time but many, and the listener's attention may shift from one pattern of repetition to another, from one performer to another, while being aware of the overarching community—the musicians here act together more like speakers in an unfolding conversation than like orchestral players, all and only concerned with the composer's thought. It would thus be impossible for African musical ensembles to have a conductor: their narrative is always in the process of *becoming* (and it is the musicians—and their audience—who must decide, as they go along, what it will become).

> The repetition of a style is important as a way of maintaining the tension of an ensemble's beat, and the duration of the style is important in terms of the crucial decision of when to change to get the maximum effect. In the timing of the change, the drummer demonstrates his own awareness of the rhythmic potential of the music and his personal control of its inherent power, but most important, *he demonstrates his involvement with the social situation* in a dramatic *gesture* that will play upon the minds and bodies of his fellow performers and his audience . . . As the music engages people to participate by actively and continuously integrating the various rhythms, a change at just the appropriate moment will pace people's exposure to the deeper relationships of the rhythms, involving an audience for different lengths of time with the various rhythms that have been judged to fit most properly . . . *The music is perhaps best considered as an arrangement of gaps where one may add a rhythm, rather than as a dense pattern of sound.*[8]

Second, what are the communicative implications of *crowd-pleasing?* To put it crudely, can music lie? On the one hand, the answer must be no: music works through the sharing of "inner time"; such sharing cannot rest on a deception. But, on the other hand, all communication, by definition, can be misunderstood; and such misunderstanding can, in turn, be manipulated. Jonathan Kramer usefully distinguishes between sounds that take their meanings from their place in a musical structure (climaxes, endings, recapitulations, and so on) and sounds that are, in fact, *gestures* at such moments *in themselves*, and not because of their structural position (the most obvious example is the "false ending"). Such sounds signify transition, climax, contrast, and so forth, but they do so conventionally (that's what these things usually sound like), without actually functioning as such in this particular score. Composers, in other words, can play with "gestures of time"; they can suggest a contrast *between* "absolute" and "gestural" time. A piece can "end" gesturally before it is actually over.[9]

Time gestures are particularly significant in pop songs, the appeal of which rests, in a sense, on their ability to project "inner time" beyond their material limits (as, for example, in the fade-out). Keir Keightley suggests that from this perspective there are "only two tenable genres of vocal popular songs, ballads and fast (or rhythm) numbers . . . ballads (slow songs) may be seen to involve a greater sense of the past, compared to the emphases on an enhanced and exclusive present in rhythm numbers (fast songs)." In organizing the appropriate rhetorical accounts of time—the ballad seeming to envelop everything that has already happened; the rhythm number expanding to fill the moment—pop songs are as dependent on musical as on lyrical devices.[10]

Kramer generalizes that all music has (or may refer to) at least two temporal continua: both an order of succession and the conventional meaning of gestures. Music's account of past/present/future can therefore be distinguished from the actual note order of earlier/simultaneous/later; in narrative (or rhetorical) terms, music's beginning, middle, and end is determined as much by gestural shape (its "theory" of time passing) as by the actual order of succession: "the time structure of music, at least of tonal music, can thus be profoundly multiple, paradoxical, and contradictory."[11]

Kramer, then, supplements Schutz's concept of inner time with a concept of "moment time"; he emphasizes the importance in music of the "now," an experience of the *continuous* present. Moment time, that is to say, makes memory impossible (or, the same thing, irrelevant): it doesn't offer rehearsals of what is to come or rehearings of what has been; it does not contain developments or returns or "expositions," the elements of musical communication that Schutz took for granted. Duration is divorced from content, from the memory of durations. Nonetheless, we cannot separate linearity and non-linearity completely: we hear the music in time, in succession, even if its meaning, its "impact" is non-linear, in moments: "Moment time may deny the waves of tension and release, of upbeats and downbeats, that are the essence of linear musical time. But in their place moment time offers its ultimate paradox: *Moment time uses the linearity of listening to destroy the linearity of time.*"[12] This is as pithy a description of disco as I know, and it helps to explain disco culture's obsession with the technology of time, with those devices (the double deck, the extended mix, the 12" single, the measured beats-per-minute) which enable moment time to be lengthened *non-linearly*, as it were.

What both Jonathan Kramer and the disco deejay understand is the importance of music as offering us an experience of *time passing*. In the most general terms, music shapes memory, defines nostalgia, programs the way we age (changing and staying the same).[13] But here I want to focus specifically on the musical experience itself, on Stravinsky's suggestion that "music is given to us with the sole purpose of establishing an order in things, including, and particularly the coordination between man and time."[14] Once music is "unencumbered," in Kramer's words, by plot, character, narrative, or representation, then it really is only about time, about "tonal relationships existing and transforming in time." For twentieth-century art composers, at least, music has meant *confronting* time.[15]

John Blacking goes on from Stravinsky's claim to argue that if "ordinary daily experience takes place in a world of actual time, [the] essential quality of music is its power to create another world of virtual time."[16] Music thus enables us to experience time aesthetically, intellectually, *and* physically in new ways. From this perspective (this is Stravinsky's point) music is essentially *about* time and its meaning. Swing, Gary Giddins once wrote, is "a graceful way of advancing time that suggests ironic distance from time itself." And if swing is unique for its grace (and irony), all music, I would say, is a way of advancing time that also implies a distance from time itself. Music, to put this another way, allows us to stop time, while we consider how it passes.[17]

The first point to make here concerns the basic peculiarity of "time" itself, as a concept which depends on spatial metaphors, on implications of distance (a *long* time ago; it will be happening *shortly*) and movement (the times they are a-changin')—even though, as St. Augustine puts it, "time is not the movement of a body," not even the regular movement of a body in space (the hands going around a clock) with which we "measure" it (measure, that is, both movement and length). The past is no longer here; the present has no duration by definition; the future is not here yet.

What, then, is time? I know well enough what it is, provided that nobody asks me; but if I am asked what it is and try to explain, I am baffled. All the same I can confidently say that I know that if nothing passed, there would be no past time; if nothing were going to happen there would be no future time; and if nothing *were*, there would be no present time.

Of these three divisions of time, then, how can two, the past and the future *be*, when the past no longer is and the future is not yet? As for the present, if it were always present and never moved on to become the past, it would not be time but eternity. If, therefore, the present is only time by reason of the fact that it moves on to become the past, how can we say that even the present *is*, when the reason why it *is* is that it is *not to be*? In other words, we cannot rightly say that time *is*, except by reason of its impending state of *not being*.[18]

Time, in short, does not exist. Nor does it exist at length. ("Its duration is without length. For if its duration were prolonged it could be divided into past and future. When it is present it has no duration.") Past and future exist only as the "present," in memory and anticipation. ("If the future and the past do exist, I want to know where they are . . . at least I know that wherever they are, they are not there as future or past, but as present . . . the present of past things is the memory; the present of present things is direct perception; and the present of future things is expectation.")[19] We can't "measure" the future (it does not exist), the past (it no longer exists), or the present (it has no duration). But we do measure time—"'How long did he speak?' we ask. 'How long did he take to do that?'" And such questions make clear that "what we measure is the interval between a beginning and an end." We can only measure something "in time" when it no longer exists in time; when it is over. We can only be measuring something "which remains fixed in memory."

For St. Augustine our sense of time depends on the mind performing three functions, "those of expectation, attention, and memory." And it is these which are being measured when we use spatial metaphors—"a long future is a long expectation of the future"; "a long past is a long remembrance of the past."[20] But even here the spatial metaphor is misleading: memory and expectation aren't so much long as full—the memory of a long time ago is a more encrusted memory than the memory of a short time ago; the further off the future, the greater the possible number of expectations. The question, perhaps a peculiar one, that this approach raises is this: how *long* is the present? More specifically, can music extend this? The answer, not so peculiar

Performing Rites

after all, is that if "the present" is actually defined by a quality of *attention*, then music does indeed expand the moment, by framing it. And it is precisely this "time attention" which defines musical pleasure.[21]

Edward Cone argues that rhythm is that aspect of music that connotes least outside itself, that most insistently draws our attention to "music itself."[22] David Epstein adds that time is not "about" music (a way of describing "music itself"), it *is* music: "music *structures* time, incorporates it as one of its fundamental elements. Without time—structured time—music does not exist."[23] And I would add (following St. Augustine) that without music, structured music, time does not exist.

Repetition (which is central to our understanding of rhythm) is equally central to our understanding of time—it is only as things recur that there can be said to be movement *in time*. Musically speaking, repetition means repeating—referring to—elements of the music itself, and Richard Middleton distinguishes here between the "discursive" and the "musematic." In African-derived musics, "musemes" are repeated sound particles that provide the rhythmic "layers" of jazz and r&b. In white pop, "in music hall and Tin Pan Alley songs," rhythm is "an aspect of harmonic narrativity," while "in bourgeois song in general, sequence is a way of holding on to at least some of the power of repetition while, as it were, *cutting it down* to size, and *stitching it into* other structural processes. Sequence *composes* time (rather than marking time or obliterating it, as straight repetition, especially if musematic, seems to do)."[24] To be meaningful as a concept, then, time must be differentiated, and such demarcation "invokes two different orders of time: metrical—time unqualified by experience, marked off by mensural means external to a subject or living viewer; or experiential—time qualified by human experience."[25]

Time is "perceived as intrinsically related to motion or flow," but musical "movement" can only be defined relative to a "constant" background (this is to echo Chernoff's point about African music). The issue here isn't subjective time (experiential, variable) versus objective time (metrical, fixed)—both of these are, as we've seen, constructed by the music—but what Epstein defines as "chronometric time" (mechanistic, evenly spaced) versus "integral time" (the unique organization of time in a particular piece). Like Kramer, if with a different approach to musical rhetoric, Epstein challenges the common sense of Schutz's "stream of consciousness." Given that "the temporal is intangible," we can only perceive Schutz's "inner time" of music in a "trained, *intelligent* act," as a kind of *deduction* from what we see and hear. Nothing done in music is ever "purely" rhythmic: even the simplest percussive instruments have pitch or timbre; even the most boring rock drummer has an individual percussive movement.[26] And nothing is completely unrhythmic—the human brain has a wonderful capacity for perceiving regularity in even the most randomly distributed noises (in the workplace, for example). "A beat," as Eisenberg puts it, "is like a Kantian category, a matrix that lets us perceive things as things instead of chaos."[27]

> Thus time in music poses a contradiction: in a world of physical sound, it is a basic element that is itself nonsonic, yet dependent for its statement and demarcation upon sound. More than any other musical dimension, time in music depends totally on forces outside its own proper domain—namely upon sound.[28]

It is clear by now that one problem of discussing musical time is the plethora of descriptive terms involved (a metaphorical abundance reflecting the problem that what is being described doesn't really exist). Even the simplest measuring words (describing the "rate" or "speed" of the music) such as "tempo" or "beat" really only refer to the recurrence of a particular sound or break or emphasis. As Robin Maconie puts it, "What the ear interprets as fast or slow has less to do with speed than with contour, contrast, texture, and rhythm." Musical tempo, in other words, is not something objectively *in* the music (a metronome setting, beats per minute) but an effect of the listener's (or player's or conductor's or deejay's or dancer's) "aural sensibility."[29]

Then there are words that refer to a quality of the production of sounds—"accent," "stress." These words describe "the tension of musical articulation." They refer to what Charles Keil and his colleagues call the "participatory discrepancies" in music making—"a PD is 'a slight human inconsistency' in the way that a musician executes rhythm, pitch and timbre"—and the immediate contrast being made here is between the human and the mechanical, between the drummer and the drum machine. David Epstein notes, for example, that Hollywood session musicians have problems with "click tracks"—no one can play "naturally or 'musically' in this fashion,"—while J. A. Prögler describes the various ways in which digital instrument makers have sought to "humanize" their programs, have become concerned with "'imperfections,' 'inaccuracies,' 'perturbations,' 'offsets,' 'adjustments,' 'shifts' and 'feel.'"[30]

Finally, there are words like "meter" and "rhythm" itself which refer to the resulting sound patterns, and thus seem to describe both musical events, things we actually hear as taking place in time, and something more abstract, the musical logic "behind" what we hear. On the one hand, as David Epstein notes, "rhythm" is thus "a primordially physical aspect of music, largely kinaesthetic and muscular," and dependent on musicians' intuitive judgments (the split-second decisions regarding when to bang or blow or bow). On the other hand, "rhythm" has come to mean, analytically, "the musical organization of time" encoded in the score structurally, as a matter of harmonic progression and resolution, pitch instructions, tension and release, principles of control.[31]

To grasp the "rhythm" of a piece of music (which is, in the end, to listen to it) means both participating actively in its unfolding and trusting that this unfolding has been (or is being) shaped—that it will lead us somewhere. It is at once a physical and mental process; it involves aesthetic and ethical judgments. By entering this world of "virtual" or "inner" time we effectively (willingly, trustfully) leave the world of "real" time: hence the common experience of music as timeless (the common use of music to achieve the state *of* timelessness).

In art music one recurrent concern of the avant-garde, whether modernist or postmodernist, Webern or Terry Riley, has been to reject both the classical account of musical time as leading to a resolution (whether in terms of cycle or goal) and the Romantic treatment of musical time as "destiny," and instead to use music to take control of time in the present, to intensify our perception of time-as-it-is-passed. The stress here is, as with Stockhausen, on time experienced through musical *action* (music as "not perpetually ready-made but perpetually to-be-made")[32] or, as with Cage, on time experienced as musical *process* (an effect of "random" sound choices). Either way, time is treated as "a frame to be filled," and how it is filled (actively, randomly) determines its shape (not vice versa). Music is thus a way of *experimenting* with time (to what else does "experimental music" refer?)—with chance events, order without sequence, sequence without order, juxtaposition without story. In Michael Nyman's words, "form thus becomes an assemblage, growth an accumulation of things that have piled up in the time-space of the piece." He cites an experiment by John Cage and George Brecht. They composed a piece in which each musician had to do two things, each once only, at a time of their own choice. The performance took place in the dark, so that performers couldn't see when someone was about to play or had played, couldn't anticipate what would happen next or, indeed, when the piece was "over" (the last sound made). Afterwards the performers were asked how long they thought they had been in the dark: "guesses ranged from four to twenty-four minutes: the actual duration had been nine minutes."[33]

So-called minimalist composers (like Nyman himself) developed a different defense against "teleological" music. If, in the latter tradition (the norm of Western classical music), everything leads to an end, with each work an "argument," the minimalists sought to compose "objectively," to put into play music that moved free of intent or human purpose, developed strictly according to formal logic. The emphasis is not on chance (and random sound events) but on mathematics (and necessary sound events), on quantitative rather than qualitative judgments. Minimalist music is thus "self-generating," neither expressive nor representational.[34]

Both chance and minimalist music require "aimless" listening too. The listener is placed in a virtual time which has no history (no story line), no architecture (no outline), no apparent beginning, middle, or end; there is neither musical resolution nor musical expectation, nothing to help us make narrative sense of what we hear. In Wim Mertens's words, minimalist music is thus a "field of intensity," a "free flow of energy," less a human statement than a kind of eternal force: the music was there before we started listening and will continue after we stop. In Philip Glass's words,

> When it becomes apparent that nothing "happens" in the usual sense, but that, instead, the gradual accretion of musical material can and does serve as the basis of the listener's attention, then he can perhaps discover another mode of listening—one in which neither memory nor anticipation (the usual psychological devices of programmatic music . . .) have a place in sustaining the texture, quality, or reality of the musical experience. It is hoped that one would be able to perceive the music as a . . . pure medium of sound.[35]

As Kramer argues, if the experience of "timelessness" actually describes an out-of-the-ordinary attention *to* time, this can, in turn, take different forms: he describes both a three hour experience which seemed like forty minutes, and a twenty-five minute performance which felt as if it had lasted two hours. In the latter case, a multimedia performance piece, Kramer experienced "a vastly extended present" because of "sensory overload" (the same metaphor as keeping busy in order "to fill time"); in the former case, listening to the "Vexations" section of Erik Satie's *Pages mystiques* (four eight-bar phrases played 840 times in succession), time initially got "slower and slower, threatening to stop."

> But then I found myself moving into a different listening mode. I was entering the vertical time of the piece. My present expanded, as I forgot about the music's past and future. I was no longer bored. And I was no longer frustrated because I had given up expecting. I had left behind my habits of teleological listening. I found myself fascinated with what I was hearing . . . True, my attention did wander

and return, but during the periods of attending I found the composition to hold great interest. I became incredibly sensitive to even the
smallest performance nuance, to an extent impossible when confronting the high information content of traditional music. When
pianists traded off at the end of their twenty-minute stints, the result
was an enormous contrast that opened a whole new world, despite
their attempt to play as much like each other as possible. What little
information I found in the music was in the slight performance
variability, not in the notes or rhythms.

I never lost touch with myself or my surroundings. Although I
listened deeply enough to the music to accept its extended present,
I never ceased to be aware of my mental and physical environment.[36]

There is in this respect a thin line between minimalist music and ambient
music. Satie suggested that his "furniture music" *(musique d'ameublement)*

hopes to contribute to life the way a casual conversation does, or a
picture in the gallery, or a chair in which one is not seated . . . We
want to establish a music designed to satisfy "useful" needs. Art has
no part in such needs. Furniture music creates a vibration; it has no
other goal; it fills the same role as light and heat—as *comfort* in every
form.[37]

Satie's concept of furniture music (like Brian Eno's idea of "music for
airports") is more complex than it might at first seem. There are images of
both culture and nature here (a chair, casual conversation; heat and light),
the suggestion both that music shapes itself, usefully, to bodily needs, and
that individual bodies are themselves absorbed into a kind of implacable sonic
flow.[38] Virtual time here describes an experience of bodilessness, an indiffer-
ence to materiality (minimal composers have a declared interest in Eastern
religions), and Mertens notes the paradox that rhythmic regularity may well
have exactly the same effect in dance music: disco, he suggests, also works
like a "narcotic," "individuating" musical experience through repetition but
leaving the listener/dancer "floating in cosmic soup," with no aims, no desires
at all. Bodily excess—as at a rave: the sheer volume of the beat, brightness of
the lights, intensity of the drugs, depth of the sweat and exhaustion—becomes
bodily transcendence; an obsessively repetitive dance floor track like Kool and
the Gang's "Get Down On It" is every bit as *mentally* absorbing as, say, Steve
Reich's *Drumming*.[39]

But the most interesting aspect of the concept of "ambient" sound is the
questions it raises about our experience of time as *space*. Kramer describes

the ways in which experimental performers in the 1960s sought to focus audiences' attention on the present by blurring the distinction "between piece and environment." The model here, Cage's silent *4'33"*, made "music" out of the ordinary sounds of the environment simply by getting people to give them a special, concert-hall attention. Such pieces, Kramer notes, "may at first take advantage of listeners' expectations of what a concert should entail, but after the initial impact is gone their world remains as an unchanging entity to be explored during the extended present." Audiences found there was "nothing to listen to," and so got to hear Philip Glass's "pure sound event": "an act without any dramatic structure," referring to nothing outside itself.[40]

In dance culture the distinction between music and environment is blurred in other ways, by transforming space itself into a kind of moving sonic image. Lights and mirrors, darkness and deception, are used so that what one sees seems always an effect of what one hears; space becomes movement as dance hall, club, and warehouse are shaped by the dancing bodies that fill them; when silence falls, the setting disappears. The dancers are performers, programmed by the deejay; the music stops, play time—the *scene*—is over.[41]

As every clubber knows, to dance is not just to experience music as time, it is also to experience time as music, as something marked off as more intense, more interesting, more pleasurable than "real" time. To put this another way: how we experience time as music, as special, cannot be disentangled from how we hear time routinely, as ordinary; how we interpret time musically depends on how we make sense of it normally. Time passing, time returning, the rhythm of night and day, work and play, determine what it means to have time *free,* and musical time sense is thus as much a matter of history and sociology as of sound and rhythm.[42]

At the very least music is thus about temporal *possibility;* it suggests that time can be organized intentionally, as a matter of accent and stress, pulse and phrasing, rather than having to be experienced only as a matter of industrial discipline, or of menstrual and seasonal cycles, or of inexorable aging. But, further, music also works as a commentary on—an experiment with—our everyday experiences of time. As Philip Tagg suggests, it is in making and listening to music that we pay attention to—take pleasure in— temporal shifts from the static to the dynamic, the regular to the irregular, the quick to the slow, the empty to the full, the sudden to the gradual, the rough to the smooth.[43]

Popular music has a special interest in two common forms of time-experience in particular: boredom and fashion. To describe a situation as "boring" is to say that nothing is happening, nothing to engage our attention—time *drags*. Fashion, by contrast, "is the perception of a recurring process in time in which, while newness is seen as being of value, that which is new is constantly being swept away at a dizzying pace and replaced by a different newness. This is called 'industrialized eternal return.' In this sense, the essence of time is ephemerality and repetition."[44]

Popular music addresses these issues simultaneously. On the one hand, pop songs fill the hole that the bored stare into; fun is the time that one doesn't notice passing till afterwards. On the other hand, popular music works to stop time, to hold consumption at the moment of desire, before it is regretted. Even as it is enjoyed, though, popular music is confirming the premises on which its pleasures depend—that times change and nothing happens, that this is a momentary diversion. Pop is nothing if not fashionable (drawing our attention to its transience, to the ever-familiar shock of the new); and it is centrally—from cabaret to punk, from Billie Holiday to Kurt Cobain—*about* boredom, about the vanity of believing that cheap music is potent enough to take on nothingness.[45] From one perspective (Adorno's, say), pop music thus colludes with its own negation. A popular cultural critic like Abraham Kaplan argues that "popular art, far from countering boredom, perpetuates and intensifies it," while "there is a nostalgia characteristic of the experience of popular art, not because the work as a form is familiar but because its very substance is familiarity."[46]

But my conclusion is different. Music is not, by its nature, rational or analytic; it offers us not argument but experience, and for a moment—for moments—that experience involves *ideal time*, an ideal defined by the integration of what is routinely kept separate—the individual and the social, the mind and the body, change and stillness, the different and the same, the already past and the still to come, desire and fulfillment. Music *is* in this respect like sex, and rhythm is crucial to this—rhythm not as "releasing" physical urges but as expanding the time in which we can, as it were, *live in the present tense*.

Songs as Texts

8

Building in any successful rock 'n' roll record is a sense of the power of the singer to say what he or she means, but also a realization that words are inadequate to that task, and the feeling of fulfillment is never as strong as the feeling of frustration. The singer goes as far as she or he can go; the singer even acknowledges the quandary, gives in to its tension, abandons words and screams. But the singer still comes up short; the performance demands the absolute lucidity it has already promised, a promise from which it is already falling back, and so an instrument takes over. It is a relief: a relief from the failure of language. The thrill is of entering a world where anything can be said, even if no one can know what it means.

   Greil Marcus[1]

But people don't use songs according to anyone's intent. In the truest moments, songs like microbes—without intent, without brains—use people.

Greil Marcus[2]

Most contemporary popular music takes the form of song (even acid house), and most people if asked what a song "means" refer to the words. In examining what the words do mean we can follow two obvious strategies, treating songs either as poems, literary objects which can be analyzed entirely separately from music, or as speech acts, words to be analyzed in performance.

But in listening to the lyrics of pop songs we actually hear three things at once: *words,* which appear to give songs an independent source of semantic meaning; *rhetoric,* words being used in a special, musical way, a way which draws attention to features and problems of speech; and *voices,* words being spoken or sung in human tones which are themselves "meaningful," signs of persons and personality. In this chapter I will focus on words and rhetoric; in the following chapter I will consider the voice.

Until relatively recently, most academic analysts of Anglo-American popular music assumed, like commonsense listeners, that pop's meaning lay in the lyrics.[3] This is the tradition of content analysis, a tradition still faithfully followed in the pages of *Popular Music and Society;* and arguments about pop's political and social value are still more likely to refer to pop words than to pop sounds (think, for example, of the debate about rap). There are mundane reasons for this—fans, academics, and moralists alike are more used to dealing with verbal than with musical meaning, and find it easier to talk about (and censor).[4] But this does mean—and this is my starting point—that words matter to people, that they are central to how pop songs are heard and evaluated. In the most comprehensive survey I know of teenage use of music television, for example, the most cited reason for watching a video was not to see what the performers looked like but "in order to find out what the words mean."[5] Richard Rodgers made the essential point nearly fifty years ago: "For never does a song achieve any sort of public unless the words have at some point made a joint impact with the music on the individual and public ear . . . The old defensive and competitive cry of the composer, 'Nobody whistles the words!' is simply not true."[6]

What was clear to Rodgers, what remains obviously true, is that in everyday terms a *song*—its basic melodic and rhythmic structure—is grasped by people through its words, even if these words come to us in fits and fragments (or, more commonly and deliberately, in hooks and chorus lines); the best version of Queen's "Bohemian Rhapsody," for example, is Fuzzbox's a cappella reading, which translates all the instrumental bits into half-heard words too.[7]

Nicholas Tawa has shown how words—titles, hook phrases—became the basis of popular songs' market "punch" in the early days of Tin Pan Alley:

E. M. Wickes said a good title can have punch and make the song into a hit. A title tag lingered in memory after one heard the piece; it conjured up related images and revived past recollections and associations. Some of the best titles were adverbial clauses, like "When the harvest days are over," "When the meadow lanes are green again," and "Where the sweet magnolias bloom." Titles connected to the events of the day were valuable because they received free publicity. At any rate, a fine title suggested or conveyed a definite idea. It helped to attract the attention of performers, especially if they were selecting songs to be sent to them from a catalog. Amateurs in a music store would ask to see and hear a song whose title caught their eye.

Not surprisingly, the title was almost invariably used as a punch line by placing it in the first line and, less often, also towards the end of the chorus. Nearly without exception, it was set to one of the most appealing melodic phrases, and in most cases the most winning phrase, of the song.[8]

As this suggests, the words without the music were usually (quite literally) unmemorable. Unlike lyrical poems (a comparison to which I'll return), song words are only remembered in their melodic and rhythmic setting, as anyone knows who has followed the TV pop quiz question in which panelists are asked to identify a lyric that winds along the bottom of the screen as a plain print text. They usually can't, but it only takes a couple of notes of the music to be faded in and everyone (listeners at home too) can immediately recall it.

The first systematic content analysis of the American pop song that I know of was carried out by one of the Frankfurt School scholars in exile, J. G. Peatman, for Paul Lazersfeld's 1940s Radio Research project. Perhaps not surprisingly, Peatman found the same sort of standardization in song words that Adorno found in radio music: such a finding is, one could say, a necessary result of the coding process. The description of the pop song as a formula song is familiar enough in the music industry too. Tawa notes that even in the 1830s (when the modern song business began) critics accused the new songs of "a vitiating sameness," and Peter Etzkorn's study of professional songwriters in the United States in the early 1960s revealed that

> the composing activity of songwriters would seem to be constrained by their orientation towards the expectations of significant "judges" in executive positions in the music business whose critical standards are based on traditional musical clichés. In their endeavor to emulate the norms of successful reference groups, songwriters (even with a variety of backgrounds) will produce compositions virtually homogenous in form and structure, thereby strengthening the formal rigidity of popular music.[9]

One aspect of this in the early days, as Tawa notes, was that the song, as a commodity, had to have a particular sort of use value—it had to be *adaptable*.

> A copy of a very popular song, "Anona," published in New York by Feist in 1903, advertises: "This famous composition is also published as an Intermezzo—Two Step—for Piano, also for Band, Orchestra, Mandolin, Guitar, Banjo, Zither, etc." The song's key, tempo, and dynamics were also flexible, thus freeing the performer and making a winning presentation dependent on his or her interpretation.[10]

The pop song "formula," in other words, was indeed (as the Frankfurt scholars argued) an effect of market forces. But content analysis has consistently revealed the way in which the pop formula is also dominated by a particular sort of romantic ideology. The pop song is the love song, and the implication, putting these two findings together, is that what pop songs are really about are *formulas of love*. Two analytic strategies can then be adopted. The first is to argue that these romantic formulas (and, in particular, the way they change over time) somehow *reflect* changing social mores, and thus give us useful evidence as to how "the people" regard love (and associated social mores). For Stuart Chase, for example, popular song "is the sum of all the patterns of behavior" which "keep the group from flying into a thousand fragments, and help it adapt to nature and survive its environment." Popular songs, from this perspective, express "commonly held values" and speak for "the millions who treasure them." "Popular recordings," as B. Lee Cooper has put it more recently, "are pieces of oral history."[11]

Alternatively, one can make a *contrast* between the standard pop account of love and something else, something more real and complex and individual. "Standard" lyrics, "sentimental" and "banal" words, are routinely measured against "realist" lyrics, against songs which deal with the actual world and lived emotions.[12] Lawrence Levine, replicating S. I. Hayakawa's famous 1955 study of American popular songs (which had been entitled, symptomatically, "Popular Songs versus the Facts of Life"), comes to much the same conclusion about both the sentimental vapidity of these songs and the contrasting "truthfulness" of the blues:

> In a period when divorce rates were rising, family stability declining, pastoral life styles disappearing, bureaucratic impersonality and organization increasing, popular music constructed a universe in which adolescent innocence and naiveté became a permanent state. Men and women (often referred to in the songs as boys and girls) dreamed

pure dreams, hopefully waited for an ideal love to appear (the gift of some beneficent power that remained undefined and unnamed), and built not castles but bungalows in the air complete with birds, brooks, blossoms, and babies.

Adults were being socialized to a world constructed out of childhood fantasies or, more accurately, adult views of childhood fantasies:

> You're right out of a book,
> The fairy tale I read when I was so high.
> No armored knight out of a book,
> Was more enchanted by a Lorelei than I.

As in the fairy tales, so too in popular songs, life was not purely idyllic. Reality was allowed to intrude: often lovers were faithless, promises broken, hopes unfulfilled. But the reality proved as insubstantial as the dream. Tears were shed and self-pity expressed, yet little was learned and less resolved. Fatalism prevailed and the fantasies went on and on.[13]

Levine compares white song lyrics with the blues, "the closest Negro equivalent to American popular music."

Any such comparison shows important and revealing differences. While both blues and popular music were dominated by lyrics concerning love, black consciousness of and attitudes towards this relationship differed considerably from those of the larger society.

The blues were far less pervaded by self-pity, the profound fatalism, and the very real disillusionment that marked American popular music.

For all their "pathos," then, the blues were "saved" from white narcissism "by the strong sense of humor and proportion which frequently prevented even the most pitiable lover from posturing." In the blues, "love seldom resembled the ethereal, ideal relationship so often pictured in popular songs. Love was depicted as a fragile, often ambivalent relationship between imperfect beings." It was, in other words, "portrayed realistically as a multidimensional experience."[14]

Levine concludes that the differences between black and white songs in the 1920s and 1930s had less to do with supposed differences between black and white sensibilities (or sexual behavior) than with the different uses and functions of popular music in different cultural settings, and his argument is thus subtler (and more convincing) than Hayakawa's (though he also has a tendency to leap from lyrical analysis to ideological effect without much pause for thought about how the songs were actually heard and used). Levine is clear, for example, that the lyrical contrasts he describes had as much to do with convention as intention: black song had different lyrical possibilities open to it because it served different purposes than white song, because it circulated in a different sort of cultural economy.[15]

Interviewed in *New Musical Express* in 1982, Elvis Costello made a similar point about the emotional constraints of pop formulas and functions, but put the emphasis on listeners being deprived of songs which articulate reality rather than being duped by songs into believing in daydreams.

> Most people, I think, are confused regarding their identities, or how they feel, particularly about love. They're confused because they're not given a voice, they don't have many songs written about them. On the one hand there's "I love you, the sky is blue," or total desolation, and in between there's this lack of anything. And it's never that clear-cut. There's a dishonesty in so much pop—written, possibly, with an honest intent—all that starry stuff. I believe I fulfil the role of writing songs that aren't starry eyed all the time.[16]

These are important arguments for any evaluation of song lyrics, and are familiar from both rock criticism and people's everyday accounts of why some songs are silly, others profound. At the same time, though, while the terms of such criticism may be familiar, their application often seems somewhat eccentric: one person's silly lyric touches another person's real feelings, and vice versa, particularly when we're talking about love songs. We need, in particular, to consider two further points about the sort of real/unreal argument used, in their different ways, by Levine and Costello.

First, it is important to remember that the distinction between "real" and "unreal" lyrics is, at least in part, arbitrary. Songs, after all, are not mostly general statements of sociological or psychological truth (as even Levine sometimes seems to imply); they are more likely to be examples of personal rhetoric.[17] And even in life (which is, after all, imbued by romantic ideology, organized sexually around the idea of "being in love"), one is more likely to say "I love you more than there are stars in the sky" than "there are ambiguities in the way I feel about you." The question becomes, in other words, why some sorts of words are *heard* as real or unreal, and to understand this we have to understand that how words work in song depends not just on what is said, the verbal content, but also on how it is said—on the type of language used and its rhetorical significance; on the kind of voice in which it is spoken.

Second, much of the argument that starts from lyrical content analysis assumes that the "content" (or "meaning") of songs as revealed by the analyst is the same as their content (or meaning) for other listeners. There is a very quick slippage in this analytic tradition from a summary of the lyrical content as revealed by academic survey to a moralistic denunciation of the effects of pop songs on their listeners—this is the strand of the argument that links Frankfurt School accounts of the psychology of consumption to Leavisite anxiety about the commercial corruption of childhood, which informs both Hayakawa's account of "demoralization" and Levine's account of "fatalism"; it is this argument that supports contemporary moralists' claims that heavy metal lyrics make white adolescents suicidal and that rap lyrics make black adolescents violent. All these things may be true, but they are certainly not demonstrated by content analysis alone.

There is, in fact, no firm empirical evidence that song words determine or form listeners' beliefs and values (any more than there is really much evidence that they reflect them). The few sociological investigations of teen-agers' response to song words show either that they don't understand them (as American researchers soon found to be the case with 1960s "protest" songs like "Eve of Destruction") or that they "don't really notice them" (semantically, that is).[18]

What this suggests, I think, is the difficulty we face if, in interpreting how songs "mean," we attempt to separate the words from their use as speech acts. I would put the argument this way: song words are not about ideas ("content") but about their expression. And I can best clarify this with two examples.

First, then, songs don't *cause* people to fall in love, but provide people with the means to articulate the feelings associated with being in love.[19] Levine's argument is, in a sense, back to front. It is not that love songs give people a false, sentimental, and fatalistic view of sexual relationships, but that romantic ideology requires such a view and makes love songs necessary (and the question that Levine really raises concerns the different place of romance in black and white American cultural histories). Historically speaking, after all, the love song *followed* the social diffusion of romantic ideology (rather than vice versa), and, interestingly, has had to take account of the male as well as the female investment in love (unlike other popular cultural forms, such as romantic fiction).

The realist critique of the love song is therefore problematic because of its implication that romantic fantasies aren't real. But people really do fall in love—really do engage, that is, in the pleasure of idealizing themselves and an other, fantasizing perfect and lasting relationships, equating sex and sympathy, sentimentalizing differences, and so on. The fact that love doesn't last, that the divorce rate is high, that passion causes as many pains as pleasures, doesn't mean that romantic fantasies aren't true, aren't felt, don't have consequences. If pop songs are narratives of love, and we do indeed fall in love, then songs are in this respect narratives of our lives, of the ways in which we engage in—and *realize*—fantasies. Silly love songs have certainly been as realistic—and helpful—in making sense of the romance in my life as so-called musical realism.

The second indication that songs concern not so much ideas as their expression can be found in the historical fate of "protest" songs. In pop terms, these don't function to convey ideas or arguments but slogans. And the paradox here is that the political power of a pop song—as a slogan—need not bear any relationship to its intended message at all. Irony, in particular, seems to be a doomed lyrical strategy. The Strawbs' 1973 single "Part of the Union," for example, was meant as an anti-union song, but its ironic chorus ("they can't get me, I'm part of the union!") became a gleeful picket line chant; while Tom Robinson's 1978 "Glad to be Gay," an ironic tag line to verses spelling out the oppression of homosexuals in Britain, became a triumphalist shout, and was even used as such by tipsy heterosexual students at the end of the Saturday night college disco. And I could point to numerous other examples of such lyrical drift: Pink Floyd's "We don't want no education," taken up as a slogan by black youth in South Africa, protesting about compulsory Afrikaans schooling; a pre-election Tory Party rally joining hands for John Lennon's "Imagine"; the Republican Party's attempt to hijack Bruce Springsteen's "Born in the USA" in the 1984 presidential election.[20]

This last example is particularly illuminating. "Born in the USA" is, lyrically, clearly a protest song. It is about growing up working class, being shipped off to fight in Vietnam and coming back to nothing—a standard scenario in American popular film and song, a populist formula. The lyrical theme was also tied to Springsteen's star persona—this was not his own story, but it was the story of the people with whom he identified, whom he was taken to represent (as indicated by his iconography on stage and album). The record did, then, lay claim to a certain sort of truth of veterans' experience, to a political realism. Formally, though, the song is organized around a chorus line—"Born in the USA!", a musical phrase which is, in rock convention (its texture, its rhythmic relentlessness, its lift), not bitter but triumphant. In other words, for a rock listener what comes across from this song is not the intended irony of the chorus line, but its pride and assertiveness. And it was as such a patriotic boast that Ronald Reagan wanted to use it. Although Springsteen dismissed this reading, in performance his own trappings (the American flag, the celebration of American working-class masculinity) could also serve to confirm it.[21]

Once we grasp that the issue in lyrical analysis is not words, but words in performance, then various new analytical possibilities open up. Lyrics, that is, are a form of rhetoric or oratory; we have to treat them in terms of the persuasive relationship set up between singer and listener. From this perspective, a song doesn't exist to convey the meaning of the words; rather, the words exist to convey the meaning of the song. This is as true of the "story song" or the *chanson* as of the most meaningless house or rave track, just as political and love songs concern not political or romantic ideas, but modes of political and romantic expression. Pop songs, that is, work with and on *spoken* language.

This means, first of all, that song language is used to say something about both the singer and the implied audience. Lyrical language is an important aspect of genre convention—the conversational colloquialism of the country song (a "storyteller" like Tom T. Hall reminiscing at the bar) works very differently from the raucous colloquialism of punk (a ranter like Joe Strummer agitating in the streets). Nicholas Tawa describes the linguistic conventions of the late nineteenth century commercial American popular song, conventions that were to be even more formulaically applied in twentieth-century Tin Pan Alley:

> Language is kept plain, graphic, relevant and concrete. Abstract and unusual references are avoided. Generally, an informal conversational tone is adhered to, and subject and expression are kept recognizable for easier comprehension. The title evokes the chorus; the chorus summarizes the content of the verse. The sense of each line is normally complete; the end of each line comes to a natural stop before a new line is taken up. The change from verse to chorus is managed so as not to perturb the listener, the latter appearing as a reasonable epilogue to the verse that has come before.[22]

But lyrical plain speaking may cover any number of linguistic variations. Peter Trudgill's study of "the sociolinguistics of British pop-song pronunciation" is illuminating in showing that it is not just words but also accents which situate singer and listener. Trudgill's starting point is the obvious one that British pop singers "employ different accents when singing from when they are speaking." The reason seems clear:

Most genres of twentieth-century popular music, in the western world and in some cases beyond, are (Afro-)American in origin. Americans have dominated the field, and cultural domination leads to imitation: it is appropriate to sound like an American when performing in what is predominantly an American activity; and one attempts to model one's singing on that of those who do it best and who one admires most.[23]

Such a sense of linguistic fitness is familiar in popular genres—folk singers adopt "quasi-rural" accents, white reggae singers a Jamaican lilt, European rappers New York street tones, and so on. But, as these examples make plain, such "language modification" does not always work. In the case of British pop singers' "American" voices, "one obvious measure of their lack of success is that many American listeners are utterly unaware that this is what British singers are trying to do." The problems here are manifold: for British singers to copy their vocal models accurately (often Black and/or Southern singers rather than "Americans" in general) they would need "sufficient access" (and the analytic ability) to work out the rules of their preferred linguistic behavior, and the discipline to modify their own pronunciation accordingly. As this was hardly the case, voices that were heard as "American" by British listeners still seemed—in their very peculiarity!— obviously British (or, at least, non-American) to Americans. Trudgill adds that "from around 1964 on, British singers generally began trying less hard to sound like Americans," as "British pop music acquired a validity of its own." Singers now sought to cross class barriers rather than the Atlantic. Punk, for example, introduced "features associated with low-prestige south of England accents":

> The use of these low-status pronunciations is coupled with a use of nonstandard grammatical forms, such as multiple negation and the third-person singular *don't,* that is even higher than in other sub-genres of pop music, and the intended effect is assertive and aggressive. There is also clearly an intention to aid identification with and/or by British working-class youth, and to appeal to others who wish to identify with them, their situation and their values.[24]

The desire to sound low-class English did not so much replace the desire to sound American as compete with it, and different groups handled the conflict differently. (Trudgill confirms linguistically my critical belief that the Stranglers weren't really a punk band: their "Americanisms" meant that "they closely resemble[d] 'mainstream' groups in their linguistic behaviour.")

The conflict is between a motivation towards a supposedly American model, and a motivation towards a supposedly British working-class model—which can be glossed as a conflict between "how to behave like a genuine pop singer" and "how to behave like British urban working-class youth."[25]

Which is a good a summary as one could have of the aesthetic dilemma of British rock, which has mostly been performed anyway by nice boys from the suburbs.

Two final points from Trudgill are relevant here. First, as he makes clear, linguists cannot explain why in particular cases particular choices are made in pronunciation—why is this word American-inflected, this one not? Since these are acoustic choices—decisions as to what words will *sound* like—we obviously have to consider other, musical reasons why a singer or lyricist might decide that "this sounds right." Second, Trudgill notes that "pop-music is a field where language is especially socially symbolic, and typically low in communicative function, high on the phatic and self-expressive." In other words, the use of language in pop songs has as much to do with establishing the communicative situation as with communicating, and more to do with articulating a feeling than explaining it.[26]

I can make the same point following a different route, from the study of rhetoric. There is, from this perspective, an inevitable tension in the popular lyric between its colloquial, vernacular language and its use in a "heightened," elevated way, framed by music. A pop song is ordinary language put to extraordinary use. Two issues arise from this.

On the one hand, the popular performer has a recurring problem of *sincerity*. In popular cultural terms, good talkers are mistrusted as well as admired: people who have a "way with words"—the seducer, the salesman, the demagogue, the preacher—are people with power, and the power to use words is a power to deceive and manipulate.[27] Sincerity may then be best indicated by an *inability* to speak (as in soul vocal convention) or through an aural *contradiction* between the glibness of the lyric and the uncertainty of the voice (as in much male country music).

On the other hand (and in other genres), singers and writers may deliberately use heightened language to draw attention to their art, to their individual sensibility. Here there is a deliberate use of non-colloquial language (as in Bob Dylan's early songs, for example), or else ordinary words are "framed," held up and examined, everyday clichés liberated by being taken literally or turned inside out.

Either way, songs can be used to explore the relationships of *different* languages—different ways of speaking—and in pop terms this has often meant challenging linguistic hierarchies, subverting the way words are used to dominate—"song texts," as Roland Barthes put it, "provide a framework for permissive language behavior."[28] This was obviously an aspect of the imitation of African-American and working-class accents by British pop singers, but voices can also be made to move between languages within a song. This was a key aspect of Gracie Fields' comic technique as a music hall singer;[29] and it is now a crucial component of rap, a song form which is word-rich in its obsession with the empowering and disempowering effects of language.[30]

Take Public Enemy's "Don't Believe the Hype."[31] As with "Born in the USA," the power of this lies in its chorus phrase—"Don't Believe the Hype!"—a slogan that could be of use to listeners in all sorts of circumstances. But the line is also an intervention in the debate about Public Enemy's music itself, about the meaning of rap, about the value of African-American male youth culture. The song is an *argument*, drawing on rap's conventional use as a form of conversation—between performer and performer, between performer and audience, between performer and media. And this is the context in which power is being defined as *a way with words*. Rap as a necessarily mass mediated form, a commodity, is in effect releasing all the forces of contemporary communications technology onto language, onto the clichés of corporate and political power (appropriated directly, via sampling), onto the vitality of the slang and the fragmented, reactive, ugly, utopian language of the streets. A rap like "Don't Believe the Hype" is significant less for its logical unfolding than for its investment of key words with force. And given the nature of these words—their obvious coding as urban black—they are being invested with urban black force; they are at once a threat and a promise, according to who's listening.

This brings us back to the point of the protest song. The most significant political effect of a pop song is not on how people vote or organize, but on how they speak. And this becomes a particularly interesting (and complex) effect in a rap, which foregrounds the problematic relationship of sung and spoken language. Rap acts like Public Enemy imply that such musical (or poetic) devices as rhythm and rhyme are material ways of organizing and shaping feeling and desire; they offer listeners new ways of performing (and thus changing) everyday life.

Lyrics, to put this another way, let us into songs as stories. All songs are implied narratives. They have a central character, the singer; a character with an attitude, in a situation, talking to someone (if only to herself). This, as Leon Rosselson argues, is one reason why songs aren't poems. The only way they can be introspective is if "the 'I' in the song is a fiction," and the lyric is about introspection. "Song," in this respect, "is theatre."

> The language of song, like the language of drama, is not a literary language; it embraces the idioms and rhythms of everyday speech while looking for ways of enriching that language . . . Song, like drama, is about the invention of characters and stories; people—not issues, arguments, slogans, abstractions or soul-searching—are at its centre. And because people do not live in a vacuum, song, like drama, is at home in the public arena.[32]

The most obvious narrative song is the French *chanson*. In Ned Rorem's words, "Fluid states of mind are what French popular songs portray: they have always told stories that develop in a straight line, *a-b-c*, towards a delicious or catastrophic resolution. Which is why their words haunt us more than their melodies. French song is thus not bound to set forms: the subject imposes the pattern. Often the music shifts to (or is entirely within) a regular 3/4—the dance of experience."[33] Rorem points out that generically the *chanson* derives from the troubadour epic via the "naturalistic *fin de siècle* café-concert narrations of Yvette Guilbert." It was always as much a verbal as a musical form. Edith Piaf's songs

> spoke of love fermenting into murder, then of redemption and of love's return in heaven. They spoke of Sunday fairs in the squalid Vincennes park as reward for the barmaid's six-day week. They spoke of injustice in Pigalle's underworld—what Parisians call *le milieu*. They told also, like Jerome Kern's song "Bill," of life sustained through fidelity to the unfaithful, but, unlike "Bill," that life was prolonged more through words than music. More as *littérateuse* than as *musicienne* is the Sparrow recalled today, as she was applauded in her prime.

Chanson singers, in other words, effectively "'talk' their tunes, beguiling through anecdote rather than through a formal development of sound."[34]

But this is not a simple matter of telling a story; or, rather, telling a story is not a simple thing to do. As Ginette Vincendeau argues, the *chanteuses* also took a part *within* their narratives: on the one hand, the imagery of the songs (which had an obvious cinematic source in terms of both character and setting) determined *how* they were performed—the singer lit and staged as if she too were on screen; on the other hand, the singers were taken to live the same lives as their characters, with the same melodramas, the same oppressions, the same romance, the same sadness. Edith Piaf's stories were authenticated by her own story; and her story was as much shaped by her songs as were those of her lyrical protagonists. People flocked to her shows not just to hear good tales well told, but also for the spectacle of *narrative-in-action*, for the sight of someone hanging onto life, pummeling and defying it, by putting it into words. And this pleasure was, from the beginning, imbued with nostalgia.[35]

It is notable that when *chanson* has been taken up by rock singers it has been as theatrical song—David Bowie sings Jacques Brel songs as if they were written by Brecht and Weill; Marc Almond treats them as high camp. For both Almond and Bowie the "character" of the song, the person they enact, is the *chansonnier* himself; and (putting aside the generic peculiarities of the *chanson*) this is a point that can be generalized: to sing a song is to tell a story, and to tell a story is to be a storyteller. One of pop's principle pleasures is being buttonholed in the first place.

In the British (as opposed to the French) tradition popular music has always featured the character song, a form which links music hall artists like Marie Lloyd and Gracie Fields to a cabaret act like Noel Coward, and which has been the most obviously "British" component of rock from Ray Davies and Mick Jagger to Elvis Costello, Morrissey, and Blur. The lyrical and narrative convention here is to use a song to portray a character while simultaneously drawing attention to the art of the portrayal. The singer is playing a part, and what is involved is neither self-expression (the equation of role and performer, as in *chanson* or the blues) nor critical commentary (as in the German theater song) but, rather, an exercise in style, an ironic—or cynical—presentation of character *as* style. The art of this sort of singing becomes a matter of acting, and there is always a question concerning the singer's relationship to his own words (an obvious question for Mick Jagger, for example).

Elvis Costello, probably the best contemporary writer of character songs, uses a person (and in this context even "his own character" is clearly an act) and a situation to encapsulate particular sensations—lust, jealousy, meanness, betrayal—but, at the same time, his songs are about the enactment of those sensations, about the embarrassment, humiliation, and frustration of trying to make such feelings known. Even at their most emotionally intense Costello's songs are self-conscious (a self-consciousness reflected, most obviously, in the drawing-attention-to-itself cleverness of his word schemes). For Costello, character songs are not so much (as Rosselson would have it) about people as about characterization.

A different approach to lyrical narrative can be found in the African-American blues tradition, which works less with incidents building to a climax or through gestures shaping a character than by the accumulation of images as feeling. For obvious historical reasons the expressive African-American use of the English language, originating in slaves' talk, has always been metaphorical, has always been dependent on double meanings, on allusion, indirection, and puns, on symbolism, and on the surrealism of language organized as *sound*.[36] And this leads to the central question about the song as a form of persuasive communication. What does it mean to *sing* words? How is their meaning changed from when these same words are spoken?

As I've already suggested, to sing words is to elevate them in some way, to make them special, to give them a new form of intensity. This is obvious in the use of singing to mark off religious expression from the everyday use of words. But note also our discomfort at hearing banal conversation sung. Opera (and oratorio) composers have always faced the problem of what to do with those words which are needed to move the audience from one (heightened) scene to another: hence the stylization of the recitative, which confirms musically the conventional distinction between "ordinary" talk and the emotion of song—however realist an opera or musical might otherwise be, it is a humorous device to get someone to sing, say, "Pass the salt!" One of the few attempts to defy this convention, the Jacques Demy/Michel Legrand musical film *Les Parapluies de Cherbourg*, opens with a man going into a garage and singing his request for his car (which is being serviced); the uneasy (and usually laughing) audience suddenly realizes that everything here is going to be sung. I love this film (and *Les Demoiselles de Rochefort*) because the effect *is* soon magical: sung, the most ordinary transactions seem to float across the pastel backdrops.[37]

Another way of getting at the difference between talking and singing is our own practice. Most people are happier to talk in public than to sing; singing (in a seminar, for instance) is a source of embarrassment. There are obviously social reasons for this—we're taught to speak in ways we're not usually taught to sing; talking has, in that respect, been naturalized (and there remain places and situations in which it is equally embarrassing to speak publicly, just as there are situations—a drunken party or a sports event or in church—where singing seems natural). But whatever the sociological reasons, the fact is that most of us experience singing (unlike speaking) as a *performance* (to see this just visit a *karaoke* bar).[38] A performance in two respects: singing draws a different sort of attention to the words, the "special" effect I've already noted; and it draws a different sort of attention to the singer, hence the embarrassment. Singing seems to be self-revealing in a way that speaking is not.

This is a paradoxical situation: by singing words we subject them to a control that they're not used to: they have to take their part in a rhythmic and melodic frame; how and where they are pitched is suddenly an open question. And so we, as their users, experience a loss of control—we may not be able to do what we want with the words (or with the sounds of our voices). To sing is to feel vulnerable (and to be a trained singer, to enjoy singing in public, is, precisely, to feel in control). Singing seems both less natural than speaking (involves a different, less familiar sort of self-consciousness) and at the same time more natural—more bodily, more exposing, more revealing of who we "really"—naturally—are.

I'll come back to issues of voice, subjectivity, and embarrassment in the next chapter; here I want to focus on the effect of singing on language. The challenge of setting words to music is that two principles of the organization of sound have to be made to cohere. The rhythm of speech, the way in which a stress pattern is determined by syntax, is not necessarily appropriate to the rhythm of music, which follows its own structural rules. Similarly, the sound of the word that is necessary semantically (to make a statement meaningful) may not be the sound of the word that is desirable musically, to make the musical statement attractive. As Dryden once complained (about his libretto for Purcell's *King Arthur*), "the Numbers of Poetry and Vocal Musick, are sometimes so contrary, that in many places I have been oblig'd to cramp my Verses, and make them rugged to the Reader, that they may be harmonious to the Hearer."[39]

There is a distinction, in Stockhausen's words, between words as "speech-symbols" and words as "sound-symbols," although, as he points out, words-as-sound-symbols can, in fact, take on their own semantic significance, as marks of ritual expression, for example—this is particularly obvious in religious music, where the meaning of words becomes their meaning as sounds. (It is, likewise, difficult to avoid hearing intelligible words in vocal sounds: we find a meaning for songs sung in a strange language, and spontaneously interpret Lewis Carroll's "Jabberwocky" or Hugo Ball's Dada "Seepferdschen und Flugfische.")[40]

In pop terms this problem is routinely solved by rhyming—the craft of the lyricist is find the word which both sounds and means right, and one sort of pop pleasure is simply observing the cleverness with which this is done. The theater song tradition, for example, from Gilbert and Sullivan to Stephen Sondheim, is in part a celebration of the lyricist's artifice. A song like "Bewitched" (from *Pal Joey*) cannot just be discussed in terms of emotional realism: the song is about a mood (love as lust) and a situation (older woman/younger man), but it expresses the character of its singer (a character, in this case, in a musical play) and, even more overtly, the nature of her performance, her performance not just as an actress in a play but also as a singer to an audience. In the end the song is about a use of language; it draws our attention to its puns and rhymes, to the way this piece of spontaneous stage business was crafted lyrically—through repetition, contrast, changing verbal pace.[41]

The relation of spoken and sung language has undoubtedly been explored most fruitfully in African-American music, both because song was culturally important for so long as a means of expression of all sorts, and because, for the same oppressive historical reasons, oral (rather than print) culture remained for so long the source of social identity. By the turn of this century blues singers could draw on an accumulated store of lyrical resources: phrases, images, and clichés, elevated and mundane, stylized and familiar. As Levine notes:

> Many pages could be filled with familiar floating lines like these which appeared in different arrangements and contexts in song after song: I'm worried now but I won't be worried long; Got de blues but too damn mean to cry; Out in dis wide worl' alone; Brown-skin woman, she's chocolate to de bone; I got de blues an' can't be satisfied; I got a rainbow tied 'roun my shoulder; You don't know my mind; I'm laughin' to keep from cryin'; Woke up this mornin', blues all around my bed; Look down that lonesome road; I been down so long, it seems like up to me; If you don't think I'm sinking look what a hole I'm in.[42]

Words here are used as aphorisms (another way of making ordinary words special, framing them); or, in a reverse process with the same effect, common phrases which have lost their metaphorical power are taken seriously and so recharged. But this isn't just a matter of linguistic politics. "Ordinary language" also stands here for a kind of accumulated knowledge, a shared way of being (and a shared way of being denied political, cultural, and human rights), and blues singers have certainly treated language like this, as cultural memory. As Levine explains:

> The blues allowed individuals greater voice for their individuality than any previous form of Afro-American song but kept them still members of the group, still on familiar ground, still in touch with their peers and their roots. It was a song style created by generations in the flux of change who desired and needed to meet the future

without losing the past, who needed to stand alone and yet remain part of the group, who craved communication with and reassurance from members of the group as they ventured into unfamiliar territories and ways.[43]

Rap offers another sort of example, also deriving from a musical use of spoken language rather being a lyrical form as such. Its origins lie in long-established rituals of insult in which language is subjected to rules of rhyme and meter, is treated with the skill with words that is a necessary aspect of an oral culture (where stories and songs have to be stored in the mind and the body, not on the page or in print). If, in rap, rhythm is more significant than harmony or melody, it is rhythm dependent on language, on the ways words rhyme and syllables count.[44]

As insults became more and more elaborately rhymed (in Philadelphia "jones" was the local ritual term), more surreal metaphorically, more personalized in their use of the put-down, so, noted Ulf Hannerz in the 1960s, they came closer and closer to "song jones." Words were increasingly chosen, that is to say, for their sound (for their sound in a particular voice, according to a specific rhythm of contempt) rather than for their meaning.[45] And whatever other explanations anthropologists or historians or psychologists might come up with for the insult ritual, its most obvious function is to develop participants' verbal skills—skills not just in verbal invention or virtuosity, but also in what one might call verbal discipline, the ability to follow rules of rhyme and meter. In this respect, an insult form like "the dozens" must be related to other verbal skills that are a part of African-American linguistic culture— the toastin' and testifyin' that have equally fed into rap.

I'll come back to the importance of these verbal performing skills in Chapter 10. What I'd like to note here, as a final twist to the discussion of how words are made fit for music, is that musical forms have, in practice, adapted themselves to languages, to ways of speaking. This is particularly obvious in the global movement of rock music. There are clearly ways in which rock musical conventions, in terms of melodic form, use of verse/chorus, mode of vocal attack, and so on, reflect—or at least gesture at— patterns of Anglo-American and Afro-American speech (as Trudgill's analysis made clear). These musical conventions may not be appropriate for other languages. The use of rhyme as the basic rhythmic device in rock lyrics, for example, creates problems for those languages (like Italian) which don't usually finish sentences with "hard," blunt-edged consonants. This is one reason why most non-English-speaking rock musicians compose in English (it is not just their pursuit of international sales)—and why punk was liberating for young bands in, say, Finland: the "ugliness" and incoherence of the punk sound meant that Finnish words sounded good sung too![46]

Genre sound rules, in other words, are as important in deciding what words can be sung as genre rules of what it is right to sing about—rock sung in, say, an upper-class English accent doesn't just sound unconvincing in terms of character, it also sounds wrong as a noise. And this seems a suitable point from which to turn finally (and I have deliberately left this issue till last) to a consideration of song lyrics as poetry.

In the academy, to study special or elevated uses of language is to study poetry, and from early on in rock history the highest critical compliment—the way to take lyrics seriously—was to treat them as poetry, as print texts. During the 1970s a spate of college-aimed rock poetry books appeared, with claims so heartfelt that it is impossible to resist the temptation of quotation:

> Then the phenomenon of rock burst forth. It was perhaps crude and unpoetic in its infancy, but as the sixties progressed, lyrics of increasing sophistication and skill appeared. Once more, the lyric voice is flowering. The great creative energy of man's stubborn attempt to penetrate the meaning of his existence is surging forth in voices from the streets, voices that weave the sounds of the present with the age-old questions of man in relation to his *loved one*, his *society*, and the *cosmos*.[47]

Or, again,

> Over the past few years there has indeed emerged something we can call "the poetry of rock," something that at times can be quite good. The beginnings, of course, were far from promising. Despite the fertile sources on which rock music of the 1950s drew, it was musically innovative and vibrant but lyrically almost unbelievably banal and trivial. If it contained any poetry at all, that poetry was pedestrian adolescent doggerel full of unrefined slang and trite neoromantic convention. But in the early 1960s there burst upon the scene a number of exceptionally talented artists, perhaps even poets, who managed to bring together in various degrees all the many elements of what we now call rock and to make something of quality.[48]

Now in one respect what we see here seems familiar: the high cultural judgment of pop. Pichashe compares the Stones' "No Expectations" favorably to the treatment of similar themes in country songs because "the Stones' song is not sentimental at all . . . The reaction of the singer, like the tone of the song, is a refreshing change from the gush we'd expect to get in this situation." And Bob Sarlin, having defined "song poetry" as a new form, and contrasted it with the "slick" and "insincere" Cole Porter, and the "self censorship," "stock imagery," and "worthlessness" of rock 'n' roll (song poetry's values are derived from the folk refusal to compromise), admits to his doubts about Don McLean's "American Pie": "I would be suspicious of a record or a song that appeals to everyone." He can't help concluding that McLean's work, like Carole King's, is "shallow."[49]

But in the end the rock-as-poetry books don't really value their chosen lyrics in terms of contemporary literary critical arguments but, rather, according to the middlebrow criteria that New Criticism successfully drove out of the academy in the 1930s.[50] There's not really much difference, in other words, in their understanding of poetry, between these 1970s accounts of rock lyrics and Theodore Dreiser's comments on his brother Paul's successful popular songs at the beginning of the century. Theodore admired Paul's "sighings over home and mother and lost sweethearts and dead heroes such as never were in real life . . . They bespoke . . . true poetic feeling for the mystery and pathos of life and death, the wonder of the waters, the stars, the flowers, accidents of life, success, failure."[51]

For more sophisticated approaches to lyrics as poetry—for close textual reading, the pursuit of ambiguity, the reference of lyrical devices to poetic history, the focus on form rather than feeling—we have to turn to Dylan studies, to Michael Gray's *tour-de-force ragout* of pop criticism, New Criticism, and Leavisism, *The Art of Bob Dylan* ("this calculated lack of specificity becomes, in Dylan's hands, a positive entity grown out of and beyond the specific; and it opens up the way for the recreation of many different universal relationships") or to Aidan Day's more theoretically and thematically austere *Jokerman* ("the present book concentrates on providing close readings of individual lyrics selected principally from that side of Dylan's lyrical writing which takes up questions of identity").[52]

Day starts from the assumption that although Dylan's lyrics are written to be sung, they nonetheless contain the "poetic richness of signification" and "density of verbal meaning" that characterize modernism; Day is therefore concerned primarily with "the semantic properties of the words of the lyrics," which "excludes consideration of the expanded expressive range belonging to performances of those lyrics." He concentrates on "obscurities in structure and verbal texture," on the "indirectness of language in the stanzas," on the "density of allusion and pun," on "lyrics whose framing of the multiform and bizarre energies of identity constitutes Dylan's most distinctive achievement."[53]

Day is helpfully clear here about the assumptions that inform most academic studies of rock lyrics. What is taken for granted is that (modern) poetry is something read, not something heard; that it is defined by page layout rather than by performing voice—and Derek Attridge has pointed to the irony of the fact that "high" poetry became primarily a visual form at precisely the moment when "the easy availability of recordings and recording devices" gave the human voice "a cultural centrality" it hadn't had since "printing became the dominant representation of language."[54]

There may well be cause and effect operating here: high cultural authority is, for all sorts of reasons, more easily challenged and subverted by the spoken than by the written word. But I want to take another point from Attridge: to treat the distinction between poetry and lyric as a distinction between the written and the spoken word is aesthetically misleading. There is, to put this another way, a continuity between poetry and song, rather than a clear division. Between the two lie various sorts of "performed" language, whether "oral poetry" as technically defined by anthropologists, or public and formalized uses of words for special ends as in nursery and playground and advertising rhymes; whether in insult rituals like the dozens, or in poetry "recitals." It is, after all, precisely the refusal to draw a clear boundary between poetry and song that has made African-American musicians so important for twentieth-century mass culture.

There are two contexts in which the "crossover" between poetry and song has been usefully explored. The first is the problem of the art music setting of "high" verse. Edward Cone, for example, makes the point that poetry as read is much more "open" for the reader, in terms of both sound and pace, than poetry as heard (whether being read aloud or set to music). The reader makes her own decisions about "speed, emphasis, tone, accent and inflection." Now obviously the poet plants clues or instructions—the original choice of words was partly made to cause the reading to work one way or another; but Cone argues, I think rightly, that in reading (unless the poem is a nonsense poem—and this is the definition of a non-sense poem) we balance sonic logic against semantic logic: we're trying to make sense of the poem as we read it, we're thinking about it, thinking back about it, rereading a line accordingly, shifting our emphases: the reading is the interpretation, and it is as much affected by a posited meaning behind the words as by the words themselves. A performance of the poem doesn't allow such flexibility; once a verse is set to music, "the mind is so to speak chained to the vehicle of the moving sound." We can't stop the music. We have to move from beginning to end and be satisfied with what we immediately perceive; our compensation is that the music makes the words more "vivid." A musical setting of a poem, then, is a *choice* of meaning given a special intensity, such that, in Mark Booth's words, the "content" of the song becomes its effect, becomes what it makes us feel.[55]

Such intensity no more guarantees that this is the "correct" or "best" reading of the poem, than the fact that it is being read aloud by its author. In Ned Rorem's words, "a poet declaiming his own verse is no more definitive, no more *inevitable,* than some composer's setting of that verse." Rorem recalls arranging Elizabeth Bishop's poem "Visits to St. Elizabeth's" for performance by a mezzo-soprano. "The tact of Elizabeth's disappointment was touching," but she eventually explained what she felt about it:

> My complaint is that it sounds too hysterical. I hadn't imagined it that way, somehow. Yes, I had thought of a male voice, I suppose— but I don't believe that is what bothers me. It is the fast tempo and the increasing note of hysteria. Because the poem is observation, really, rather than participation . . . something like that. Two friends have said rather the same thing to me. It is awfully well sung, nevertheless. I don't know whether it could be *slowed* down, or not? Probably not.[56]

Bishop's problem, as Rorem ruefully notes, is that "poets' work ends with their poems," and one difference between a poem and a lyric is that whereas both only exist when they are performed, the former can never be fixed by or to a performance. Every reader will perform it differently, and the poet herself cannot determine that her performance will be definitive (she can't even ensure that the voice, the "I" in which she speaks her poem when writing it, will be the voice that anyone will use when reading it). Bishop was shocked to hear Rorem's setting only because she wasn't used to hearing what her readers made of her verse: *every* reading the poem has had might be just as shocking![57]

Rorem puts it like this: "poetry is self-contained, while lyrics are made to be sung and don't necessarily lead a life of their own." And he adds that "when 'real' poets write with song in mind they fail both as poets and lyricists because, in 'helping' the composer, they overindulge in presumably felicitous vocables that emerge as self-conscious banality."[58] Which is to echo a point made by a lyricist, P. G. Wodehouse: "If I write a lyric without having to fit it to a tune, I always make it too much like a set of light verse, much too regular in meter. I think you get the best results by giving the composer his head and having the lyricist follow him."[59]

This leads us to the second way of thinking about music and poetry. The question is not now how musicians understand poetry, but how poets understand music. Northrop Frye notes that what is conventionally called "musical poetry" describes poetry with a particular sort of sound: sensuous, languorous, alliterative. Poets such as Poe or Swinburne are said to write verse that "flows" over us, envelops us, like music. But, Frye suggests, this actually describes the most unmusical sort of poem. Poetry that works as music should be concerned not with sound but with rhythm; it should be interested in "throwing the ear forward," not in encouraging us to bask in the words' presence. To be musical, poetry needs a dance rhythm, discordant textures and stressed accents, not balanced vowels and "a dreary, sensuous flow of sound."[60]

In considering the transitions from spoken English to poetry to music, Frye raises two different issues. One concerns poetry as such: a poet, that is to say, occupies a space *between* music and speech; she chooses words for reasons to do with both meaning and sound, to satisfy what she wants to say as well as the formal conventions of how she wants to say it. The more the choice is concerned with sonic rather than semantic factors, the more "musical" the verse. Frye's point is that the "musical" choice here is not simply a matter of sound (a sensuous decision) but also of movement. What's really involved in "musical poetry," then, is a poet trying to impose a performance on us, trying to persuade us to follow a certain sort of interpretive logic. As the poet John Ashbery puts it, "What I like about music is its ability of being convincing, of carrying an argument through successfully to the finish, though the terms of this argument remain unknown quantities. What remains is the structure, the *architecture* of the argument."[61] There is, in short, an issue of rhetoric here too: poets aren't the only people for whom sound-patterns are significant for meaning. We can recognize a sales patter or a sermon or a seduction without needing to understand the language (as any European tourist can testify). And lyricists are as interested in using these rhetorical devices as in following so-called "poetic" conventions.

A "rhythmic" poem, one which causes us to beat time whether through reading emphasis or with a literal tapping of the foot, occurs, in Attridge's words, not because a rhythmic structure, such as a melody, has been imposed upon the language, but because the language, read aloud (even read aloud "in our heads") produces "a rhythmic organization that encourages regular muscular movement." Our appreciation of what's expected of us rhythmically when faced with an order of words thus depends as much on our general knowledge of language as spoken as on our educated experience of poetry as written, and Attridge notes (like Frye) the particular rhythmic sophistication of English speakers because of "the coexistence, in some degree of tension, of *two* series of energy pulses in speech—those that produce the syllables, and those that augment certain syllables with stress. Both these series of pulse incline toward rhythmic repetition, but in the random syllabic arrangements of prose, neither can be fully satisfied."[62]

English is, in this sense (and unlike, say, Japanese), an inherently rhythmic, or at least syncopated, language, and this is the linguistic context in which music imposes on words its own way of reading, through its own production of rhythmic stress, its own power over how syllables are sounded, a power which may determine, in turn, what those words mean, syntactically, semantically, and rhetorically. And in this respect Frye's pitching of words-as-meanings against words-as-sounds seems too simple. A statement may be heightened in its intensity precisely because, musically, it departs from its "natural" linguistic rhythm.

The point is that as speakers we create meaning through stress; music creates stress; therefore music creates meaning. As a spoken phrase, for example, "she loves you" shifts its narrative meaning (if not its semantic sense) according to whether the emphasis is placed on "she" (rather than someone else), "loves" (rather than hates), or "you" (rather than me or him). In setting the words to music the Beatles had to choose one stress, one dominant implication. The song becomes the preferred reading of the words.

Rhythm, as Attridge explains it, is also relevant to my earlier point about how people grasp and remember songs—as words via music, as music via words. What's actually involved here is the way we grasp something *bodily*, store it physically so that we can reproduce it physically, by using our voices. Such grasping is, as Attridge suggests, an embodied perception of periodicity, but the point to stress is that this is a perception (not reality). It is periodicity as measured not by a metronome but by a sort of recognition via meaning (which is why words matter)—and for most of us such song memories are incomplete: we can reproduce songs internally, for ourselves, but wouldn't be able to reproduce them, to sing them, for anyone else.

And this brings me to my final point, the reason why lyrics aren't poetry and why no song words, in my opinion, stand up as print texts. Good song lyrics are not good poems because they don't need to be: poems "score" the performance or reading of the verse in the words themselves, words which are chosen in part because of the way they lead us on, metrically and rhythmically, by their arrangement on the page (a poem is designed to be read, even if in an out-loud performance, and such reading directions are just as much an aspect of "free" as of formally structured verse forms). Lyrics, by contrast, are "scored" by the music itself. For a lyric to include its own musical (or performing) instructions is, as Ned Rorem observes, to over-determine its performance, to render it infantile.

Ruth Finnegan makes the same point about the difference between oral and written poetry. Because oral poetry is performed in particular ritualized ways, part of its meaning and effect is taken from the performing context, from the "live" emotional atmosphere, the immediate pleasures of identification and suspense which are, in a sense, *tangible* (oral poetry is almost inevitably therefore flat and monotonous when written down and read). The performance, in other words (as with a song), is a necessary aspect of its "poetic" quality. Oral poetry doesn't need the devices written poetry must use to hold the reader's attention; that is the job of the poet herself, *as performer.*[63]

Good lyrics by definition, then, lack the elements that make for good lyric poetry. Take them out of their performed context, and they either seem to have no musical qualities at all, or else to have such obvious ones as to be silly (this goes as much for Lorenz Hart and Cole Porter as for Bob Dylan and Elvis Costello, as much for Curtis Mayfield and Smokey Robinson as for Hank Williams and Tom T. Hall). And this is most obvious (to return to Greil Marcus) in those songs in which the pleasure—the exhilaration—comes from the singer's failure to integrate musical and semantic meaning. The best pop songs, in short, are those that can be heard as a *struggle* between verbal and musical rhetoric, between the singer and the song.

The Voice

Let us imagine for this double function, localized in one and the same site, a single transgression, which would be generated by a simultaneous use of speech and kissing: *to kiss while embracing, to embrace while speaking.* It would appear that such a pleasure exists, since lovers incessantly "drink in speech upon the lips of the beloved," etc. What they delight in is, in the erotic encounter, the play of meaning which opens and breaks off: the function *which is disturbed:* in a word: *the stammered body.*

Roland Barthes[1]

We came to listen to that voice of difference likely to bring us *what we can't have* and to divert us from the monotony of sameness.

Trinh T. Minh-ha[2]

"Yeah," Scott said, "a singer like Ella says, 'My man's left me,' and you think the guy went down the street for a loaf of bread or something. But when Lady says, 'My man's gone' or 'My man's left me,' man, you can see the guy going down the street. His bags are packed, and he ain't never coming back. I mean like *never.*"

Tony Scott on Billie Holiday[3]

Look at a song's lyrics on the page: whose "voice" is there? Who's talking? The answer seems to start with the pronouns, the "shifters," not just the "I," the apparent speaker, but the "you" and "we" and "she" which reveal various things about the speaker. Even without an explicit "I," that is, we have an implicit one, someone who's doing the addressing: "*you've* got a lot of nerve, to say that *you're* my friend." The "voice" in the printed lyrics is thus articulated by the text itself, by a process that is both self-expressive and self-revealing, both declared openly and implied by the narrative.[4]

But even from the reader's point of view there's more to the voice than this. The printed lyric is already a double act, both the communicative process it describes or enacts—the "I" of the lyric speaking to the "you" of the

183

lyric—and the communicative process it entails, writing and reading. As readers do we necessarily become the "you" of the writer's "I"? Do we take onto ourselves her love or contempt? Do we have to take a place in her story? The answer is obviously no; or, at least, there are certainly other options. We can refuse to become involved at all, read the lyric as an overheard conversation between other people, take it to be reported speech, put quotation marks around it. Or we can read it as if speaking it, become the "I" ourselves. (I think it would be impossible to read Bob Dylan's "Positively 4th Street" as if we were the "you" at issue—and this is a song positively *obsessed* with the word. The pleasure of these lines is as a means of sounding our *own* feelings of contempt and hauteur.)

How we read lyrics is not a completely random or idiosyncratic choice. The lyricist sets up the situation—through her use of language, her construction of character—in a way that, in part, determines the response we make, the nature of our engagement. But once we say that, we admit that there's another "voice" here, the voice of the lyricist, the author, the person putting the words in the "I's" mouth, putting the protagonists into their lyrical situation. And the authorial voice can be more or less distinctive; we may recognize—respond to—that voice (Cole Porter, Elvis Costello, Morrissey, P. J. Harvey) even when reading a lyric. "Voice" in this sense describes a sense of personality that doesn't involve shifters at all, but is familiar as the special way a person has with words: we immediately know who's speaking.

Now stop reading the lyrics, and listen to the song. Whose voice do we hear now? Again there's an obvious answer: the singer's, stupid! And what I argue in the rest of this chapter is that this is, in fact, the stupid answer. We hear the singer's voice, of course, but how that voice relates to the voices described above is the interesting question. To sing a lyric doesn't simplify the question of who is speaking to whom; it makes it more complicated.

In *The Composer's Voice*, Edward Cone asks whose voice we hear when we listen to a Schubert setting of a poem by Goethe. We hear a singer, Thomas Allen say, with a distinctive physical voice; we hear the protagonist of the song, the "I" of the narrative; we hear the poem's author, Goethe, in the distinctive organization of the words and their argument; and we hear Schubert, *in whose voice* the whole thing is composed.[5] And this last definition of voice, as the stylistic identity of the composer, is undoubtedly the dominant definition of "voice" in classical music criticism: a Schubert song is a Schubert song, regardless of whose words he has set to music and which singer is singing them. Schubert's "voice" thus refers to a personal quality—a quality of his personality—apparent in all his musical work.[6]

Even in this phrasing, though, a new question is raised. What is the relationship between Schubert's characteristics *as a composer* (his distinctive use of musical language which can be traced across different works, enabling us to speak of his musical "identity" and "development") and his characteristics *as a person?* This is, of course, to raise the long-debated question (long debated in literary criticism, at any rate) of the relationship between someone's life and their work. This issue tends to be put aside in music criticism because of the belief that music is a more directly emotional form of expression than literature, and is therefore more directly (or unconsciously) revealing of the composer's character. One of Anthony Storr's casual comments can thus be taken as typical: "The listener doesn't even have to be able to read music to recognize Haydn's robustness and humour, combined with his capacity for deep feeling."[7] Is music really so transparently expressive of personality? Is a voice?

The same questions can be addressed to popular music. What is the relationship between the "voice" we hear in a song and the author or composer of that song? Between the voice and the singer? This relationship has, of course, different complications in different genres, but two general issues arise immediately. First there is, as in classical music, the problem of biography: what is the relationship of life and art? On the whole, pop fans are less simple-minded than classical music critics about this. While one can certainly find Hollywood biopix of pop stars (Oliver Stone's *The Doors,* say) to match its biopix of classical composers—the life pouring out in the sounds—this tells us more about Hollywood (and the attempt to turn Jim Morrison into a Real Artist) than it does about pop music.

The up-front star system means that pop fans are well aware of the ways in which pop performers are inventions (and the pop biographer's task is usually therefore to expose the "real" Bob Dylan or Madonna who *isn't* in their music). And in pop, biography is used less to explain composition (the writing of the song) than expression (its performance): it is in real, material, singing voices that the "real" person is to be heard, not in scored stylistic or formulaic devices. The pop musician as interpreter (Billie Holiday, say) is therefore more likely to be understood in biographical terms than the pop musician as composer (Mark Knopfler, say), and when musicians are both, it is the performing rather than the composing voice that is taken to be the key to character. As Robert O'Meally asks about Billie Holiday, "She was the greatest jazz singer of all time. With Louis Armstrong, she invented modern jazz singing. Why do these accounts [all the books about her], which tell us so much about her drug problems, no-good men, and supposedly autobiographical sad songs, tell us so little about Billie Holiday, artist?"[8]

And the answer is because as listeners we assume that we can hear someone's life in their voice—a life that's there despite and not because of the singer's craft, a voice that says who they really are, an art that only exists because of what they've suffered. What makes Billie Holiday an artist from this perspective is that she was able to give *that which she couldn't help expressing* aesthetic shape and grace.[9] Compare Gregory Sandow on Frank Sinatra:

> Even before Kitty Kelley's unauthorized biography it was hardly a secret . . . that Sinatra hasn't always been the nicest of guys. So it's a commonplace of Sinatra criticism to separate Sinatra the artist from Sinatra the man. But I've always thought that his character slips through in his performance . . . And in fact it slips through precisely because of his art. Because he *is* an artist, he can't help telling a kind of truth; he can't help reaching towards the root of everything he's felt. He makes his living singing love songs; like any great popular singer, he can expand even a single sigh in those love songs into something vast. But he's also got his own story to tell, a story that goes far beyond what any love song could express: it's a story a little bit about triumph, partly about a lust for power, often about loss, and very much about humiliation and rage.[10]

The first general point to make about the pop voice, then, is that we hear singers as *personally* expressive (even, perhaps especially, when they are not singing "their own" songs) in a way that a classical singer, even a dramatic and "tragic" star like Maria Callas, is not. This is partly a matter of sound convention. As Libby Holman once put it, "My singing is like Flamenco. Sometimes, it's purposefully hideous. I try to convey anguish, anger, tragedy, passion. When you're expressing emotions like these, you cannot have a pure tone."[11].

In classical music, by contrast, the sound of the voice is determined by the score; the expression of anguish, anger, tragedy, and passion is a matter of musical organization. As Umberto Fiore writes, "In this context, the voice is in fact an instrument: bass, baritone, tenor, soprano and so forth. Individual styles can only *improve* these vocal masks, not really transgress them . . . the creation of a person, of a character, is substantially up to the music as such; if truth is there it is a *musical* truth."[12]

But if we hear the pop singer singing "her self," she is also singing a song, and so a second question arises: what is the relationship between the voice as a carrier of sounds, the singing voice, making "gestures," and the voice as a carrier of words, the speaking voice, making "utterances"? The issue is not meaning (words) versus absence of meaning (music), but the relationship between two different sorts of meaning-making, the tensions and conflicts between them. There's a question here of power: who is to be the master, words or music? And what makes the voice so interesting is that it makes meaning in these two ways simultaneously. We have, therefore, to approach the voice under four headings: as *a musical instrument;* as *a body;* as *a person;* and as *a character.*

I'll begin with the voice as a musical instrument. A voice obviously has a sound; it can be described in musical terms like any other instrument, as something with a certain pitch, a certain register, a certain timbral quality, and so forth. Voices can be used, like any other instrument, to make a noise of the right sort at the right time. Both these terms (right sort, right time) are apparent in the most instrumental use of the voice, as "backup." Here the singers' sound is more important than their words, which are either nonsensical or become so through repetition; and repetition is itself the key to how such voices work, as percussive instruments, marking out the regular time around which the lead singer can be quite irregular in matters of pitch and timing, quite inarticulate in terms of words or utterances.[13]

Even in this case, though, the voices can't be purely sound effects; at the very least they also indicate gender, and therefore gender relations (the aggressive-submissive attitude of the Raelettes to Ray Charles; the butch male choral support for Neil Tennant on the Pet Shop Boys' "Go West"), and it is notable that while rock conventionally uses other male voices, other members of the band, to sing close harmonies, backup singers are almost always female—and remarkably often black female at that.[14] This raises questions about the voice as body to which I'll return; but in talking about the voice as musical instrument I'm not just talking about sound, I'm also talking about skill and technique: neither backup nor lead singers simply stand on stage or in the studio and open their mouths. For the last sixty years or so, popular singers have had a musical instrument besides their voices: the electric microphone. The microphone made it possible for singers to make musical sounds—soft sounds, close sounds—that had not really been heard before in terms of public performance (just as the film closeup allowed one to see the bodies and faces of strangers in ways one would normally only see loved ones). The microphone allowed us to hear people in ways that normally implied intimacy—the whisper, the caress, the murmur. O'Meally notes the importance of the mike for the development of Billie Holiday's singing style, "as she moved from table to table in speakeasies . . . Whether in clubs or on recording dates, she continued to deliver her lyrics as if only for one or two listeners whom she addressed face to face."[15]

The appearance of the female torch singer and the male crooner had a number of consequences both for musical sexuality (crooners were initially heard as "effeminate" and unmanly, for example; the BBC even banned them for a time) and for what one might call musical seduction (radio advertisers took immediate note of "the performer's capacity to make each member of the audience perceive the song as an intimate, individual communication," and Rudy Vallee quickly became "one of the biggest radio and advertising successes").[16] As Bing Crosby, probably the greatest musical entrepreneur of the twentieth century (or at least the one with the best understanding of the implications of technology) realized, crooning made a singer the perfect salesman of his own song.[17]

This wasn't a matter of singers just going up to a microphone and opening their mouths, either. Mike technique had to be learned. Take the case of Frank Sinatra:

> As a young singer, he consciously perfected his handling of the microphone. "Many singers never learned to use one," he wrote later. "They never understood, and still don't, that a microphone is their instrument." A microphone must be deployed sparingly, he said, with the singer moving in and out of range of the mouth and suppressing excessive sibilants and noisy intakes of air. But Sinatra's understanding of the microphone went deeper than this merely mechanical level. He knew better than almost anyone else just what Henry Pleasants has maintained: that the microphone changes the very way that modern singers sing. It was his mastery of this instrument, the way he let its existence help shape his vocal production and singing style, that did much to make Sinatra the preeminent popular singer of our time.[18]

One effect of microphone use is to draw attention to the technique of singers *as singers* in ways that are not, I think, so obvious in classical music or opera, as they move with and around the instrument, as volume control takes on conversational nuances and vice versa.[19] Another is to draw attention to the *place* of the voice in music, to the arrangement of sounds behind and around it, as the microphone allows the voice to dominate other instruments whatever else is going on.[20] Consider these three descriptions of the popular musical voice.

Gregory Sandow on Alex Stordahl's arrangements for Frank Sinatra:

> I didn't know if I'd ever heard music at once so rapt and so shy. I searched for images. Could the arrangements be like waiters in a

restaurant? They took on shape only when they emerged briefly into view to fill pauses in Sinatra's phrasing; they might have been clearing plates away, making room on the table for the next course to be served. Or better still, were they like a wife? That made sense. Stordahl's arrangements, I decided, were like an adoring wife who says nothing in public but works patiently at home, cooking, mending, tending a spotless refuge for her man . . . but it might be more accurate to say that they're like a perfect dance partner, or, better still, like a woman lost in a dream because she's dancing with a perfect man.

Violins introduce "Embraceable You," and I hear her open her arms to surrender. "Embrace me," he sings; she lets him guide her, and, after an all but imperceptible breath, nestles more closely in his embrace. Now he sings ". . . my sweet embraceable you," and in response she whispers, almost to herself, "Oh YES, Frank." "Embrace me," he goes on, and she anticipates his step, moving with him almost before he knows where he himself will go. Then she hears him pause for an instant as he sings "my silk . . . and laceable you"; she waits, suspended, secure that when he resumes he'll know exactly what to do. "I'm in love with you, I am," he croons, and when from far in the distance she hears him add "and verily so," she closes her eyes and dances almost in place, hardly moving in his arms.[21]

Aidan Day on Bob Dylan:

Typically, the voice engages the line of the melody but its simultaneous jarring, atonal separation from the music, together with the relentless subordination of musical elements to the exigencies of verbal order, opens a space which registers a distance and unease involving both singer and listener. The singing voice at once solicits and rebuffs. The gratifications it offers are uncomfortable ones. It is a pattern of invitation and rejection in which the audience—alienated from easy absorption into the music and denied relaxation—is required to attend closely to the transactions between voice and words. While the voice impinges distinctively on the listener, it simultaneously seeks to refuse an unthinking capitulation to itself and to the sense of what it is singing. It is a pattern which places special demands upon an audience, expecting it to participate actively—and to risk itself—in the play of meaning.[22]

And Glenn Gould on Barbra Streisand:

> With Streisand . . . one becomes engaged by process, by a seemingly
> limitless array of available options . . . Like [Elizabeth] Schwarzkopf,
> Streisand is one of the great italicizers; no phrase is left solely to its
> own devices, and the range and diversity of her expressive gift is such
> that one is simply unable to chart an a priori stylistic course on her
> behalf. Much of the *Affekt* of intimacy—indeed, the sensation of
> eavesdropping on a private moment not yet wholly committed to its
> eventual public profile—is a direct result of our inability to anticipate
> her intentions.[23]

Although the voices described here are only ever heard, only exist, as
musical instruments, as sounds in arrangements of sounds, each of these
writers treats the voice as something which *has a relationship*—with an
orchestra for Sinatra, with an audience for Dylan, with the music itself, the
melody, for Streisand; the voice, that is to say, is described as if it existed—
could be heard—apart from the sounds that it does make, apart from what
we do hear. The implication is that all singers thus put "their own shape" on
the music, and it is the meaning of "their own" that interests me.

What these critics hear, to put this more plainly, is a *willed sound,* a sound
that is this way because it has been chosen so, could have been something
else. As Edward Cone suggests, a voice can never really be heard as a wordless
instrument; even when we listen to a singer in a language we do not understand, a singer making wordless sounds, scat singing, we still hear those
sounds as words we do not understand, or as sounds made by someone who
has *chosen* to be inarticulate.[24] "She accompanied herself on the piano," we
observe; not "she accompanied herself on vocals." And the matching term,
unaccompanied, which used to appear on popular concert bills, raises a
broader question still: when singing, do you accompany the music, or does
the music accompany you?

This helps explain, I think, the special status of the voice as a concept in
both musical and literary analysis. On the one hand, a musician's "voice"
need not be restricted to the voice in a physical sense: when jazz performers
are said to "speak" with their instruments, it is this same quality of willed
sound which is being described—which is why it is trickier to claim that
classical musicians, constrained in some respects by the score, have individual
"voices" (rather than styles): even Glenn Gould didn't really "speak" on his
piano (even if he sang along with it). On the other hand, to hear or read a
"voice" in a text is to assign *intention* to what we hear or read. "Authorless"

texts are those—like newspaper headlines or advertising jingles—which however carefully crafted don't bear this imprint of individual articulation.

Even when treating the voice as an instrument, in short, we come up against the fact that it stands for the person more directly than any other musical device. Expression with the voice is taken to be more direct than expression on guitar or drum set, more revealing—which is why when drums and guitars are heard as directly expressive they are then heard as "voices." And this argument has legal sanction. Lawyers in cases of musical theft assume that a voice is a personal property, that it can be "stolen" in a way that other instrumental noises cannot (James Brown's vocal swoop is recognizably his immediately; a guitarist has to prove that a melodic riff, a composition rather than a sound, is unique). The most interesting legal rulings in this context concern soundalikes, cases in which the voices used ("Bette Midler," "Tom Waits") *weren't* actually theirs, and yet because they were recognizably "the same" could nevertheless be adjudged to invade the stars' "privacy," to steal their "personality." To recognize a voice, the courts ruled, is to recognize a person.[25]

Consider now the next element of this process, *the voice as body.* The starting point here is straightforward. The voice is a sound produced physically, by the movement of muscles and breath in the chest and throat and mouth; to listen to a voice is to listen to a physical event, to the sound of a body. This is, of course, true for the sound of other instruments too, but whereas what's involved there is the relationship between the body and something else—a string or reed or piano key or drum set—the voice draws our attention to something happening to the body itself; which is why we don't think of the microphone as a musical instrument: we don't expect voices to need anything outside the body in order to be heard. And this is clearly one reason why the voice seems particularly expressive of the body; it gives the listener access to it without mediation.

The effects of "the body in the singing voice" have been explored most famously by Roland Barthes, in his essay on the "grain" of the voice, where he argues that different timbral qualities have differential bodily implications. This point is usually taken up in rock criticism as a celebration of "the materiality of the body speaking its mother tongue," in terms of the "voluptuous pleasure of its signifier-sounds," but it is just as important to take note of the other side of Barthes's argument, his suggestion that there is such a thing as an "ungrained" voice, a voice that conceals its own means of physical production. This might, for example, be one way of describing those backup singers, further drawing attention to their peculiarity: here we have three smart, fleshly women, singing "grainlessly," while a physically awkward male star waxes *bodily*.[26]

In fact, though, there are further distinctions to be made here. We certainly do hear voices as physically produced: we assign them qualities of throatiness or nasality, and, more specifically, we listen by performing, by reproducing (even if only silently, tentatively) those muscular movements for ourselves, "sympathizing" with a singer by pushing the words up against the top of our mouths when she does. A "grained" voice might, then, simply describe a voice with which, for whatever reasons, we have physical sympathy: "I am sitting in the Met at Leontyne Price's recital in 1985 and Price's vibrations are *inside my body*, dressing it up with the accouterments of interiority."[27]

The voice as direct expression of the body, that is to say, is as important for the way we listen as for the way we interpret what we hear: we can sing along, reconstruct in fantasy our own sung versions of songs, in ways we can't even fantasize instrumental technique—however hard we may try with our air guitars—because with singing, *we feel we know what to do*. We have bodies too, throats and stomachs and lungs. And even if we can't get the breathing right, the pitch, the note durations (which is why our performances only sound good to us), we still feel we understand what the singer is doing in physical principle (this is another reason why the voice seems so directly expressive an instrument: it doesn't take thought to know how that vocal noise was made).

This relates to a second point, that the voice *is* the sound of the body in a direct sense. Certain physical experiences, particularly extreme feelings, are given vocal sounds beyond our conscious control—the sounds of pain, lust, ecstasy, fear, what one might call inarticulate articulacy: the sounds, for example, of tears and laughter; the sounds made by soul singers around and between their notes, vocal noises that seem expressive of their deepest feelings because we hear them as if they've escaped from a body that the mind—language—can no longer control.[28]

Jonathan Swift put his own sardonic gloss on this three hundred years ago:

> Now the art of canting consists in skilfully adapting the voice to whatever words the spirit delivers, that each may strike the ears of the audience with its most significant cadence. The force or energy of this eloquence is not to be found, as among ancient orators, in the disposition of words to a sentence, or the turning of long periods; but, agreeably to the modern refinements in music, is taken up

wholly in dwelling and dilating upon syllables and letters. Thus, it is frequent for a single vowel to draw sighs from a multitude, and for a whole assembly of saints to sob to the music of one solitary liquid. But these are trifles, when even sounds inarticulate are observed to produce as forcible effects. A master workman shall blow his nose so powerfully as to pierce the hearts of his people, who were disposed to receive the excrements of his brain with the same reverence as the issue of it. Hawking, spitting, and belching, the defects of other men's rhetoric, are the flowers, and figures, and ornaments of his. For the spirit being the same in all, it is of no import through what vehicle it is conveyed.[29]

One way in which we hear the body in the voice, to put this more positively, is in the sheer physical pleasure of singing itself, in the enjoyment a singer takes in particular movements of muscles, whether as a sense of oneness between mind and body, will and action (a singer may experience something of the joy of an athlete) or through the exploration of physical sensations and muscular powers one didn't know one had (and the listener, like the sports spectator, enjoys the experience partly by proxy, but also aesthetically, with awe at the sheer grace of, say, Aaron Neville not exactly singing "Tell It Like It Is," but *holding* its notes, turning them over for our admiration).[30]

One effect of such pleasure is that for many singers what they are singing, a word, is valued for its physical possibilities, what it allows the mouth or throat to do. The singer finds herself driven by the physical logic of the sound of the words rather than by the semantic meaning of the verse, and so creates a sense of spontaneity: the singing feels real rather than rehearsed; the singer is responding (like the listener) to the musical event of which they are part, being possessed by the music rather than possessing it. The most obvious device here (listen to Otis Redding live, for instance) is repetition, a syllable being savored, sung again, sung with different consonants, tossed up against different harmonies; but singers may slow things down as well—the young Elvis Presley, for example, seemed to bask (like one of Swift's cantors) in the sheer voluptuousness of his own vocal noise.[31]

Hovering around all of these approaches to the voice as body is the question (Barthes's question) of music and sexuality: what makes a voice *sexy?* What gives a voice its erotic charge? How does the attraction of a singing voice relate to sexual attraction? Gender is obviously one issue here. We've learned to hear voices as male and female (in terms of a biologically based but not determining low/high register, for example), and the singing voice carries these codings with it (which means that a performance artist like Laurie Anderson confuses the-body-in-the-voice no end by using a vocoder to give herself a "masculine" pitch, while Diamanda Galas threatens biological certainties with the sheer range of her vocals).[32]

What, then, is the significance of mainstream rock's generic preference for high-pitched male voices like Robert Plant's, for the articulation of a "hard" rock sound as a man straining to reach higher? In the spring of 1994 Canada's Crash Test Dummies had a worldwide hit with "Mmm Mmm Mmm Mmm," and no one doubted that a major reason for its success was the novelty of Brad Roberts's bass voice, his swollen vowels, the noise rumbling back down in his throat. This was manly singing, authoritative and a bit potbellied. And what made "Mmm Mmm Mmm Mmm" stand out was not that this sound is unusual as such (lots of men must sing in this deep-voiced way) but that it was unusual in today's radio soundscape. Roberts's voice is, by current pop standards, a freak.[33]

In other music contexts the high male voice has been regarded as freakish. Wayne Koestenbaum argues from his operatic perspective that the falsetto is "among the greatest of singing shames." "Long before anyone knew what a homosexual was," he writes, "entire cultures knew how to mock men who sang unconventionally high."[34] And Gary Giddins suggests that

> in American pop song and jazz, the baritone has ruled since the mid '20s, when Bing Crosby sang his first solos with Paul Whiteman and was celebrated for his virility and naturalness. The tenors he displaced were considered effete or affected—unnatural. The very few pop tenors who have appeared in recent decades were treated as novelties and worse: often they were adolescents (Wayne Newton, a castrato-manqué) or lunatic throwbacks (Tiny Tim and his ukulele).[35]

It's easy enough to spot the "unnatural" and "effeminate" rock use of the falsetto too: Frankie Valli's delirious high-pitched recollection of his father's advice in "Walk Like a Man"; Jimmy Somerville's appearance as a cherub in Sally Potter's *Orlando*. But the point is that such readings are matters of convention, not biology. A falsetto is, after all, a man's voice (there's no such thing as female falsetto); and the Crosby who, according to Giddins, "was celebrated for his virility and naturalness" was also the crooner the BBC sought to ban for "going against nature" and Cardinal O'Connell denounced for being "degenerate" and "effeminate."[36]

"Natural" voices, masculine and feminine, are defined culturally and must be understood structurally, as sounds heard against other sounds, and in rock history low, not high, voices have seemed structurally odder, a Captain Beefheart more idiosyncratic than a Jon Anderson. There are some obvious reasons for this. The high voice is heard as the young voice, and rock is a youth form—Frankie Lymon and Michael Jackson remain the teen male models. And one of the lasting effects of doo-wop was to break the male voice up into its component parts such that the combination of *all* its sounds, from low to high, defined masculinity. This remains the norm of male rock group singing, the boys in the band harmonizing above the lead, oohing and aahing just like a bunch of girls (but, of course, not heard like girls at all).

On the other hand, there have been few falsetto rappers so far, and if the youth and doo-wop roots of rock accustomed us to the sound of the high-pitched male voice, it was in a specific expressive context: as the sound of seduction, of intimacy, of the private man. For Britain's soul-inflected singers in particular (Mick Hucknell out of Jackie Wilson and Smokey Robinson) a high voice means not effeminacy (man as woman) but *a ladies' man,* and we now take it for granted that a male voice will move up a pitch to register more intense feeling, that the more strained the note, the more sincere the singer.

What seems odd about this is the relationship of body and voice and sex. It's as if in rock convention (*pace* Roland Barthes and the Barthians) the sexiest male voice is the least bodily—the heaving bosom of the Neapolitan baritone now seems "male" in a decidedly unsexy way (and Demis Roussos's high-pitched tremor thus comes across far more lasciviously than Pavarotti's big-chested tenor). But then Elvis Presley, probably as sexy a male pop singer as there has ever been, for a long time sought (via Dean Martin) to be an Italian balladeer; and what is apparent from his early records is that Presley was, in fact, his own doo-wop act, his bass no more unnatural than his falsetto. I'm perpetually seduced by his voice, and start to wonder: as a man-fan, what am I being seduced by? What am I being seduced for?

There's a simple point here: we hear voices as male or female and listen to what they say accordingly—according to our own sexual pleasures and preferences (which is why gay and lesbian singers can subvert pop standards by *not* changing the words: Ian Matthews bubbling that "I met him on a Monday and my heart stood still"; Mathilde Santing realizing that "I've grown accustomed to her face").[37] The possibilities for confusion here between "natural" and "conventional" voices of desire are well realized in X-Ray Spex's "Oh Bondage Up Yours!"[38] This is one of the most important tracks from the heyday of U.K. punk; its lyric refers both to the sexual bondage items worn by punks for shock value and to a generalized feminist anger. But the politics of the song lies in its voice—which is drawn to one's attention by the spoken intro: this is a "little girl" determined to be heard. And part of our "hearing" is negative, relates to what the voice is not. It is not "feminine"; it is not sweet or controlled or restrained. Such rawness also serves to register the track's punk authenticity—there is no need to assume that this sound reflects the limits of Poly Styrene's own voice; its "unmusicality" is crafted. It is necessary for the song's generic impact. There is, in short, a clear *collusion* here with the listener. The song addresses an "other"—"Up Yours!"—but on our behalf. We can only identify with the singer, with the voice, with the aggression. And if the politics here is a sexual politics, a gender politics, a politics of female identity and desire, then male listeners too are being offered the exhilaration of female de-bondage.

X-Ray Spex deliberately challenged the taken-for-granted reading of "male" and "female" voices both biologically—in terms of what girls do "naturally" sound like—and ideologically—in terms of what girls should naturally sound like. But there was a further question in their music too (or at least in their way of performing their music): does a voice have to be embodied? Must it be gendered? Can a singer *change sex*?

Sean Cubitt has made the point that the simultaneous emergence around the turn of the century of the telephone, the gramophone, and the radio meant that people became accustomed, for the first time ever, to hearing a voice without a body (previously such an experience would have meant the supernatural, the voice of God or the devil).[39]

But, of course, in practice we don't hear telephone or radio or recorded voices like this at all: we assign them bodies, we imagine their physical production. And this is not just a matter of sex and gender, but involves the other basic social attributes as well: age, race, ethnicity, class—everything that is necessary to put together a person to go with a voice. And the point to stress here is that when it comes to the singing voice *all* such readings have as much to do with conventional as "natural" expression, with the ways in which, in particular genres, singing voices are coded not just as female, but also as young, black, middle class, and so forth. In fact, the popular musician's hardest problem has been to develop conventional sounds for the *disembodied* voice—whether the ethereal voice (which is, nevertheless, female—the Cocteau Twins' Elizabeth Fraser) or the heavenly choir (ditto—Morricone's I Cantori Moderni d'Alessandroni); whether the computer voice (which is, nevertheless, male—Kraftwerk) or the collective voice of religious submission (ditto—the Stanley Brothers).[40]

This last strategy is the most interesting (and most successful) because it suggests that to disembody a voice is to rob it of individuality, and this leads directly to the question of vocal identity, to the *voice as a person*. How does a voice signify a person? What is the relationship of someone's vocal sound and their being? As I've already noted, the voice is usually taken to be the person (to imitate their voice is a way of becoming that person—hence the art of the impressionist), and the voice is certainly an important way in which we recognize people we already know (on the telephone, for example). But it is also a key factor in the way in which we assess and react to people we don't know, in the way we decide what sort of person they are, whether we like or dislike, trust or mistrust them. This is one reason why we often think we "know" a singer as part of what we mean by "liking" their voice (and why, similarly, we may feel we "know" the author of a book we like: we hear in it a particular sort of voice).

But having said this, I must add some qualifications. First, a voice is easy to change. As a matter of personal identity it is easier to change, indeed, than one's face (or one's body movements). And this is not just a matter of "acting" in the formal sense. People's voices change over time (as they adapt to the sounds of surrounding voices, to accents, and so forth; the shifting quality of people's voices in class terms, as they are upwardly or downwardly socially mobile, has often been noticed in Britain), and, more to the point, people's voices change according to circumstances—at home or in school, in the office or in bed, with friends or strangers (just listen to how people adapt their voice on the telephone, according to who is at the other end).

The voice, in short, may or may not be a key to someone's identity, but it is certainly a key to the ways in which we change identities, pretend to be something we're not, deceive people, lie. We use the voice, that is, not just to assess a person, but also, even more systematically, to assess that person's sincerity: the voice and how it is used (as well as words and how they are used) become a measure of someone's truthfulness.

In popular music, two points about this are striking. First, "truth" is a matter of sound conventions, which vary from genre to genre. What becomes clear in David Brackett's detailed comparison of Billie Holiday's and Bing Crosby's versions of "I'll Be Seeing You," for example, is that it is almost impossible to hear both of them as sincere: the assumptions that lie behind a reading of Holiday's voice as "witheringly" sad entail our hearing Crosby's voice as "shallow." If Holiday sings "for real," then Crosby, as Brackett puts it, gives "the impression of someone playing a role in a film"; while someone hearing Crosby as reassuringly direct and friendly could only hear Holiday as mannered. How we hear a musical voice, in other words, is tied into how we hear music.[41]

Second, one of pop's pleasures has always been singers taking on other people's voices, and I don't refer here simply to parody or pastiche but also to what Bernard Gendron describes as caricature, the taking on of another voice not as homage or mockery or pretense, but in order to draw attention to its specific characteristics (in the same way that a good comic impressionist doesn't just imitate someone's voice but uses its individual shape to reveal something about its owner). This is most obvious in the white use of black voices in rock and roll history, from Jerry Lee Lewis's "Whole Lotta Shakin' Goin' On," which, as Gendron says, "presents itself as white-boy-wildly-singing-and-playing-black," to Mick Jagger's "I'm a King Bee," which, we might say, presents itself as white-boy-lasciviously-slurring-and-playing-black-sex. No listener could have thought that either Lewis or Jagger was black; every listener realized that they wanted to be.[42]

Which leads me to my second general point about vocal deception: if a voice can be made to change to deceive other people, it can also be used to deceive ourselves. Our "internal" experience of the voice, that is to say, the way we hear ourselves, may not at all resemble how it sounds "externally," to other people (which is why most people are genuinely shocked—and appalled—when they first hear themselves on tape). "Putting on voices" is not something we only do as part of a specific public performance (in a *karaoke* bar, say), or in a specific act of deception; it is, rather, a normal part of our *imaginative* activity. And, as Jonathan Rée has suggested, it may in fact be difficult to know "one's own voice" amidst the babble of the different voices in which we talk to ourselves: "You glimpse the possibility that it is quite arbitrary to try to mark off certain of your vocal performances and nominate them as one voice, the voice that really belongs to you: do you really possess an ownmost, innermost voice which has the power to clamp quotation marks round the others and shrug them off as 'funny'?"[43]

This question seems pertinent too for our experience of hearing voices, of listening to song. The musical pleasure lies in the play we can make of both being addressed, responding to a voice as it speaks to us (caressingly, assertively, plaintively), and addressing, taking on the voice as our own, not just physically, as I've already discussed—singing along, moving our throat and chest muscles appropriately—but also emotionally and psychologically, taking on (in fantasy) *the vocal personality* too.

This is the context in which the voice as character becomes significant. In taking on a singer's vocal personality we are, in a sense, putting on a vocal costume, enacting the role that they are playing for ourselves. But a singer's act in this respect is complex. There is, first of all, the character presented as the protagonist of the song, its singer and narrator, the implied person controlling the plot, with an attitude and tone of voice; but there may also be a "quoted" character, the person whom the song is about (and singers, like lecturers, have their own mannered ways of indicating quote marks). On top of this there is the character of the singer as star, what we know about them, or are led to believe about them through their packaging and publicity, and then, further, an understanding of the singer as a person, what we like to imagine they are really like, what is revealed, *in the end*, by their voice.

Such a multiplicity of voices can be heard in *all* pop forms, whatever the generic differences in how they are registered—whether by Tom T. Hall or Johnny Rotten always "being themselves," by Dory Previn being "The Lady with the Braids" (complete with nervous laughter), or by Frank Sinatra being himself being a late-night melancholic in "One for my Baby"; whether, to be more dramatic, in Patti Smith's rock and roll chronicle, "Horses," in the Chi-Lites' strip cartoon, "Have You Seen Her," or in Meat Loaf's big brother act, "Objects in the Rear View Mirror May Appear Closer Than They Are."[44]

What we take for granted, listening to all these songs, is that they involve *layers* of interpretation, and that in pop it is therefore all but impossible to disentangle vocal realism, on the one hand, from vocal irony, on the other. How does one read, for example, Randy Newman's concert performance of "Lonely at the Top"? Here we have not just a cult singer/songwriter pretending to be a superstar (listen to the audience laugh with him) but also a highly successful writer/composer pretending to be a failure (listen to him laugh at his audience). Or take Michelle Shocked's "Anchorage," the meaning of which, as Dai Griffiths argues, depends on "whether you hear in Anchorage, a place in Alaska, the natural voice of the letter writer, or in 'Anchorage,' a song by Michelle Shocked, the crafted voice of the songwriter." And the pleasure of this lies in the fact that we actually hear *both Anchorage and "Anchorage" at once.*[45]

This returns us to the point from which I started: all songs are narratives; genre conventions determine how such narratives work; words are used to define a voice and vice versa.[46] In one respect, then, a pop star is like a film star, taking on many parts but retaining an essential "personality" that is common to all of them and is the basis of their popular appeal. For the pop star the "real me" is a promise that lies in the way we hear the voice, just as for a film star the "real" person is to be found in the secret of their look. This naturally leads to the issue of performance, but first I want to address two final matters relating to the voice itself: the question of interpretation, and the use in pop music of voices speaking/singing to each other.

In his discussion of the classical song, Edward Cone, as we've seen, distinguishes a song's composer, performer, and protagonist. A number of analytic questions follow from this. For example, does a performer need to know what she's singing about? If she sings the notes correctly and expressively, according to classical convention, as instructed by the composer in the score, will this *in itself* have the character effect the composer intended?[47] Cone proposes an analytic distinction: a protagonist's character is determined by the composer (by the way the music is constructed) but interpreted by the performer, and the question becomes what the relationship is of these two processes: what does an interpreter *do?* Cone also suggests that in responding to this question for themselves, listeners effectively make a choice: either to focus on the music, the piece performed, the character as composed, or on the performance, the performer, the character as interpreted. And he implies that one of the key differences between the art and the pop aesthetic can be found here: the classical concert performance is designed to draw attention to the work; the pop performance is designed to draw attention to the performer.[48]

Does this distinction stand up to pop scrutiny? I would argue, rather, that the pop performer draws attention to performance itself, to the *relationship* between performer and work. Take the case of the torch song, the "elegy to unrequited love," which is, perhaps, the clearest example of the pop singer's interpretive art. John Moore has suggested that the torch singer is best heard as an emotional expert—not an expert on emotions as such (the assumption of the form was that such emotions were universal) but an expert on their expression. Although the torch singers presented particular feelings describing particular situations (romantic illusions and disillusion), our pleasure in the songs lies not in the drama of the event, but in the way the singers explore the nuances of the feeling; torch singing is for both singer and listener an essentially narcissistic art. Torch song lyrics were therefore just signs of the feelings that the singer was to explore through the way they were sung. The music set up a "sense of sadness," the words a "verbal space" within which a voice could tell a story; and the singer applied herself—her critical, musical faculties—to the pleasures and difficulties of interpreting feelings, atmosphere, verse.[49]

Torch singing, in short, was a highly disciplined skill; it was certainly not about "direct" emotional expression or self-abandon. It involved reflection on feeling, not the feelings themselves—Billie Holiday, writes Martin Williams, "had the ability of a great actress to keep a personal distance from both her material and her performance of it"—and part of the sexual charge of the torch song came from the fact that not only were these women singers, as the lyrical protagonists, almost always reflecting on the behavior of men, they were also, as interpreters, reflecting on the words of men. These songs, then (and perhaps this is Cone's point), clearly "belong" to their singers, not their writers. Interpretation in this context does not mean realizing what the composer (or, rather, his music) meant, but using the music to show what interpretation means. Billie Holiday's voice, writes Robert O'Meally, whatever the song she sang, "was always, *always* the heroine."[50]

"Is there actually such a thing as the love song," asks Edward Cone, "outside the conventions of the love song itself?" And the answer is no, with the proviso that conventions are only the beginning of musical expression, not its end, and thus different singers (Ruth Etting and Helen Morgan, Billie Holiday and Bryan Ferry) can take the same words, the same tune, the same situation ("Body and Soul," "These Foolish Things") and use them to provide quite different accounts of love itself, its permanence and transience, its sweetness and humiliation. Voices, not songs, hold the key to our pop pleasures; musicologists may analyze the art of the Gershwins or Cole Porter, but we hear Bryan Ferry or Peggy Lee.[51]

My final question concerns vocal difference: what is the relationship *between* voices in popular song? After all, since the mid-sixties the group (rather than the solo singer) has dominated Anglo-American popular music (at least in terms of male voices), and if such groups more often than not have a "lead" singer we rarely hear his voice completely unaccompanied. We are, that is, accustomed to the idea of a "group voice"—the appeal of both the Beatles and the Beach Boys rested on their (quite different) blend of male voices; while, to take a different genre example, the male vocal trio (on the model of the Impressions) was central to the development of reggae in the 1960s and 1970s.

Such use of voices (rather than voice) can be pushed in two directions. In male group tradition, whether traced from gospel, barbershop, doo-wop (or their intermingling), the emphasis has been, in Keir Keightley's words, on singing as "social co-operation, the submission of individuality to the service of a larger corporate structure," and the "rational" organization of male voices as *sounds*—Lennon and McCartney thus sang "as one" (and it was only later, when we and they wanted to take these songs seriously as art, not pop, that anyone could hear Beatles numbers as "a Lennon song," "a McCartney verse").[52]

In female group tradition, by contrast (and I am deliberately exaggerating this contrast here; in practice male and female groups are not so distinct), different voices are used differently, in a conversational way (which in another trajectory, out of insult ritual, also leads to rap). The voices on tracks like the Shangri-Las' "Leader of the Pack" or the Angels' "My Boyfriend's Back" function as each other's audience; the chorus, dramatically, comments on the story and the action, encouraging the lead singer, disbelieving her, egging her on. Here "corporate identity" is indicated less by harmony singing than by the sharing out of the lead voice itself, and there is a direct continuity between the Shirelles' 1958 "I Met Him on a Sunday" and Salt-n-Pepa's 1991 "Let's Talk About Sex."[53]

As a label, "girl groups" (which may include groups of boys) describes a form which is, by its nature, *dramatic:* girl group records feature—focus on—vocal rhetoric and its effects. And, though less obviously, so does the pop duet (a form which has been somewhat devalued by the current fashion of reviving old stars' careers by getting them to sing along with new stars to no dramatic effect at all). In country music, for example, the man/woman duet is usually conflictual; the male and female voices are registered separately, present their different points of view, with the chorus harmonies suggesting just a temporary truce (the classic pairing here was Conway Twitty and Loretta Lynn). In soul the duet was usually used as a way of intensifying feeling, as a means of seductive talk, male and female voices moving in and to musical and sexual union (listen, for example, to Marvin Gaye and Tammi Terrell).[54]

In rock the most effective duets work not so much with realist effects (a man and woman quarreling or making up) as with star quality and across genre lines. Sinead O'Connor, for example, has been used to brilliant effect as a voice *querying* what's being said by a rapper, on the one hand (in her song with M. C. Lyte, "I Want (Your Hands on Me)"), and by a country singer, on the other (on Willie Nelson's version of Peter Gabriel's "Don't Give Up")—and I defy anyone to listen to her first entry on the latter track without a shiver of recognition that *this* person (with all we know about her) should be telling Willie Nelson (with all we know about him), should be telling him, so surely, so sweetly, to survive.[55]

Performing Rites

Performance

One minute into this performance and she's not wearing
her heart on her sleeve: all of
her internal organs are draped
over her body like a hideous
new skin. Blood seeps through
her pores; stigmata break out
all over, making signs no one
can read. By marshalling an
array of blues and soul man-
nerisms, she contrives an act
that in certain moments—and
you can hear them coming—
ceases to be any kind of act at
all. The means of illusion produce the real, and the real is
horrible, but so vivid you
couldn't turn away to save
your life, or the singer's. It's no
fun: there's an instant in the
last chorus of the performance
when Joplin's voice goes . . .
somewhere else, and it's simply not credible that the music
then ends with an ordinary
flourish people can cheer for.
How did she get back?

**Greil Marcus on Janis Joplin's performance of
"Ball and Chain" at the Monterey International
Pop Festival, 1967**[1]

At one extreme, one finds that the performer can be fully taken in by his own
act; he can be sincerely convinced that
the impression of reality which he stages
is the real reality. When his audience is
also convinced in this way about the
show he puts on—and this seems to be
the typical case—then for the moment at
least, only the sociologist or the socially
disgruntled will have any doubts about
the "realness" of what is presented.

Erving Goffman[2]

My argument in this book is not just that in listening to popular
music we are listening to a performance, but, further, that "listening" itself is
a performance: to understand how musical pleasure, meaning, and evaluation
work, we have to understand how, as listeners, we perform the music for

ourselves. In this chapter I want to explore in detail how pop performance works. One problem here is what is meant by a "performance," particularly now that "the performative" is a familiar term in the literary critical lexicon. I should stress, then, that I am less interested in theories of text than of context, less interested in performance as a means by which a text is represented, "licensed," or made "excessive" than in performance as an experience (or set of experiences) of sociability (it has always seemed to me ironic that the academic effect of Jacques Derrida's musings on what it means to treat a text as an event has been the systematic study of events as texts).[3]

I'm sure, similarly, that postmodern theorists (also much concerned with performance issues) have more to learn from a study of popular music than popular music theorists have to learn from postmodernism. Nick Kaye, for example, concludes the most systematic survey of the "postmodern" in dance and theater by tentatively identifying the term with "an unstable 'event' provoked by a questioning that casts doubt sharply upon even itself," but his relentless attention to the institutionally defined avant-garde means that at no time does he stop to consider to what extent such instability and questioning have always been an aspect of popular performance—something as much to do with the social basis of the event as with the intentions or principles of the performers.[4]

My position, in brief, is that before trying to make sense of performance as a way of working with a text, we should first be sure we understand how performance is different, how it is "non-textual." What makes something a "performance" in the first place? What are its conditions of existence? How does performance-as-acting relate to performance-as-role-playing? What is the difference between performance on stage and performance off stage? Such questions are central to any discussion of performance in popular culture, in which the most interesting phenomenon is, precisely, the shifting boundary between the "staged" and the everyday.[5]

Sticking with a high cultural theory for a moment, then, what would it mean to treat popular musicians as performance artists? Noël Carroll has usefully suggested that the concept of performance art, as developed in the 1960s, is best understood as the entangling of two rather different practices and aesthetics.[6] On the one hand, the term described fine artists using their bodies, themselves, as the material of their art. In terms of art theory what mattered here was the *medium:* art became something living, moving, and, by its nature, changing. Work and artist were "for the time being" the same thing, and the space of art was redefined as a moment or period or *event:* now the work stopped when the artist's show was over. This was, nevertheless, still effectively an *objectifying* process, objectifying the artist herself, whose very being (her shape, her look, her "willed" acts) were constrained by the work's formal requirements. The unsettling question became: where is the "subject"?

On the other hand, performance art described stage performers (actors, dancers) who now took themselves and their bodies as the objects or sites of narrative and feeling. Such performers no longer "acted out" (or "in") a playscript or choreographic score, but effectively *subjectified* themselves: the implication of their work (which depended, as we will see, on a degree of collusion from the audience) was that what was happening on stage was determined only by the nature, shape, technique, body, and will of the performers themselves, which meant, among other things, a new emphasis on the process of putting together and taking apart a *persona*. Such performance involved the dialectic of coherence and incoherence.

Put these two lines of development together—objectifying the artist as the medium of the art; subjectifying the artist as the site of the narrative—and it is clear why performance art called into question a series of binary oppositions set up or assumed by the academic arts (though not, I think, by the popular arts): subject/object, mind/body, inside/outside. I'll come back to these distinctions in pop music terms shortly, but first I want to note two more general issues that emerge from this account of performance art.

First, the term "performance" defines a social—or communicative—process. It requires an audience and is dependent, in this sense, on interpretation; it is about meanings. To put this another way, performance art is a form of rhetoric, a rhetoric of gestures in which, by and large, bodily movements and signs (including the use of the voice) dominate other forms of communicative signs, such as language and iconography. And such a use of the body (which is obviously central to what's meant here by performance art) depends on the audience's ability to understand it both as an object (an erotic object, an attractive object, a repulsive object, a social object) and as a subject, that is, as a willed or shaped object, an object with meaning. Rhetorically, then, performance art is a way not of acting but of posing: it takes for granted an audience's ability to refer these bodily movements to others (in this respect, as in others, Madonna is the most self-consciously "arty" of pop performers, but by no means pop's only performance artist).

My second general point follows from this: the performance artist depends on an audience which can interpret her work *through its own experience of performance,* its own understanding of seduction and pose, gesture and body language; an audience which understands, however "instinctively" (without theorizing), the constant dialogue of inner and outer projected by the body in movement. For performance art to work it needs an audience of performers; it depends on the performance of the everyday.[7]

From a socio-historical perspective it would doubtless be relevant here to point to the increasing significance of performance in everyday life as an effect of urbanization and the decline of intimacy (more and more of our dealings are with people we don't know), as an effect of industrial capitalism (we no longer derive our identity from productive labor), as an effect of commodity fetishism (our consumption is now a matter of imagination, not need).[8] But whatever the material basis for contemporary performance, it is clearly culturally based. Western performance art only makes sense in terms of Western performing conventions—conventions shaped as much in the home and on the street as in the theater and the gallery.

What this means, in turn, is that the body-in-communication in performance art holds in tension not simply the subjective and the objective (the art question), but also the private and the public (the everyday question). In our experience (or imagination) of our own bodies, that is to say, there is always a gap between what is meant (the body directed from the inside) and what is read (the body interpreted from the outside); and this gap is a continual source of anxiety, an anxiety not so much that the body itself but its meaning is out of our control. In most public performances the body is, in fact, subject to a kind of external control, the motivation provided by a score or a script or a routinized social situation, which acts as a safety net for performer and audience alike. It is this safety net which the performance artist abandons, and one can therefore conclude that the essence of performance art is, in the end, embarrassment, a constant sense of the inappropriate. If, in conventional theater, one is embarrassed only when someone forgets a line or is suddenly "out of character," in performance art one is on the edge of embarrassment all the time because the performer is not "in character" to begin with (and the nervous tension among the audience at a "performance" as opposed to a "performance of a play" is palpable).

So far I have been describing performance "art," something defined in the gallery, on the one hand, and the theater, on the other. Performance itself, though, has a history in low cultural spaces too, and I'm sure that performances in popular places and genres (in the music hall and vaudeville, popular song and comedy) are much more akin to performance art than to "legitimate" art or theater. If performance artists in the 1960s turned to such popular forms as stand-up comedy and burlesque, wrestling and the circus, this was not just a postmodern breakdown of high/low cultural barriers; it was also because they had something to learn.[9]

Two aspects of this need further discussion. First, in describing something as a "live" performance we are drawing attention to a situation in which thinking and doing are simultaneous: we are watching willed activity in which it is the will that is active, so to speak. To put this another way, *all* live performance involves both spontaneous action and the playing of a role. This is obvious enough in live music: it must involve a *combination* of improvisation and note-following, with the extremes being a well-drilled orchestra (in which each player still has to will each note, just so) and a free-form solo invention (which must make a gesture at musical expectations even in flouting them). The interesting comparison here is with sports, in which performers may well feel most in control, most free, when, technically, they are playing most correctly.

The sports example is also a reminder that one of the recurring pleasures of popular culture is the difficult or spectacular act, the drama of which lies precisely in its liveness, in the resulting sense of risk, danger, triumph, virtuosity: we need to see things which we know must be live (even if we also know, as in the case of a James Brown show, that for such things to work they must be elaborately planned and rehearsed—they must always work, that is, *in exactly the same way*). What's valued here is not (as in high culture) seeing something unique, but seeing something difficult, something that *takes work*. Far from wanting the means of production to be concealed, the popular audience wants to see how much has gone into its entertainment. Performance as labor is a necessary part of the popular aesthetic.

The second point I want to make here about popular performance concerns "framing." Performance may only make sense through the everyday, but "public performance" also describes something marked off from the everyday, something in which when the everyday does appear it is as a joke, an intruder (which also means, to reverse the argument, that when the everyday turns out to have been a performance, to have been literally framed, by a viewfinder, it comes as a shock: "Smile, please! You're on *Candid Camera!*"). Public "framing," in short, involves the application of the sort of genre rules I've already discussed, rules which determine how both performer and audience should behave (rules which we can see enacted in even the most domestic of home videos).

As the anthropologist Richard Bauman has pointed out, it follows that there is not necessarily a clear distinction in terms of setting between the "staged" and the everyday. What is at issue, rather, is how activities are "staged" *within* the everyday. Thus a way of speaking can, in itself, signify a performance (which describes both an action and an event) by putting an "interpretive frame" around itself, such that listeners no longer treat what is being said as part of normal conversation. In everyday terms the most obvious example of this is probably the joke: joke telling is certainly a performance, even if it occurs within a casual conversation (or within another sort of performance altogether, a lecture, say)—hence people's claims that they "can't tell jokes." What does such "telling" involve?[10]

The relationship between the conversational and the performative is complex, then, involving not just a particular use of language but also a claim to be competent in such use, and an assumption that one's audience is also so competent, or, at least, able to recognize one's talking skills. Unlike ordinary conversation, that is, a performance can be good or bad; it is evaluated. It follows some sort of formal rule, and the anthropologist's question becomes how such a performance is "keyed". How do we know that it is a performance? That it has begun? That it is over?

The answers obviously relate to the genre rules I discussed in Chapter 4, but Bauman also makes three general points that are important here. First, he notes that in anthropological terms a performance may range, in principle, from the completely "novel" (spontaneous invention) to the completely fixed (a traditional religious rite). In practice, as I've already suggested, nearly all performances lie somewhere between these two extremes, and Bauman's point is that this is what enables an audience to *judge* them: by measuring what's original, personal to this performance, against the conventions of the performance form in general. This is one of the problems, of course, for "original" performance art: no one knows how to tell if it's any good or not. And this isn't just a problem for the audience. The success of a performance for a performer can, in the end, only be measured by the audience response (this is what makes it a performance, a kind of oratory). A joke that gets no laughs, a song that gets no response, is a bad performance by definition.

Bauman's second point follows from this: a performance is "an emergent structure"; it comes into being only as it is being performed.[11] As the dance theorist George Beiswanger puts it, performing is a "kind of activity, peculiar to art-making, in which doing and thinking are so aligned that thinking proceeds to deploy what the doing is to be, and doing provides the thinking with a manifest presence. What is thought out is precisely what is done, the thought-out dance and danced-out thought being one and the same . . . dances are events brought forth by performing."[12]

Finally, like Beiswanger, Bauman suggests that performance is an "enhancement," involving a heightened "intensity" of communication: it makes the communicative process itself, the use of language and gesture, the focus of attention. And if for the performers this means prestige (for a good performance, for their skill), for the judging audience too it means an increased sense of *control* over the usual flow of communication: performance is, in this context, a way of standing back from content and considering form. Thus pop listeners are always aware of the tension between an implied story (content: the singer in the song) and the real one (form: the singer on the stage), while pop performers use this tension to destabilize the concepts of content and form in the first place. Björk's "There's More To Life Than This," for example, a track from her fine *Debut* album, was "recorded live at the Milk Bar toilets," and the drama of her performance, its sense of immediacy—a "secret" moment of song snatched from an evening of public display—is more significant for our listening pleasure than the excuse for it, a *faux-naive* on-the-spot song *about* sneaking away from the party. The image that sticks in the mind is not from the song ("we could go down to the harbour and jump between the boats") but from its singing, Björk hiding out in the bathroom.[13]

It is arguable, then, that in this self-conscious games-playing with the musical "event" we have exemplified not the postmodern but the popular. Whereas in both high and folk cultures, performing rules tend to be naturalized (so that everybody carefully avoids noting what a very peculiar event a classical concert or a folk festival is), in popular performance the rules (and the comic or shocking possibility of breaking them) are always on the surface of performance itself.[14] Peter Bailey thus argues brilliantly that the central performing trope in late nineteenth century music hall was a kind of *knowingness*, a *collusion* between performer and (implied) audience, between audience and (implied) performer, which was both inclusive and exclusive, worrying and reassuring.[15]

Bailey's key point is that the best performers in the music halls constructed their own audiences, their own colluders, by using a mode of address which both flattered the audience's social competence and acknowledged its social wariness, its feeling that it might *get things wrong*, a feeling played on by almost every comedian. (Bailey notes the routine use of a butt in the crowd, someone who could stand for cultural incompetence.) More specifically (and it is this which makes knowingness peculiar to the music hall—other forms of popular performance use other forms of collusion), music hall comics could work in the belief that the audience understood what was *not* said, could systematically use both innuendo and parody-by-inflection or, usually, both, as "respectable" English was spoken in a way that mocked its conventions in the very act of using them (which is, again, to come close to the idea of "postmodern" performance).[16]

For contemporary popular music, though, the most significant linguistic source of performing conventions is undoubtedly "talking black," the "speaking behavior" of African-American and African-Caribbean communities described by Roger D. Abrahams, in which there is not (as in European and European-American cultures) a clear distinction between "dramatic-type performance" and "other types of interactional behavior." Rather, workaday talk and conversation are *constantly* framed as performance, as the language used becomes formalized, as speakers "get into it," as the street itself becomes the site of a "constant self-dramatization," "an entertainment of each by the other." Abrahams notes that such "performing by styling" involves the use of body as well as verbal language: "to stylize is to call attention to formal and formulaic features" of both what one says and how and in what situation one is saying it (at home or in public; as a man or a woman; to an audience of men or women; and so forth).[17]

As Abrahams further notes, black slang (often misunderstood when taken over into white talk) systematically describes performance as a collective process—"doing your own thing" means taking your own part in a group drama; to "dig it" means not to understand, to get beneath, but to get involved, to get into. And it is this everyday experience of vernacular performance which has made African-American culture so important as a source of popular performing expertise, of popular performing style.[18]

I argued in Chapter 9 that the meaning of pop is the meaning of pop stars, performers with bodies and personalities; central to the pleasure of pop is pleasure in a voice, sound as body, sound as person. The central pop gesture, a sung note, rests on the same inner/outer tension as performance art: it uses the voice as the most taken-for-granted indication of the person, the guarantor of the coherent subject; and it uses the voice as something artificial, posed, its sound determined by the music. The star voice (and, indeed, the star body) thus acts as a mark of both subjectivity and objectivity, freedom and constraint, control and lack of control. And technology, electrical recording, has exaggerated this effect by making the vocal performance more intimate, more self-revealing, and more (technologically) determined. The authenticity or "sincerity" of the voice becomes the recurring pop question: does she really *mean* it?

And there is an additional point to make here. In the gallery world, one important reason for taking up performance art was its impermanence: the performance artist mocked the ideology of transcendence and the exploitation of art as property (though, of course, tapes of performances were soon marketed). In the pop world, recording made a performance a property from the start (and what happened in a studio in 1935, on a stage in 1965, is now sold as a jazz or rock "classic"), but the most important "permanent" element of pop music culture is not the event but the star. A performance is always, that is to say, a performance in a history of performances; an "image" (like a stylistic "voice") describes change within continuity.

This raises a number of questions about the listening (or spectating or consuming) process—we don't, after all, consume the stars but their performances. If the singer's voice makes public (makes manifest, makes available) the supposed sounds of private (personal, individual) feeling, then these public gestures are consumed privately, fitted into our own narratives, our own expressive repertories.[19] Similarly, if all songs are narratives, if they work as mini-musicals, then their plots are a matter of interpretation both by performers attaching them to their own star stories *and* by listeners, putting ourselves in the picture, or, rather, placing their emotions—or expressions of emotion—in our own stories, whether directly (in this situation, in this relationship, now) or, more commonly, indirectly, laying the performance over our memories of situations and relationships: nostalgia, as a human condition, is defined by our use of popular song.[20]

Just as a singer is both performing the song and performing the performance of the song, so we, as an audience, are listening both to the song and to its performance. For me this is a literal process: to hear music is to see it performed, on stage, with all the trappings. I listen to records in the full knowledge that what I hear is something that never existed, that never could exist, as a "performance," something happening in a single time and space; nevertheless, it *is now* happening, in a single time and space: it is thus a performance and I hear it as one, imagine the performers performing even when this just means a deejay mixing a track, an engineer pulling knobs.[21]

Even without such naiveté, I think it can be argued that the "act" of singing is always contextualized by the "act" of performing; and if the latter, like any other stage role, is put together behind the scenes, the former takes place in public: we see and hear the movement in and out of character; we watch this aspect of the performance *as a performance*. The way singers put roles on and off—"the next song is a slower number"—works differently in different genres, but all methods (irony, earnestness, virtuosity, craft pride, humor)[22] draw attention to the singers' knowledge of what is going on, to their knowledge of our knowledge of what is happening. It's as if the "as if" of the song performance is foregrounded in order to naturalize the "as if" of the musical performance. A skilled rock and role player like Bruce Springsteen seems to adopt the same attitude to his songs, to his band, and to his own performance as the audience itself, and in taking our place, living our reality, he thus enacts his own star persona, as *one of us*.

And it is here that we begin to get interesting divergences from (or glosses on) performance as performance art. For a star is also (to use the industry's own language) an "act"; performance is not as self-revealing as it may seem. To begin with, because pop is primarily a song form, because it involves the use of voice and words, so it is also a dramatic form: pop singers don't just express emotion but also play it (as I argued in Chapter 8, pop songs are, in this respect, more like plays than poems). But pop singers are unlike play actors (though similar to film stars) in two respects.

First, as we've seen, they are involved in a process of *double enactment*: they enact both a star personality (their image) and a song personality, the role that each lyric requires, and the pop star's art is to keep both acts in play at once. This is most obvious in the plainest narrative forms, such as music hall or country music, where performers employ a variety of techniques (more obvious on stage than in the recording studio, though used there too) to move in and out of character. Interruption thus becomes a basic vocal device: the performer's skill is to objectify an expressive gesture at the very moment of its expression, to put quotation marks around it. The singer (Elvis Presley, say) becomes his own audience: is it really *me* singing that? (In country music, with its excessively self-conscious equation of realism and formalism, a central place in this process is occupied by songs about the past: the singer in her present persona responds to the naiveté or ambition of her past self, as expressed in the song; the performer is thus the singer and not-the-singer simultaneously, just as—and this is essential to country ideology—the past is both the present and not the present.)

The second complication in the pop singer's enactment of the pop star is that she (unlike the opera singer, say) is also the site of desire—as a body, and as a person (the film star analogy still holds). In performance, then, in the playing of their various song parts, instead of "forgetting who they are," singers are continuously registering their presence. (This is, perhaps, most obvious for performers who are most remote—Whitney Houston, for example.) Singing, as an organization of vocal gestures, means enacting the protagonist in the song (the right emotions for this part), enacting the part of the star (the moves in keeping with the image), *and* giving some intimation of a real material being—a physical body producing a physical sound; sweat produced by real work; a physicality that *overflows* the formal constraints of the performance.

This raises questions about the sexuality or erotics of performance, and its relation to possession (why do audiences dress up like the stars?), though the issue that most immediately concerns me (one that is raised by performance artists too) is this: what does it mean to make a spectacle of oneself? In the last chapter I suggested that discussion of the voice as body would always be haunted by questions of sexuality. So are discussions of the body as body. To put it simply (to return to the everyday), to perform for an audience as a woman means something different than to perform for an audience as a man—different both in terms of the *social* connotations of what it means for a woman to show her body publicly, to pose, and in terms of the power play of sexual desire.[23] As Susan McClary puts it, a woman's problem is how to keep control of herself in a space, the stage, patrolled by an objectifying sexual gaze conventionalized by hundreds of years of patriarchal command. The female performer is inevitably much more self-conscious than a male performer in that she has to keep redefining both her performing space and her performing narrative if she is to take charge of her situation.[24]

McClary's heroine in this respect is Laurie Anderson; most recent feminist discussion of the issue has focused on Madonna.[25] But women performers in all musical genres have always been conscious of what it means to be spectacularly female. As a country singer, Dolly Parton, for example, doesn't only play on a male notion of femininity, but in *performing* the signs of vulnerability—the little-girl voice, the giggle, the nervous flounce—makes their meaning problematic. Parton's remarkable vocal range—in terms of volume/power rather than pitch as such—draws attention to her art as a singer as much as to her life as a woman. As is typical in country music, her voice (as opposed to her body), though a clearly physical sound, becomes the sign, the trademark even, of her stardom, the meaning around which all her other signs (the hair, the breasts, the gowns) are organized. The song of dependence (common in her repertoire and often self-written) is therefore so obviously crafted, so clearly designed to display vocal skill rather than an emotional state, that at the very least Parton's audience has to consider her lyrical sentiments as ironic. (It is not surprising that she built up a strong camp following.)[26]

By contrast, the English music hall star Gracie Fields, an ungainly, "homely" woman by showbiz standards, took on character roles much more specifically than Parton did and, like other music hall stars, mixed sentimental ballads with comic story songs. By spoofing her voice (rather than her looks), by displaying her vocal range (in terms of style as well as pitch) as a bit of a joke, Fields became endearing, beloved—"Our Gracie"—as a kind of favorite aunt or big sister. (This meant, among other things, that in her films Fields, unlike Parton, always, only, played herself.)[27]

By contrast again (although less of a contrast than one might imagine), Millie Jackson uses the different conventions of soul feeling and the insult ritual to set up another sort of collusive relationship with her audience—or at least with its female part, speaking for it, drawing on innuendo and the unsaid to unfold a conversation that could be taking place in the launderette and then moving dramatically back to the reality of her presence, on stage, with a band, microphone, lights. Like Fields, Jackson's movement from comic routine to ballad implies that, in the end, the comedy is the assumed role, the ballad the real feeling. The message, for all the ideological aggression, is orthodox: all men are shits (laughs) but we love them anyway (sighs). Her strutting public performance acts out a private resignation.[28]

Two issues are significant here, I think. The first is *embarrassment*. Performing involves gestures that are both false (they are only being put on for this occasion) and true (they are appropriate to the emotions being described, expressed, or invoked). Even the most stylized performer, the one with the most obviously formal and artificial gestures, is expressing the self, displaying in public sounds and movements usually thought of as intimate; what the audience wants to see, as Roland Barthes puts it, is "a convinced body, rather than a true passion."[29] In judging a performer we are, as an audience, measuring her gestures against our sense of what she's really like, off stage (what her voice and body really do, in this sort of situation), and even if, from the singer's point of view, this makes it even more important to maintain a clear separation or distance between self and personality, nevertheless, what's on offer is a kind of vulnerability: we might not like her (and in most pop genres performance is, specifically, about being liked).[30]

The performer's problem here is that however carefully crafted the star persona, in performance a real body is involved: singing is not necessarily or even desirably pretty—singers sweat, they strain, they open their mouths wide and clench their throats. To make the necessary musical sounds, singers have to do things (or simulate doing things) which may not "fit" the star body, the star persona. As Koestenbaum says of opera singers, "Singers look like freaks unless they control themselves, and this possibility of looking grotesque is appealing if you choose (as I am choosing) to embrace rather than to reject a stereotypical freakishness."[31]

Performers always face the threat of the ultimate embarrassment: *the performance that doesn't work*. (I have painful memories from my rock critic days of support acts orchestrating an audience response that isn't there, a singalong in which no one else is singing; that was just embarrassing, we muttered in the interval bar.) The appropriateness of a gesture, in other words, can be decided only by its effect. (This is a normal aspect of everyday performance too: a risked intimacy—an endearment, a caress—is always a risked embarrassment; it's the response which decides whether it was, indeed, fitting.)[32]

On the other hand, we also know from everyday life that the way to deflate embarrassment is through self-mockery—we hastily pretend that the gesture was a joke, was meant ironically. As audiences too we often decide (with delight or disdain) that a performer has gone "over the top." This is, in part, the effect of the music in making expressed feelings more intense: a stage performer gets the same sort of emotional charge from her soundtrack as a screen performer gets from his. And music's enveloping effect applies to the audience too: the world can only now be perceived in this emotional state, and the narcissism of the singer, exploring her own feelings, becomes our own. We forget ourselves in the music as part of a condition of collective self-indulgence; we are alienated, as Sartre would put it, in the collective ego.[33] But, further, over-the-top artists deliberately set gestures free from their appropriate setting. The great pop performers (whether Judy Garland or Shirley Bassey, Mick Jagger or Prince) don't so much enact emotional roles as hold their enactments up before us in fragments, so we can admire the shape of the gesture itself.

It is no accident that such performers are camp idols, are beloved (following Susan Sontag) in terms "of artifice, of stylization." Such performers seem to have grasped the camp point that the truth of a feeling is an aesthetic truth, not a moral one; it can only be judged formally, as a matter of gestural grace. "Sincerity," in short, cannot be measured by searching for what lies *behind* the performance; if we are moved by a performer we are moved by what we *immediately* hear and see.[34]

This brings me to the second theme I want to pick up here, *seduction.* Guy Scarpetta suggests that a singer is in the same trade as a prostitute, publicly offering a bliss that can only be experienced privately.[35] We realize that the singer is making us an offer ("Know me!") that is essentially false, yet is true to our fantasy of what the offer might be, that it might be just for us ("To know me is to love me"). The listening fantasy, to put this another way, is that we control the music (the sexual exchange) when, in fact, the performer does. The seductive voice mediates between nature (the real person about whom we fantasize) and culture (the performing person we get); it draws attention both to the social construction of our desire, to its artificiality, and to our obdurately subjective reading of it. The presence of even a recorded sound is the presence of the implied performer—*the performer called forth by the listener*—and this is clearly a sensual/sexual presence, not just a meeting of minds.[36]

What, then, is the role of the body in our understanding of musical performance and musical response? How does the body itself (as separate from the voice) communicate and react? Paul Eckman has usefully suggested that in considering so-called body language, we should move analytically from universal, unconscious, spontaneous bodily "utterances" through a spectrum of socialized body movements to the most stylized, conventionalized, and posed.[37]

First there are the direct physical expressions of emotional states—fear, ecstasy, delight, anger, aggression, timidity, and so forth. There does seem to be a repertory of physical and facial expressions (to go with the vocal noises described in Chapter 9) which are simply human (though we also read them onto animals). In responding to such bodily signs (a baby's smile; an audience's laughter; a friend's fear) we both read their bodies as indicating their emotional state and experience their emotions by reproducing the same bodily and facial movements for ourselves (by smiling, laughing, holding our bodies in the same state of tension).

This is the essence of what John Blacking calls "fellow feeling" (and, for him, a necessary aspect of musical communication). Such movements are, significantly, the hardest to act (it is difficult to laugh or cry to order), and actors normally need to be in the right character or narrative situation to do so—to be, that is to say, in the right state of fellow feeling. Nowadays, Blacking suggests, we tend to feel such "oneness" with other people only in specifically framed situations (as an aspect of particular sorts of hedonistic or religious or aesthetic experience; at climactic moments of love or achievement): "Similar somatic states seem to be induced by drink or drugs or fasting; but I think it would be more correct to say that such devices do not induce the state so much as help suppress the cultural rules that have inhibited their natural expression."[38] And this is obviously relevant to the way in which popular performance is framed, precisely with the promise of such fellow feeling. The usual cultural constraints on expression are suspended, and at the height of enjoyment at a rock concert (or football match), one can and does hug strangers, leap into the mosh pit, turn cartwheels on the floor. Such body movements feel spontaneous, unmeaningful of anything except a diffuse joy.

Second, there are what Eckman calls "illustrative movements," movements tied to the content of a verbal narrative, to the flow of speech. These can be quite unconscious (or "integrated") movements—the hand movements we make (and can't help making) when we speak, as a kind of commentary on what we say: an emphasis here, a shrug there (and tones of voice, bodily *sound* adapted to the nature of what we're saying, are obviously an aspect of this). But even if such movements are unconscious, they are certainly not universal; they are as culturally specific as the languages in which we speak. The point here is not simply that different languages use the body differently (so that one can distinguish French, Italian, and English speakers by sight as well as sound) but also that the same bodily movements may mean different things in different cultures. (A nodded head can be "yes" or "no"; eye contact a mark of respect or contempt. How to touch someone else's body is in most societies the subject of elaborate rules of power and decorum.)

In performance terms, we could also label the "semi-conscious" or intentional acting out of a described emotion as illustrative: in conversation, that is, we find ourselves mimicking the state we describe (in saying we felt sad we "sadden" our face, and so on), and such mimicry (which quickly becomes conventionalized) becomes the basis for the enactment of emotion in mime and pantomime (in the exaggerated bodily and facial movements of the silent screen actor and actress).

Eckman's third category is bodily manipulations, movements in which one part of the body does something to another part. Here we find an odd mixture of our most unconscious movements, nervous tics like head scratching, nose picking, mouth rubbing, nail biting, and so on—actions that we both can't help doing and are embarrassed to be caught at—and the most conventionalized, the language of insults, insulting, it seems, precisely because they draw attention to bodily functions.[39]

Finally there are what Eckman calls emblems, symbolic body movements which have specific (often verbal) meanings that can only be understood by people who know the interpretive rules, the code (and such body language is often, indeed, an aspect of membership in a secret or exclusive society). Obvious examples are making the sign of the cross, auction bidding, the Masonic handshake, and the referees' rulings in American football. Such movements are entirely conventionalized, which is to say that they make no reference whatsoever either to an emotional state or, indeed, to the body as such. It is simply being used as an instrument to write with, as a site to write on.

Two issues emerge from this approach to the performing body. First, at the core of our understanding of body language must be the knowledge that even the most direct form of human expression—the unmediated articulation of fear, anger, ecstasy, and so on—can always be faked (as in the faked orgasm restaurant scene in the film *When Harry Met Sally*). To call something a language is to say that it can be used for lying, and this is a particularly disturbing aspect of body language because its "truth" is tied into our own *unable-to-be-helped* response: someone's "appearance" of laughter or anger is enough to cause our laughter or fear *for real*.[40]

This takes us back to the script as safety net and to the potential for embarrassment when it is removed. A staged performance is framed by a suspension of fellow feeling or, perhaps, by a kind of enactment of it: we know the performer is acting anger, so we act our fearful response. In performance art, though, we don't know if this is an act, and an element of our fear is therefore real—maybe she, Millie Jackson, is going to come to my table and ask my partner about my own sexual performance (and there will be further embarrassment when I reveal my fear of humiliation just as she reveals that this was only an act, after all). Or, alternatively, perhaps she, Judy Garland, is not just acting grief but is really crying, which is to embarrass us in a different way, on her behalf. This is a particularly complex issue given that in performance body language is necessarily a combination of direct and conventional expression.

It is clear, moreover, that questions of gender and sexuality must be central to any account of body language, if only because the body is the key to the social meaning of both. On the one hand, sexual differences are directly read from physical differences (A has visible breasts, B doesn't; A is a woman, B a man); on the other hand, these biological differences are coded culturally into different *uses* of the body which have nothing to do with biology at all. And it is because men and women are seen to move differently that trans-gressive performance becomes possible, as a fertile form of sexual lying.[41]

So far I've been talking about the body as an expressive site or medium, assuming that an internal state or statement is externalized as a body shape or movement which is then interpreted, given meaning, by reference to the intention or feeling that produced it. And this is certainly one way in which we routinely listen to music and read performers. But we need to consider also the body's relationships *outside,* its place in the material world.

To begin with, take clothes. Clothes offer the body its most intimate traffic with the outside world (a point brilliantly made in *Paris Is Burning*), and there is by now a well-established literature that treats clothes (or fashion) as a language too. The implication here is that it is the clothes themselves that do the talking; beneath them is a kind of universal (if aged and gendered and racialized) body. This is the Emperor's New Clothes model: clothes are the way the body speaks; without them it has nothing to say. Hence the pop significance of dressing up, making up, Madonna's endlessly "revealing" costumes.

But as Anne Hollander has argued so persuasively, the relationship of clothes and body is more complex than this model implies.[42] Bodies them-selves bear the imprint of clothes. Social signs, that is, are written on the body itself, on its shape, its size, its texture, its curves and bones and flesh and hair. Stage clothes, stage costumes, don't necessarily *transcend* physical circum-stances (think of those clodhopping British glitter bands of the early 1970s like Sweet and Slade), and band uniforms depend, for their effect, as much on the musical relationships between a group's members as on their design features. How musicians look—how casual, how smart—clearly affects how at first we hear them (and most pop fans quickly realize that the most casual clothes are carefully chosen: it's the *same* ratty T-shirt every night). But we don't just experience a musician's body as costumed. As Ornette Coleman explains,

> For me, clothes have always been a way of designing a setting so that by the time a person observes how you look, all of their attention is on what you're playing. Most people that play music, whether it's pop, rock or classical, have a certain kind of uniform so they don't have to tell you what you're listening to. I always thought that if this was the case, why wouldn't I try to design from the standpoint of the opposite of that? Have the person see what you have on and have no idea what you were going to play. I'm not playing to represent what I'm wearing, and I'm not dressing to represent what I play.[43]

The point here is that the musician's body is also an instrument. Much of the discussion of body language treats the body as an autonomous object, something defining its own space. In fact, though, much (if not most) body movement is determined by other bodies (by parents and children and lovers and friends) and by the use of tools (whether at work or play). The use of the body as an instrument involves, in fact, two components. On the one hand, the *material* we work on determines our movements (when writing, cuddling, driving, sewing)—in musical terms the instrument we play thus determines the instrument our body must be (standing up, sitting down, bowing or blowing, hitting or pulling).[44] On the other hand, our movements are also determined by our *purpose* (to write a letter, comfort a child, go to the store, make a shirt, play a certain sort of note).

To describe body movement, then, is to describe both *what* is being done and *why* it is; to read body movements, to interpret them, is always to put them in a story. The same physical acts may be described as writing or doodling, as caressing or harassing; we refer here not to what we see but to what we infer (because of the situation, the characters, the plot). And the further complication here is that bodily movements (this is particularly obvious for musicians) depend on physical capacities, on learned competence. The body can't always do what we want it to, and what we see may mark a *failure* of purpose.

In pop terms, the most commonly learned form of musical movement is dance, and the most familiar setting for performing anxiety the dance floor. The starting question here is a simple one: what does it mean to move to music? Among performers (I'll come back to the audience shortly) we can distinguish between techniques of *interruption* and techniques of *enslavement*, between devices that signal listening to music by disrupting it, and devices that signal listening to music by being absorbed in it. In some musical genres the spontaneity of a show is indicated by the performers' mistakes, their broken strings, their false starts and ruffled endings; in others the musicians' total engagement with what they're doing is indicated by the precision of their changes, the perfection of their harmonies. Then there's the question of what musicians do when they are not playing: is their interest in their colleagues' sounds best shown by movement or stillness, by concentration or abandon? Silent singers perform their continuing stage role in various ways, but most deliberately move as musicians (rather than as listeners), grab castanets rather than go into a choreographed routine.[45]

The relationship of "listening" to music and "moving" to music is, in short, a matter of convention, as is what sort of movement to make; even a spontaneous response has to be coded as "spontaneous." The next question is when does a movement-to-music become a dance-to-music, and there are two issues here: the nature of the connection between what's heard and what's done, and the question of form, the relationship between one movement and another—how free are we to move, how do we know what movement is appropriate? The issue here is control: dancing is to walking, one might say, as singing is to talking. When dancing we subject our body movements to musical rules (we are less free than when we walk), and yet in our very self-consciousness we seem to reveal more clearly our physical sense of our selves; we are more self-expressive. As Francis Sparshott puts it, "Dance, then, is a mode of behaviour in which people put themselves rhythmically into motion in a way that transforms their sense of their own existence in a way that is at once characteristic and strongly qualified according to the dance performed."[46]

The art and ballet critic Adrian Stokes once noted that to add music to a scene is to frame it, to make the movements in it (people walking to and fro) look different, less natural. As spectators we become more aware of people's body movements (trying without thinking to relate them to a musical shape), and they look to us themselves more self-conscious. Movement to music seems more willed than movement without it; more thought is going into it—when to put one's foot down, when to pause and turn—and even when holding still one's posture now seems more consciously crafted. The analogy that comes to mind here is listening to a strange tongue: we distinguish between someone babbling and someone speaking an unknown language according not to what we hear but to what we assume about what we hear: language, unlike babble, is taken to be ruled, the words consciously chosen for their meaning. Adding music to a scene gives all the movements in it an implied intention: babble becomes speech, a walk becomes a dance, even if we don't understand it.[47]

Dance is not simply a heightened or more intense form of movement, then; rather, it is movement which *draws attention to itself,* in the very act of ceding control to the music—this is the difference between a movement that coincides with a beat and a movement that submits to it. (In the video of "Papa Don't Preach," for example, when does Madonna stop walking to the rhythm and start dancing to it?)[48] For Adrian Stokes, a balletomane, the question becomes: is a ballet dancer totally in control of her movements (all of which are decidedly unnatural, depending on years of training, skill, and self-discipline) or totally out of control of them (with *everything* she does determined by the score and the choreographer)? The dancer's technique, that which allows her body to do whatever the dance requires, is precisely that which allows her to forget about her body altogether and just think the music (the parallel with sport is again applicable here: the unnatural fitness to which a soccer player brings his body enables him to forget it, as a body, when he's playing—which no doubt explains why soccer players, like dancers, are recurrently injured: they also forget what frail things their bodies really are).

Dance, in short, is willed movement (people only dance on hot bricks by analogy), but it is also unnecessary movement, an end in itself rather than a means to another end (like walking to the store for milk or passing the ball to the inside right).[49] Dance movements are chosen for aesthetic rather than functional reasons—dancing to the store isn't the quickest way to get there, and dancing back may well mean dropping the bottle; there's an analogy here with the poetic use of language: describing the fire in sonnet form is not the most efficient way of clearing the building, even if the sonnet is still about the fire, just as dance is still about moving across a space. The anthropologist Roderyk Lange thus describes dance as "poeticised" walking—a form of movement in which we are "carried" by the music, and experience an "unusual degree of continuity" in our actions. They relate to each other now according to the logic of shape and sound rather than means and ends; again there's an obvious analogy with the "poetic" use of language, words chosen for the logic of a poem's rhythm, shape, and sound, not just to convey meaning.[50]

What makes a dance movement attractive or, to use the key word, graceful? To some extent such a judgment depends on genre conventions, but whether we're describing Margot Fonteyn or Michael Jackson, Cyd Charisse or John Travolta, Will Crooks or Siobhan Davies, the common factor seems to be ease of movement, a sense of bodies become somehow *immaterial*—as if the music flows through them without any physical hindrance at all. As Sarah Jeanne Cohen notes, "To be dramatically compelling on stage, the dancer cannot allow *involuntary* movement to distract the viewer."[51] The dancer, in other words, conceals her efforts, draws attention to the created form rather than the process of creation.

On the other hand (given the aesthetic of effort), at the populist end of dance there clearly is pleasure to be taken in virtuosity and spectacle, in high leaps and difficult turns.[52] The work that goes into these is certainly not concealed, and this is as true for Russian ballet dancers as for New York break dancers.

Sally Banes describes what happened to break dance when it became "art":

> The media hype about break dancing has changed both its form and its meaning. So to talk about break dancing you have to divide it into two stages: before and after media. Before the media turned breaking into a dazzling entertainment, it was a kind of serious game, a form of urban vernacular dance, a fusion of sports, dancing, and fighting whose performance had urgent social significance for the dancers. After media, participation in break dancing was stratified into two levels: professional and amateur. For the pros, break dancing had become a theatrical art form with a technique and vocabulary that, like ballet's, could be refined and expanded. On this level, competition took on new meaning. It was no longer a battle for control of the streets, for neighbourhood fame, or to win your opponent's "colors" (tee-shirt with crew insignia). Now cash prizes, roles in Hollywood movies, and European tours were at stake. For the amateurs, the element of competition had diminished. The appeal was a mixture of getting physically fit, tackling the challenge of breaking's intricate skills, and even becoming more like street kids, who've suddenly become stylish thanks to the meteoric vogue of hip hop.[53]

In tracing the way the meaning of break dance changed as it moved from an amateur to a professional setting, Banes raises general questions about the differences between various forms of stylized movement. What is the difference, for example, between dance and gymnastics? Answer: the different factors controlling the body's moves: music rather than equipment, choreographic convention rather than competitive rules. What makes dancing different from ice dancing? Answer: in principle, nothing (ice dancing is mostly performed as a competitive sport, but that is not necessary to the form). But we're beginning to touch now on the aesthetic problem at the heart of dance analysis: if dance is a communicative art, what does it communicate, what is it about? Why, as Sparshott asks, should we attend to it? What, for example, do we mean by a good dancer? What are we describing? A physical skill? The dancer's ability to make us feel that she is somehow exempt from the law of gravity? Or something else—an interpretive skill, the ability to use the body to say something?[54]

In terms of physical display, there was a direct continuity between break dance as street and as theater art, but in terms of dance meaning there was an equally clear change of focus. As Banes notes, its "body symbolism" had made break dancing "an extremely powerful version of two favorite forms of street rhetoric—the taunt and the boast," but such rhetoric lost its point once staged for the art audience: the dance now represented the boast and the taunt, rather than being them.[55]

When we talk about dance we are almost always talking about movement to music.[56] The question therefore comes back to this: does a dancer, any sort of dancer, express the music, or respond to it? If, as Lange suggested, to dance is to let oneself to be carried by the music, to be moved by it (rather than by where one wants to go), then in what sense is this a personal matter? Does one have a heightened sense of oneself when one dances, or no sense of oneself at all? I don't know the answer to that question (both, I think), but one does, without a doubt, have a heightened, more intense, above all more concentrated sense *of the music.* Dancing (if not watching dancing), is, in this respect, a form of enhanced listening, which is why a good club deejay can play a club as if choreographing a dance (and why disco dancers on the floor are no more dancing apart than ballet dancers on the stage).

A question still remains, though: how do dancers know how to listen to the music, what to listen for? And clearly the answer depends on the genre. Conventions of dance performance are genre-based; they follow a combination of stylized and naturalized movements, of learned and spontaneous responses. (In my own experience, it is in learning how to dance to a music—watching what other people are doing and copying them—that we learn how best to listen to it.) And conventions also determine what the dance is "about." In classical ballet, after all, the dancer is not just dancing the music, but dancing a character, a narrative role, and Edward Cone thus distinguishes the "art dance" from the "natural dance" and the "ritual dance." But certain pop performers too (Madonna, Prince, Mick Jagger, most obviously) dance a part, dancing *to* the music but *in* character, and much vernacular dance has used mime, the dancer representing the movements of an animal, a work process, a social type.[57]

Dance is an ideological way of listening; it draws our attention (not least in its use of space and spaces) to arguments about its own meaning (think of the difference between classical, modern, and postmodern ballet, between ballroom and break dancing, between a hop and a rave). And dancing, like listening, doesn't come naturally: to dance to music is not just to move to it but to say something about it—whatever else the performer may tell us from stage, what they really think about their music is shown by how they move to it. The meaning of heavy metal is best articulated by head-banging, male bonding in futility, just as the most profound statement of what Motown meant in the twenty-fifth anniversary Motown TV show was Michael Jackson's glide across the stage in front of footage of old Jackson 5 stagecraft, a movement both exhilaratingly free and frighteningly precise.

It is somewhat ironic, then, that in self-consciously studying "performance," cultural analysts have paid far more attention to pop videos than to stage shows. There are various reasons for this: performance is taken to be a postmodern topic, pop videos are taken to be a postmodern medium, and so the two naturally go together; videos are now ever-present in the home: they're probably the way most teenagers now see most performances, and they're certainly the way most academics do; the most interesting contemporary performers (that is to say, Madonna) use music video as their performing medium, and therefore video is the source of pop's most interesting performance practices.

There's truth in all these assumptions, but there's also (as so often with postmodern theory) a willful ignorance of history: videos are analyzed as if pop stars didn't perform before there was a camera to record them (and as if pop's performing conventions weren't long ago established in both cinematic and televisual terms). The pop video is important, in other words, not because it compels musicians to perform in quite new ways (though it may sometimes do this), but in the way it necessarily draws on (and therefore brings to our attention) established performing conventions and adapts them to new technological and selling circumstances.[58]

From my perspective, then, music videos are less interesting as mini-films, as visual narratives, than as ideal types of performance, as visual frames, and the most obvious differences between video styles reflect musical rather than filmic conventions. As we've seen, different pop genres offer quite different accounts of the relationships between performer and audience, performer and song, performer and performer. These distinctions must be articulated in video: a credible heavy metal musician looks and acts quite differently than a credible country star.[59] And, just as important, a heavy metal crowd registers its pleasures quite differently than country music fans do. In framing performance for television, pop videos (like TV music shows before them) pull away from the stage (if only metaphorically) to show the auditorium as well. They reveal as much about the meaning of the music in the shots of people listening to it as in the footage of the people playing it.[60]

My conclusion from this is that videos are ideologically important not because they bring new concerns to pop performance (and certainly not as some sort of postmodern disruption of musical narratives) but because they enable musicians (or their record companies) to translate their performing ideals into televisual terms directly, without having to be mediated by the established norms of TV entertainment. However, two innovative aspects of video production are worth noting. First, video performance isn't restricted to the usual performing settings. While most videos do, in fact, set their stars front stage and in the recording studio or back stage and in the rehearsal room, they also move them out of a musical context—into the everyday (the street, the home); into the fantastic (the dream, the wilderness). And what makes such movement coherent is not the song (the closer the match between setting and lyric, the more banal the video) but the performer (whose ability to impose herself on all visual circumstances parallels the ability of the live performer to impose herself on all musical circumstances, to register the continuity between sad and happy song, rocker and ballad).

As video stars, pop performers have to play themselves. They are not acting out stories (videos are not operas). Video foregrounds the performance of music rather than the music itself. We don't take the musicians to be interpreting the song; rather, our response is to interpret the musicians. Video performers are taken to be the authors of what we see (videos are not watched as examples of either directors' or songwriters' art), which is why video was an empowering medium for female acts, whatever the sexist or "objectifying" visual elements involved.[61] Pop videos, in short, foreground performance-as-seduction and forestall performance-as-embarrassment. If nothing else (and this relates to the long history of music photography, framing the musician as pinup as well as stage star), video is now a key component in our understanding of music as erotic.

Technology and Authority

Not the voices of animals but their entrails are important to us, and the animal to which music is most indebted is not the nightingale but the sheep.

Eduard Hanslick[1]

The life of the touring blues musician, Charles Keil has observed, furnishes all the loneliness and jealousy he needs to sing the blues authentically. It is a strong extract of modern life. The recording situation is an even stronger and more representative extract. The glass booths and baffles that isolate the musician from his fellow musicians; the abstracted audience; the sense of producing an object and of mass-producing a commodity; the deconstruction of time by takes and its reconstruction by splicing—these are strong metaphors of modern life. Their mirror images in the listener's experience are solitude; the occlusion of the musician; the use of music as an object and a commodity; the collapse of a public architecture of time and the creation of a private interior design of time. Since they contradict everything that music-making once seemed to be, they are paradoxes.

Evan Eisenberg[2]

Who said that musicians are the only ones that can make music?

Hank Shocklee[3]

In its most basic definition, the technology of music simply refers to the ways in which sounds are produced and reproduced. From this perspective the history of music can be divided into three stages, each organized around a different technology of musical storage and retrieval.[4]

In the first (or "folk") stage, music is stored in the body (and in musical instruments) and can only be retrieved through performance. Music is either marked off from the everyday as ritual and ceremonial, or is so totally integrated into everyday social practices (work song, for example, or lullabies) as to be part of their meaning. In the second (or "art") stage, music is stored through notation. It can still only be retrieved in performance, but it also has now a sort of ideal or imaginary existence (against which any individual performance can be measured—and found wanting). Music becomes a potentially sacred experience; it gives us access to the transcendent (and, as in the appreciation of classical music, the musical mind is thus elevated over the musical body). In the final (or "pop" stage), music is stored on phonogram, disc, or tape and retrieved mechanically, digitally, electronically. This transforms the material experience of music: it can now be heard anywhere; it is mobile across previous barriers of time and space; it becomes a commodity, a possession. And yet ideologically—as a matter of interpretation and fantasy—the old values remain (presence, performance, intensity, event), and listening to recorded music becomes contradictory: it is at once public and private, static and dynamic, an experience of both present and past. In the world of recordings there is a new valorization of "the original." It is as if the recording of music—its closeup effect—allows us to recreate, with even greater vividness, the "art" and "folk" experiences which the recording process itself destroys.

It is clear, for example, that recording technology (particularly following electrical recording and the development of magnetic tape) allowed classical record producers to claim that their work represented the perfect (or impossible) musical object embedded in the score. Using tape splices, retakes, remixes, and so on, it became possible for a performer like Glenn Gould to set aside the usual "hazards and compromises" of concert performance, and to take to the recording studio "in a quest for perfection."[5]

Walter Legge, the pioneering British classical record producer, thus claimed,

> I was the first of what are called "producers" of records. Before I established myself and my ideas, the attitude of recording managers of all companies was "we are in the studio to record as well as we can on wax what the artists habitually do in the opera house or on the concert platform." My predecessor, Fred Gaisberg, told me: "We are out to make sound photographs of as many sides as we can get during each session." My ideas were different. It was my aim to make records that would set the standards by which public performances and the artists of the future would be judged—to leave behind a large series of examples of the best performances of my epoch.[6]

This involved not only "artificial" events in the sense of assembling performers just for the recording session, in halls and studios organized for recording-suitable acoustics, but also the creation of ideal performances from the fragments of real ones, from the assemblage of different takes and re-recordings. Records made available musical experiences which were unrealizable "live." At Decca in the 1950s and 1960s, for example, John Culshaw "demonstrated that the three-dimensional spatial illusion created by stereo could be used to sharpen dramatic focus, that varied acoustical ambience could articulate and colour individual scenes." Benjamin Britten "actually composed into [the *War Requiem*] the effects of placement and distance that Culshaw and his team had become so expert at realizing."[7]

The debate on classical music technology orchestrated by Glenn Gould in *High Fidelity Magazine* in 1966 focused on the question of the recording as a musical object: was it an event (a real or fake live performance) or a work (a score, the piece of music itself)? The resulting arguments reflected the ongoing implications of classical music ideology: on the one hand, the orchestral concert had been held up for well over a century as being, in itself, the transcendent musical experience; on the other hand, the recorded works at issue were pieces of music composed long before recording technology was available, pieces of music long familiar *as* live performance. Even in the 1960s, then, the classical music world was wary of musical perfection achieved through studio "cheating," and the suggested analogy between a much spliced or over-dubbed record and a much revised or edited manuscript (see the quote by Babbitt below) didn't quite work: we don't measure our individual experience of reading a book against even an imaginary public reading.[8] The 1960s arguments would have been different (as they were in pop and rock) if the classical works at issue hadn't already had a "live" existence quite apart from their recording. (As we'll see, there are doubts about recording technology in all musics that are ideologically committed to performance as collective *event*.)

Take the suggested elevation of the work as it "ought" to exist, as it *could* exist, above any particular performance of it. Milton Babbitt, composer:

> I can't believe that people really prefer to go to the concert hall under intellectually trying, socially trying, physically trying conditions, unable to repeat something they have missed, when they can sit home under the most comfortable and stimulating circumstances and hear it as they want to hear it. I can't imagine what would happen to literature today if one were obliged to congregate in an unpleasant hall and read novels projected on a screen.[9]

Adorno, interestingly, used a similar analogy in arguing that opera is a musical form best suited to the LP:

Shorn of phoney hoopla [the hoopla of both live stagings and radio and television opera broadcasts], the LP simultaneously frees itself from the capriciousness of fake opera festivals. It allows for the optimal presentation of music, enabling it to recapture some of the force and intensity that has been worn threadbare in the opera houses. Objectification, that is, a concentration on music as the true object of opera, may be linked to a perception that is comparable to reading, to the immersion in a text. This offers an alternative to that which opera does in the best case—and which is just what an artwork ought not do—that is: cajole the listener. The form of the gramophone record comes into its own as a form of sound figures. The ability to repeat long-playing records, as well as parts of them, fosters a familiarity which is hardly afforded by the ritual of performance. Such records allow themselves to be possessed as one previously possessed art-prints . . . LPs provide the opportunity—more perfectly than the supposedly live performances—to recreate without disturbance the temporal dimension essential to operas . . . The form of the LP makes it possible for more than a few musically engaged people to build up such a museum [of opera] for themselves. Nor need they fear that the recorded works will be neutralized in the process, as they are in opera houses. Similar to the fate that Proust ascribed to paintings in museums, these recordings awaken to a second life in the wondrous dialogue with the lonely and perceptive listeners, hibernating for purposes unknown.[10]

"Liveness," in short, whether defined in social or physiological terms, is *not* essential to musical meaning.

On the other hand, it is equally clear that to record a work is just as much to interpret it as to perform it in any other way. Glenn Gould himself defended tape-splicing in these terms: "One cannot ever splice style—one can only splice segments which relate to a conviction about style." But one can then criticize engineers for "misinterpreting" the music, for being poor "performers." Goddard Lieberson, record company executive:

I don't believe the engineer should intrude between the composer, or performer, and the listener and suddenly make you hear a flute or trumpet. I think the next step will be a regression back to the old days, with fewer microphones placed further away both to give perspective and to let the ears listen on their own. If a composer wants to write the other way, he should frankly call his piece a String

Quartet for Four Instruments and Four Microphones; that is quite a different sound than for instruments alone.[11]

The question begged here is the relationship between the "perspective" of the recording studio, that of the concert hall, and that of the living room. Even if people want the concert hall experience in their homes, the living room is a different acoustic setting, and the acoustic organization of the sounds must therefore change, even if only to have the same effect, to give "the illusion of the concert hall illusion" as RCA's Richard Mohr calls it. Gould quotes the pianist Claudio Arrau as objecting to concert hall recordings on the grounds that "stratagems . . . designed to fill acoustical and psychological requirements of the concert situation, are irritating and anti-architectural when subjected to repeated playbacks." The problem here is not just a shift of musical space (from concert hall to living room) but a change in musical time (from an experience of the unique to an experience of the repeated).[12]

And musical space-time is, as we have seen, itself an ideological construct. LeMahieu quotes a 1926 *Gramophone* review of *Adeste Fideles,* one of the first Columbia releases using electronic recording technology: "The result overwhelmed me. It was just as if the doors of my machine were a window opening on to the great hall in which the concert was held."[13] Obviously what was at critical issue here was the acoustic status of the "as if": a statement of an ideal, not an actuality. Meanwhile, from a popular cultural perspective, Philip Brophy suggests (with reference to the move from silent to talking pictures) that "sound may have set dramatic film back on a course of *theatrical mechanics* due to its reinstatement of the human voice in the narrative space."[14] We take it for granted now, that is, that the voice will dominate the film soundtrack (just as we take it for granted that the voice will dominate the song soundtrack). Films or records for which this isn't true sound "difficult" or shoddy, badly produced and badly mixed, whether deliberately or not. But, again, what's at issue isn't a "natural" sound badly recorded, but an ideological acoustic hierarchy, in which some sounds are just "naturally" more important.

Gould thus argues against live recordings as being, by their nature, "archive" recordings: they reveal in documentary fashion something about their times—how Beethoven was interpreted *then*—but they are therefore "indisputably of and for their time. They spurn that elusive time-transcending objective which is always within the realization of recorded music."[15]

While technology may liberate the music work from its performance in one way, it opens it up to new possibilities of humiliation in another. In Gould's words, "at the centre of the technological debate, then, is a new kind of listener—a listener more participant in the musical experience. The emergence of this mid-twentieth-century phenomenon is the greatest achievement of the record industry." Consumer choice means we decide what to listen to from among our records. (The gramophone, wrote Percy Scholes in 1924, "allows every man to decide for himself.") It means we decide which tracks to play and in which order. And it means we decide how loudly to play them, with what balance (left to right), what tone (treble to bass), what mix.[16]

Even in the 1960s, before digital recording and domestic equalizing devices, Goddard Lieberson was disturbed by the implications:

> I believe the listener should leave his phonograph alone; if he wants to get into the picture, let him play the piano. I would like to see a standard set with phonographs whereby even the volume could not be changed. Then you would finally have what the artist wanted. If you carried the opposite to its ultimate, you would end up with a printed piece of music to be played mechanically, with instructions to the customer to set his own tempo and dynamics; then everybody would be his own Beethoven interpreter.[17]

The folk arguments about technology and the "original" sound are different. Charles Keil, for example, argues that "in class society the media of the dominant class must be utilized for [a vernacular] style to be legitimated." In the 1920s, for example, the new media of radio and records seemed to "call forth" new forms of "ethnic" music (his examples are polka and blues), distinct American sounds that "could not be created and legitimated without being part of the new mainstream channels of communication." Polish musicians had to produce something that would still sound authentically Polish to their Polish immigrant communities *on the radio.* "The legitimating function of records and radio for blues is less clear," according to Keil, but he suggests that there is evidence that "all the best known blues artists from 1930 forward learned as much or more from records as from oral transmission." Evan Eisenberg pushes this point further with respect to jazz:

> I will argue that records not only disseminated jazz, but inseminated it—that in some ways they created what we now call jazz. It is important to remember, first of all, that numbers were often "composed" just before a recording session. As record companies did not like to pay royalties unless they had to, published tunes were avoided; but if one of the musicians came up with a tune, that came under his flat fee. So even regularly performing bands, when they recorded, often put aside their well-worn, worked-out routines and threw

together fresh ones . . . Armstrong said of Oliver, "When he started makin' records, he started bein' a writer. Ha ha ha!"[18]

In considering the relationship between technology and origin in vernacular culture, Keil himself makes two important points. First, rather than a "folk" style developing "naturally," as it were, out of sight or hearing of the media until it becomes too big or noisy to be ignored (the supposed rock 'n' roll story, for example), it actually develops *in* the soundscape mapped by the media—whether providing different pleasures to those of mainstream mass culture, or offering opportunities to local media entrepreneurs (providing "residual cultural resources" for "petty capitalists"). Noting the emergence of distinctively "rough" polka and blues styles in the 1950s, Keil asks, "Does the simultaneous opening up of the radio and record industries invite the 'down-home' blues and 'village' polkas out of the little taverns and into a redefined and more subtly mediated public space, or do these rough and ready styles rudely push themselves forward from the bottom up?"[19]

Second, Keil takes up Nietzsche's suggestion that Apollonian and Dionysian arts emerge from "the separate art worlds of *dreams* and *intoxication*." Keil suggests that in the vernacular art worlds of polka and blues, there were, indeed, two aesthetics. Rather than the recording achieving the perfection that the performance couldn't (the Glenn Gould model), the recording offered one sort of pleasure (the perfection of a form, a dream state) while live performance offered another (the pleasure of a process, risk and excitement, intoxication). Keil was originally curious about why there was so little live recording of polka and blues: was it really true, as it seemed, that these vernacular communities (unlike the classical audience) didn't want their records to represent live events?

> I suspect that the perfectionism in blues and polka recordings is an expression of people's preferences, musicians and their audiences wanting the cleanest and most sophisticated versions of their music in public space. Once norms are established, "recorded blues" and "recorded polkas" [recorded down-home blues; recorded honky-tonk-style polkas] take on a perfectible Apollonian dreamlife of their own. In polkas, for example, bands routinely record with upright string bass and a regular piano twenty years after these instruments disappeared from live performance because "that's the way polka records should sound." Many polka bands rehearse only when they have a recording session to prepare; the shared tradition of evergreen standards can sustain any band in live performances without rehearsing and through any changes in personnel.[20]

Kenneth Goldstein comes to similar conclusions from his experience as a folk record producer for the Riverside, Electra, and Folkways labels in the 1950s and 1960s: "I had to figure out what my responsibilities were to (1) the public, which is a record that is good to listen to, easy to listen to, straight through; (2) to the folklorist, an actual representation, an ethnographic record, if you will; and (3) to the singer, which is the best that he bloody well can do, which is what the singer wants to present to the world." Goldstein quickly identified primarily with the singers: "They had heard records, all of them had heard records. They didn't hear background noises on those records. That became the standard to them for what a good record was." The singers, in short, wanted the best possible sound in formal terms (Keil's perfection), and "there was never a question to me about splicing if it made the performance better."[21]

The basic point here is that in popular (unlike classical) forms, live and recorded practices are not necessarily seeking to realize the "same music" (even if people's expectations about what a band can and should do may carry over from one form into the other—one of the great pleasures of a pop concert is hearing the "hits": songs with which we have a long and sometimes profound intimacy suddenly sound both just the same and quite different). There is a sense, as Keil suggests, in which the record in popular music takes on the role of the score in art musics—as a kind of register of what the music is *ideally*—but then the music's live performance takes on its own value as a unique, audience-involving *contingent* experience: "the normative recordings intensify live performance as something extraordinary, abnormal, and magical as well."[22] And, put like that, this is obviously true for classical music too.

The arguments explored by Glenn Gould in the art music world and by Charles Keil in the folk or (his preferred term) people's music world address the same underlying question: how has musical experience been changed by recording technology? What are its aesthetic effects? It is important to note right away that the issue is not just about the transformation of music making and listening by the invention of recording—we can't simply divide the technological history of music into the periods before and after Edison.

On the one hand, we need to remember that recording is in fact an aspect of the long history of *musical instruments* (with the player piano—a much more important music machine culturally than is now remembered—acting as a kind of bridge between "productive" and "reproductive" instruments). Alan Durant notes that "with the exception of promotional and review literature, discussions [of new sound technologies] tend to be vague on matters of practical detail; they are rarely anchored in close attention to the music-making techniques they claim to be about, or to the terminology and relations of work which will define whatever new conditions of music emerge."[23] The point here is not simply that we should avoid technological determinism, but that musical technologies always describe means of sound production as well as reproduction—musicians, that is to say, are as significant for their development as consumers (even as the meaning of what it is to be a "musician" changes). Technology, in short, is a means of communication, and what people want to say has its own effects on the means they have to say it. As Durant points out, *all* musical instruments have a history "related to ideas of what they should sound like and when and how they should be played, as well as to economic and technical conditions of how they can be manufactured."[24]

On the other hand, the internal developments of recording processes themselves have been every bit as significant aesthetically as the first capture of the voice in the machine. The pursuit of "high fidelity," the best recording as the most "faithful" to the "original" sound, has thus been an increasingly misleading description of the recording process, a description rooted in the original wax processes (when the recording made, indeed, a highly imperfect reference to a performance which the listener had to imagine for herself, to reconstruct from these crackly notes).[25] Electrical recording (and amplification) broke the previously necessary relationship between the sound and the body; tape recording broke the previously necessary relationship between a musical object in space and a musical object in time. Recording perfection ceased to refer to a specific performance (a *faithful* sound) and came to refer, as we've seen, to a constructed performance (an *ideal* sound). The "original," in short, ceased to be an event and became an idea.

A number of difficult and contradictory points follow from this. Take the idea of "permanence" and history. The early ideology of recording stressed that music was now being made to last; there was much talk of subsequent generations, posterity, and so forth; performers could "speak" to future generations like writers. LeMahieu quotes Sergei Rachmaninov from 1931, "Formerly, the artist was haunted by the knowledge that with him his music must also vanish into the unknown. Yet, today, he can leave behind him a faithful reproduction of his art." In practice, though, as LeMahieu goes on to observe, the technological improvements in recording, plus the drive to high turnover and lowered production costs characteristic of mass production, meant that "old" records were soon heard as outdated, primitive, unlistenable; they broke, ceased to be produced, became rare items, of interest only to collectors.[26]

Enter the CD. Or, rather, enter digital technologies, which allow engineers to retrieve the information "packed into the grooves of waxen discs in the land before tape." Gary Giddins cites the example of a 1925 Sidney Bechet sarrusophone solo (the only one in jazz recording history): on the original record "he produced a clamorous rumble suggesting the kind of internal combustion caused by bad diet"; on the remastered digital version "you can hear the staccato tonguing and the ebullient control; the overall impression, once of frenzy, is now of audacious wit."[27]

Here the "original" sound was in the "original" recording, but was inaudible, because of the surface noises and crackles, because no equipment could get at it. Now the surface noise can be eliminated; now the information can be retrieved. This is, though, still to assume that we can distinguish between the original sound and its recording. In fact, practically speaking, that sound only existed—only exists—as a recording: the distinction between the noise that is necessary and noise that is unnecessary to an old recorded performance is an aesthetic as well as a technical judgment. Remastered records, whether from the jazz or the classical back catalogue, may still hold up the ideal of some historical "live" performance, but in fact they are providing something new: a performance reconstructed according to today's sound values. David Schiff has thus rightly observed that "analog recordings of avant-garde pieces sound 'older' than digital recordings of early music," while Keith Johnson, one of America's leading digital audio engineers, explains why his job is not just technical:

> If I've done my job, there's what I call a "thereness." You really have that sense like the performer is *there;* there's a human element. And there's something magical about that when it really works.
>
> Once I've gone through the digital system, if everything is working right in the digits, the most obvious thing that happens right away is that the human element seems to be more distant. The artist doesn't seem to be quite as present, and the recording has become kind of cold and hard and analytical on the digital playback. It'll be very quiet, it'll be very pure, it'll have a very low distortion, it'll be very clean—it'll have those features—but in a way that's an awfully high price to pay for silence. The analytical character—what I call a dull, brittle character—in my mind takes away more than I would like to have taken away.[28]

The question is who now has the power to decide what the original performance sounded like. As Johnson makes clear, the sound judgment that determines what we hear on such CDs is that of neither the original musicians nor the original studio producer/engineer but of the contemporary remaster.[29] The "original" sound that is being revealed in such cases is certainly not that, whatever else it may be.

Whatever the complications of music's recording history, we can, I think, reach some general conclusions about its social effects. First, music is now *everywhere* (an effect still best symbolized, perhaps, by soldiers' use of portable gramophones to play the latest metropolitan hits at the front in the First World War). Music no longer needs to be framed by a special place or time (it is, in this respect, no longer necessarily an event). It increasingly moves, one might say, from foreground to background. As Glenn Gould puts it, recordings do not depend, like concerts, "upon the mood of a special occasion." They are suitable as background, and, as such, music can now draw upon "an incredible range of stylistic reference," sounds which have a new validity precisely because they are out of context, "unobtrusive." Most commentators take this as music's loss of power—the more it's heard, the less it means. Background music has no sense of history or authority; it is anonymous, artificial, electronically enhanced, and so forth. It encourages "regressive" hearing in Adorno's terms—"alienated, narcotized listening"; listening that is, in Joseph Horowitz's words, "mentally supine."[30]

Gould disagreed:

Those who see in background music a sinister fulfilment of the Orwellian environment control assume that it is capable of enlisting all who are exposed to it as proponents of its own vast cliché. But this is precisely the point! Because it can infiltrate our lives from so many different angles, the cliché residue of all the idioms employed in background becomes an intuitive part of our musical vocabulary. Consequently, in order to gain our attention any *musical* experience must be of a quite exceptional nature. And, meanwhile, through this ingenious glossary, the listener achieves a direct associative experience of the post-Renaissance vocabulary, something that not even the most inventive music appreciation course would be able to afford him.[31]

There is, in fact, less and less sense of music being "appropriate" to certain times and places (except in occasional tones of outrage—most noisily expressed, in my experience, by European tourists surrounded by blaring local radios in the foothills of the Himalayas). At the same time music has become entirely mobile: it can follow us around the house, from living room to kitchen and bathroom; on journeys, as "in car entertainment" and "the walkman effect"; across national and political boundaries; in and out of love and work and sickness.

The second aspect of this is the sheer *quantity* of music that is now around—the same work, the same event, the same performance, is endlessly repeatable, it is never lost; and music from all sources, from a hundred years ago, from a hundred thousand miles away, is equally available. The "past" of music is endless re-experienced in its presence; the most distant or strange music is heard in our most familiar surroundings. Simply in its accumulation music ceases to be special. It can no longer be defined against the everyday as something unusual; music *is* now the everyday (and silence becomes the mark of the special moment: a minute's silence to observe death; the silence in a film which accompanies the most intense tension or ecstasy).

A third point is that the musical experience has been *individualized.* Music is no longer a necessarily social or collective affair materially (though it may be in the imagination). There seems to be a long-term trend here: the street and concert hall piano of the mid-nineteenth century giving way to the domestic piano of the late nineteenth century which, in turn, gave way to the living room record player and radio, to the bedroom transistor and Dancette, to the boombox, Walkman, and Discman. One aspect of this is obviously the commodity effect: we can now possess music as obsessively, as madly, as music once possessed us. On the one hand, we have the collector (the collector as traveler and anthropologist, gathering up other people's music; the collector as archivist, tracing lineage, genealogies, catalogue numbers; the collector as investor, in pursuit of the odd, the rare, the first pressing—exchange value as use value).[32] On the other hand, we have what one might call the domestic stage manager: we can now decide for ourselves when and where to hear music, which music to hear, which sounds go together, how sounds will sound.

Musical taste, in short, is now intimately tied into personal identity; we express ourselves through our deployment of other people's music. And in this respect music is more like clothes than any other art form—not just in the sense of the significance of fashion, but also in the sense that the music we "wear" is as much shaped by our own desires, our own purposes, our own bodies, as by the intentions or bodies or desires of the people who first made it. Koestenbaum notes that the early phonograph was sold as "a kind of confessional" or as a mirror reflecting "your soul—and what is hidden deep within it." Eisenberg quotes his friend Nina: "'When I play a record,' she once told me, 'it's as though someone else were expressing my feelings. When I play the piano, it's as though I were expressing someone else's feelings.'"[33] Public sounds are thus brought into private situations and given new meanings: the domestic interior becomes a vaudeville stage, the vaudeville stage a domestic interior.

This means, in turn, a new dialectic in music: absence of performer/presence of performer (absence of audience/presence of audience) as against the classical, score-based dialectic of absence of composer (in the performance)/presence of composer (in the notes). Dave Laing reminds us how peculiar it first seemed to listen to "a voice without a face," and Adorno concluded that "what the gramophone listener actually wants to hear is himself, and the artist merely offers him a substitute for the sounding image of his own person which he would like to safeguard as a possession. The only reason that he accords the record such value is because he himself could also be just as well preserved. Most of the time records are virtual photographs of their owners, flattering photographs—ideologies."[34]

One question raised here concerns the relationship of visual and aural pleasures. Adorno argued in 1928 that

> male voices can be reproduced better than female voices. The female voice easily sounds shrill—but not because the gramophone is incapable of conveying high tones, as is demonstrated by its adequate reproduction of the flute. Rather, in order to become unfettered, the female voice requires the physical appearance of the body that carries it. But it is just this body that the gramophone eliminates, thereby giving every female voice a sound that is needy and incomplete. Only there where the body itself resonates, where the self to which the gramophone refers is identical with its sound, only there does the gramophone have its legitimate realm of validity: thus Caruso's uncontested dominance. Wherever sound is separated from the body—as with instruments—or wherever it requires the body as a complement—as is the case with the female voice—gramophonic reproduction becomes problematic.[35]

This is suggestive, if wrong—even as Adorno was writing, American female singers like Bessie Smith and Ethel Waters were making records on which they hardly sounded "needy and incomplete," and John Corbett has more recently suggested that in recording culture the look (or body) of the performer is replaced by the look of the record and record-playing equipment itself. ("For it is the lack of the visual, endemic to recorded sound, that initiates desire in relation to the popular music object.") We listen by way of the treasured record jacket, in a form of "fetishistic audiophilia" (the hi-fi freak), or as collectors with our cherished objects, those slithers of plastic themselves.[36]

On the other hand, as Philip Brophy points out, technology has also transformed the sound of *live* musical performance and changed audiences' sense of themselves in that sound. If, in classical music, the concert and the record are distinctive acoustic events (the problem is the relationship between them), the rock aesthetic, at least, is as much based on the technology of concert amplification as on studio equipment. "Live" rock music has thus become music that is super-live! "Electrical amplification," in Brophy's words, "is integral to the cultural and social growth of Rock. It changed not only the sound of instruments but also the scale of the live event which contained them, thereby determining the nature of the audience experience." For Brophy, the audience was thus amplified every bit as much as the musicians: "The guitar 'feedback' of the latter 60s *symbolizes* a distortion of audience 'feedback' pre-Beatles: both deal with an overload in the producer/production/product chain . . . If noise is essentially an overload of sounds, then Rock truly is noisy. In effect, the sound of its live concert—produced by audience-performer feedback and amplified electric instruments—is the *noise* of spectacle; the *noise* of communicated signals and audible responses."[37]

Brophy thus traces the role of the live rock recording in training consumers "how to become listeners and how to recognise themselves in the recordings," which were, in effect, recordings of their own performances (not those of the musicians, who might just as well be recorded in the studio). The record becomes the ideal performance in terms of its ideal staging—"the fusion of the best performance with the best response"—and if the best performance can be faked by the tape splicer, so can the best staging be faked by the digital engineer:

> Today, record production still speaks the essential technical dialect of digital delay and digital reverb: the two seminal components in creating space, location, perspective and dimension in sound in *post-production*. In effect, this is like a Frankenstein experiment in reviving the dead (with—surprise—electricity) . . . The void space of the studio is thus reconstructed through the *effecting* of sounds, making them occur in phantom spaces which do not exist within the physical confines of the actual studio.[38]

As Brophy suggests, "the sound of a space" thus becomes "more desirable and more effective than an actual space," and, one might add, following Adorno, that its desirability lies in the sense that this is *our* sound, the sound of the listener—the audience—in that space. "You are there!"

From another perspective one could add, finally, that we also have a new socio-technological form of music, *public records:* musical events, social gatherings, discos, and clubs in which sounds on disc are the entertainment.[39] Here, whether in terms of volume, spectacle, sociability, or emotional intensity, the private fantasies of record listening are, in a sense, enacted, felt *for real*. Dancing in public—listening in public—thus seems to be *more* expressive of how we feel about our music, more truthful, than dancing, listening, alone.[40]

From the listener's perspective, technology has clearly affected not just where and when and how we listen to music, but also what we hear. For a start, we now hear music in much more detail than ever before. This is not just a matter of sound quality (the elimination of extraneous noises; the "closeness" of sounds through headphones and speakers contrasted with the distant acoustic tones heard at the back of a hall), but also because we can now stop sounds, listen to them again and again, break them up into parts for analysis. In popular musical terms, this has meant, in particular, concentration on the "personal" touches of specific performers; music is heard in new ways as expressive of personality. Star quality in music, as we've seen, is thus a perception of intimacy. And the point here is not just that details of sounds lost in live settings, imperceptible in the passing of a musical event, become available through a new sort of technological attention (just as a TV playback and slow motion enable us to see the detail of a goal which is otherwise experienced only as a blur and a desperately rationalizing memory) but also that such sounds were heard in the twentieth century *for the first time*—as the pioneering recording engineer Fred Gaisberg suggested, recording revealed "tones hitheto mute to us."[41]

Similarly, amplification has enabled us to hear the detail of loud sound in quite new ways, and if the distinction between music and noise depends on our ears being able to find order in chaos, then technology, in allowing us to attend to previously indistinguishable sonic detail, has greatly expanded our sense of what music is and can be—at high as well as low volume. This is, perhaps, most obvious in popular music in the habit of listening, as it were, from the bottom. As Philip Brophy notes:

> The lineage of Caribbean music is founded on bass: from ska (the Caribbean distortion of East Coast R'n'B) to reggae (the latter being the first major instance of subsonic bass intruding upon white rock's favoured mid-range aural spectrum) to black disco (which continental Europe technologically colonized into Eurodisco and sold back to white America) to the eventual bass explosion in Eighties' hip hop. This explosion is regional: booming drum machines, pounding disco bass drums, cheesy subsonic synthesizer bass lines and creative distortions of bottom-end effects travelled from the East Coast (the New

York state of electro, rap, hip hop, Latin hip hop) throughout the nation (Chicago house and acid, Detroit techno, Miami bass) and over to the West Coast (LA hard core rap and jack-beat swing). And on it will go.[42]

At the same time we also now take for granted a kind of musical sonic *purity*. This relates to the history of recording technology referred to earlier, to the audio-engineer's drive to get rid of "extraneous" sounds, the hiss and crackle of the recording itself, the rumbles and pop of amplification. The implication is that we can now get to the kernel of the "musical sound" itself—the sound that no one before recording technology had ever actually heard (however well designed the room, however well behaved the audience, a live concert is always awash with small noises, small movements, of the people, of the building).[43]

The ideology of musical "purity" is what links the digital sound mixer to the piano tuner, and I don't need to repeat the points I've already made about the resulting confusion between musician and technician, between aesthetic and engineering sound decisions. What is clear is that Glenn Gould's championing of the perfect recording over the imperfect live performance is misleading insofar as it implies that the "perfection" of the record is a strictly musical matter. Joseph Horowitz points out that as classical recordings moved away from the simulation of live performances, so the resulting "good" sound reflected as much a technological or engineering ideal as the determination now to realize the *composer's* best intentions. Recordings "were engineered and edited to ensure clarity, precision, and brilliance," and these values began to be pursued by conductors like Toscanini (using live performance to sell the recorded sound) in the concert hall too. We ended up, in Eduard Steuermann's words, with "the barbarism of perfection."[44]

Making music has always involved not just the planning of notes on paper, but also the realization of those notes as sounds *in particular settings*, particular aural spaces. And if a musical score is obviously an unfinished object, its realization dependent on specific sound judgments made in specific sound settings (judgments by a conductor or record producer considering the audio-dynamics of the performing space), then so is the pop record. The music it stores is also only realized in specific settings—a radio transmission, a dance club, one's living room. It will sound different accordingly, whether as determined by a choice of record company mixes or as the listener shifts volume and tone controls.[45]

Music thus has a new effect on space. The recording studio (note the term—referring not just to the painter's *atelier* but also, as Keir Keightley puts it, to "a carpeted den") was a new musical location, and the record listener was given a new musical place: we're now somehow (thanks to the use of reverb, delay, and all the other engineering tricks) *in* the music, not constrained by the concert hall model of listening *at* it.[46] Whatever the familiar ideology of "active" (concert) listening and "passive" (home) listening, acoustically it is, in fact, as record listeners that we seem to be musical participants.[47]

Jonathan Tankel argues that the remix engineer creates a new work in reconceptualizing a record's "sonic atmosphere." This is a more drastic act than rearranging an existing tune because it changes the essence of what we hear—a remix is, in this respect, akin to a jazz player's improvisation on a standard tune: "Remixing *is* recoding, the reanimation of familiar music by the creation of new sonic textures for different sonic contexts . . . The remix recording creates a new artifact from the schemata of previously recorded music. It is *prima facie* evidence of Benjamin's contention that to 'an ever greater degree the work of art reproduced becomes the work of art designed for reproducibility.'"[48]

We certainly do now hear music as a *fragmented* and *unstable* object. The earliest phonographs had varying and unreliable speeds (had to be wound up, were quickly wound down); music became something to which things happened (rather than just being in itself the happening). As we have taken power over music on records, as they have become ubiquitous (every entrepreneur using music for her own ends), so the musical work has ceased to command respectful, structural, attention. All music is more often heard now in fragments than completely; we hear slices of Beatles songs and Bach cantatas, quotes from jazz and blues. Such fragmentary listening may have as much to do with—may be particularly suited to—industrialization and urbanization as with recording technology as such. Michael Ondaatje imagines Buddy Bolden reminiscing as follows:

> When I played parades we would be going down Canal Street and at each intersection people would hear just the fragments I happened to be playing and it would fade as I went further down Canal. They would not be there to hear the end phrases . . . I wanted them to be able to come in where they pleased and leave when they pleased and somehow hear the germs of the start and all the possible endings at whatever point in the music I had reached *then*. Like your radio without the beginnings or endings. The right ending is an open door

you can't see too far out of. It can mean exactly the opposite of what you are thinking.[49]

If listening to a piece of music from beginning to end is these days unusual, the exception rather than the rule, this presumably has some effect on our sense of musical progression. At the same time, because *all* our experiences of time are now fragmented and multilinear, fragmented music is also realistic music (this is Ondaatje's point); it represents experience grasped in moments. One aspect of this is, in Hosokawa's words, to direct "the listener's attention to 'sound,'" what is heard immediately, rather than to "music," notes as they make sense in a structure. "Technology," Kramer concludes, "has liberated listeners from the completeness of musical form." (Just as film has liberated us from the completeness of visual form.) Composers, knowing now that their music will be repeated on record and radio, no longer have to build "repeatability" into the score, into each performance. In the popular music aesthetic, at least, Hosokawa suggests, "perception of sound is more important than consideration of the 'composition' as an entity in and of itself." Hence the rise in the 1980s of popular music made up of fragments, of samples: "Such quoting establishes a connection that builds authenticity, a kind of italicizing that identifies the author, *by means of authorship, as it undoes it.*"[50]

The commonsense (Romantic) belief that recording technology has systematically undermined the authority of the composer is thus more problematic than it may at first seem. Consider these remarks by Milton Babbitt:

Somebody will ask those of us who compose with the aid of computers: "So you make all these decisions for the computer or the electronic medium, but wouldn't you like to have a performer who makes certain other decisions?" Many composers don't mind collaborating with the performer with regards to decisions of tempo, or rhythm, or dynamics, or timbre, but ask them if they would allow the performer to make decisions with regard to pitch and the answer will be "Pitches you don't change." Some of us feel the same way in regard to the other musical aspects that are traditionally considered secondary, but which we consider fundamental. As for the future of electronic music, it seems quite obvious to me that its unique resources guarantee its use, because it has shifted the boundaries of music away from the limitations of the acoustical instrument, or the performer's coordinating capacities, to the almost infinite limitations of the electronic instrument. The new limitations are the human ones of perception.[51]

There seem to be three issues here. First, the question of musical *origins.* Today all sounds from all sources can be relatively easily taken apart (through digital sampling) and reassembled; none of them therefore any longer carries any necessary realist or expressive weight (which becomes, instead, an ideological judgment). All sounds, that is, carry an equal value as signs; there is a flattening out of even the difference between human and non-human sounds; natural and unnatural noise; intended and found sounds; music and noise. No sound, in short, can any longer guarantee truth (no folk sound, no proletarian sound, no black sound).[52] However, one can also interpret this both as a new form of imitative realism (as accurately reflecting the noise of the contemporary street) and as a new opportunity for compositional freedom (Babbitt's point) as all physical constraints on sound making are removed.

Second, the question of the musical *author.* What's startling here is that just as it seems that a "self" can no longer possibly be expressed in the ever more socially and technically complex processes of pop production, so artistic authority is rediscovered—in the person of the producer, the engineer, the image maker, the deejay. We're not only desperate but still successful in finding voices in the machine—hence, for example, the academic idolization of Madonna.[53]

Third, the question of the musical *object.* There's no doubt here that the fetishization of the recording has meant the demystification of the work. Even in classical music, the accumulation of versions (now available, thanks to CD, for continuous historical comparison) has led to what I'll call *interpretive relativism:* everyone can hear that the readings of scores change, that the "ideal" performance is variable (old recordings are odd or incomplete or just plain "wrong" in the same way as old readings of literature or art). Our sense of the "timelessness" of great music has thus become the belief (eagerly fostered by the music industry) that it must be continually updated.[54]

In popular music, where the focus is on the work-as-performance rather than the work-as-score, the recording effect that interests me is different. (The CD here has, in fact, confirmed the "timelessness" of classic jazz and rock tracks.) Digital storage has reinforced the feeling both that music is never finished (with every cut the starting point for a variety of mixes) and that it is never really *integrated*—we are always aware of the parts that make up the (temporary) whole.[55] Multi-track recording, that is to say, has had a long-term aesthetic effect: we now hear (and value) music as layered; we are aware of the contingency of the decision that put this sound here, brought this instrument forward there. It's as if we always listen to the music *being assembled,* and the paradox is that pop listeners thus have a clearer sense than classical listeners of music in composition (music as it is conceived, that is, by a composer).

For Milton Babbitt the promise of technology was to give the composer complete control of his composition even through the contingencies of its performance. Technology offered a solution to longstanding problems of musical power and authority. But what's clear from a popular music perspective is that technology doesn't so much resolve the politics of musical meaning as change the context—the sense of musical time and space—in which the traditional arguments take place, the arguments *about* the transcendent and the contingent, about the freedom of artistic intention, the freedom of listener response. If we should resist easy arguments about technological determinism (the machines making meaning), so we should resist equally eager arguments about technological fertility (everything now possible). As Chris Cutler has long argued, even if musical technology in the abstract did make new—"liberated"—ways of composing and performing and listening possible, it doesn't work in the abstract, but as a commodity force, a matter of equipment to be bought and sold, and there are powerful interests (the electronics industry) working to ensure that whatever else may happen to music it remains a source of profit.[56] The detailed effects of technology may be unpredictable (nothing is used in the way the industry expected), but the general trend is undeniably conservative. What is most startling about the history of twentieth-century sounds is not how much recording technology has changed music, but how little it has. If music's meanings have changed, those changes have taken place within the framework of an old, old debate about what musical meaning can be.

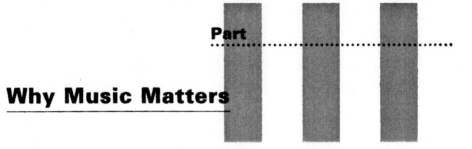

Part

Why Music Matters

The Meaning of Music

But much of Schumann and Chopin, saving some of the fine tumultuous pieces, should be laid aside for a while. Of Wagner, too, there is much question. Indeed, the morbidity, the servile melancholy, the frenetic sexuality, the day-dreaming flight from reality that permeates much of the music of the nineteenth century cannot be regarded as fit for a class with a revolutionary task before it.

Charles Seeger[1]

With its major tonality and foreshortened melodic range, "Tom Dooley" is a kind of sober, almost a pious duty, like planting a tree. With the simplicity of a bugle call, its tune climbs sadly in four nearly identical phrases from a grave fifth below the tonic to a weary second or third above it, where it pauses to rest. Lingering in one of the two chords, tonic or dominant, that resignedly bear away the stanza.

Robert Cantwell[2]

All truly meaningful music is a swan-song.

Friedrich Nietzsche[3]

My argument in this book rests on a simple enough premise. As a sociologist I'm happy to assume that "meaning" can only be defined institutionally: the term describes not simply discursive conventions—agreements to agree—but regulated forms of social behavior. Arthur Danto's philosophical point—"To see something as art requires something the eye cannot decry—an atmosphere of artistic theory, a knowledge of the history of art: an artworld"—is the guiding principle of the sociology of culture too.[4]

To grasp the meaning of a piece of music is to hear something not simply present to the ear. It is to understand a musical culture, to have "a scheme of interpretation." For sounds to be music we need to know how to hear them; we need "knowledge not just of musical forms but also of rules of behaviour in musical settings."[5] The "meaning" of music describes, in short, not just an interpretive but a social process: musical meaning is not inherent (however "ambiguously") in the text. As Lucy Green argues persuasively, "Both experience of the music and the music's meanings themselves change complexly in relation to the style-competence of the [listener], and to the social situations in which they occur . . . music can never be played or heard outside a situation, and every situation will affect the music's meaning."[6]

John Cage's suggestion that "the wisest thing to do is to open one's ears immediately and hear a sound suddenly before one's thinking has a chance to turn it into something logical, abstract, or symbolical" is therefore futile: to adopt such a listening position is, in itself, a social gesture; what we hear will therefore already be meaningful.[7] Ola Stockfelt has shown how the meanings of musical works (Mozart's Symphony No. 40 is his example) change as they enter new "listening situations," as listeners apply different "modes of listening," appropriate for concert hall, walkman, car, cinema, café, sports contest, or airplane waiting to take off. The "appropriate" here is partly a social matter:

> For example, to dance during a symphony concert (which is practically impossible because of the fixed seats, etc.) is to commit a *gaffe*, a breach of social convention, even if one is hearing Viennese waltzes or other music originally meant to be listened to in connection with dancing. It is likewise inappropriate to sink into prolonged intramusical contemplation when one is squeezed into a 7–11 type convenience store.[8]

But it's also partly an ideological matter. Even if nowadays "one can listen to march music in the bathtub and salon music in the mountains," nevertheless specific musical styles are still "implicitly bound to specific environments and specific relationships between the performer and the listener," and it is not true to say that "all music has an equal relation to each different environment." A rave track on the BBC Radio 1 breakfast show still means something different from the rock ballads played around it, still refers to an *ideal* listening situation, still constructs one sort of musical space even as it is being heard in another one altogether.[9]

Once fantasy enters the picture the sociological model gets complicated. One can (I do) love rave music without ever having been to a rave, and this changes the argument I've been making. If the standard sociological position is that (real) social processes determine what music means, now the suggestion is that a musical experience "means" by defining (imagined) social processes. I'll discuss this further in the final chapter. Here I want to focus on one issue, the question of value. Sociological orthodoxy, following Bourdieu, is that "aesthetic" listening is itself a socially determined process, describes a particular sort of listening behavior in a particular sort of listening situation, means the right sort of listeners pursuing the right sort of listening aims. Rose Subotnik notes, for example, that her students hear the "Soldiers' March" from Stravinsky's *Histoire du Soldat* as better than Sousa's "Washington Post March" not because they like it any better (nor because they know what the pieces are), but because the Stravinsky piece signals "art music" and is therefore listened to in a specific way, with an ear for complexity, authority, and so forth.[10]

As Kyle Gann puts it,

> You like Milton Babbitt's music? It's probably not so much because you can hear the way he juggles hexachords as the fact that 12-tone music expresses the "serious-intellectual" values of the scientific/academic community you identify with . . . I like new music, successful or not, that tries things never heard before; I want to think of myself as independent, as having escaped the inauthenticity of mass consciousness.[11]

The suggestion here is that the conventional high cultural way of evaluating what one hears is a way of declaring who one is: a listener of distinction. And it is then a short step (the step Bourdieu takes) to explaining the meaning of music entirely in terms of its social function, its organization of taste. I have two problems with this position. First, it seems to deny (or ignore) the difference between the musical experience and other sorts of cultural processes. Music may, indeed, be used (or articulated) in functional terms, but that does not account for the undeniable ways in which it moves us, does not explain the ways in which to listen to music is, indeed, to be taken *out* of oneself (and one's society). Second, the argument about taste may undermine high culture's eternal categories, but it preserves high/low cultural difference: the implication is that the popular audience is unconcerned with aesthetic evaluation, with individual distinction. This is nonsense—all cultural life involves the constant activity of judging and differentiating—but, further, it is to miss the point that the peculiarity of the musical experience—its specialness as a form of sociability—makes it necessarily an aesthetic matter. In John Blacking's words, "Music is essentially about aesthetic experiences and the creative expression of individual human beings in community, about the sharing of feelings and ideas."[12]

For popular music listeners just as much as for classical music listeners, "good music" describes something unusual, unusual because it cannot easily be explained away in terms of everyday social practice, as a matter of class or commerce or functional routine. Which is why, when popular musical values are articulated, they are so often phrased in art musical terms (terms devised specifically to account for the meaning of music as music). This is Alec Wilder, for instance, waxing Romantic: "Arlen, like Rodgers, reveals in his melodies a deep rooted need to express himself. In both men there is a very personal, almost private approach to creation, rather than the professional capacity to contrive and produce reasonable facsimiles of the real thing."[13] And this is Keir Keightley expanding the boundaries of the pop musical text by drawing on any number of high critical conventions: "The 'thrilling sadness' mentioned above is produced in/by the song [The Beach Boys' "All Summer Long"] at a number of levels: the passing shift from major to minor, the falling movement of the group and the resistance and alienation of the falsetto, the situation of the lyric in traditions of summer songs concerned with passing seasons and moments of loss, the fragmentary construction of an imaginary montage, as well as other, less easily specified elements. The construction of both the lyric and the album cover in particular may be situated with traditions of criticism which see melancholy and loss as associated with fragments."[14]

This is the sociological paradox: musical experience is socially produced as something special; the importance of music is therefore taken to be that its meaning is not socially produced, is somehow "in the music." Pop fans too have an aesthetic mode of listening. Pop fans too believe that music derives its value "from its inner and private soul."[15]

It is not surprising, then, that the aesthetic theory developed in art music to distinguish what real musicians (and listeners) do from the market exchanges between pop's producers and consumers should provide the terms (and arguments) in which popular music becomes meaningful too. The error in high cultural attitudes toward low music is the condescending assumption that popular listening describes a quite different sort of experience. In his impeccably liberal humanist *Music and the Mind,* for example, Anthony Storr, while constantly stressing that Western art music is just one form of expression among many others "equally valid," also casually assumes that "much popular music today" is "trivial" and "monotonous," popular only because its listeners are "unsophisticated."[16] Or take this passage from Roger Scruton: "Consider modern pop music, and compare it with New Orleans Jazz and ragtime, and then with the folk music, African and American, from which both derive; you will see therein a tragic history of decline. Aggression and fragmentation have come in place of comfort and community."[17]

I find myself bristling at this not because of the aesthetic judgment involved (I'd happily argue for the value of aggression and fragmentation in art, certainly as against comfort—and, given his brand of conservatism, "community" means something rather different to Scruton than it does to me), but because of Scruton's obvious ignorance of the musics mentioned. He presumes that a high theorist can talk about the meaning of low music without listening to it, without liking it, without needing to know anything much about it at all. But then the concept of expertise, the relationship of knowledge and pleasure, is unclear in all musical worlds. As Nicholas Cook puts it, "What I find perplexing, and stimulating, about music is the way in which people—most people—can gain intense enjoyment from it even though they know little or nothing about it in technical terms."[18]

And so I find myself bristling equally when I read this:

> It is, for example, extremely important to hear Led Zeppelin's "The Crunge" (from *Houses of the Holy*) not only as a more-sophisticated-than-usual instance of heavy metal, but also as a sarcastic commentary on James Brown's more involuted performances. This is not simply collateral knowledge about the piece; it involves hearing certain modulations and syncopations in special ways. One who does not hear this has yet to understand the piece totally.[19]

Is such understanding necessary? This question has perplexed me ever since I became a rock critic and realized that I had no hesitation about pronouncing authoritatively on new releases and live performances while, formally, I could offer no convincing theoretical account of musical value at all. My questions in this book reflect personal as well as sociological curiosity: how do people come to value and assess particular sounds and styles and stars? How does music give pleasure (or pain)? In what terms do I make sense of my musical experiences? Where do these terms come from? What *is* musical understanding? "To understand music," suggests Peter Kivy, "seems in significant part to be able to describe it," and for the rest of this chapter I want to consider the problems of such description.[20]

In the eighteenth century argument about musical meaning focused on the relative value of instrumental and vocal or operatic works. The problem of instrumental music lay in its apparent inadequacy as a means of "imitation":

> Instrumental Music, though it may, no doubt, be considered in some respects as an imitative art, is certainly less so than any other which merits that appellation; it can imitate but a few objects, and in even those so imperfectly, that without the accompaniment of some other

art, its imitation is scarce ever intelligible: imitation is by no means essential to it, and the principle effects which it is capable of producing arise from powers altogether different from those of imitation.[21]

And most commentators assumed that instrumental music was therefore inferior to music accompanied by words or gestures.[22] It took the Romantic move—from theories of imitation to theories of expression—to reverse this judgment. In the nineteenth century instrumental music came to be valued above vocal music for its ability to release feeling "from the confinements of prosaic everyday reality," that is, from its attachment to particular objects or states.[23] By 1828, in his *Lectures on Music*, Hans Georg Nageli was celebrating instrumental music *because* it neither represents nor imitates. Music, he suggested, has no content but is simply "a being at play," and it is this which enables it to move the listener, to invoke "indefinite and ineffable feelings": "The soul hovers, carried along by this play of forms, in the whole immeasurable realm of emotions, now ebbing, now flowing up and down, plunging with the gently echoing breath of tones to the utmost depths of the heart and then soaring again with the rising impetus of tones to supreme feelings of bliss."[24]

For Adam Smith, writing fifty years earlier, such an appreciation of music necessarily involved intellectual understanding: we don't so much feel music's emotional meaning as admire its emotional shape.[25] Even when we contemplate a painting, he suggests, something clearly representational, we don't simply see what's represented; rather, we see how the picture differs from its object while suggesting it. We marvel, that is, at the skill with which one thing has been made to represent another. In contemplating instrumental music, which is not representational, we marvel at its order and method—and thus at the order and method of the mind itself: "Whatever we feel from instrumental music is an original and not a sympathetic feeling: it is our own gaiety, sedateness or melancholy; not the reflected disposition of another person."[26]

As Kevin Barry shows, Adam Smith here followed other eighteenth-century philosophers in valuing music for those qualities that discredited it to the empiricists—its obscurity, instability, and incompleteness. Because music is experienced temporally, what we perceive is always in a state of becoming. For James Usher this was why music, rather than painting, is sublime. The aesthetic experience is constituted by desire, a state of mind in which an object is known by its absence, in which the contemplation of perfection is not tainted by the flaws of its material presence. Music expresses this contemplative principle best. Its significance depends on absence, on sound already gone or yet to come; its "perfection" is always a matter of memory and anticipation.[27]

Adam Smith himself was less interested in the sublime than in the beautiful. The value of instrumental music (like the value of art in general) lay for him in its integration of the intellectual and the sensual. If music was the highest form of art, this was because it offered the most complete experience of the harmony of thought and feeling. The difference between the "nobler works of Statuary and Painting and the phenomenon of Nature," Smith wrote, is that the former "carry, as it were, their own explication along with them, and demonstrate, even to the eye, the way and manner in which they are produced."[28] Similarly,

> a well composed concerto can, without suggesting any other object, either by imitation or otherwise, occupy, and as it were fill up, completely the whole capacity of the mind, so as to leave no part of its attention vacant for thinking of anything else. In the contemplation of that immense variety of agreeable and melodious sounds, arranged and digested, both in their coincidence and in their succession, into so complete and regular a system, the mind in reality enjoys not only a very great sensual, but a very high intellectual pleasure, not unlike that which it derives from the contemplation of a great system in any other science.[29]

Smith is anticipating here one strand of Romantic thought—the belief in "absolute music." "Must not purely instrumental music create its own text?" asked Friedrich von Schlegel in 1798. "And is not its theme developed, confirmed, varied and contrasted, just as is the object of a sequence of philosophical speculation?" Or, as Jules Combarieu put it a hundred years later, music "is the art of thinking in sounds."[30]

In her study of the rise to dominance of the nineteenth-century concept of the "musical work," Lydia Goehr suggests that Adam Smith's writings "mark a transitory phase."[31] The transition was from the analysis of music as rhetoric to the analysis of music as art. Central to this change in perception were two metaphorical shifts. First, music began to be described in terms of space rather than time. Second, aesthetic attention moved from the listening subject to the musical object. By 1892 Edward Baxter Perry was writing in *Music* that "silence is to music what light is to painting—the first absolutely essential condition, upon which all its effects and impressions depend . . . The slightest noise, even involuntarily produced . . . blurs the outline of the work, like a shadow falling across a picture."[32]

Both of these changes meant the clear elevation of the intellectual over the sensual response. For Eduard Hanslick, the most influential champion of the new approach, "aesthetic value in music" meant "experiencing a piece of music as a kind of beautiful object through 'the voluntary and pure act of contemplation which alone is the true and artistic method of listening.'"[33] Hanslick argued—and this took him beyond Smith's position—that the value of music lay in the formal qualities of the work itself, and not in the quality of the listener's experience. Musical appreciation is thus a matter of reason (or, in Hanslick's terms, science); it means knowing what to listen to, rather than how to feel about it. In his words, "Certainly with regard to beauty, imagining is not mere contemplating, but contemplating with active understanding, i.e. conceiving and judging."[34]

This argument has had two obvious consequences. First, it has moralized the musical experience: it is now customary to distinguish "good" and "bad" listeners; musicology in the nineteenth century became a study not of how people did listen to music but of how they ought to. Second, this moral distinction was rooted in a distinction of mind and body, which became, in turn, a way of distinguishing between "serious" and "popular" listeners, between ideal and "flawed" listening. Rose Subotnik describes the effects of being taught to listen properly:

> In my college harmony course, use of piano was forbidden. Whereas scoreless listening was unheard of in my university education, sound-less keyboards were fairly common . . . In numerous seminars on early music I transcribed reams of manuscripts of which I never heard a note or discussed the musical value. As a music major, and later as a teacher, listening to scratched and otherwise dreadful monophonic recordings, I developed a strategy of listening which I have never entirely shaken, whereby I mentally "correct" for inadequacies of sound or performance that distract from my structural concentration . . . Yet I am not at all sure that any of this structural discipline has made me a more competent listener than my brother, who travels eight hours a week to the opera houses of New York to hum the tunes and listen to certain sopranos.[35]

The nineteenth-century shift from music as rhetoric to music as art meant devaluing the listener's role in musical judgment. As Mark Bonds shows, in the eighteenth century the purpose of music had been to "elicit an intended emotional response," "to move, persuade and delight the listener," and musical "form" thus referred to qualities of "coherence and persuasiveness." In this context, the listener had been "the only true arbiter" of musical value. Now the arbiter became the work (and its composer):

As an organism, the musical work is an object of contemplation that exists in and of itself. As an oration, the musical work is a temporal event whose purpose is to evoke a response from the listener. We can be moved by both modes of experience; but the metaphor of the oration necessarily emphasizes the temporality of the work, the role of the listener, and the element of aesthetic persuasion, whereas the model of the biological organism has no need to account for a work's effect upon its intended audience. Indeed, the audience, for all practical purposes, is irrelevant to the organic model. The organic metaphor implies that the standards by which any given work is to be judged will be found within the work itself.[36]

Lydia Goehr suggests that we must understand the nineteenth-century definition of the musical work as a "regulative concept," that is, it meant not only a rewriting of musical history (to turn eighteenth-century composers into artists) but also the formulation of behavioral rules for both musical performers and audiences.[37] But while there is certainly plenty of evidence that such regulation was an aspect of developing bourgeois cultural practice, at the same time the difficulty of enforcing such rules suggests that, hard as they might try to suppress their feelings, even the most respectable listeners were still hearing music sensuously.

No doubt it is the sheer aesthetic obstinacy of music listeners (and players) which accounts for musicologists' occasional contemptuous tone. Hanslick set the pattern:

Slouched dozing in their chairs, these enthusiasts allow themselves to brood and sway in response to the vibrations of tones, instead of contemplating tones attentively. How the music swells louder and louder and dies away, how it jubilates or trembles, they transform into a nondescript state of awareness which they naively consider to be purely intellectual. These people make up the most "appreciative" audience and the one most likely to bring music into disrepute. The aesthetic criterion of intellectual pleasure is lost to them; for all they would know, a fine cigar or a piquant delicacy or a warm bath produces the same effect as a symphony.[38]

In its materiality, music, in Kant's words, "lacks good breeding," and the final logic of the music-as-music position is that it should be neither heard nor played, only contemplated. Sound, mused Adorno, is a "layer of music" using historically conditioned resources—instruments and technology and performers—which "bear the imprint of social ideology and allow the 'neutralisation' of structural individuality." "Why can't music go out the same way it comes into a man," wondered Charles Ives, "without having to crawl over a fence of sounds, thoraxes, catgut, wire, wood and brass?"[39]

Ives voices here the note of Romantic individualism that originally undermined accounts of music as oration and helped define the "serious" as the "unpopular." In his 1802 life of J. S. Bach, Johann Forkel suggested that "the public merely asks for what it can understand, whereas the true artist ought to aim at an achievement which cannot be measured by popular standards. How, then, can popular applause be reconciled with the true artist's aspirations towards the ideal?"[40] And Schoenberg believed that "those who compose because they want to please others, and have audiences in mind, are not real artists . . . They are merely more or less skilful entertainers who would renounce composing if they did not find listeners."[41]

Popularity is defined here not just by reference to quantity (the size of the audience) but also to quality (the nature of the response). The proper listener—the listener paying aesthetic attention—has to translate a temporal experience into a spatial one. Music has to be appreciated organically, in terms of its internal structure, and the question becomes how we can grasp an architecture from the immediate flow of sounds. "The listener," Heinrich Kostlin declared sternly in 1879, "needs a firm observation post from which he can review the march-past of those harmonies, like a general reviewing his troops on parade."[42]

Structural listening is necessarily dependent on music's spatial representation, on the score. "By legislating for pitch," notes the composer Robin Maconie, "notation could be said to have freed musical invention from the tyranny of the ear," just as "regulation of time values in its turn liberated player and composer from the limitations of memory and the tyranny of succession."[43]

But the score isn't the music, and in what is still the most interesting analytic exploration of musical "autonomy," Roman Ingarden suggests that the nineteenth-century argument involved two elements: the score, which fixes the work but does not constitute a musical experience nor even part of it; and an infinite set of performances, each one a distinct and unique experience, but nevertheless drawing its meaning from its "truth" to the score. Given that in practice no single performance is judged to be "the absolute, faultless, genuine embodiment of the score," least of all the first performance or the composer's own version, the musical work can only be said to exist in its potential. As Ingarden puts it, a musical work is an *intentional object*—it originates in a creative act which gives the score its purpose—and a *schematic object*—the score leaves open different possibilities of completion, aesthetically significant areas of indeterminacy.[44]

A musical work, in short, is neither real (it is not defined simply by its performances) nor ideal (it is brought into existence by material processes of composition and realization); it is neither the score nor its realization, but the relationship between the two. Bringing music into aesthetic line with the other arts in the nineteenth century meant building an "imaginary museum of musical works," a concert hall equivalent of the galleries in which the meaning of painting and sculpture was being redefined.[45] And the power of this metaphor is reflected in the musicological approach to popular music: the first task is transcription, the translation of sound into score, whether the score of an imaginary event (most contemporary recorded music is not performed but constructed) or an improvised one (Ornette Coleman is said to have looked aghast at a transcription of one of his solos, knowing that he would be quite unable to play it).[46]

From this perspective, musical listening is, by definition, a double process, involving both the immediate experience of sound and an abstract, comparative exercise of judgment. Music turns out to be, after all, an imitative art: a performance is an imitation of a score. But the possibility of such imitative listening depends on certain material conditions. To put it simply, a musical work must be heard repeatedly, and it was both a cause and an effect of the new approach to music in the nineteenth century that people began to think in terms of the musical repertoire (the imaginary museum), to take it for granted that "great" music was regularly performed music. In the eighteenth century even the most committed listener would not have expected to hear any particular piece more than once—it had to do its aesthetic work immediately.

My own conclusion from these philosophical arguments is that the aesthetics of twentieth-century popular music relates more obviously to eighteenth-century interests in oration, performance, and gesture than to the nineteenth-century concern with structure, but the question underlying the last two hundred and fifty years' debate about music remains: what does a listener to music actually *do?* Adam Smith wrote at a time when there was confidence—at least among intellectuals—that this question could be answered by systematic self-analysis, and it is, perhaps, unfortunate that since then experimental psychology has displaced the philosophy of the mind. "The intense influence of music upon the nervous system is fully accepted as fact by psychology as well as physiology," wrote Hanslick in 1854. "Unfortunately an adequate explanation of this is still lacking."[47] And, as John Sloboda comments, it is nowadays equally unfortunate that "musical reception, the one area of music psychology in which research is flourishing, should be characterised by a relative insensitivity to the problem of relating research findings to normal musical listening."[48]

So what is "normal" listening? It is noteworthy that the two great European rationalists of the early twentieth century, Freud and Lenin, were both disturbed by their response to music. Lenin was reluctant to listen to Beethoven because the music made him want to pat people on the head; Freud remarked that his pleasure in art lay in comprehension: "Whenever I cannot do this, as for instance with music, I am almost incapable of obtaining any pleasure. Some rationalistic, or perhaps analytic, turn of mind in me rebels against being moved by a thing without knowing why I am thus affected, and what it us that affects me."[49]

Laurence Kramer has suggested that to call music "meaningless" is a response "less to an absence of thought than to the presence of danger."[50] The danger—the threat posed by music and dance to aesthetics—is not so much the absence of mind as the presence of body. The ideology of the musical work leads, as we've seen, toward a repression of the sensual. In the words of one psychoanalyst, "it is a prerequisite to the *aesthetic* response to musical art work that we free ourselves of [such] sensuous feelings and let the work exert its influence unimpeded, in the full beauty of its aesthetic form."[51]

But, in the words of another, the musical experience is an essentially sensual "pleasure in motion": "The joyous freedom and inexplicable obedience to will in the play of musical movement is, according to my opinion, a regressive repetition and idealised intensification of bodily pleasure in that early period of infancy, when the discovery of limbs is followed by the gradual mastery of the whole body."[52]

The obvious solution to the contradiction here is to integrate the intellectual and the sensual. This strategy lay behind Adam Smith's refusal to refer the value of music to anything extra-musical. Music, argued Smith, may evoke feelings, but only as objects for contemplation. To feel music directly is to understand it less well than to concentrate on how these feelings are produced. To put it another way, music which is designed to arouse feeling is clearly inferior to music which stimulates feeling *through* thought. The latter works by suggesting nothing "that is different from its melody and harmony."[53]

There are a number of strands in this argument, but the most important is the suggestion that what we hear as the "sensuality" of music is actually the effect of following musical "thoughts." Rather than an immediate sensual response, and then its contemplative interpretation, musical listening means grasping a piece intellectually and then taking sensual pleasure in the "movement" of the mind. Music offers, it seems, the experience of *feelings under control,* and this model has become the norm (in various guises) of classical music ideology. Consider, for example, these remarks by Deryk Cooke:

> We may say then that, whatever else the mysterious art known as music may eventually be found to express, it is primarily and basically a language of the emotions, through which we directly experience the fundamental urges that move mankind, without the need of falsifying ideas and images—words or pictures. A dangerous art in fact . . . But under the guidance of the intellect and enlightened moral sense, it is surely as safe as anything human can be—as safe at least, shall we say, as religion or science.[54]

Two questions remain. First, why should following the motion of music be described as an *emotional* activity? And, second, if "the musical experience" is so clearly rooted in subjectivity, how can we say that anyone's response to music is "wrong"? The fact that most people don't hear (or describe) music as the movement of sounds that is represented by the score does not mean that they don't hear (and reflect pleasurably upon) music—sounds moving. "When we come down to the fundamental musical experience," concedes Cooke, "the transformation of sound into emotion, the professional is as tongue-tied as the layman."[55]

It was established in the eighteenth century that there couldn't be a direct link between sound and feeling. Sir William James pointed out that "no man, truly affected with love or grief, ever expressed the one in an acrostic, or the other in a fugue." James Beattie asked: "What is the natural sound of devotion? Where is it to be heard? What resemblance is there between Handel's 'Te Deum' and the tone of voice natural to a person expressing, by articulate sound, his veneration of the Divine Character and providence?"[56]

On the other hand, neither can it be denied that music makes us feel, nor that we can label those feelings—as gaiety, tranquillity, or melancholia, in Adam Smith's example. The eighteenth-century move was therefore to distinguish between general and specific feelings. Music, suggested Archibald Alison, was "limited indeed in the reach of its imitation or expression and far inferior to language, in being confined to the expression only of general emotions, but powerful within these limits beyond any other means we know, both by the variety which it can afford, and the continued and increasing interest which it can raise."[57]

For Hanslick, who believed that the content of music was simply "tonally moving forms," it thereby embodied "the motion of feeling, abstracted from the content itself, i.e. from what is felt." Music concerns the "dynamic of feeling" rather than feeling itself, and Hanslick made a telling analogy with dance: "The more it abandons the beautiful rhythmicity of its forms, in order to become gestures and mimicry to express specific thoughts and feelings, the more it approaches the crude significance of mere pantomime."[58]

Two different sorts of distinction are being made in these attempts to define emotion abstractly. On the one hand, the suggestion is that musical emotion is profound but vague—we have the feeling but not its occasion; in Adam Smith's terms, music doesn't make us sad but makes us feel sadness; in von Hartmann's words, "Music reveals ineffable depths of the emotional life, such as poetry simply cannot express, whereas poetry presents not only the emotion itself but a perception of the situations, characters and actions that determine the emotions."[59] This is, as we saw in Chapter 5, the working assumption of film scorers, who use music to arouse the general feelings which the audience then interprets according to the film's narrative; we are first made to feel and then given a reason for doing so. For Hollywood pragmatists, it doesn't much matter why certain sounds cause certain feelings, it's enough that they do. But the question remains as to how the analogy between musical and emotional shapes works—and whether there is anything more to this than an analogy.

The second way of approaching this is to suggest not that music somehow expresses the shape of feelings, but, rather, that in describing musical experiences we are obliged to apply adjectives, and that we therefore attach feeling words conventionally and arbitrarily to what is, in fact, a purely aural experience. This would explain why, for example, in music (unlike the other arts) a child prodigy can move us. As Max Dessoir says, "Children of eight can perform prodigies of understanding, performing, even creating music . . . There is virtually no parallel to this in the other arts, since even the most gifted can only gradually acquire that understanding of the world and of humanity which is needed by the poet and the painter. Music, on the other hand, has no essential need of any relationship with reality."[60]

But what interests me here is another point—not music's possible meaninglessness, but people's continued attempts to make it meaningful: to name their feelings, supply the adjectives. In the early nineteenth century the French critic François Joseph Fétis noted that

> with the large audience, colouring will always pass as expression, for
> unless it consist of individuals capable of forming an abstract ideal—
> something not to be expected of a whole auditorium, no matter how

select it may be—it will never listen to a symphony, quartet, or other composition of this order without outlining a programme for itself during the performance, according to the grandiose, lively, impetuous, serenely soothing, or melancholy character of the music.[61]

The issue here, to return to my starting point, is that to ascribe meaning to a musical work is to provide a certain sort of *description*. Roland Barthes may have been contemptuous of the use of adjectives in bourgeois music criticism, but music is, in fact, an adjectival experience. Henry Kingsbury notes, for example, that "in the bulk of contemporary theoretical texts, music is not so much an entity occasionally described with anthropomorphic terms as it is itself an anthropomorphic, figurative representation." He quotes Heinrich Schenker, the guru of structural analysis: "We should get accustomed to seeing tones as creatures. We should learn to assume in them biological urges as they characterize living beings."[62]

Kingsbury is interested in the way in which music theorists assign motives and character to "the music itself" (rather than to the performers who produce the music, or to the composer who wrote it), and Frank Sibley has developed this argument, showing how important figurative adjectives are to musical analysis, adjectives which can't be read as implicit descriptions of either music makers or listeners. He quotes Hanslick, who referred to "those imposing and sombre pyramids of sound of the old Italian and Dutch schools, and the finely chased salt cellars and silver candlesticks, so to speak, of venerable Sebastian Bach."[63] Sibley's point is that "purely musical" descriptions (more or less technical accounts of what is "actually" heard) "fail to articulate what, following others, I have been calling the 'character' and qualities of music, and do little to explain why music may engage us as appreciative listeners—which is why non-musicians and musicians alike employ figurative characterizations."

As Sibley suggests, someone could describe a piece of music perfectly accurately in technical terms while being quite unable to appreciate it; while someone quite unable to read music can perfectly well convince us that they've "understood" a work: they make sense of our own experience of it through their figurative description. This is the job of the rock critic, for example.

This view, that grasping the character of a piece involves hearing it in such a way that some possible extra-musical description(s) would be appropriate to our experience, would stand sharply opposed to the belief that extra-musical description is always improper. Much that is centrally appealing about music would be, paradoxically, essentially extra-musical.[64]

Two points follow from this. First, such descriptions must be "apt" rather than true. An inapt description is evidence of a musical misunderstanding, and Sibley suggests that description here is something like an actor's or director's interpretation of a dramatic role: each musical description may be personal, but it can, nevertheless, be used as evidence of whether someone has understood the work (in this respect describing a piece of music is analogous to playing it). Conversation—argument—about musical meaning is, then, possible: the adjectives describe the music and not people's responses to it; they are not a way of declaring how we feel (declarations that no one could deny). Second, though, "we do not grasp, realize, or perceive the character of music—or of faces, paintings or scenery—in words or in any-thing else . . . *Having* grasped its character, however, or while trying to, we may try to describe it in either [musical or figurative] terms."[65] And our skill here will be as much a skill with words as a skill "at listening."

The point to stress here is that this use of adjectives is not confined to professional writers about music and professional talkers about music, to musicians and critics. Rather, it is a necessary aspect of all musical listening; it defines the musical experience. John Sloboda remarks on

> someone who has just listened to a performance of a long and complex symphonic work. It is quite possible that he or she cannot recall a single theme from the work (I have often been in this situation myself), yet he or she certainly remembers *something* about the work, and can make some appropriate response to it. When this response is expressed in words it characteristically contains remarks about the substance of the music which are neither descriptive ("it was loud") nor reactive ("I liked it") but embody an attempt to *characterize* the music through metaphor ("it had the feeling of a long heroic struggle triumphantly resolved"). It seems less significant that people often disagree about their characterizations than that they nearly always have *some* comment to offer. This is not an arbitrary reaction, but a genuine attempt to describe some real thing or experience.[66]

Music does not have a content—it can't be translated—but this does not mean that it is not "an object of the understanding."[67] Or, to put it another way, the gap in music between the nature of the experience (sounds) and the terms of its interpretation (adjectives) may be more obvious than in any other art form, but this does not mean that the pleasure of music doesn't lie in the ways in which we can—and must—fill the gap. "After playing Chopin," wrote Oscar Wilde,

> I feel as if I had been weeping over sins that I had never committed, and mourning over tragedies that were not my own. Music always seems to me to produce that effect. It creates for one a past of which one has been ignorant, and fills one with a sense of sorrows that have been hidden from one's tears. I can fancy a man who has led a perfectly commonplace life, hearing by chance some curious piece of music, and suddenly discovering that his soul, without his being conscious of it, had passed through terrible experiences, and known fearful joys, or wild romantic loves, or great renunciations.[68]

To follow the history of music theory since Adam Smith is to follow an attempt to constitute both a definition of music and a way of listening. The peculiarity of this history is that it has, in a sense, been successful discursively and unsuccessful materially—in the academy, at least, people talk about music in ways which make little sense of how they listen to it. We take it for granted, for example, as I noted at the beginning of this chapter, that a clear distinction can be made between "serious" music and music as entertainment, or, at least, between serious listening and listening as entertainment. But in practice, as a listener, I'm much less clear about this difference. Can I really distinguish between the pleasure that I take in Bartok and the pleasure that I take in Hüsker Dü? Am I describing something quite different when I say that I'm moved by Fauré's *Requiem* and by Sharon Redd?

The debate about musical meaning in which Adam Smith took part was a debate about what we should say about music. Aesthetic argument is a matter of lexical regulation. "We may doubt," writes Roman Ingarden, "whether so-called dance music, when employed only as a means of keeping the dancers in step and arousing in them a specific passion for expression through movement, is music in the strict sense of the word."[69] But the point of music, whether in club or concert hall, is, precisely, to flout the strict sense of the word, and Roger Scruton has thus argued that "dancing to music is an archetype of the aesthetic response":

> When we dance to music we move in response to it, with the same dispassionate absorption with which we move to another's dancing . . . and our more "civilized" habits in the concert hall are in many ways like truncated dances, in which our whole being is absorbed by the movement to which we attend, inwardly locked in incipient

gestures of imitation. There is no doubt in our feeling that the object of this imitation is a human life, presented somehow through the music. We could not remove this thought from our response without destroying the whole place of music in our culture.[70]

Scruton suggests that the "aesthetic character of music" can be grasped in a variety of ways—by listening to it, playing it to oneself, performing it for others, moving to it. This differentiates music from other art forms, and Scruton concludes that to get at the peculiarity of music "we should not study listening, which has so much in common with reading and looking, but dancing, which places music in the very centre of our bodily lives." Anthony Storr, writing from a psychologist's point of view, makes a similar point: "The formalist analysts are trying to make the appreciation of music purely cerebral, whereas music is rooted in bodily rhythms and movement." Echoing Scruton, he notes that music, unlike poetry or paintings, "makes us want to move our bodies."

> If music is rooted in the body, and closely connected with bodily movement, even though modern listeners in the concert hall may have to inhibit such movement, then Schopenhauer's view that both our experience of the body and our experience of music possess a depth, an immediacy, and an intensity which cannot be obtained in other ways becomes comprehensible and persuasive.[71]

For Storr, the psychologist, the point here is that music affects our emotions bodily as well as engaging our feelings mentally. He cites Darwin: "So a man may intensely hate another, but until his bodily frame is affected he cannot be said to be enraged."[72]

For Scruton, the philosopher, the argument is put more coolly:

> In responding to the meaning of a piece of music, we are being led through a series of gestures which gain their significance from the idea of a community that they intimate, just as do the gestures of a dance. As with a dance, a kind of magnetic field is created which shapes the emotions of the one who enters it. We move for a while along the orbit of a formalized emotion and practise its steps. Our truncated movements [in listening without dancing] are also acts of attention: we do what we do in response to the sounds that we hear, when we attend to them aesthetically . . . And if it is worth anything, the music does not leave us there [with the little fragments of human life that musical elements may suggest], but leads us on, through its own powers of development. As we move with these elements, there-

fore, we are lead by our sympathies into a wholly new totality: a musical bridge is created, spanning distant reaches of human life.[73]

I've used these two anti-pop thinkers deliberately to show that even for them the meaning of music comes back to emotion, the body, movement, dance (all the things that are supposed to characterize African rather than European musics). But I want to return, finally, to a sociological point. Different musical activities (listening, playing, performing, dancing) produce different aesthetic objects. In particular, as Nicholas Cook has argued so effectively, the music produced by the composer must be distinguished from the music produced by the listener (with performers, critics, and analysts occupying uneasy positions between the two).[74]

This is reflected in the academic study of popular music: musicology produces popular music for people who want to compose or play it, sociology produces popular music for people who consume or listen to it; these approaches are different because they are concerned with different sorts of musical experience (which is why, in this chapter, I've been more concerned with the writings of philosophers and psychologists than with those of music analysts and sociologists). Cook quotes Schoenberg:

> Music is an art which takes place in time. But the way in which a work presents itself to a composer . . . is independent of this; time is regarded as space. In writing the work down, space is transformed into time. For the hearer this takes place the other way round; it is only after the work has run its course in time that he can see it as whole—its idea, its form and its content.[75]

I'll quote Ned Rorem:

> For myself, I no longer hear new music except visually: if it pleases me, I inscribe it on a staff in the brain, photograph that notation, take it home, and develop the film which can be preserved indefinitely. This manner of musical recall is not, I think, unusual to many composers.[76]

And what's at issue here is not just different musical practices, different musical experiences, different musical situations, but a single musical culture *defined by such differences.*[77] As Roland Barthes put it,

> I record myself playing the piano; initially, out of curiosity to *hear myself;* but very soon I no longer hear myself; what I hear is, however pretentious it may seem to say so, the *Dasein* of Bach and of Schumann, the pure materiality of their music; because it is my utterance,

the predicate loses all pertinence; on the other hand, paradoxically, if I listen to Horowitz or Richter, a thousand adjectives come to mind: I hear *them* and not Bach or Schumann.—What is it that happens? When I listen to myself *having played*—after an initial moment of lucidity in which I perceive one by one the mistakes I have made—there occurs a kind of rare coincidence: the past of my playing coincides with the present of my listening, and in this coincidence, commentary is abolished: there remains nothing but the music (of course what remains is not at all the "truth" of the text . . .)[78]

Toward a Popular Aesthetic

What, after all, do I put down when I put down notes? I put down a reflection of emotional states: feelings, perceptions, imaginings, intuitions. An emotional state, as I use the term, is compounded of everything we are: our background, our environment, our convictions. Art particularizes and makes actual these fluent emotional states. Because it particularizes and because it makes actual, it gives meaning to *la condition humaine*. If it gives meaning it necessarily has purpose. I would even add that it has moral purpose.

Aaron Copland[1]

The Beatles were all ours, from a Northern town, and we in our provincial towns all over the country could understand them.

Carol Dix[2]

The academic study of popular music has been limited by the assumption that the sounds somehow reflect or represent "a people." The analytic problem has been to trace the connections back, from the work (the score, the song, the beat) to the social groups who make and use it. What's at issue is homology, some sort of structural relationship between material and cultural forms. From this perspective musical meaning is socially constructed; our musical pleasures are defined by our social circumstances. Marxist and Weberian musicologists alike argue that music is a form of ideological expression, not just in broad institutional terms (how it is played and heard), but also aesthetically, through the expressive dependence of the organizing principle of the music as a structure of willed sounds on the organizing principle of society as a structure of power. As the semiotician

Theo van Leeuwen puts it, "Music can be seen as an abstract representation of social organization, as the geometry of social structure."[3]

The problem of the homological argument, as van Leeuwen himself notes, is that "music not only represents social relations, it also and simultaneously enacts them"; and too often attempts to relate musical forms *to* social processes ignore the ways in which music is *itself* a social process. In other words, in examining the aesthetics of popular music we need to reverse the usual academic argument: the question is not how a piece of music, a text, "reflects" popular values, but how—in performance—it produces them.[4]

Let me make this point in a different way, by quoting at length an exemplary piece of pop criticism, Frank Kogan's fanzine celebration of Spoonie Gee (written sometime in the mid-1980s).

> "Spoonin Rap" and "Love Rap" by Spoonie Gee are my favorite American-made records of the last ten years. They came out about five years ago, "Spoonin Rap" in late '79 and "Love Rap" in '80. I've never read a review of either.
>
> Rap music centres on the human voice. The voice is a rhythm instrument as well as a melodic one, capable of emphasizing beats as if it were a set of drums. Spoonie Gee bears down hard on the words, achieving a mesmerizing intensity akin to hard rock—yet he also puts a hanging drawl in his phrasing. So he sounds tough and funky/graceful simultaneously. His first producers, Frank Johnson and Peter Brown of Sound of New York and Bobby Robinson of Enjoy Records, were smart enough to emphasize Spoonie's voice: "Spoonin Rap" is just bass and drums, sound effects and voice; "Love Rap" is just voice, drums and percussion.
>
> On the basis of his voice alone, the way it balances coolness with angry passion while keeping a dance beat, Spoonie is a major artist; in addition, he's a writer. His lyrics are as intense as his singing, and embody the same tensions. Example: both "Spoonin Rap" and "Love Rap" start with detailed and explicit bragging—about how cool and sexy he is, about how the girls go for him, how they're impressed with his rapping and his car. He puts on his eight-track. He makes love to the girl in his car. In his Mercedes. The seat's so soft, just like a bed. At the moment of sexual triumph the lyrics make a jarring change, as if there's a second song hidden behind the first, as if the bragging were a set-up for something else. "Spoonin Rap": "Then I got the girl for three hours straight / a'but I had to go to work a'so I couldn't be late / I said, 'Where's your man?' She said 'He's in jail'

/ I said 'A'come on baby cuz you're tellin' a tale / Cuz if he comes at me and then he wants to fight / See I'm a get the man good and I'm a get him right . . .'". "Love Rap": "When I got into my house and drove the female wild / The first thing she said is 'Let's have a child' / I said 'No no baby I only got time / To make a lot of money and to save my pride / And if I had a baby I might go broke / And believe me to a negro that ain't no joke.'" And then it's like the first part of the song, but turned inside out—the guys and girls are drawn to his flashy clothes and car only so they can rip him off and leave him in the gutter. The girls are gonna play him for a fool . . . Then it shifts back to what a great lover he is, nice descriptions of his girl friends. "Spoonin Rap" shifts around in the same way. It's about how cool he is, about how sexy women are; then it's about don't do dope, don't steal, you'll go to jail and they'll fuck you in the ass. Then it's about jumping the turnstile and the cop pulls a gun but he doesn't shoot.

There's a lot of precedent in black lyrics for jarring emotional juxtapositions—in the blues particularly, also in Smokey Robinson's deliberate paradoxes. But the nearest emotional equivalent isn't in black music, it's in punk—early Stones, Kinks, Velvets, Stooges, Dolls—where a song will seem to be one thing, then be another. The ranting part of "Love Rap" could be Lou Reed in one of his bad moods—except that, unlike a Jagger or a Reed, Spoonie hasn't cal- culated—may not even be aware of—his juxtapositions. Which adds to his power. The feelings have great impact because they come from an unexpected source. If Spoonie were in punk or rock his alienation and rage would fill an expectation of the genre. In disco, they seem truer.

. . . Spoonie's not one of us. He has nothing to do with punk culture or post-punk culture. I don't know if I could carry on an interesting conversation with him, if we could find any cultural or moral common ground. But there is a common ground . . . However much I admire current heros like Mark Smith and Ian Mackaye, people I identify with, I know they don't make music as strong as this. Listening to Spoonie is like hearing my own feelings, and I have to confront my own fear. This means maybe that I'm not really unlike him. Maybe I'm more like him than I am like you.[5]

I've quoted this at length, partly because this is how it works as criti- cism—the move from description to emotion to identity—and partly to show how the concerns of this book (the ease and necessity of evaluation, the consideration of voice and genre, text and performance, knowledge, truth and feeling) can be focused on one artist, on a couple of tracks. What Kogan assumes—what I assume—is that music gives us a way of being in the world, a way of making sense of it: musical response is, by its nature, a process of musical identification; aesthetic response is, by its nature, an ethical agreement. The critical issue, in other words, is not meaning and its interpretation—musical appreciation as a kind of decoding—but experience and collusion: the "aesthetic" describes a kind of self-consciousness, a coming together of the sensual, the emotional, and the social *as* performance.[6] In short, music doesn't represent values but lives them. As John Miller Chernoff concludes from his study of drumming in Ghana,

> African music is a cultural activity which reveals a group of people organizing and involving themselves with their own communal relationships—a participant-observer's comment, so to speak, on the processes of living together. The aesthetic point of the exercise is not to reflect a reality which *stands behind it* but to ritualize a reality that is *within* it.[7]

And if music is particularly important in the history of black identities, such value is not confined to diasporan African cultures.[8] Philip Bohlman, for example, has explored the role of chamber music in forming German Jewish identity, in both articulating cultural values and enacting a form of collective commitment to them. In this context the scored basis of "absolute music" is as socially fecund as the improvised basis of jazz:

> Viewed from a performative perspective, the absence of specific meaning within the text allows meaning to accrue only upon performance, thus empowering any group—for example, an ethnic community—to shape what it will from absolute music. A gap therefore forms between the content of chamber-music repertories and the style of performance situations. It is within the mutability allowed by style that differences in meaning and function of music arise, thereby transforming chamber music into a genre that can follow numerous historical paths. These paths may be as different as, say, the ethnic associations in Israel and the practices of amateur music making found in many American academic communities. Clearly, such cases reflect different attitudes towards both the repertories of chamber music and the communities that lend the music its distinctive functions and form its different histories.[9]

And Gina Arnold describes how in the American indie scene in the 1980s, "deep in the heart of our very own small towns, we took the tools of our culture and hewed them into our very own road . . . Nirvana has dragged us all up along with them, and now here we stand, looking down at the past, at a mental map of our traversal of the route that brought all this to pass."[10]

In responding to a song, to a sound, we are drawn (haphazardly, as Arnold suggests) into affective and emotional alliances. This happens in other areas of popular culture, of course; in sports, for example, or in fashion and style—social constructions which provide keys to the ways in which we, as individuals, present ourselves to the world. But music is especially important for our sense of ourselves because of its unique emotional intensity—we absorb songs into our own lives and rhythm into our own bodies. In John Blacking's words, "Because music is concerned with feelings which are primarily individual and rooted in the body, its structural and sensuous elements resonate more with individuals' cognitive and emotional sets than with their cultural sentiments, although its external manner and expression are rooted in historical circumstances."[11] Music, we could say, provides us with an intensely subjective sense of being sociable. Whether jazz or rap for African-Americans or nineteenth-century chamber music for German Jews in Israel, it both articulates and offers the immediate *experience* of collective identity.[12]

Paul Gilroy remarks that while growing up he was "provided by black music with a means to gain proximity to the sources of feeling from which our local conceptions of blackness were assembled."[13] But he also notes that "the most important lesson music still has to teach us is that its inner secrets and its ethnic rules can be taught and learned," and as a child and teenager I also learned something about myself—took my identity—from black music (just as I did later, in the disco, from gay music). What secrets was I being taught?

First, that identity comes from the outside, not the inside; it is something we put or try on, not something we reveal or discover. As Jonathan Rée puts it, "The problem of personal identity, one may say, arises from play-acting and the adoption of artificial voices; the origins of distinct personalities, in acts of personation and impersonation."[14] And Rée goes on to argue that personal identity is therefore "the accomplishment of a storyteller, rather than the attribute of a character . . . The concept of narrative, in other words, is not so much a justification of the idea of personal identity, as an elucidation of its structure as an inescapable piece of make-believe."[15]

Identities are, then, inevitably constrained by imaginative forms—"structured by conventions of narrative to which the world never quite manages to conform," in Kwame Anthony Appiah's words[16]—but also freed by them. As Mark Slobin suggests, cultural imagination is not necessarily restricted by social circumstances: "We all grow up with *something,* but we can choose just about *anything* by way of expressive culture."[17] And as I have argued elsewhere, with reference to literary forms and social identities (black writing, women's writing, gay writing), the question is not whether such writing can be mapped back onto the reader (reading as a woman, a man, a black) but whether literary transformation—the process of writing *and* reading—doesn't subvert all sociological assumptions about cultural position and cultural feeling.[18]

This seems an even more obvious question to ask about popular music, of which the dominant forms in all contemporary societies have originated at the social margins—among the poor, the migrant, the rootless, the "queer." [19] Anti-essentialism is a necessary part of musical experience, a necessary consequence of music's failure to register the separations of body and mind on which "essential" differences (between black and white, female and male, gay and straight, nation and nation) depend.

It follows that an identity is always already an ideal, what we would like to be, not what we are. In taking pleasure from black or gay or female music I don't thus identify as black or gay or female (I don't actually experience these sounds as "black music" or "gay music" or "women's voices") but, rather, participate in imagined forms of democracy and desire, imagined forms of the social and the sexual. And what makes music special in this familiar cultural process is that musical identity is both fantastic—idealizing not just oneself but also the social world one inhabits—and real: it is enacted in activity. Music making and music listening, that is to say, are bodily matters; they involve what one might call *social movements.* In this respect, musical pleasure is not derived from fantasy—it is not mediated by daydreams—but is experienced directly: music gives us a real experience of what the ideal could be.

In his discussion of black identity, Paul Gilroy argues that it is neither "simply a social and political category" nor "a vague and utterly contingent construction" but "remains the outcome of practical activity: language, gesture, bodily significations, desires."

> These significations are condensed in musical performance, although it does not, of course, monopolise them. In this context, they produce the imaginary effect of an internal racial core or essence by acting on the body though the specific mechanisms of identification and recognition that are produced in the intimate interaction of per-

former and crowd. This reciprocal relationship serves as a strategy and an ideal communicative situation even when the original makers of the music and its eventual consumers are separated in space and time or divided by the technologies of sound production and the commodity form which their art has sought to resist.[20]

And once we start looking at different musical genres we can begin to document the different ways in which music works materially to give people different identities, to place them in different social groups. Whether we're talking about Finnish dance halls in Sweden, Irish pubs in London, or Indian film music in Trinidad, we're dealing not just with nostalgia for "traditional sounds," not just with a commitment to "different" songs, but also with experiences of alternative modes of social interaction. Communal values can only be grasped as musical aesthetics in action.[21] "Authenticity" in this context is a quality not of the music as such (how it is actually made), but of the story it is heard to tell, the narrative of musical interaction in which the listeners place themselves.

We all hear the music we like as something special, as something that defies the mundane, takes us "out of ourselves," puts us somewhere else. "Our music" is, from this perspective, special not just with reference to other music but, more important, to the rest of life. It is this sense of specialness (the way in which music seems to make possible a new kind of self-recognition, to free us from everyday routines, from the social expectations with which we are encumbered) that is the key to our musical value judgments. "Transcendence" is as much part of the popular as of the serious music aesthetic, but in pop transcendence articulates not music's independence of social forces but a kind of alternative experience of them. (Of course, in the end, the same is true of "serious" music too.)

Music constructs our sense of identity through the experiences it offers of the body, time, and sociability, experiences which enable us to place ourselves in imaginative cultural narratives. Such a fusion of imaginative fantasy and bodily practice marks as well the integration of aesthetics and ethics. John Miller Chernoff has eloquently demonstrated how among African musicians an aesthetic judgment (this sounds good) is necessarily also an ethical judgment (this is good). The issue is "balance": "the quality of rhythmic relationships" describes a quality of social life.[22]

Identity is necessarily a matter of ritual: it describes one's place in a dramatized pattern of relationships—one can never really express oneself "autonomously." Self identity *is* cultural identity; claims to individual difference depend on audience appreciation, on shared performing and narrative rules.[23] Such rules are organized generically: different musical genres offer different narrative solutions to the recurring pop tensions between authenticity and artifice, sentimentality and realism, the spiritual and the sensual, the serious and the fun. Different musical genres articulate differently the central values of the pop aesthetic—spectacle and emotion, presence and absence, belonging and difference.

In her study of music making in the town of Milton Keynes, *The Hidden Musicians*, Ruth Finnegan persuasively argues that these days people's voluntary, leisure activities are more likely to provide their "pathways" through life than their paid employment. It was in their musical activities that her town dwellers found their most convincing narratives; it was in their aesthetic judgments that they expressed their most deep-seated ethical views.[24]

This is, perhaps ironically, to come to the aesthetics of popular music as performance by way of a spatial metaphor: what makes music special—what makes it special for identity—is that it defines a space without boundaries. Music is the cultural form best able both to cross borders—sounds carry across fences and walls and oceans, across classes, races, and nations—and to define places: in clubs, scenes, and raves, listening on headphones, radio, and in the concert hall, we are only where the music takes us.

In this book I have suggested ways in which we can use a sociology of music as the basis of an aesthetic theory, how we can move from a description of popular music as a social institution to an understanding of how we can and do value it. One of my working assumptions has been that people's individual tastes—the way they experience and describe music for themselves—are a necessary part of academic analysis. Does this mean, in the end, that the value of popular music is simply a matter of personal preference?

The usual sociological answer to this question is that such preferences are themselves socially determined—that individual tastes are really examples of collective taste, reflecting consumers' gender, class, and ethnic backgrounds—and I don't want to deny that our cultural needs and expectations are, indeed, materially based. All the personal terms I have been using (identity, emotion, memory) are, of course, socially formed. But this is only part of the story. Pop tastes do not just derive from our socially constructed identities; they also help to shape them.

For the best part of this century, pop music has been an important way in which we have learned to understand ourselves as historical, ethnic, class-bound, gendered, national subjects. This has had conservative effects (primarily through nostalgia) as well as liberating ones. What music does (all music) is put into play a sense of identity that may or may not fit the way we are placed by other social forces. Music certainly puts us in our place, but it can also suggest that our social circumstances are not immutable (and that other people—performers, fans—share our dissatisfaction). Music is not in itself revolutionary or reactionary. It is a source of strong feelings which, because they are also socially coded, can come up against common sense. It may be that, in the end, I want to value most highly that music, popular and serious, which has some sort of disruptive cultural effect, but my argument is that music only does this through its impact on individuals, and that this impact is obdurately social.

I began this book at a dinner party in Stockholm. I'm ending it in a hotel room in Berlin. Across the street is the Hard Rock Café, and the local bars feature '50s and '60s North American pop. I desultorily watch the pop video shows on German television, but only Ace of Base's "Eyes of a Stranger" (intrigue on the Stockholm underground) holds my attention. I trawl the dial on my walkman and, pushing past the ubiquitously ingratiating Elton John, find things I do want to hear. Beethoven's Violin Concerto, played faster than usual so that the moments when the soloist returns to earth and the rest of the string section are there to catch her seem more exhilarating, more reassuring, than ever. A New Orleans version of "Nobody Loves You (When You're Down and Out)" with, I think, Louis Armstrong on trumpet, shaping pathos so lovingly that it becomes something else, a refusal of the human spirit to be laid low. Old pop songs with unexpected resonance: Rick Astley solemnly marking time to a cheap '80s disco beat; Cat Stevens' "Father and Son," well-meaning '70s advice; Whitney Houston swinging through a ballad like a trapeze artist. A big, brassy *schlager*, oompah music with a hint of Viennese mockery. German-Turkish music, the ululating voice picked out by a techno pulse. And then, spine-tingling coincidence, a track from Portishead's *Dummy*, a new British album with a strong critical buzz, to which I'd been listening on tape as I sat around in airports.[25]

This is my favorite track on *Dummy*, "Sour Times." The sampled sound from a Lalo Schifrin *Mission Impossible* LP places the track in space, not time, in the suspended space of the traveler, caught between West and East, past and future. Beth Gibbons' voice—high, sweet, thin—has the tone of a torch singer's but not the anxiety. She sounds matter-of-fact (like the Dutch singer Mathilde Santing), feminine without tears. And all the time behind her a babble of noise, the talk of the 1990s British dance floor, the movement of traffic between soul and house, white and black, Europe, America, the Caribbean, background and foreground. I decide that no record better captures the pop aesthetic at this time, in this place—not for its utopian (or dystopian) vision, but for its determination to be heard, to give cultural confusion a social voice. And I wish there were someone here to play this to.

"Human attitudes," Percy Grainger once argued, "and specifically human ways of thinking about the world are the results of dance and song."[26] I cast my mind back a few days. Another night and I'm in a small town in the British midlands, at a charity event in a community center. There's locally prepared Mexican food and a salsa band from Birmingham—the singer from South America (country unspecified), the musicians local session players. I meet people I haven't seen for a decade, friends from punk promoting days in Coventry. This is a community brought together by shared political interests (to benefit the environment and education in Nicaragua) but fused together, on the dance floor, by the obstinate insistence of the rhythms (this is a good salsa band) and by the sexual charge of the vocals. Memories dance with the music too—old ideological bust-ups and alliances, parties and love affairs. A flash of the lights offers a snapshot, of bodies held in motion, parents and children, friends and enemies, the successful and the unsuccessful, of where we've been together. This is what I mean, I think, by music both taking us out of ourselves and putting us in place, by music as both a fantasy of community and an enactment of it, by music dissolving difference even as it expresses it. The sounds on that Leamington dance floor, like the sounds now in this Berlin hotel room, are at the same time rootless, cut free from any originating time and place, and rooted, in the needs, movement, and imagination of the listener.

Another coincidence: "La Bamba" is on the radio. "La Bamba" was the encore spot of the salsa night, a track whose winding forty-year journey from 1950s Mexican Los Angeles to 1990s Berlin and Leamington Spa, through the mass media of rock 'n' roll, radio, TV, Hollywood, is matched by its winding journey through our own bodies, through the memories of what we once wanted to be that make us what we are. "La Bamba," I think restlessly, this is where I came in.

Notes

Index

Notes

1. The Value Problem in Cultural Studies

1. Ned Rorem, *Settling the Score* (New York: Harcourt Brace, 1988), p. 258.
2. Thanks to Frank Kogan for this quote.
3. Levin L. Schücking, *The Sociology of Literary Taste* [1931] (London: Kegan Paul, 1944), p. 32.
4. Ex-members of the band From Eden, who went on to form, respectively, Pop Will Eat Itself and The Wonder Stuff. Quoted in Martin Roach, *The Eight Legged Atomic Dustbin Will Eat Itself* (London: Independent Music Press, 1992), pp. 18, 89.
5. Patrick Kane, *Tinsel Show: Pop, Politics, Scotland* (Edinburgh: Polygon, 1992), p. 59.
6. Frank Kogan is quoted here, as elsewhere in this chapter, from private correspondence.
7. For further discussion of some of these issues see Sarah Thornton, *Club Cultures: Music, Media and Subcultural Capital* (Cambridge: Polity, 1995). And see Pierre Bourdieu, *Distinction: A Social Critique of the Judgement of Taste* [1979] (London: Routledge, 1984). The most illuminating application of Bourdieu's ideas to popular music is Mats Trondman, "Rock Taste—on Rock as Symbolic Capital. A Study of Young People's Music Taste and Music Making," in Keith Roe and Ulla Carlsson, eds., *Popular Music Research* (Göteborg: Nordicom-Sweden, 1990).
8. For the last three years I've chaired the judging panel of the Mercury Music Prize (for the British "album of the year"). My fellow judges have all been authoritative music industry types, and much of my understanding of how argument works in everyday musical evaluation is drawn from our disputatious shortlisting sessions (I was unable to convince my colleagues, for example, to put the Pet Shop Boys' *Very* on the 1994 shortlist).
9. Peter Van Der Merwe, *Origins of the Popular Style* (Oxford: Clarendon Press, 1989), p. 3.
10. Allan Bloom, *The Closing of the American Mind* (New York: Simon and Schuster, 1987), pp. 73–74.
11. Mark Crispin Miller, "Where All the Flowers Went." Reprinted in his *Boxed In: The Culture of TV* (Evanston, Ill.: Northwestern University Press, 1989), p. 175.
12. Gordon Legge, *The Shoe* (Edinburgh: Polygon, 1989), p. 36. The three albums listed were recorded by Van Morrison, Joy Division, and Roxy Music.
13. Barbara Herrnstein Smith, *Contingencies of Value* (Cambridge, Mass.: Harvard University Press, 1988).
14. As Derek Scott has pointed out, this sort of argument has proved problematic in the music academy too. The music of Sir Arthur Sullivan, for example, has done rather

better in terms of "longevity" than that of Schoenberg: how long should we wait for the latter to be properly appreciated "by posterity"? See Derek B. Scott, "Music and Sociology for the 1990s: A Changing Critical Perspective," *Musical Quarterly* 74(3) (1990): 389.

15. For the value issue in film theory see David Bordwell, *Making Meaning: Inference and Rhetoric in the Interpretation of Cinema* (Cambridge, Mass.: Harvard University Press, 1989). For the peculiar (and peculiarly British) concept of "quality television" see Charlotte Brunsdon, "Problems with Quality," *Screen* 31(1) (1990).

16. Many thanks to Judith Williamson for discussing her experience with me. Her collected film criticism is published as *Deadline at Dawn* (London: Marion Boyars, 1993).

   I discuss the problems of treating popular culture as an academic object in much greater detail in *Pearls and Swine: Instituting Popular Culture* (Manchester: Manchester University Press, forthcoming).

17. Frank Kogan, *Why Music Sucks* 7, 1991, pp. 3–4.

18. See Joke Hermes, *Reading Women's Magazines: An Analysis of Everyday Media Use* (Cambridge: Polity, 1995).

19. Theodor W. Adorno, "On the Fetish Character in Music and the Regression of Listening" [1938], reprinted in *The Culture Industry*, ed. J. M. Bernstein (London: Routledge, 1991), p. 26.

20. See John Fiske, "Popular Discrimination," in James Naremore and Patrick Brantlinger, eds., *Modernity and Mass Culture* (Bloomington: Indiana University Press, 1991).

21. See Dave Harker, "Still Crazy After All These Years? What *Was* Popular Music in the 1960s?" in Bart Moore-Gilbert and John Seed, eds., *Cultural Revolution? The Challenge of the Arts in the 1960s* (London: Routledge, 1992), and "Blood on the Tracks: Popular Music in the 1970s," in Bart Moore-Gilbert, ed., *The Arts in the 1970s: Cultural Closure?* (London: Routledge, 1994).

22. Lawrence Levine, *Black Culture and Black Consciousness* (New York: Oxford University Press, 1977), p. 233.

23. Brian Jackson, *Working Class Community* (London: Routledge and Kegan Paul, 1968), p. 34.

24. Richard Shusterman, *Pragmatic Aesthetics: Living Beauty, Rethinking Art* (Oxford: Blackwell, 1992), pp. 179, 183–187, 193–200. David Novitz argues equally persuasively that we also cannot distinguish high and low art in terms of formal difference (the complex vs. the simple), effective difference (the challenging vs. the confirming), or creative difference (individual vs. collective production). See his "Ways of Artmaking: The High and the Popular in Art," *British Journal of Aesthetics* 29(1) (1989).

25. See Fiske, "Popular Discrimination."

26. For a typical assertion of the assumptions here take this comment, in *The Independent*, on the financial support by the Grateful Dead's Phil Lesh (through the group's Rex Foundation) for recordings by "forgotten" and "neglected" twentieth-century British composers: "Most significant of all, it has opened a dialogue between creative musicians on opposite sides of the commercial schism, dissolving the difference between those who make music for instant gratification and those who patiently await the verdict of eternity." Norman Lebrecht, "The Grateful and the Dead," *The Independent Magazine*, June 22, 1991, p. 60.

Of all rock groups, the Grateful Dead (and their fans) probably think the least in terms of "instant gratification."

27. Shusterman, *Pragmatic Aesthetics,* pp. 212–213.

28. See Richard Hoggart, *Uses of Literacy* (London: Chatto and Windus, 1957), and Raymond Williams, "Culture Is Ordinary," [1958] in his *Resources of Hope* (London: Verso, 1989).

29. The clearest statement of this problem in recent cultural studies (clear at least in part because she is quite unable to resolve the contradiction) is Janice Radway's *Reading the Romance* (Chapel Hill and London: University of North Carolina Press, 1984).

2. The Sociological Response

1. Quoted (from *A travers chants*) in Carol MacClintock, ed., *Readings in the History of Music in Performance* (Bloomington: Indiana University Press, 1979), pp. 430–432.

2. Barbara Herrnstein Smith, *Contingencies of Value* (Cambridge, Mass.: Harvard University Press, 1988), p. 13.

3. John Culshaw, *Putting the Record Straight* (London: Secker and Warburg, 1981), p. 317.

4. Lovat Dickson, *Radclyffe Hall at the Well of Loneliness* (London: Collins, 1975), pp. 45–46. Thanks to Gill Frith for this reference.

5. Sheila Davis, *The Craft of Lyric Writing* (Cincinnati, Ohio: Writer's Digest Books, 1985).
   Carl Dahlhaus describes the same sort of discursive clash in the historically shifting aesthetic of classical music: "The concept of originality which grew up in the late eighteenth century established itself in the nineteenth as an unquestioned aesthetic doctrine, whereas the idea of *ars inveniendi,* the theory of musical invention which was taken for granted in the seventeenth and earlier in the eighteenth, was condemned in the nineteenth as if it were a blasphemy against the cult of genius. Until the end of the eighteenth century a musical idea could be a platitude, something quite commonplace, without attracting the charge of being meaningless; convention—recognizable dependence on precedent—was still regarded as aesthetically legitimate." Quoted in Janet M. Levy, "Covert and Casual Values in Recent Writings About Music," *Journal of Musicology* 6(1) (1987): 25.

6. This was already the case, of course, for radio listeners, and it was a problem of which the BBC, at least, was well aware: much of its music programming policy under John Reith in the 1920s and early 1930s was designed to promote "active" listening.
   The Gramophone (like the BBC's *Radio Times*) is a rich source of examples of how bourgeois musical discourse changed to meet changing technological and commercial circumstances. See D. L. Le Mahieu, "*The Gramophone:* Recorded Music and the Cultivated Mind in Britain between the Wars," *Technology and Culture* 23(3) (1982).

7. As Richard Mohr, musical director of RCA Victor's Red Seal label, puts it, "The ideal for a phonograph record is the concert hall illusion or rather the illusion of the concert hall illusion because you can't transfer the concert hall into the dimensions of a living room. What you can do is record a work so that you think you're in a concert hall when you listen to it at home." See Glenn Gould, "The Prospects of Recording," *High*

Fidelity Magazine, vol. 16, April 1966, p. 49. My thanks to Paul Thèberge for bringing this to my attention.

8. Robert Stradling and Meirion Hughes suggest that a similar distinction within classical music itself was put into play by the BBC at the end of the 1920s, when it created the "categories of 'light' and 'light classical' music, which had previously been unknown." "Light composers" like Ketèlby and Coates could no longer appear on the same programs as "serious" composers such as Holst and Vaughan Williams. See *The English Musical Renaissance* (London: Routledge, 1993), pp. 89–90.

9. Dave Russell, *Popular Music in England, 1840–1914* (Manchester: Manchester University Press, 1987), p. 4.

10. Peter Van Der Merwe, *Origins of the Popular Style* (Oxford: Clarendon Press, 1989), pp. 16–19.

11. William Weber, *Music and the Middle Class: The Social Structure of Concert Life in London, Paris and Vienna* (London: Croom Helm, 1975), pp. 19–21.

12. Ibid., pp. 30–38, 60, 85–88, 113.

13. Lawrence M. Levine, *Highbrow/Lowbrow* (Cambridge, Mass.: Harvard University Press, 1988), p. 107.

14. Ibid., pp. 120, 146.

15. Paul Di Maggio, "Cultural Entrepreneurship in Nineteenth Century Boston. Part II: The Classification and Framing of American Art," *Media Culture and Society* 4(4) (1982): 317. And see Di Maggio, "Cultural Entrepreneurship in Nineteenth Century Boston: The Creation of an Organizational Base for High Culture in America," *Media Culture and Society* 4(1) (1982).

16. Quoted in Weber, *Music and the Middle Class,* p. 26.

17. Russell, *Popular Music in England,* pp. 6–7.

18. Ibid., pp. 7–8.

19. Katherine K. Preston, *Music for Hire: A Study of Professional Musicians in Washington (1877–1900)* (Stuyvesant, N.Y.: Pendragon Press, 1992), pp. 241–242.

20. Quoted in Jeremy Crump, "The Identity of English Music: The Reception of Elgar 1898–1935," in Robert Colls and Philip Dodd, eds., *Englishness: Politics and Culture, 1880–1920* (London: Croom Helm, 1986), p. 167. And see Van Der Merwe, *Origins of the Popular Style,* pp. 3–4, and Russell, *Popular Music in England,* pp. 7–8.

21. Levine, *Highbrow/Lowbrow,* p. 108.

22. See Irving Wallace, *The Fabulous Showman* (London: Hutchison, 1960), pp. 120–122. For Barnum's own account see *Struggles and Triumphs of P. T. Barnum By Himself* [1882] (London: Macgibbon and Kee, 1967), chap. 9. His Jenny Lind story is an uncanny preview of the Beatles' "invasion" of America to come.

23. Janice Radway, "The Scandal of the Middlebrow: The Book of the Month Club, Class Fracture and Cultural Authority," *South Atlantic Quarterly* 89(4) (1990). See also Joan Shelley Rubin, *The Making of Middlebrow Culture* (Chapel Hill and London: University of North Carolina Press, 1992).

24. Max Horkheimer and Theodor W. Adorno, *Dialectic of Enlightenment* [1944] (London: Allan Lane, 1973), p. 143.

25. Joseph Horowitz, *Understanding Toscanini* (New York: Alfred A. Knopf, 1987), p. 7. For Horowitz's analysis of classical music as mass music (and middle-class sociability)

in the postwar period, see his study of Van Cliburn, *The Ivory Trade: Piano Competitions and the Business of Music* (Boston: Northeastern University Press, 1990).

26. Horowitz, *Understanding Toscanini*, pp. 197–198.

27. Ibid., pp. 202, 208–209. And see T. W. Adorno's "Analytical Study of the NBC *Music Appreciation Hour*," reprinted in *Musical Quarterly* 78(2) (1994).

28. See Horowitz, *Understanding Toscanini*, p. 224. For the gramophone societies in Britain in this period, loosely organized by *The Gramophone* to encourage classical music appreciation among new listeners, see Le Mahieu, "*The Gramophone*: Recorded Music and the Cultivated Mind."

29. John F. Kassan, *Rudeness and Civility: Manners in Nineteenth Century Urban America* (New York: Hill and Wang, 1990), pp. 252–256. The best study of the same process in Britain remains Peter Bailey, *Leisure and Class in Victorian England* (London: Routledge and Kegan Paul, 1978).

30. Kathy Peiss, *Cheap Amusements: Working Women and Leisure in Turn-of-the-Century New York* (Philadelphia: Temple University Press, 1986), p. 136.

31. Geoffrey Nowell-Smith, "On Kiri Te Kanawa, Judy Garland, and the Culture Industry," in Naremore and Brantlinger, eds., *Modernity and Mass Culture* (Bloomington: Indiana University Press, 1991), p. 78.

32. Howard S. Becker, *Art Worlds* (Berkeley: University of California Press, 1982); Pierre Bourdieu, *Distinction: A Social Critique of the Judgement of Taste* [1979] (London: Routledge, 1984). For an earlier sociological approach which, drawing on Schutz, implicitly employs concepts of both art worlds ("musical cultures") and cultural capital ("musical competence") see Derrick F. Wright, "Musical Meaning and its Social Determinants," *Sociology* 9(3) (1975). A musical culture, Wright suggests, involves "knowledge not just of musical forms and interpretative schemes but also of rules of behaviour in musical settings." It means knowing "how, when and where to hear music" (p. 428).

33. I sometimes wonder whether my compulsion to think in threes is an effect of the BBC's division of my music listening experience into Radios 1, 2, and 3 (or, before that, the Home Service, the Light Programme, and the Third Programme), but my folk/art/pop distinction is, in fact, routine in the field, as I'll describe. Van Der Merwe, for example, defines "parlour music" by contrast to "art" music, on the one hand, and "folk" music, on the other, while Booth and Kuhn, using a very different musicological model, also come up with a tripartite division of folk/art/pop, which they root in different economic bases of support and transmission (art music is defined as patronized music). Musical forms can then be related to the constraints imposed by different production/transmission systems, in terms of levels of complexity and novelty, the nature of the audience, who's paying for the music, and so on. See Gregory D. Booth and Terry Lee Kuhn, "Economic and Transmission Factors as Essential Elements in the Definition of Folk, Art and Pop Music," *Musical Quarterly* 74(3) (1990).

34. Quoted in Kyle Gann, "Pulitzer Hacks," *Village Voice* (date unknown), p. 84.

35. I owe this point to Gregory Sandow. The great majority of art music professionals, of course, are players and not composers, but they face a similar problem in earning a living: *someone's* got to pay their way, and Cyril Ehrlich has argued that the necessity to give lessons to make a living had an entirely debilitating effect on art music culture

in Britain (he is thinking specifically about piano lessons, which became a normal part of middle-class childhood for 75 years or so from the turn of the century). See Cyril Ehrlich, *The Music Profession in Britain since the Eighteenth Century* (Oxford: Clarendon, 1985), chap. 6.

36. Henry Kingsbury, *Music, Talent and Performance: A Conservatory Cultural System* (Philadelphia: Temple University Press, 1988).

37. I take this list from Kingsbury, *Music, Talent and Performance*, pp. 17–18. He also includes as a conservatory characteristic "highly privatised teacher-student dyads."

38. Quoted in Horowitz, *Understanding Toscanini*, p. 212.

39. For a scathing account of how the pantheon of Great British Composers of the twentieth century was thus constructed, in "a selection process in which something less abstract than aesthetic judgement was involved"—on down the crown of the road march Parry, Elgar, and Vaughan Williams; out on the sidelines sit Rutland Boughton, Samuel Coleridge Taylor and Sir Arthur Sullivan—see Stradling and Hughes, *The English Musical Renaissance*, chap. 6.

40. In *Understanding Toscanini*, Joseph Horowitz is entertainingly rude about the "music appreciation" broadcasts and books issued by such American classical music popular- izers as Walter Damrosch in the 1920s and 1930s, seeing their approach as banal, parochial, and run through with an oily religiosity (pp. 203–210). Intellectuals were similarly quick to laugh at the ignorance and deplore the pronunciation of the presenters on Britain's first national commercial radio station, Classic FM, which was designed (successfully) to capture the popular audience for classical music that the BBC had eschewed. On the other hand, it remains striking that on newspaper arts pages it is still assumed that critics of popular forms (TV, film, and to some extent pop) need know nothing about such forms except as consumers: their skill is to be able to write about ordinary experience. Critics of high art forms, by contrast—music, art, and even literature—are expected to be educated in the form (book critics by having written books themselves). Music critics, in other words, are still seen as deriving their authority from their education rather than their individual sensibility or writing skills.

41. Quoted in Stradling and Hughes, *The English Musical Renaissance*, p. 234. Their emphasis.

42. Christopher Jackman, "Some Sociological Issues of Live Music Performance," Ph.D. thesis, Department of Sociology, Brunel University, 1992. For further thoughts on concert conventions see Christopher Small, "Performance as Ritual: Sketch for an Enquiry into the True Nature of a Symphony Concert," in A. L. White, ed., *Lost in Music*, Sociological Review Monograph 34 (London: Routledge, 1987). For the com- plex negotiations between bandleader and caterer on the New York private party circuit see Bruce A. Macleod, *Club Date Musicians* (Urbana and Chicago: University of Illinois Press, 1993), pp. 97–100.

43. Niall MacKinnon, *The British Folk Scene* (Buckingham: Open University Press, 1993). Direct quotes are from pp. 81, 94, and 112.

   Compare Robert Cantwell's argument from the United States: "As Dave Guard [of the Kingston Trio] recalls, the untutored, but far from amateur, vocal sound [of the 1950s folk revival] was the conscious production of professional coaching in phrasing, vowel sounds, and speech accent." See his "When We Were Good: Class and Culture in the Folk Revival," in Neil V. Rosenberg, ed., *Transforming Tradition* (Urbana and Chicago: University of Illinois Press, 1993), pp. 43–44.

44. MacKinnon, *The British Folk Scene*, p. 81.

45. For the significance of these resources for folk "revivals" see Rosenberg, *Transforming Tradition*, passim. The liner-note quote is from Kenneth S. Goldstein, "A Future Folklorist in the Record Business," p. 109.

 The original folk revival in Britain, at the beginning of the century, was heavily dependent on Cecil Sharp's exercise of authority through the English Folk Dance and Song Society; he and his trained teachers took on "the role of expert in the legitimation of performance." See Georgina Boyes, *The Imagined Village* (Manchester: Manchester University Press, 1993), p. 105.

46. Cantwell, "When We Were Good," p. 57.

47. MacKinnon, *The British Folk Scene*, pp. 19, 40, 53.

48. Boyes, *The Imagined Village*, p. 241; Bruce Jackson, "The Folksong Revival," in Rosenberg, *Transforming Tradition*, pp. 76–77. And see MacKinnon, *The British Folk Scene*, pp. 57, 72.

49. Simon Frith, *Sound Effects* (New York: Pantheon, 1981).

50. See, for example, Wilfrid Mellers, *Twilight of the Gods* (London: Faber and Faber, 1973) (on the Beatles); *A Darker Shade of Pale* (London: Faber and Faber, 1984) (on Bob Dylan); and *Angels of the Night* (Oxford: Basil Blackwell, 1986) (on popular female singers).

51. Frith, *Sound Effects*, chap. 3.

52. Ernest Borneman, *A Critic Looks at Jazz* (London: Jazz Music Books, 1946), p. 48.

53. I'm assuming here (unlike Bourdieu) that we can't map these discourses onto social class, or trace "homologies" between aesthetic values and social situations. If nothing else, the historical work on high and low culture should make the critic wary of treating mass culture (and all these discourses concern mass culture) in simple class terms.

54. Charles Keil has suggested that commercial media have been important in legitimating ethnic musics in the United States, in providing them with that weight, that history, that assures their "authenticity." See "People's Music Comparatively: Style and Stereotype, Class and Hegemony," *Dialectical Anthropology* 10 (1985).

55. See Robert Cantwell, *Bluegrass Breakdown* (Urbana: University of Illinois Press, 1984).

56. George Steiner, *In Bluebeard's Castle: Some Notes Towards the Re-definition of Culture* (London: Faber and Faber, 1971), p. 92.

57. Quoted (from a bandsmen's magazine) in Brian Jackson, *Working Class Community* (London: Routledge and Kegan Paul, 1968), p. 25. For Romanticism and rock see Simon Frith and Howard Horne, *Art into Pop* (London: Methuen, 1987), chap. 2. For the historical origins of these various ideals see Morag Shiach, *Discourse on Popular Culture* (Cambridge: Polity, 1989).

58. See Ruth Finnegan, *The Hidden Musicians: Music-Making in an English Town* (Cambridge: Cambridge University Press, 1989).

59. Borneman, *A Critic Looks at Jazz*, p. 12.

60. See Frith, *Sound Effects*, and Frith and Horne, *Art into Pop*.

61. Howard Rye, "Fearsome Means of Discord: Early Encounters with Black Jazz," in Paul Oliver, ed., *Black Music in Britain* (Milton Keynes: Open University Press, 1990), p. 47.

62. Quoted in Rye, "Fearsome Means of Discord," p. 49.

63. See Simon Frith, "Playing with Real Feeling—Jazz and Suburbia," *New Formations* 4 (1988).

64. See Ron Welburn, "Duke Ellington's Music: The Catalyst for a True Jazz Criticism," *International Review of the Aesthetics and Sociology of Music* 17 (1986).

65. Borneman, *A Critic Looks at Jazz*, p. 14.

66. Welburn, "Duke Ellington's Music," pp. 114–115.

67. Ibid., p. 122.

3. Common Sense and the Language of Criticism

1. Ernest Borneman, *A Critic Looks at Jazz* (London: Jazz Music Books, 1946), p. 7. Borneman the jazz fan doesn't always follow the advice of Borneman the anthropologist. While he does attempt to establish an "objective" criterion of jazz value, which depends first on establishing what "makes this music different from all other forms of music," and second on asserting that "the best musician is the one who shows the least compromise with alien forms of music; who gives the widest development to the traditional framework; who shows the greatest variety within the unity of the chosen idiom" (p. 14), his views often stray across such clear generic boundaries and express obvious "subjective" views—"in jazz, as in all art, the great masterpieces are invariably lucid, serene and perfectly poised" (p. 15); "Tin Pan Alley tunes are not only poorly invented and generally in bad taste, but also insufficient in rhythmic, melodic and harmonic tension to provide a musical stimulus for jazz improvisation" (p. 16).

2. From a letter commenting on my arguments in this chapter.

3. For a useful discussion of the methodological issues raised here for taste research, see Jackie Stacey, "Textual Obsessions: Methodology, History and Researching Female Spectatorship," *Screen* 34(3) (1993).

4. See Fred Vermorel and Judy Vermorel, *Starlust: The Secret Fantasies of Fans* (London: W. H. Allen, 1985); and Lisa A. Lewis ed., *The Adoring Audience: Fan Culture and Popular Media* (London and New York: Routledge, 1992).

5. One observer, interested in courtship routines, was unceremoniously chased off the beach by angry lovemakers, and Graham Greene made full use of the spy/observer confusion in *The Confidential Agent* (London: William Heinemann, 1939). For an early overview of M-O's findings see Mass-Observation, *Britain* (Harmondsworth, Middlesex: Penguin, 1939).

6. For an example of this sort of research, see Herbert Blumer, *Movies and Conduct* (New York: Macmillan, 1933). Even in the Lynds' Middletown research, the emphasis tended to be more on cinema's effect on social mores, or, rather, on the Lynds' reading of this, than on Middletowners' own account of their movie pleasures—see, for example, Robert Lynd and Helen Lynd, *Middletown* (New York: Harcourt, Brace and Company, 1929), pp. 267–268.

7. See Jeffrey Richards and Dorothy Sheridan, ed., *Mass-Observation at the Movies* (London: Routledge, 1987). There are obvious precursors here of the way television researchers in the 1970s began to concentrate on television viewing as a social practice, one which might have very little to do with what was on the screen, and which was

shaped by particular sorts of domestic relationships. For a useful survey of the arguments see Dave Morley, *Television, Audiences and Cultural Studies* (London: Routledge, 1992).

8. There is some supporting evidence that the tastes described by the Mass-Observation projects were typical in a questionnaire survey carried out through *Picturegoer* a few years later. See J. P. Mayer, *British Cinemas and Their Audiences* (London: Dennis Dobson, 1948), pp. 153–244. Mayer looks at the film preferences of a sample of 50 moviegoers (the earlier part of the book concerns the effect of moviegoing on people's lives as revealed by their "motion picture autobiographies").

9. On this point see Robert B. Ray, "The Twelve Days of Christmas: A Response to Dudley Andrew," *Strategies* 3 (1990): 284.

10. There is not much academic research on popular musicians, but the few existing studies are rather good. In the United States Howard Becker's work on dance musicians became the model for a number of subsequent studies. See Howard S. Becker, *Outsiders* (Glencoe, N.Y.: Free Press, 1963); Robert A. Stebbins, "The Jazz Community: The Sociology of a Musical Subculture," Ph.D thesis, University of Minnesota, 1964; Robert R. Faulkner, *Hollywood Studio Musicians: Their Work and Career in the Recording Industry* (Chicago: Aldine-Atherton, 1971); H. Stith Bennett, *On Becoming a Rock Musician* (Amherst: University of Massachussetts Press, 1980).

In Britain Mavis Bayton's "How Women Become Rock Musicians," Ph.D. thesis, University of Warwick, 1989, provides a useful corrective to Bennett's picture of an entirely masculine world, and there are two outstanding anthropological studies of local music making: Ruth Finnegan, *The Hidden Musicians* (Cambridge: Cambridge University Press, 1989), and Sara Cohen, *Rock Culture in Liverpool* (Oxford: Clarendon Press, 1991).

All these studies (not least for methodological reasons) deal with the journeymen and women of the popular music world rather than with its stars, though Robert Walser's *Running with the Devil: Power, Gender and Madness in Heavy Metal* (Hanover and London: Wesleyan University Press, 1993) does something to redress the balance. He, like any serious researcher on this topic, is reliant on the magazine *Musician,* by far the best source of information on rock star values. See the interviews collected in Bill Flanagan, *Written in My Soul* (Chicago: Contemporary Books, 1986).

11. Borneman, *A Critic Looks at Jazz,* p. 12.

12. Geoff Wills and Cary L. Cooper, *Pressure Sensitive: Popular Musicians under Stress* (London: Sage, 1988), pp. 80–81.

13. A point first made by Howard S. Becker. See "The Professional Dance Musician and His Audience," *American Journal of Sociology* 57(2) (1952).

14. For an early sociological description of this problem see Carlo L. Lastrucci, "The Professional Dance Musician," *Journal of Musicology* 3(3) (1941).

15. Art Hodes and Chadwick Hansen, *Hot Man: The Life of Art Hodes* (Urbana and Chicago, University of Illinois Press, 1992), p. 109.

16. Bruce MacLeod, *Club Date Musicians: Playing the New York Party Circuit* (Urbana and Chicago: University of Illinois Press, 1993), p. 92.

17. As one of Wills and Cooper's interviewees puts it, "Most people regard musicians as one step up the 'social ladder' from rapists and muggers, and it's this 'alienation' from the non-musician that I believe creates most of the problems. The prolonged experi-

ence of being regarded as 'unclean' by 'civilians' is what causes the musician to retreat into himself, and causes a build-up of neuroses which can all-too-easily lead to a nervous breakdown. This is compounded by many facts . . . There is no standard set. The public wouldn't know a good player from a bad one, the media largely promote mediocrity, and the Musicians' Union have no set standard to conform to: pay your subs', and you're in! In any other profession, it's a fair bet that as you become more skilful, you move up, and do better quality work. Not so for the musician." Quoted in *Pressure Sensitive*, p. 46.

18. Quoted in Dr. Licks, *Standing in the Shadows of Motown: The Life and Music of Legendary Bassist James Jamerson* (Wynnewood, Pa.: Dr. Licks Publishing, 1989), p. 41.

19. It is interesting to read John Culshaw's views on this. From his perspective as a classical music producer, he concluded that it was the *situation* of performer/audience that was bad for music: "I really doubt that anyone plays better with an audience than without. They may think they do. But actually they only feel better. Listen to a transcription of a recorded concert that had the audience feeling 'My God, that was wonderful' and you will find that it really wasn't that good. But it was an occasion, like a funeral, and one is excited and moved by having been part of the audience. When somebody buys the record he feels that he has been swindled if he doesn't go crazy like the audience of 2,000 to 3,000 that was present and so he doesn't apply his usual critical faculties . . . He is a conditioned dog." Quoted in Glenn Gould, "The Prospects of Recording," *High Fidelity Magazine*, vol. 16, April 1966, p. 54.

20. They were more likely to be represented by American Equity. See George Seltzer, *Music Matters: The Performer and the American Federation of Musicians* (Metuchen, N.J.: Scarecrow Press, 1989), p. 263.

21. Quoted in Dr. Licks, *Standing in the Shadows of Motown*, p. xiii.

22. Konstantin Economou, *Making Music Work* (Linkoping, Sweden: Linkoping University, 1994), p. 200.

23. For an interesting sociological description of how this feels from the inside, see H. L. Goodall, Jr., *Living in the Rock N Roll Mystery* (Carbondale and Edwardsville, Ill.: Southern Illinois University Press, 1991).

24. As Economou's research suggests, young musicians, like any other young fans, value their idols as standing for "a certain way of looking at life." This is what the music (and the musical genre concerned) is taken to mean; such meanings must be shared by one's fellow players in a group. See Economou, *Making Music Work*, pp. 101, 202–205.

25. Quoted in MacLeod, *Club Date Musicians*, p. 141.

26. Many thanks to Greg Sandow for this point.

27. Norman Lebrecht observed Rodney Friend, leader of the BBC Symphony Orchestra, getting increasingly irritated as he rehearsed a piece by Harrison Birtwistle: "'The only pleasure I get,' expostulated Friend, unable to fathom the structure of the music sitting on his stand, 'is actually being able to play it from beginning to end more or less accurately.' . . . Both men, beneath the professional courtesies, were exceedingly angry. Friend felt he was being forced to abuse his instrument; Birtwistle heard his music being attacked." Norman Lebrecht, "Knights at the Opera," *The Independent Magazine*, May 18, 1991, p. 59.

28. Jon Frederickson and James F. Rooney, "The Free-Lance Musician as a Type of Non-Person: An Extension of the Concept of Non-Personhood," *Sociological Quarterly* 29(2) (1988).

29. In British critical ideology the ideal creative force is thus taken to be the guitarist/ singer writing partnership—Jagger/Richard, Morrissey/Marr.

30. The resulting confusions in Britain's "indie-rock" scene are well brought out in Cohen's *Rock Culture in Liverpool*.

31. John Miller Chernoff, *African Rhythm and African Sensibility* (Chicago and London: University of Chicago Press, 1979), pp. 126–127.

32. Quoted in Brian Jackson, *Working Class Community* (London: Routledge and Kegan Paul, 1968), p. 25. Emphasis in the original.

33. For sociological studies of the recording studio see Edward R. Kealy's "From Craft to Art: The Case of Sound Mixers and Popular Music" (*Sociology of Work and Occupations* 6 [1979]), which shows how professional values shifted in the 1960s as sound engineers took on a more self-consciously artistic (rock-derived) attitude to their work; and Antoine Hennion's "The Production of Success: An Antimusicology of the Pop Song" (*Popular Music* 3 [1983]), a subtle account of Paris recording studios which draws attention to the ever-present arbitrating role of the person not there, the consumer, as everyone present tries to judge sounds against what she or he might like.

34. For a lucid and instructive account of "the production of culture" in country music, showing how at each stage the "work" at issue—the piece of music—becomes a different discursive object, see John Ryan and Richard A. Peterson, "The Product Image: The Fate of Creativity in Country Music Songwriting," in J. Ettema and D. Whitney, eds., *Individuals in Mass Media Organisations* (Newbury Park, Calif.: Sage, 1982).

35. I'm generalizing here both from my own conversations, and from Keith Negus's excellent study of the British recording industry, *Producing Pop* (London: Edward Arnold, 1992), which suggests that the key value clash is not that between musicians and companies, but between A&R and marketing departments, which define musical value differently and are equally eager to claim sales success for themselves (and blame market failure on each other).

36. For record company Romanticism see Jon Stratton, "Capitalism and Romantic Ideology in the Record Business," *Popular Music* 3 (1983). For copyright law, see Simon Frith, ed., *Music and Copyright* (Edinburgh: Edinburgh University Press, 1993).

37. Nicholas Tawa notes the importance of the man with an ear "like the public's" (and the actual commercial unreliability of his taste) for song publishers in turn-of-the-century Tin Pan Alley. See Nicholas Tawa, *The Way to Tin Pan Alley: American Popular Song, 1866–1910* (New York: Schirmer Books, 1990), p. 42.

38. Chrysalis Records Press Release, August 29, 1990.

39. BMG press release for Raging Slab, January 16, 1990.

40. See, for example, Paul Willis, *Profane Culture* (London: Routledge and Kegan Paul, 1978); and Dick Hebdige, *Subculture: The Meaning of Style* (London: Methuen, 1979).

41. See, for example, Vermorel and Vermorel, *Star Lust*; Sheryl Garratt, "Teenage Dreams," in Sheryl Garratt and Sue Steward, *Signed, Sealed and Delivered* (London: Pluto, 1984); and Sue Wise, "Sexing Elvis," *Women's Studies International Forum* 7 (1984).

42. See, for example, Donna Weinstein, *Heavy Metal: A Cultural Sociology* (New York: Lexington, 1991); Johan Fornäs, "Popular Music and Youth Culture in Late Modernity," in Keith Roe and Ulla Carlsson, eds., *Popular Music Research* (Göteborg: Nordicom-Sweden, 1990).

43. One of the more interesting examples of such a "functional" aesthetic concerns the South Korean genre of the "demo-song," songs used for demonstrations (and therefore banned by the state): "Generally speaking, demo-songs fall into three types. First, the lyric song, which has the Korean structure of feeling. What is important here are the words, which describe Korean political reality. We generally sing these songs in the bar or at home alone. Second, the folk song, translated into contemporary terms. We always sing the folk song before the political demonstration, along with group dances which represent unity. Here what is important is not the lyric but the empowering rhythm. Finally the direct demo-song. We sing these songs when we take part in a demonstration and fight the police and the army. The songs in this category are lyrically political but contain simple and repetitive rhythms. What is significant about demo-songs is not pleasure or fun but an experience in which I, the song, and reality become one. Of the three types I like the lyric song best, since such songs are most emotionally affecting. The more the grief expressed, the deeper the song's echo." Quoted, with thanks, from an unpublished essay by Chang Yun Joo.

44. Weinstein, *Heavy Metal*; Walser, *Running with the Devil*.

45. Nicholas Cook, *Music, Imagination and Culture* (Oxford: Clarendon Press, 1990), pp. 58–59. Compare Kyle Gann: "At a conference two years ago, I overheard a professor, who had just delivered a lecture on the structure of an Elliott Carter orchestral work, admit to a colleague that while Carter's music analyzes beautifully on paper, you can't hear in the music the nice things you've analyzed. His colleague sorrowfully agreed." (Kyle Gann, "Pulitzer Hacks," *Village Voice* [date unknown], p. 84.)

   The Italian musicologist Gino Stefani makes a similar distinction in terms of the different sorts of "musical competence" involved, contrasting "popular" competence and "high" competence in terms of a grid of interpretive codes moving from the general/functional to the formal/specific. See Gino Stefani, "A Theory of Musical Competence," *Semiotica* 66(3) (1987). I'm not convinced that there's a continuity here, rather than two quite different conceptions of music. My favorite example of what (to an ordinary listener) seems like musicological madness is cited by Janet M. Levy in "Covert and Casual Values in Recent Writings about Music," *Journal of Musicology* 6(1) (1987). This is Charles Rosen on Beethoven and "his continuous attempt to strip away, at some point in each large work, all decorative and even expressive elements from the musical material—so that part of the structure of tonality is made to appear for a moment naked and immediate, and its presence in the rest of the work as a dynamic and temporal force suddenly becomes radiant . . ." As Levy asks, what on earth does this mean? (p. 16).

46. Cook, *Music, Imagination and Culture*, p. 85.

47. Ibid., p. 223.

48. See William Mann, "What Songs the Beatles Sang . . .," *The Times*, December 27, 1963; Deryck Cooke, "The Lennon-McCartney Songs," *The Listener*, February 1, 1968; Wilfrid Mellers, *Twilight of the Gods* (London: Faber and Faber, 1973).

   As to who was laughing at whom, I can't resist quoting at length Glenn Gould's brilliant musicological review of Petula Clark. Parody? Serious? Or both?

But for Tony Hatch, tonality is not a worked-out lode. It is a viable and continuing source of productive energy with priorities that demand and get, from him, attention. "Downtown" is the most affirmative diatonic exhortation in the key of E major since the unlikely team of Felix Mendelssohn and Harriet Beecher Stowe pooled talents for "still, still with Thee, when purple morning breaketh, / When the bird waketh and the shadows flee" . . . Motivically, "Who Am I?" plays a . . . game of reverse "Downtown"-ism. The principal motivic cell unit of that ebullient lied consisted of the interval of a minor third plus a major second, alternating, upon occasion, with a major third followed by a minor second. In "Downtown," the composite of either of these figures, the perfect fourth, became the title motive and the figures themselves were elongated by reiterated notes ("When/you're/a/lone/and/life/is"), shuffled by commas ("down-town, where") ("to help, I") (["Pret]-ty, how can"), and constantly elaborated by the sort of free-diatonic transpositioning which seems entirely consistent with the improvisatory fantasies of youth.

In "Who Am I?", however, the same motive, though introduced and occasionally relieved by scale-step passages ("The build-ings-reach-up—to-the-sky") is most often locked in a diatonic spiral—the notes F-E-C and C-A-G serving to underline "I walk alone and wonder, Who Am I?" Furthermore, the bass line at this moment is engaged with the notes D-G-E and G-E-A, a vertical synchronization of which would imply a harmonic composite of the title motive. Now, admittedly, such Schoenbergian jargon must be charily applied to the carefree creations of the pop scene. At all costs, one must avoid those more formidable precepts of Princetonian Babittry such as "pitch class," which, since they have not yet forded the Hudson unchallenged, can scarcely be expected to have plied the Atlantic and to have taken Walthamstow studio without a fight. Nevertheless, "Downtown" and "Who Am I?" clearly represent two sides of the same much-minted coin. The infectious enthusiasm of the "Downtown" motive encounters its obverse in the somnambulistic systematization of the "Who Am I?" symbol, a unit perfectly adapted to the tenor of mindless confidence and the tone of slurred articulation with which Petula evokes the interminable mid-morning coffee-hour laments of all the secret sippers of suburbia. ("Petula Clark," *High Fidelity*, November 1967. Quoted from Tim Page, ed., *The Glenn Gould Reader* [1984] [London: Faber and Faber, 1987], pp. 300–307.)

49. J. A. Westrup, Editorial, *Music and Letters* xlix(1), January 1968.
50. See Walser, *Running With The Devil*, passim.
51. Levin L. Schücking, *The Sociology of Literary Taste* [1931] (London: Kegan Paul, 1966), p. 57.
52. And it raises a recurring laugh among musicians. Bruce MacLeod notes that "the phrase 'Best band I've ever heard' has become a standard in-joke among club date musicians, who use it as an ironic response to questions about how the music was at a recent job. The reply makes it clear that it was pretty bad, although the audience liked it—as usual." (MacLeod, *Club Date Musicians*, p. 152.)
53. Andrew Porter, "Opera," *The New Yorker*, November 12, 1990, pp. 108–109.
54. Schoenberg quoted in Scott, "Music and Sociology for the 1990s," p. 389. Nicolas Slonimsky records an early example of this (and of the fact that "new music always

sounds loud to old ears") in a review of the first London performance of Beethoven's Ninth Symphony: "Beethoven finds from all the public accounts that noisy extravagance of execution and outrageous clamor in musical performances more frequently ensures applause than chastened elegance or refined judgement. The inference, therefore, that we may fairly make, is that he writes accordingly." See Nicolas Slonimsky, *Lexicon of Musical Invective* [1953] (Seattle and London: University of Washington Press, 1969), p. 18.

55. Borneman, *A Critic Looks at Jazz*, p. 52.

56. Letter to the *Voice Pazz and Jop Music Supplement,* March 5, 1991, p. 7.

57. For an entertaining and helpful account of these arguments among turn-of-the-century writers see Peter Keating, *The Haunted Study: A Social History of the English Novel, 1875–1914* (London: Secker and Warburg, 1989).

58. Perhaps the most striking feature of the resulting standoff between the aesthete and the philistine is that for both sides the other is feminine. The woman as materialist corruptor of the artist is a consistent theme of Henry James's stories and of subsequent bohemian mythology (in Bob Dylan's early songs, for instance), just as the high cultural description of mass culture as feminine by theorists from Horkheimer and Adorno to Baudrillard is echoed in rock fans' contemptuous dismissal of commercial pop as "teenybop." (See Andreas Huyssen, "Mass Culture as Woman: Modernism's Other," in his *After the Great Divide* (Bloomington: Indiana University Press, 1986.)

Meanwhile, from the philistine side, the American bandmaster John Philip Sousa once stressed to a Houston reporter that "the people who frequent my concerts are the strong and healthy. I mean healthy of both mind and body. These people like virile music. Longhaired men and shorthaired women you never see in my audience. And I don't want them." (Quoted in Levine, *Highbrow/Lowbrow*, p. 238.) Nicholas Tawa suggests that the philistine treatment of high art as "effete" was a central theme of the late nineteenth century popular song (see Tawa, *The Way to Tin Pan Alley*). This equation of high art with sissiness and perversion remains familiar in populist prose.

59. Borneman, *A Critic Looks at Jazz*, p. 13.

60. See Roland Barthes, "The Grain of the Voice" [1972] in *The Responsibility of Forms* (Berkeley and Los Angeles: University of California Press, 1991), p. 267: "If we examine the current practice of music criticism (or of conversations 'on' music: often the same thing), we see that the work (or its performance) is invariably translated into the poorest linguistic category: the adjective."

61. Kingsbury, *Music, Talent and Performance*, p. 87.

62. Lebrecht, "Knights at the Opera," p. 57.

63. Robert Sandall, "Lou Reed's *Magic and Loss*," Q, 65 (February 1992).

64. Reviews by Stephen Dalton from the "Short Circuit" album round-up, *New Musical Express* (date unknown).

65. Simon Reynolds, "Smells Like Teen Spirit," *Village Voice,* December 3, 1991, p. 69.

66. *Voice Pazz and Jop Supplement,* March 5, 1991, p. 7.

67. The most common arguments about musical effects are rather different. Popular music has, for example, been held responsible for sexual arousal and/or hysteria; delinquency and violence; despair and suicide; fascism and political mindlessness; sexism and homophobia; bourgeois ideology generally (and romantic heterosexualism in particular).

Such readings tend to be made by people from outside the music worlds concerned, and they therefore don't depend on any pop or rock knowledge at all (which is why such arguments so often seem plain silly to the fans and musicians themselves). Despite (or maybe because of) this, such arguments, unlike production arguments, tend to be remarkably effective materially, in terms of labelings, bannings, and censorship. The effects critics do influence what music is and can be produced and heard, and a necessary part of such judgments is, indeed, the assertion that something "should be done": stop Skrewdriver concerts! Ban Shabba Ranks tracks from the radio! This even though very little evidence usually exists that the music has the effects it is purported to have, whether on crowd behavior, individual attitudes, social beliefs, or whatever. It follows, paradoxically, that effects criticism focuses much more closely than production criticism on the music itself. The "effects" of the music, that is to say, have to be deduced from the music itself because there is no independent evidence of them. In this context "the music itself" is reduced to a rather small number of effective elements: rhythm; lyrics; performance.

68. See Howard S. Becker, "Art as Collective Action," *American Sociological Review* 39 (1974).

69. See Susan D. Crafts, Daniel Cavicchi, and Charles Keil, *My Music* (Hanover and London, Wesleyan University Press, 1993).

This is not Charles Keil's first venture into such research. In 1965 he "sponsored a contest in *Spear* magazine . . . which had a wide circulation in various levels of Nigerian society . . . Readers were asked to respond in thirty words or less to the question 'Who is your favourite musician—and why?'" The results are reported as an appendix to Chernoff, *African Rhythm and Sensibility.* The following quotes indicate the variety of technical and functional judgments:

"My favourite musician is I. K. Dairo. He begins moderately, sings moderately, ends moderately. No mixing of language. No mumble. Different tones, tunes, and beating in each music. His tunation, tone and beating moulded together keep music unfaded" (p. 174).

"My favourite musician is Mr Cardinal Jim Rex Lawson because his music can make the unhappy to be happy and a divorced couple to be reengaged and an angry lion to be calmed" (p. 174).

"Jim Lawson is my favourite . . . The underground sound of instruments thrills even a mad person to dance and escape madness meanwhile" (p. 175).

"In fact the moment I am annoyed with my girlfriend or feel unhappy with everything on earth and fed up with life, but as soon as I put on my radio and hear I. K. Dario's music, I will be just very happy and forget all sorts of bad thinking and start kissing my girlfriend" (p. 178).

"The late Jim Reeves is my music idol. His cool sentimentality, his heart-awakening compositions, the voice and the instruments which make you feel the angels around, surely win your heart" (p. 177).

70. Crafts, Cavicchi, and Keil, *My Music,* pp. 61, 168, 140, 144.

71. Ibid., p. 49 (and compare pp. 69, 103, 118, 137) and pp. 193, 85, 90–91.

72. Ibid., pp. 97–98.

4. Genre Rules

1. Quoted in Nicholas Tawa, *The Way to Tin Pan Alley: American Popular Song, 1866–1910* (New York: Schirmer Books, 1990), p. 85.
2. Quoted in Christopher Ballantine, *Music and Its Social Meanings* (New York: Gordon and Breach, 1984), p. 26.
3. Cited in Tawa, *The Way to Tin Pan Alley*, p. 162.
4. I always enjoy looking for my brother's records in strange record stores: as an "avant-garde" guitarist who has performed in a great variety of idioms, Fred Frith may turn up as jazz or rock or contemporary classical, as alternative, New Age, or Euro pop.
5. This information was taken from *Variety: The Complete Book of US Show Business Awards* (New York: Garland, 1985). Thanks to Alex Doty for bringing this to my attention.
6. This list was taken from Ken Barnes, "Top 40 Radio: A Fragment of the Imagination," in S. Frith, ed., *Facing the Music* (New York: Pantheon, 1988).
7. David Zimmerman, "Adult Top 40 Makes Waves in Radio," *USA Today*, date unknown.
8. There's a particular problem here of genre boundaries. On the one hand, radio stations are loath to play anything too different from their basic sound (the first principle of programming is to ensure that no one is moved to switch off); on the other hand, neither do they want to seem too exclusive (the second principle is to entice the straying listener to stay). The effect (as many a bemused European visitor will testify) is that, for all the fine demographic distinctions, American commercial radio stations sound much the same. This is not much help to record sellers—and helps explains the rise of MTV, which maps the music market in much more record company–friendly ways.
9. Government of Canada, *Loi sur la Radiofusion*, 1983, Schedule II, Content Categories and Subcategories, pp. 2573–4. On Canada's insistence, Canadian content requirements were not an issue in the Free Trade Agreements between Canada and the United States and Mexico. Thanks to Will Straw for clarification of Canadian radio policy.
10. For an interesting answer see Line Grenier, "Radio Broadcasting in Canada: The Case of 'Transformat' Music," *Popular Music* 9(2) (1990).
11. The words of EMAP's David Hepworth, quoted in Judy Rumbold, "Rock plays it riff and ready," *Media Guardian*, September 10, 1990.
12. The Independent Radio Authority, which is responsible for awarding broadcasting licenses, later put its own gloss on this clause, by defining music recorded or composed before 1960 as "non-pop music" even if it was both strongly rhythmic and amplified.
13. House of Lords *Weekly Hansard*, October 16, 1990, columns 752–754. The amendment was passed and accepted by the House of Commons; the FM license was awarded to Classic FM, a classical music station.
14. The rock/pop distinction was, in fact, taken from sociology—see my *Sound Effects* (New York: Pantheon, 1981). The ideological implications were obvious in media discussion at the time. Judy Rumbold quotes Danny Kelly, then editor of *New Musical Express* (now editor of *Q*): "Pop is bought by teenage girls. Rock is bought by everybody else." And Mark Fisher, then Labour Party spokesman for the Arts: "Pop music is rock music without the sex or soul." See Judy Rumbold, "Rock plays it riff and ready."

15. Barry Walters, "A Better Best Top 100," *Village Voice*, September 6, 1988, p. 73.

16. See Jason Toynbee, "Policing Bohemia, Pinning Up the Grunge: The Music Press and Generic Change in British Pop and Rock," *Popular Music* 12(3) (1993); and Sarah Thornton, *Club Cultures* (Cambridge: Polity, 1995).

17. *Folk Roots* press release, March 7, 1988. Readers' letters pages become particularly interesting (and angry) when a magazine moves genre boundaries—as in *The Wire*, the British jazz magazine, which extended its definition of jazz to cover all "interesting" contemporary music at about the same time as *Southern Rag* became *Folk Roots*.

18. Quoted from the first WORLD MUSIC press release, n.d. [1987]. And see Peter Jowers, "Beating New Tracks: WOMAD and the British World Music Movement," in Simon Miller, ed., *The Last Post: Music after Modernism* (Manchester: Manchester University Press, 1993), pp. 61–64.

19. I discuss this in much greater detail in "The Naked and the Dead," in Georgina Born and David Hesmondhalgh, eds., *Western Music and Its Others* (Berkeley: University of California Press, forthcoming).

20. This becomes a particularly complex argument in the marketing of "crossover" acts, when the same music has to be sold as fulfilling different functions for different audiences. The crossover appeal of Michael Jackson's *Thriller* to a rock audience, for example, depended on a particularly subtle mix of Eddie Van Halen's guitar against Jackson's voice.

21. For discussion of these issues in an American context see Holly Kruse, "Subcultural Identity in Alternative Music Culture," *Popular Music* 12(1) (1993); and Stephen Lee, "Re-examining the Concept of the 'Independent' Record Company: The Case of Wax Trax! Records," *Popular Music* 14(1) (1995).

22. In Britain a reliable sign of an "indie" band is that its albums top the charts on release and then fall straight out—such bands have devoted followers but fail to cross over.

23. The list is based on a questionnaire funded by Nescafe and administered by student radio stations. I'm taking the information from a press release dated October 1, 1988.

24. Quotes from *WRPM*, Autumn 1991. Thanks to Caroline Hutton for making this available to me.

25. For an example of an ideological category bringing together some even odder bedfellows, see Janos Marothy, *Music and the Bourgeois, Music and the Proletarian* (Budapest: Akadémiai Kiadó, 1974), pp. 536–538. At one point Marothy discusses "new folk singers" or "political folk singers," musicians who are not "lured by the commercial showbusiness" but "continue the proletarian folk tradition in the original spirit . . . so as to make it part and parcel of the conscious socialist movements of our modern age." These singers included Merle Travis (U.S.A.), Ernest Busch (Germany), Yves Montaud (France), Ewan McColl (Britain), and, from Italy, Margot and the Cantachronacle movement (which at this time included Italo Calvino). Some enterprising political nostalgic should put together a celebratory CD.

26. This is obvious, for example, in the musicians' conversations recorded in Sara Cohen, *Rock Culture in Liverpool* (Oxford: Clarendon Press, 1991).

    In an article examining the blurred boundaries between contemporary rock and art musics (and the increasing use of the term "new music"), Kyle Gann quotes Robert Ashley's simple formula: "Anything over five minutes is classical music, anything under that is rock." But even such an objective measure turns out to have an evaluative underpinning. Ashley explains that "Over five minutes a piece begins to need a structural foundation to hold together on a deeper-than-surface level." Add the suggestion that art music is also defined by its concert setting, a setting providing the necessary quietness, concentration, and intimacy, and we're back with a distinction that is really about art music's *superiority* to rock. See Kyle Gann, "Boundary Busters," *Village Voice*, September 3, 1991, p. 87.

27. Every critic is ambitious to fix a genre with a new label, to *conventionalize* a set of comparisons. My best attempt was the term "Hip Easy Listening," used in *Time Out* in April 1977 to describe Californian soft rock—Fleetwood Mac, etc. It was, however, redundant; the American radio label AOR described the same sort of music more efficiently. For a useful discussion of the same process in the book trade, see Susanne Kappeler, *The Pornography of Representation* (Cambridge: Polity Press, 1986), pp. 116–122.

28. Hence, for example, the continuing importance of *Maximum Rock'n'Roll* for the American since-punk scene, or the role of such little magazines as *Girl Germs* and *Girlymag* in the making of Riot Grrrl.

29. This clearly relates to the long-established truism of postwar popular music history that small, local, independent entrepreneurs pick up on new sounds and markets first (are "closer to the streets"). The majors only come in when new money-making possibilities are confirmed—the pattern from rock 'n' roll to rave.

30. Sarah Thornton makes this point about London's '90s dance club magazines, like *Boys' Own*—see *Club Cultures*. I am also indebted for the arguments here to Franc Donohoe's unpublished study of industrial music and Seona Slevin's unpublished work on Riot Grrrl.

31. For an excellent discussion of parallel arguments about the use of genre labels in film theory see Steve Neale, "Questions of Genre," *Screen* 31(1) (1990).

32. This is, perhaps, most obvious in country music. In Katie Stewart's words, "So it is that in country music the saddest of sad songs have come to represent the source or origins of 'country' as an other world or lyrical space that some people, and not others, inhabit. The music is filled with self-referential images of 'places' and 'types of people.' It fashions lyric images into a country world by indiscriminately mixing the metaphoric with the literal or the allegorical with the actual so that the subjects and objects of the songs appear as if in quotes and the categories themselves become objects of discussion to be reproduced, carried to excess, parodied, or taken to heart." Katie Stewart, "The Narrative Poetics of American 'Country' Lament: A Re-presentation of Country Music's Lost Love and Appalachia's Litanies of the Dead," unpublished paper, n.d., pp. 16–17. And see Aaron Fox, "The Jukebox of History: Narratives of Loss and Desire in the Discourse of Country Music," *Popular Music* 11(1) (1992).

33. See Paul Oliver's comments on the problems bequeathed by blues collectors to historians of African-American popular music: "Perceiving the blues as central to black secular song has had the effect of minimizing and even totally ignoring other vocal traditions, or of placing them in a relationship dependent upon their bearing on blues." Paul Oliver, *Songsters and Saints: Vocal Traditions on Race Records* (Cambridge: Cambridge University Press, 1984), pp. 3–12.

34. See Ruth Finnegan, *The Hidden Musicians* (Cambridge: Cambridge University Press, 1989), passim.

35. Ibid., pp. 68–69. One problem with Finnegan's research is that Milton Keynes is a rather white town, and she is not therefore able to say much about music and ethnicity. Common sense suggests that there are close ties between ethnicity and musical tastes and activities, though even here perhaps not as clear-cut as might be thought. For the relationship of different ethnic groups to reggae and ragga worlds see Simon Jones, *Black Culture, White Youth* (London: Macmillan, 1988); and Les Back, "X Amount of Sat Siri Akal! Apache Indian, Reggae Music and Intermezzo Culture," *New Formations* 26 (1995).

36. The second flaw of Finnegan's study is the lack of attention she pays to the media and what one might call genre's fantasy communities. How such fantasies work varies from genre to genre, and they affect musicians (who may or may not have ambitions for wider audiences) differently than consumers (who are involved in this wider world just by buying its artifacts, its sounds and its media). No musical scene these days, least of all most of those with which Finnegan was concerned, is simply local. For an important discussion of these issues see Will Straw, "Systems of Articulation and Logics of Change: Communities and Scenes in Popular Music," *Cultural Studies* 5 (1991).

37. Franco Fabbri, "A Theory of Musical Genres: Two Applications," in David Horn and Philip Tagg, eds., *Popular Music Perspectives* (Göteborg and London: IASPM, 1982), p. 52.

38. Ola Stockfelt, "Adequate Modes of Listening," *Stanford Humanities Review* 3(2) (1993): 160.

39. Lawrence Levine, *Black Culture and Black Consciousness* (New York: Oxford University Press, 1977), pp. 232–233.

40. Fabbri, "A Theory of Musical Genres," p. 70.

41. For an illuminating discussion of how such behavioral rules, such expectations of "good manners," constrain performers and audiences in the folk club, see Niall MacKinnon, *The British Folk Scene* (Buckingham: Open University Press, 1993).

42. Jeff Todd Titon notes, for example, the ways in which blues singers changed their off-stage stories to meet the behavioral conventions of their new white "revival" audiences in the 1960s, while Mark Fenster has documented the effects of video promotion on behavioral and semiotic rules in country music. See Jeff Todd Titon, "Reconstructing the Blues: Reflections on the 1960s Blues Revival," in Neil V. Rosenberg, ed., *Transforming Tradition* (Urbana and Chicago: University of Illinois Press, 1993), p. 234; and Mark Fenster, "Genre and Form: The Development of Country Music Video," *Popular Music* 7(3) (1988).

43. Helfried C. Zrzavy, "Issues of Incoherence and Cohesion in New Age Music," *Journal of Popular Culture*, 24(2) (1990): 39, 51.

44. Charles Hamm, "Genre, Performance and Ideology in the Early Songs of Irving Berlin," *Popular Music* 13(2) (1994): 149.

45. This is not just an issue in popular music. Hans Keller, most acerbic of classical music critics, once commented that: "The background of a composition is both the sum total of expectations a composer raises in the course of a piece without fulfilling them, and the sum total of those unborn fulfilments. The foreground is, simply, what he does instead—what is actually in the score . . . The background boils down to form, which many pieces have in common, and which can be found in the textbooks; the

foreground is the individual structure, which happens instead of the form, unless the music is a bore and fulfils all expectations—in which case you can write it yourself after the first few bars; you don't need a composer for it." Quoted in Storr, *Music and the Mind*, p. 85.

46. For a particularly interesting example of this argument, see James Parakilas, "Classical Music as Popular Music," *The Journal of Musicology* III(1) (1984). Parakilas compares performing conventions in "classical music" ("the classical style of playing Beethoven is not Beethoven's style of playing but a style about Beethoven," p. 7); "early music" (in which "style" ideally becomes "inaudible"); and "new music" (in which the composer's "style" has to be "discovered"). Parakilas's point is not just that one can't separate how these musics are played and heard from ideological arguments about their meaning (about the meaning of performance) but also that "performance" in this context has to be widely defined. Early music performers, for example, talk to the audience, drawing attention to their performance; classical performers act as if what they do is already approved by "authority"—it needs no justification; the unpredictable reception of new music, by contrast, makes "concert notes" of particular significance. Parakilas concludes that there are many uses of classical music: "Each use makes classical music popular in a different way, and every form of popularity feeds the others" (p. 13), while noting that the most common use of the music today is as "background," for reasons that haven't really been examined empirically. Because of its wordlessness? Its familiarity? Its prestige? But the theoretical question is this: how can the same music be the subject of both the most concentrated and the least concentrated listening? Is the "same" music really part of two quite different genres? Or do the boundaries of the classical genre need rethinking?

5. Where Do Sounds Come From?

1. Richard Norton, *Tonality in Western Culture* (University Park, Pa.: Pennsylvania University Press, 1984), p. 105.

2. Ned Rorem, *Settling the Score* (New York: Harcourt Brace, 1988), p. 357.

3. As Richard Norton puts it with reference to Western art music: "tonality is a *decision* made against the chaos of pitch" (his emphasis). See Norton, *Tonality in Western Culture*, pp. 4–5.

4. See Philip Tagg, "Reading Sounds: An Essay on the Soundscape and Music, Knowledge and Society," unpublished paper, 1986, p. 5. The most profound study of music from this perspective remains Murray Schafer, *The Tuning of the World* (New York: Alfred A. Knopf, 1977). For more recent work see Helmi Järviluoma, ed., *Soundscapes: Essays on Vroom and Moo* (Tampere: Department of Folk Tradition, 1994).

5. Ronald Radano thus suggests that Muzak is "a sonic form standing at the nexus of music and noise . . . a natural ambient music-noise of the indoor public environment . . . Muzak becomes a shadow—a likeness of music—for which the formalist arguments of value and quality are simply irrelevant." Ronald M. Radano, "Interpreting Muzak: Speculations on Musical Experience in Everyday Life," *American Music* 7(4) (1989): 457. And see Joseph Lanza, *Elevator Music: A Surreal History of Muzak, Easy Listening and Other Moodsong* (New York: St. Martin's Press, 1993); and James

Parakilas, "Classical Music as Popular Music," *The Journal of Musicology* III(1) (1984).

Deborah Cameron has pointed out to me in this context that "the age of the musical foreground" (and silent, contemplative listening) may actually be the historical anomaly. Court musicians, for example, primarily produced background sounds for other activities, and eighteenth-century opera goers seemed to have moved, talked, and dined throughout the performance.

6. Quoted in Gillian B. Anderson, "The Presentation of Silent Films, or Music as Anaesthesia," *The Journal of Musicology* 5(2) (1987): 269.

7. Philip Tagg, "*The Virginian*," from unpublished work in progress (with Robert Clarida), p. 7.

8. Rom Harré (who also refers to storms and horses) suggests that "in acquiring one's competence as a listener (and a composer) one accumulates a repertoire of musical devices, with, so to say, standard meanings in the culture." He is not, though, very clear as to where these meanings come from. See "Is There a Semantics for Music?" in Michael Krausz, ed., *Music and Philosophy* (Oxford: Clarendon Press, 1992), pp. 206–207.

9. Philip Tagg, "'Universal' Music and the Case of Death," *Critical Quarterly* 35(2) (1993): 76.

10. Ibid., pp. 74–45. (His emphases.)

11. See, in particular, Susan McClary, *Feminine Endings: Music, Gender and Sexuality* (Minneapolis: University of Minnesota Press, 1991). For a useful overview of the subsequent academic debate about musicology, gender, and sexuality, see Paula Higgins, "Women in Music, Feminist Criticism, and Guerilla Musicology: Reflections on Recent Polemics," *Nineteenth Century Music* XVII(2) (1993). The most crusty (and least convincing) male response to McClary's arguments was undoubtedly Pieter C. Van Den Toom, "Politics, Feminism and Contemporary Music Theory," *Journal of Musicology* IX (1991). And see Ruth A. Solie's "What Do Feminists Want? A Reply to Pieter Van Den Toom" in the same issue.

12. Susan McClary, "Comment: Getting Down Off the Beanstalk," *Minnesota Composers' Forum Newsletter*, February 1987, no page numbers. For a later version of this essay see *Feminine Endings*, chap. 5.

13. McClary, "Comment." And see *Feminine Endings*, pp. 77–78.

14. I find McClary's figurative musical descriptions immensely suggestive, but I do wonder sometimes where the adjectives come from—the "sluttish" second theme in Tchaikovsky's Fourth Symphony, for example. For helpful discussion of McClary's work in these terms see Mary Ann Smart's review of *Feminine Endings* in *Journal of Musicological Research* 14(1/2) (1994), and Charles Rosen, "Music à la Mode," *New York Review of Books*, June 23, 1994.

15. Leonard Bernstein, *The Unanswered Question: Six Talks at Harvard* (Cambridge, Mass.: Harvard University Press, 1976), pp. 178–179.

16. Graham Bruce, *Bernard Herrmann: Film Music and Narrative* (Ann Arbor: UMI Research Press, 1985), p. 118.

17. Nöel Carroll, *Mystifying Movies* (New York: Columbia University Press, 1988), pp. 218–219, 222.

18. Ibid., p. 223. (My emphases.) For the views of film scorers themselves on this, see the

interviews in Irwin Bazelon, *Knowing the Score: Notes on Film Music* (New York: Arco, 1975), and Royal S. Brown, *Overtones and Undertones: Reading Film Music* (Berkeley: University of California Press, 1994).

19. Carroll, *Mystifying Movies*, p. 219. (My emphasis.)

20. Fred Karlin and Rayburn Wright, eds., *On the Track: A Guide to Contemporary Film Scoring* (New York: Schirmer, 1990), pp. 228–236.

21. McClary, "Comment."

22. Hans Keller, *Criticism* (London: Faber and Faber, 1987), p. 153.

23. Note by Stephen Taylor, "New Music by Cornell Composers," February 23, 1991.

24. Note by Brian Robison, "New Music by Cornell Composers," February 23, 1991.

25. Nicholas Cook, *Music, Imagination and Culture* (Oxford: Clarendon Press, 1990), p. 171.

    And composers may be no more reliable in fixing their own music's meaning. Haydn's biographer, G. A. Griesinger, asked him what he was trying to "express" in his music: "He said that he oftentimes had portrayed moral characters in his symphonies. In one of his oldest, *which, however, he could not accurately identify,* 'the dominant idea is of God speaking with an abandoned sinner, pleading with him to reform. But the sinner in his thoughtlessness pays no heed to the admonition.'" (My emphasis.) Quoted in David P. Schoeder, *Haydn and the Enlightenment* (Oxford: Clarendon Press, 1990), p. 125.

26. See Leonard B. Meyer, *Emotion and Meaning in Music* (Chicago: University of Chicago Press, 1956).

27. See, for example, Deryck Cooke, *The Language of Music* (Oxford: Oxford University Press, 1959).

28. Philip Tagg uses "listening tests" to get at how musical connotations work empirically. He is interested, on the one hand, in measuring to what extent people's musical interpretations are shared (does everyone hear this melody as "angry"?) and, on the other, what elements of the music carry this implication (which combinations of melody, harmony, instrument, beat). See Philip Tagg, "Analysing Popular Music: Theory, Method and Practice," *Popular Music* 2 (1982). For an illuminating example of Tagg's analytic use of his method see *Fernando the Flute: Musical Meaning in an Abba Mega-Hit* (Liverpool: Liverpool University Institute of Popular Music, 1991).

    For an earlier version of the listening test (using a more directed set of questions than Tagg's, based on Charles Osgood's "semantic differential test") see Charles Keil and Angeliki Keil, "Musical Meaning: A Preliminary Report. (The Perception of Indian, Western and Afro-American Musical Moods by American Students)," *Ethnomusicology* X(2) (1966). And for an important critique of the method, arguing that musical interpretation also derives from how people "frame" the music, derives that is from the *social* circumstances of listening, and not just from the possible (fixed) semantic codes of the music itself, see Steven Feld, "Communication, Music, and Speech About Music," *Yearbook for Traditional Music* 16 (1984).

29. David Schoeder notes the same use of quotation from folk, church, and dance music in Haydn, and suggests that Haydn's "extraordinary achievement" was thus "to devise procedures for instrumental music that would allow it an intelligibility previously thought possible only if words were present." See Schoeder, *Haydn and the Enlightenment*, pp. 74, 68–71, 146–157.

30. Christopher Ballantine, *Music and Its Social Meanings* (New York: Gordon and Breach, 1984), p. 73, and see his analysis of Charles Ives' *Central Park in the Dark*, p. 87.

Robert Stradling and Meirion Hughes point out that folk quotations are the basis for assertions of music's supposed national expressiveness. They quote random examples from BBC Radio 3 program notes: "The music [of Guy Ropartz] gives off the authentic flavour of Brittany—indeed its last movement is based on a Breton folk tune." "Nielsen's music utilised a great deal of material from his island homeland of Fünen . . . which is why it sounds so Danish." And add George Bernard Shaw's tart comment: "Grieg's music does not remind me of Norway, perhaps because I have never been there."

31. Rap thus self-consciously draws attention to the act of quotation itself. As Paul Gilroy suggests, "the aesthetic rules that govern it are premised on a dialect of rescuing, appropriation and recombination that creates special pleasures." These are pleasures in which "aesthetic stress is laid upon the sheer social and cultural distance that formerly separated the diverse elements now dislocated into novel meanings by their provocative aural juxtaposition." See Paul Gilroy, "Sounds Authentic: Black Music, Ethnicity, and the Challenge of a *Changing* Same," *Black Music Research Journal* 10(2) (1990): 128–131; and compare Ballantine's analysis of Bob Dylan's use of vernacular musical quotes, his "way with signs," in *Music and Its Social Meanings*, p. 105.

32. Keir Keightley, "The History and Exegesis of Pop: Reading 'All Summer Long,'" M.A. thesis (Communications), McGill University, 1991, p. 15.

33. The pioneering work on film music from the direction of film studies was Claudia Gorbman's *Unheard Melodies: Narrative Film Music* (Bloomington and London: Indiana University Press and the BFI, 1987); and, from the direction of musicology, Philip Tagg's *Kojak: 50 Seconds of Television Music* (Gothenberg: Institute of Musicology, 1979). I have learned most of what I understand about film music from Gorbman and Tagg, as much through conversation as through their published work, and I hope that what follows does justice to their suggestions.

34. I take this list from David Mayer, "The Music of Melodrama," in David Bradby, Louis James, and Bernard Sharratt, eds., *Performance and Politics in Popular Drama* (Cambridge: Cambridge University Press, 1980), p. 62.

35. Schopenhauer quoted in Carroll, *Mystifying Movies*, p. 216; Bresson quoted in Jonathan Rosenbaum, "Sound Thinking," *Film Comment*, Sept.-Oct. 1978, p. 40.

36. Quoted in Anderson, "Presentation of Silent Films," p. 279.

37. Carroll, *Mystifying Movies*, p. 220.

38. Pop videos are thus much more like operas than like films, a point to which I'll return in Chapter 11.

39. For this approach to opera (drawing on the semiotics of Charles William Morris and C. S. Pierce), see Fritz Notske, *The Signifier and the Signified: Studies in the Operas of Mozart and Verdi* (The Hague: Martinus Nijhoof, 1977). Notske shows, for example, how Mozart uses the flute in his operas "as the disturber of balance, serving the intrigue and often revealing subconscious desire" (p. 125). And he analyzes the way Verdi uses the "musical figure of death" unconventionally, thus "renewing" its meaning as a topos (pp. 171, 214). From Notske's semiotic point of view, the meaning of music is not "intrinsic" to the text, but produced in the reading of it; from his perspective

the "sign giver" or composer is no more significant for the interpretation of a work of art than any other reader.

For discussion of relations between musical and narrative structure from the film composer's perspective (film composition as a craft), see George Burt, *The Art of Film Music* (Boston: Northeastern University Press, 1994).

40. Bruce, *Bernard Herrmann*, p. 216.
41. Quoted in John Broeck, "Music of the Fears," *Film Comment* 12 (1976): 56–60.
42. Nicholas Cook, "Music and Meaning in the Commercials," *Popular Music* 13(1) (1994): 35, 38.
43. Michel Chion, *Audio-Vision: Sound on Screen* [1990] (New York: Columbia University Press, 1994), p. 68.
44. This list taken from Carroll, *Mystifying Movies*, p. 216.
45. Quoted in Broecks, "Music of the Fears." (My emphasis.)
46. Chion refers to "la façon dont la musique *tombe* sur l'image (comme une robe tombe sur un corps)." Michel Chion, *Le Son au Cinéma* (Paris: Cahiers du Cinéma/Etoile, 1985), p. 119.
47. For this argument see Anne Hollander, *Seeing Through Clothes* (New York: Viking, 1978).
48. For this approach to film music see Gorbman, *Unheard Melodies;* Tagg, *Fernando the Flute;* Simon Frith, "Hearing Secret Harmonies," in my *Music for Pleasure* (Cambridge: Polity, 1988); Anahid Kassabian, "Songs of Subjectivities: Theorizing Hollywood Film Music of the 80s and 90s," Ph.D. thesis, Stanford University, 1993.
49. Anderson, "The Presentation of Silent Films," pp. 274–275. And see Preston, *Music for Hire*, pp. 93–96.
50. Max Winkler, "The Origin of Film Music," in James L. Limbacher, ed., *Film Music from Violins to Video* (Metuchen, N.J.: Scarecrow Press, 1974), p. 17.
51. Winkler, "The Origin of Film Music," pp. 21–22.
52. For an extremely interesting discussion of the impact of classical music on Hollywood in the 1930s see Caryl Flinn, *Strains of Utopia* (Princeton, N.J.: Princeton University Press, 1992). Flinn stresses the class and historical/nostalgic basis of this music, but underplays, I think, the use of the argument from "transcendence" that was at this time also selling classical music to middle-class America on record and radio.
53. Quoted in Anderson, "Presentation of Silent Films," pp. 261–262.
54. Carroll, *Mystifying Movies*, pp. 223–224.
55. Leith Stevens, "The Wild One," in Limbacher, ed., *Film Music from Violins to Video*, pp. 120–121.
56. Miklós Rózsa, "Quo Vadis," in Limbacher, ed., *Film Music from Violins to Video*, pp. 147–153.

One of the more interesting aspects of such conventions concerns "diegetic" music, music which is produced as part of the screen action itself, whether directly, by actor as performer, or as part of the setting (in the use of a radio or jukebox, for example). Do we believe that the performer is really playing the music (as in bio-pics of classical composers) or that he is "enacting it," but for real (as in bio-pics of pop performers)? What is the different effect? What is meant by realism here? See, for example, Charlie Gillett's comments on the Tina Turner bio-pic, *What's Love Got To Do With It,* "Truth and Tina," *Sight and Sound* 4(1) (1994): 64. For a general discussion of this issue see Irene Kahn Atkins, *Source Music in Motion Pictures* (East Brunswick, N.J.: Associated Universities Press, 1983).

57. Kathryn Kalinak, "The Fallen Woman and the Virtuous Wife: Musical Stereotypes in *The Informer, Gone with the Wind,* and *Laura,*" *Film Reader* 5 (1982): 76–77. And see her *Settling the Score: Music and the Classical Hollywood Film* (Madison: University of Wisconsin Press, 1992.

58. For film music's "representation symbolique du temps" see Charles J. Boilès, "La Signification dans la Musique de Film," *Musique en Jeu,* 1975, pp. 74–75. For music and space see Chion, *Audio-Vision,* chaps. 2–3.

59. See Philip Tagg, *"The Virginian,"* passim, and Alan Williams, "The Musical Film and Recorded Popular Music," in Rick Altman, ed., *Genre: The Musical* (London: Routledge and Kegan Paul/BFI, 1981).

60. Chion, *Audio-Vision,* p. 107.

6. Rhythm: Race, Sex, and the Body

1. Edmund Burke, *A Philosophical Enquiry into the Origin of our Ideas of the Sublime and the Beautiful* [1757] (Oxford: World's Classics, 1990), p. 112.

2. *Melody Maker,* March 9, 1988.

3. In the 1990s, the message was reversed again. Tee shirts now read: "Fuck Dance, Let's Art!"

4. Quoted in John F. Kassan, *Rudeness and Civility* (New York: Hill and Wang, 1990), p. 246.

5. Ibid., p. 246. Even today, performers or conductors who draw attention to themselves physically are thought to be a little vulgar—"Flash Harry" was the unaffectionate nickname for the British conductor Malcolm Sergeant, for example.

6. The rock equivalent to the classical experience is, I suppose, the psychedelic show: I remember the 1960s Grateful Dead audience, for example, as surprisingly quiet— "spaced out." But then this was a drug experience, and the mind/body split didn't hold.

7. Carl Dahlhaus notes that in the nineteenth century "the folk" and "nature" thus came to be connoted musically simply as a contrast to the orderly, romantic model of classical composition. See *Realism in Nineteenth-Century Music* [1982] (Cambridge: Cambridge University Press, 1985), p. 107.

8. Frank Howes, "A Critique of Folk, Popular and 'Art' Music," *British Journal of Aesthetics* 2(3) (1962); Peter Stadler, "The Aesthetics of Popular Music," *British Journal of Aesthetics* 2(4) (1962).

9. This seems to have been a well-established view among British educators. A 1945 textbook for youth club leaders concerned about their charges' low musical tastes explained that jazz "required no thought for its understanding, and relies entirely for its appeal on rhythm and sentiment." "One of the great weaknesses of jazz," the author elaborated, "is that it appeals only to the motor activities of man (i.e. as a stimulant to dance), or to the sentiment of the heart (i.e. sex) and is seldom, if ever, related to the head . . . Jazz expresses no great truths or depth of emotion, but is a stimulant to

the cheaper and more superficial sensations." Desmond Macmahon, *Youth and Music* (London: Thomas Nelson, 1945), pp. 89–90.

10. Raymond Durgnat, "Rock, Rhythm and Dance," *British Journal of Aesthetics* 11(1) (1971). This still seems to be the established aestheticians' view of rock—see, for example, Bruce Baugh, "Prolegomena to an Aesthetics of Rock Music," *The Journal of Aesthetics and Art Criticism* 51(1) (1993).

11. Guy Scarpetta, *L'Impureté* (Paris: Bernard Grasset, 1985), p. 77–78. Compare Ned Rorem: "In November 1961, the evening before I left France, Nora Auric took me to hear Johnny [Halliday] at the Olympia. Still ignorant of Presley—of Presley's *art* if you will—I was sceptical about meeting it second hand. Yet from the moment that handsome kid appeared and for the solid hour of his gyrations, Nora and I were as drugged by the mass hysteria loosened by his superbly whorish musicality as were the five thousand adolescents that jammed the hall." (*Settling the Score,* p. 257. Note the word "whorish.")

12. I'm not just thinking of jazz here. The late nineteenth century British music hall was constantly condemned by middle-class moralists as a haunt of prostitutes.

13. Bernard Gendron, "Jamming at La Boeuf: Jazz and the Paris Avant-Garde," *Discourse* 12(1) (1989–90): 11–12.

14. For a stimulating antidote to this (still widely believed) myth of the primitive, see Robert Farris Thompson's overview of African and African-American art and philosophy, *Flash of the Spirit* (New York: Random House, 1983). This is not to say that Western myths don't themselves feed into African musical ideologies. Among the replies in *Spear* to Charles Keil's 1965 question about Nigerian musical tastes was this: "Roy Chicago is my favourite musician and has been since February 1962. There is yet to appear a musician to equal his exhilarating brand of music which is peculiarly African. The absence of such music in Europe, psychologists claim, is responsible for so many Psychic cases over there. With Roy's music about the place, even the most reserved of persons forgets being shy and really does let go." Quoted in John Miller Chernoff, *African Rhythm and African Sensibility* (Chicago and London: University of Chicago Press, 1979), p. 177.

15. Marianna Torgovnick, *Gone Primitive: Savage Intellects, Modern Lives* (Chicago: University of Chicago Press, 1990), p. 228.
    Even a such a well-respected blues writer as Samuel Charters casually refers (in *The Country Blues*) to "the direct expression of sexuality in black culture," thus eliding a point about conventional differences between African-American and European-American expressive cultures, with a suggestion that in black cultures (but not white cultures) sex just comes naturally. For a general discussion of such assumptions in blues writing, see Jeff Todd Titon, "Reconstructing the Blues: Reflections on the 1960s Blues Revival," in Neil V. Rosenberg, ed., *Transforming Tradition* (Urbana and Chicago: University of Illinois Press, 1993).

16. D. L. LeMahieu, *A Culture for Democracy: Mass Communication and the Cultivated Mind in Britain Between the Wars* (Oxford: Clarendon Press, 1988), pp. 116–117.

17. Quoted in Torgovnick, *Gone Primitive,* p. 111.

18. Lawrence Levine, *Black Culture and Black Consciousness* (New York: Oxford University Press, 1977), pp. 293, 295. His emphasis.

19. Robert O'Meally, *Lady Day: The Many Faces of Billie Holiday* (New York: Arcade, 1991),

p. 154; and see Ted Gioia, "Jazz and the Primitivist Myth," in his *The Imperfect Art: Reflections on Jazz and Modern Culture* (New York and Oxford: Oxford University Press, 1990), pp. 30–31; Kathy J. Ogren, "Prudes and Primitives: White Americans Debate Jazz," in her *The Jazz Revolution* (New York and Oxford: Oxford University Press, 1989); and Neil Leonard, *Jazz and the White Americans: The Acceptance of a New Art Form* (Chicago: University of Chicago Press, 1962).

20. Charles Shaar Murray, *Crosstown Traffic* (London: Faber and Faber, 1989), p. 78.

21. Quoted in Linda Martin and Kerry Seagrove, *Anti-Rock: The Opposition to Rock'n'Roll* (Hamden, Conn.: Archon Books, 1988), p. 53. Other quotes from pp. 35, 47, 51.

   One of the more bizarre variations of the arguments here can be found in the liner notes by Dr. Sigmund Spaeth ("America's Most Popular Speaker and Writer on Music") to *Rock and Roll,* volume 1 in The Music Appreciation Library. (Volume 2 contained the *Sleeping Beauty* ballet suite, and volume 3 Beethoven's Fifth and Schubert's Unfinished Symphonies). Spaeth writes: "This highly controversial but immensely popular type of music is as characteristic of our times as comic books, western films and gangster who-dun-its. It has been called everything from a sublimation of rhythm to a reversion to savagery, and its adherence to current codes of violence is unmistakeable." Spaeth goes on to argue that musically there is nothing new about rock and roll at all. He concludes: "The violence of syncopated percussion is perhaps most obvious in 'Rock and Roll' but it also utilizes the established patterns of Boogie and revels in discord as enthusiastically as a Schoenberg or a Varèse. It is actually close to jungle music, and as such it completes a cycle which went the rounds of Rag Time, Jazz, Swing, Boogie, Be Bop and 'Progressive' back to a primitive glorification of Rhythm as such. Similarly the formulas of classicism followed the cycle of romanticism to the Modern, Ultra-Modern and Atonal styles, only to return at last to so-called 'Neo-classicism,' with Bach and Beethoven still its models." Thanks to John Street for drawing this to my attention.

22. Milton Bracker, "Experts Propose Study of 'Craze,'" *New York Times,* February 23, 1957, p. 1. Thanks to Dave Marsh and Greil Marcus for drawing this to my attention.

23. Kohut thus questions the artistic value of Ravel's *Bolero,* while also noting that as "modern" art music has no discernible rhythm so it offers no discernible pleasure! See Heinz Kohut, "Observations on the Psychological Functions of Music," *Journal of the American Psychoanalytic Association,* V(3) (1957): 391. A decade later Pinchas Noy confirmed this psychoanalytic equation of the "primitive," the "rhythmic," and the "infantile." See "The Psychodynamic Meaning of Music. A Critical Review of the Psychoanalytic and Related Material. Part II," *Journal of Music Therapy* 4(1) (1967): 14–16.

24. Eric Lott, *Love and Theft* (New York and Oxford: Oxford University Press, 1993), p. 53.

25. Bernard Gendron, "Rock and Roll Mythology: Race and Sex in 'Whole Lotta Shakin' Going On,'" University of Wisconsin, Center for Twentieth Century Studies Working Paper No. 7, Fall 1985, pp. 5, 7, 9.

26. Alice Echols, "White Faces, Black Masks," *Village Voice,* February 15, 1994, p. 92. Echols notes that even in the 1930s light-skinned black jazz musicians (Billie Holiday, for instance) were still required, on occasion, literally to black-up, to darken their skins so as to be recognized as "black."

27. Gendron, "Rock and Roll Mythology," p. 10.

28. Chernoff, *African Rhythm and African Sensibility,* pp. 150, 141.

29. Ruth Finnegan, *Oral Poetry* (Cambridge: Cambridge University Press, 1977), pp. 91–92. Halbwachs is cited by Alfred Schutz (who disagrees with his position), "Making Music Together," in *Collected Papers, Volume 2* (The Hague: Martinus Nijhoff, 1964), p. 164.

30. See Maurice Bloch, "Symbols, Song, Dance and Features of Articulation," *Archives Européennes de Sociologie,* 15(1) (1974). Bloch argues that all formalized or ritualized means of communication (all art) involves (through the use of repetition, in particular) a *restriction* on available choices of sounds and gestures (which now must form a pattern). In this respect, "art is an inferior form of communication" (p. 72). On the other hand, "when nearly all this generative potential of language (or bodily movement) has been forbidden, removed, the remaining choices left are so simple that they can suddenly be apprehended consciously. Creativity has suddenly become controllable, hence enjoyable." (As against those everyday communicative processes that are complex and unconscious) (p. 73). *All* performance is consciously structured, whatever the communicative rules or communicative elements involved.

31. Lawrence Levine, *Highbrow/Lowbrow* (Cambridge, Mass.: Harvard University Press, 1988), pp. 220–221.

32. Quoted in Charles Keil, "Motion and Feeling through Music," *The Journal of Aesthetic and Art Criticism* 24 (1966): 347.

33. For the most sophisticated version of this argument see John Shepherd, *Music as Social Text* (Cambridge: Polity, 1991), chaps. 6–8. For the most persuasive see Ishmael Reed's history of "jes grew," *Mumbo Jumbo* (New York: Doubleday, 1972).

34. Andrew Chester, "Second Thoughts on a Rock Aesthetic," in Simon Frith and Andrew Goodwin, eds., *On Record: Rock, Pop, and the Written Word* (New York: Pantheon, 1990), p. 315. Richard Norton makes a similar distinction between "high" and "low" music, noting that in popular song one doesn't listen for "the uniqueness of its harmonisation": "Harmonic utterance is collectively understood in such music as a formal structure in which components other than harmonic ones are utilised as a means for individual expression." (Norton, *Tonality in Western Culture,* p. 229.)

35. See Philip Tagg, "Open Letter: Black Music, Afro-American Music and European Music," *Popular Music* 8(3) (1989); and Van Der Merwe, *Origins of the Popular Style.* It is interesting to note how Aaron Copland moves in his Norton Lectures from a description of rhythm as "the most primitive element in music," to a discussion of the richness and variety of the American composer's unique rhythmic heritage. Aaron Copland, *Music and Imagination* (Cambridge, Mass.: Harvard University Press, 1952/1980), pp. 71, 83–90.

36. Ernest Borneman, *A Critic Looks at Jazz* (London: Jazz Music Books, 1946), p. 29.

37. The pioneering anthropologist in this respect was A. M. Jones, whose first essay on African drumming was published in 1934. His work is gathered in *Studies in African Music* (Oxford: Oxford University Press, 1959). For an exhaustive treatment of the problems of musical description raised here, see Simha Arom, *African Polyphony and Polyrhythm: Musical Structure and Methodology* [1985] (Cambridge: Cambridge University Press, 1991).

38. Borneman, *A Critic Looks at Jazz,* p. 30.

39. Chernoff, *African Rhythm and African Sensibility,* p. 92.

40. Borneman, *A Critic Looks at Jazz*, pp. 8, 31.

41. Quoted in Charles Keil, "The Theory of Participatory Discrepencies: A Progress Report," *Ethnomusicology* 39(2) (1995).

42. Levine, *Black Culture and Black Consciousness*, p. 198.

43. Art Hodes and Chadwick Hansen, *Hot Man* (Urbana and Chicago: University of Illinois Press, 1992), p. 24.

   Alec Wilder makes a similar point: "If a film composer is asked to write 'storm' music as one of the many cues in a movie score, no one is surprised to find he can do it. For it is primarily a trick. Maybe he hates both storms and music describing them. But his profession demands that he be able to devise and contrive.

   "But a swinging song is much more than a trick. For if you don't feel it, in fact love it, you can't write it. Oh you may write an imitation, but it will sound false and phony." (Wilder, *American Popular Song*, p. 119.)

44. Christopher Small, *Music of the Common Tongue* (London: John Calder, 1987), pp. 45–46.

45. Ibid., p. 480.

46. Keil, "Motion and Feeling through Music," pp. 338–339. For his later thoughts on the issues here see Charles Keil, "Participatory Discrepancies and the Power of Music," *Cultural Anthropology* 2(3) (1987), and "The Theory of Participatory Discrepancies."

47. Alan Durant, "Improvisation in the Political Economy of Music," in Christopher Norris, ed., *Music and the Politics of Culture* (London: Lawrence and Wishart, 1989). Boulez suggests elsewhere that left to their own devices players will always produce clichés—"If the player were an inventor of forms or of primary musical material, he would be a composer. If he is not a composer, it is because he is by choice and capacity a performer; so that if you do not provide him with sufficient information to perform a work, what can he do?" Pierre Boulez, *Orientations* [1981] (Cambridge, Mass.: Harvard University Press, 1986), p. 461.

48. Chernoff, *African Rhythm and African Sensibility*, p. 60. His emphasis.

49. Ibid., p. 67. My emphasis.

50. "Could it be that in some cultures children learn to dance before (or even while) they learn to listen?" asks Charles Keil ("Motion and Feeling through Music," p. 339). Watching friends' children, I'd say this was true in all cultures, and this has implications which Keil does not spell out. Could it be that insofar as the high cultural audience makes the right contemplative concert response it is not really having a *musical* experience; and that insofar as it has a musical experience this is not purely contemplative? I'll return to this point in Chapter 12.

51. Quoted in Dr. Licks, *Standing in the Shadow of Motown*, p. 95. And see Chernoff, *African Rhythm and African Sensibility*, p. 95.

52. Quoted in Gunther Schuller, *Early Jazz: Its Roots and Musical Development* (New York and Oxford: Oxford University Press, 1968), p. 22.

53. Chernoff, *African Rhythm and African Sensibility*, p. 54.

54. Ibid., p. 50.

55. John Blacking, *How Musical Is Man?* (Seattle and London: University of Washington Press, 1973), p. 27.

56. See Keil, "Motion and Feeling through Music," pp. 341–343.

57. Quoted in Keil, "Motion and Feeling through Music," p. 339.

58. For this point see Henry Pleasants, *Death of a Music? The Decline of European Tradition and the Rise of Jazz* (London: Victor Gollancz, 1961), p. 172.

59. Chernoff, *African Rhythm and African Sensibility,* p. 143. And see Robert Farris Thompson, "An Aesthetic of Cool: West African Dance," *African Forum* 2(2) (1966). From the other side of this process, O'Meally suggests that Billie Holiday's "incredibly poised sense of rhythm" derived from her early experience of having to respond vocally to the immediate rhythmic demands of juke joint dancers; see *Lady Day,* p. 38.

60. Zora Neale Hurston distinguished white and Negro dance in these terms: "The difference in the two arts is: the white dancer attempts to express fully; the Negro is restrained, but succeeds in gripping the beholder by forcing him to finish the action the performer suggests." See her "Characteristics of Negro Expression," in Nancy Cunard, ed., *Negro* (London: Nancy Cunard at Wishart and Co., 1934), pp. 41–42.

61. For a brilliant discussion of "the politics of dancing" in the post-punk era, see Will Straw, "The Booth, The Floor and The Wall: Dance Music and the Fear of Falling," *Public* 8 (1993). As Straw notes, "In any number of interviews in the early 1980s, musicians spoke proudly of their music as being about thinking *and* dancing," implying both that "thinking music" (i.e., indie-post-punk) wasn't usually danceable and that "dancing music" (i.e., disco) was usually thoughtless: "In fact, one did *think* on the dance floor of the early 1980s post-punk club; but, in thinking, one was mapping out the acceptable ranges of gesture and expression. Post-punk dancing was shaped in no small measure by the lingering and horrific memory of two precursors: the free-form obliviousness of late-hippy dancing and the extravagant displays of disco. The self-conscious control required of postures in order that they not recall these earlier moments lent itself easily to the conviction that dancing was now an activity with intellectual substance. Thus there is a smooth passage from the sense of dance as that which involves a thoughtful constraint to the belief that it might embody a disciplined militancy" (p. 177).

62. Concert hall bouncers will thus confidently tell you (with no evidence at all) what sort of music causes trouble, by which they mean what sort of music draws a "troublesome" crowd, a crowd which is overly black or young or proletarian.

63. See Philip Tagg, "Understanding Musical Time Sense," *Festschrift for Jan Ling* (Göteborg: Institute of Musicology, 1984).

64. Chernoff, *African Rhythm and African Sensibility,* p. 148. And see Richard Dyer, "In Defence of Disco" [1979], in Frith and Goodwin, *On Record.*

65. See Simon Frith, "The Sound of *Erotica*: Pain, Power and Pop," in Lisa Frank and Paul Smith, eds., *Madonnarama: Essays on Sex and Popular Culture* (Pittsburgh: Cleis Press, 1993).

Will Straw suggests that "records such as these perpetuate one of the central aesthetic principles of dance music: that high-end sounds (vocals, strings and so on) represent the playful, outrageous moments within dance music, and that for the connoisseurist, credible exercises happen at the low end, in the bass and percussion. The former endow records with their novel singularity, the latter anchor them within an ongoing history of styles."

Even within dance music, then, we find the familiar, gendered opposition of immediate response and informed appreciation: "Dance music culture's association of the feminine with the commercial and the debased is further evidence of that culture's status as one of the last modernist artworlds." (Straw, "The Booth, The Floor and The Wall," p. 181.)

7. Rhythm: Time, Sex, and the Mind

1. Quoted in Robert O'Meally, *Lady Day: The Many Faces of Billie Holiday* (New York: Arcade, 1991), p. 52.
2. Henri Lefebvre, *Everyday Life in the Modern World* [1968] (London: Allen Lane, 1971), pp. 19–20.
3. Alfred Schutz, "Making Music Together," in *Collected Papers, Volume 2* (The Hague: Martinus Nijhoff, 1964), pp. 171, 170.
4. Ibid., pp. 171–172, 175. For a similar argument about "dance time" and "real time" see David Michael Levin, "Balanchine's Formalism," in George Beiswanger, Wilfried A. Hofman, and David Michael Levin, "Three Essays in Dance Aesthetics," *Dance Perspectives* 55 (Autumn 1973). Levin is equally concerned with how a dance "communicates," and shows that to "understand" a modern dance, audiences have to experience the dancers' movements in the choreographer's time (not according to the clock)—it is the *dance* which determines whether a movement is fast or slow, rough or smooth, willed or "accidental."
5. Note Schutz's inclusion of poetry here: his point, with which I agree, is that what is semantically meaningful about a poem, its content, is not its meaning *as a poem*, which is its meaning as a timed object, a performance (even in one's head). The poem as poem only exists as experienced in inner time.
6. Schutz, "Making Music Together," p. 173. Interestingly, though, the composer will almost certainly not experience this stream of consciousness herself until she hears the first performance.
7. Ibid., p. 177. Schutz thus notes the difficulty of making music with someone one can't see. His example is the blind musician, but this also raises questions about contemporary recording studio practices and the communicative role of the producer.
8. John Miller Chernoff, *African Rhythm and African Sensibility* (Chicago and London: University of Chicago Press, 1979), pp. 95–97, 112–114 (his emphases). In his 1952 Norton Lectures at Harvard, Aaron Copland similarly distinguished "American" from European rhythmic sensibility. For Europeans, he suggested, rhythm is always applied to a phrase; for Americans rhythm is "disembodied," works as a frame or continuous possibility. Americans could work with—imaginatively hear—"minute metrical units" that Europeans couldn't. Europeans, in short, can't swing: "Of course you cannot stay off the beat unless you know where that beat is." (*Music and Imagination*, p. 87.) The contemporary British rock audience is still apt to clap on the on rather than the off beat, with dire rhythmical consequences.
9. Jonathan D. Kramer, *The Time of Music* (New York: Schirmer Books, 1988), pp. 140, 150–151. Kramer borrows from Judy Lochead the useful analogy of "breakfast," which is defined as both the first meal of the day (one can have anything for breakfast) but also by its conventional content (restaurants advertise "all-day breakfasts"; one can eat "breakfast" as a meal at 10 P.M.).
10. Keir Keightley, "The History and Exegesis of Pop," M.A. thesis (Communications), McGill University, 1991, pp. 28–29.

11. Kramer, *The Time of Music*, p. 161. I think one can delete Kramer's defensive "at least."

12. Ibid., p. 219. (His emphasis.) The concepts of moment and linear time help explain the process Michel Chion describes, the use of sound in the cinema to enable us to perceive *time in the image*—what we hear determines how we read time in the moving picture: as exact or vague, going forward or back, dramatic or stuck. See Chion, *Audio-Vision* [1990] (New York: Columbia University Press, 1994), pp. 13–14.

13. In this respect music, as Jacques Lacan noted, is not "without analogy" to psycho-analysis, and musical understanding, we might add, is not without analogy to the analyst's grasp of the unconscious. In André Michel's words, "Music, then, ceases to be only the sublimation of the sensible and becomes the perception of the sublime." "Psychoanalysis of Music," *Music Review* XI(4) (1950): 276. And see Lacan, "De l'objet musical dans le champ de la psychanalyse" [1974], *scilicet* 617 (1976), p. 334. For elaboration of the same point with regard to Freud's own account of musical and psychoanalytic time, see Jacques Caïn and Anne Caïn, "Freud, 'Absolument Pas Musicien . . .,'" in Jacques Caïn, Anne Caïn, et al., *Psychanalyse et Musique* (Paris: Société d'Édition, 1982), pp. 134–136.

14. Quoted in John Blacking, *How Musical Is Man?* (Seattle and London: University of Washington Press, 1973), p. 26.

15. See Kramer, *The Time of Music*, p. 167.

16. Blacking, *How Musical Is Man?*, p. 27.

17. Gary Giddins, *Rhythm-A-Ning* (New York: Oxford University Press, 1985), p. 246. Carolyn Abbate asks of nineteenth-century opera, "Can music, though it exists always in the present moment, create the sound of pastness? . . . Can music possess—aside from discursive space—the human, epistemological or moral complexities of a narrating voice?" (*Unsung Voices* [Princeton: Princeton University Press, 1991], p. 54). The convolution of her answers (yes and yes) reflects the problems of the "long tradition of musical analysis rooted in Hanslick's aesthetics of form" which "would argue that repetition actually creates structure, architecture, and hence stasis: time frozen" (p. 55). In popular music temporal gestures, rooted in repetition, work to make the music simultaneously past and present, to place the listener both inside and outside it. My favorite example of this narrative process remains Abba's "The Day Before You Came" (Epic, 1982), tedium recollected in tranquillity (or, rather, in emotional turmoil!), and its subtle adaptation to the even more mechanical banalities of electro-pop by Blancmange (London, 1984).

18. St. Augustine, *Confessions* [397–398] (Harmondsworth: Penguin, 1961), Book XI, section 14; and see section 24, pp. 264, 273.

19. Ibid., Book XI, sections 15, 18, 20, pp. 266–269.

20. Ibid., Book XI, section 28, p. 277.

21. One aspect of this, as Philip Tagg notes, is that "faster" pieces of music tend to be thought longer than they really are (in clock time), slower pieces judged shorter— more seems to be happening in the former; our attention is more engaged. And this is what we mean by something taking "more time." "Understanding Musical 'Time Sense,'" in *Festschrift for Jan Ling* (Göteborg: Institute of Musicology, 1986), p. 30.

22. See Edward T. Cone, *The Composer's Voice* (Berkeley: University of California Press, 1974). One complication in the study of popular music is that "rhythm" is taken to describe particular sounds—drums, bass, percussion—and a particular kind of beat,

and these don't just draw our attention to the music itself, but have all the ideological and physical connotations I discussed in Chapter 6.

23. David Epstein, *Beyond Orpheus: Studies in Musical Structure* (Cambridge, Mass.: MIT Press, 1979), p. 55.

24. Richard Middleton, *Studying Popular Music* (Milton Keynes: Open University Press, 1990), pp. 269, 272–275, 281. The suggestion that repetition might obliterate time echoes Roland Barthes's argument that "to repeat excessively is to enter into loss, into the zero of the signified." Barthes features "extravagant repetition" (formal, literal, obsessive repetition) in his semiotic erotics—the unexpected is now "succulent in its newness." *The Pleasure of the Text* [1975] (London: Jonathan Cape, 1976), p. 42.

25. Epstein, *Beyond Orpheus*, p. 55.

26. One reason why both avant-garde art composers and dance music producers have found electronic sounds interesting is that they seem to offer the possibility of sounds which are, in a sense, purely rhythmic. Stockhausen, for example, once claimed that "electronic music has liberated the inner world, for one knows that there is nothing to be seen outside oneself and that there can be no sense in asking with what and by what means the sounds and acoustical forms are produced." (Quoted in Evan Eisenberg, *The Recording Angel: Explorations in Phonography* [New York: McGraw-Hill, 1987], p. 134). But then electronic sounds soon connoted "electronics," sounds produced by machines, with (at least in the rock world) a whole series of implications about their "coldness" and inhumanity.

27. Eisenberg, *The Recording Angel*, p. 236.

28. Epstein, *Beyond Orpheus*, p. 57.

29. Robin Maconie, *The Concept of Music* (Oxford: Clarendon Press, 1990), p. 70. And see Philip Tagg: "The basis for all such conceptual units of musical duration is *recurrence*, either as repetition or reprise (the latter implying that there are *changes* which mark the recurrence), i.e. the measure and manner in which the same or similar musical structure can be regarded by a given musical-cultural community as establishing a pattern of occurrence." "Understanding Musical 'Time Sense,'" p. 23.

30. Epstein, *Beyond Orpheus*, p. 97 (note 14), and see p. 75; Allen Farmelo, "The Completing Consequences of Groove," and J. A. Prögler, "Searching for Swing: Participatory Discrepancies in the Jazz Rhythm Section," both in *Ethnomusicology* 39(2) (1995).

31. Epstein, *Beyond Orpheus*, pp. 55, 195–196. For an example of the "rhythm" of a piece being deduced from a structural reading of its score, see Ray Jackendoff and Fred Lerdahl, *A Generative Theory of Tonal Music* (Cambridge, Mass.: MIT Press, 1983), pp. 283–285. Though these authors do refer to what people hear, this "listening" is deduced from what would be necessary to make sense of the music structurally rather than from what people do actually think they're hearing when they listen.

32. Henri Pousseur, "Music, Form and Practice," in Herbert Eimert and Karlheinz Stockhausen, eds., *Die Reihe—Speech and Music* [1960] (Bryn Mawr, Pa.: Theodore Presser, 1964), pp. 80–82.

33. Michael Nyman, *Experimental Music: Cage and Beyond* (London: Studio Vista, 1974), p. 12, and see pp. 2, 26.

34. This argument is the theme of Wim Mertens, *American Minimal Music* (London: Kahn and Averill, 1983). For a highly critical review of Mertens's position see Gregory Sandow, "Minimal Thought," *Village Voice* (date unknown), which suggests that the

book is "full of confusion and mistakes." Sandow is particularly unconvinced by the suggestion that American minimalist music lacks "structure and direction," an argument which, for Sandow, reflects the weakness of Mertens's musical analysis rather than an insight into minimalist philosophy. Technically Sandow is probably right; emotionally I'm with Mertens: his argument does make sense of how at least this "unmusical" listener makes sense of minimalism. In terms of a close structural analysis the music of Philip Glass, Steve Reich, and Terry Riley undoubtedly does "develop," but such development is not what its listeners listen for.

35. Quoted in Kramer, *The Time of Music*, p. 376.
36. Ibid., pp. 378–381.
37. Quoted in Nyman, *Experimental Music*, p. 31.
38. New Age clearly draws on both minimalist and ambient sounds and ideas. For Brian Eno's ongoing thoughts on these issues see his occasional magazine, *Opal*.
39. Kool and the Gang, "Get Down On It," De-Lite 12", 1974; Steve Reich, *Drumming*, Elektra/Nonesuch LP, 1987.
40. See Kramer, *The Time of Music*, pp. 382–384. Philip Glass is quoted on p. 384.
41. Gary Jardim's *Blue: Newark Culture, Volume Two* (Orange, N.J.: De Sousa Press, 1993) contains an oral history of club music in Newark in which the dance floor is routinely treated as a stage setting. Jardim's interviewees remember how Richard Long constructed "the sonic environment" of the Zanzibar in Newark and the Paradise Garage in Manhattan (p. 94), while Kevin Hedge ("Growing up with Club") and Ace Mungin ("The Roots of Club in Newark") argue that the pioneering art of such deejays as Larry Levan was as "programmers"—their skill, in Jardim's words, was "to take the crowd on a journey." As he notes (p. 145), the essentially theatrical nature of the dance club also meant its use of all the "elements of style pioneered in the pre-disco gay club scene."

For disco/club/rave settings in Britain, see Sarah Thornton, *Club Cultures* (Cambridge: Polity, 1995). The politics of space has always been central to public dancing—in Britain, at least, there is a long history of the state seeking to regulate the dance floor (most recently, in 1994, in legislation seeking to prevent the unauthorized rave). See also Will Straw, "Systems of Articulation, Logics of Change: Communities and Scenes in Popular Music," *Cultural Studies* 5(3) (1991), which shows how important the (abstract) concept of "the scene" is for dance cultures.

42. Tagg, "Understanding Musical 'Time Sense,'" is illuminating on these issues. It should be stressed here that there is, from this perspective, no such thing as "real time," and composers who seek to work with it are therefore already involved in an ideological project. There is a significant difference, for example, between John Cage's and Olivier Messiaen's understandings of God and nature, and therefore of their musical uses of "natural time"—see Bayan Northcott, "Notes on the Music of Time," *The Independent*, May 25, 1991. Robert Morgan makes the further point that if music were really to use "ordinary" time then it would cease to be music, which is defined by a "special" temporal attention. Even Cage's 4'31" is, after all, necessarily timed—what makes it a musical composition is that it does *not* take place in real time; the music here is not the environment but the environment as framed by Cage and his audience. (The arguments here obviously parallel those about art as that which is looked at as art.) See Robert P. Morgan, "Musical Time/Musical Space," *Critical Inquiry* 6 (1980).

43. Tagg, "Understanding Musical 'Time Sense,'" p. 30.

44. Shuhei Hosokawa, *The Aesthetics of Recorded Sound* [in Japanese] (Tokyo: Keisó Shobó, 1990), English summary, p. 6.

45. The best discussion of boredom in rock is Jon Savage's *England's Dreaming* (London: Faber and Faber, 1991). And see Ilene Strelitz, "'Repetition' as Cultural Rebellion: 'Boredom,' the Avant-Garde and Rock and Roll," *OneTwoThreeFour* 4 (1987).

46. Abraham Kaplan, "The Aesthetics of Popular Arts," in James B. Hall and Barry Ulanov, eds., *Modern Culture and the Arts*, 2nd ed. (New York: McGraw-Hill, 1972), p. 55.

8. Songs as Texts

1. Greil Marcus, "Speaker to Speaker," *Artforum*, March 1987, p. 11. Compare Wayne Koestenbaum: "At the opera, we must forget that language and music aren't mutually exclusive. *We want the border between music and words to exist, so that opera can erase the border in an act of apparent transgression*" (his emphasis). *The Queen's Throat: Opera, Homosexuality, and the Mystery of Desire* (London: GMP, 1993), p. 177.

2. Greil Marcus, "Days Between Stations," *Interview*, April 1994, p. 70.

3. For a general survey of academic approaches to pop lyrics see my "Why Do Songs Have Words?" in *Music for Pleasure* (Cambridge: Polity, 1988).

4. For a hilarious account of the FBI's desperate search for the real meaning of the lyrics of "Louie Louie," see Dave Marsh, "Combating Merchants of Filth: The Role of 'Louie Louie,'" in *Louie Louie* (New York: Hyperion, 1993), chap. 10.

5. Keith Roe and Monica Löfgren, "Music Video Use and Educational Achievement," *Popular Music* 7(3) (1988): 311. And compare Rom Harré: "Recently the lead singer of the Moody Blues explained why pop music needed the visual images that have been introduced through the use of pop video. The audience is forced to contemplate, according to him, 'what the songs really mean.'" (Harré, "Is There a Semantics for Music?", in Krausz, ed., *Music and Philosophy*, pp. 212–213.)

6. Richard Rodgers, "Introduction," in Oscar Hammerstein II, *Lyrics* (New York: Simon and Schuster, 1949), p. xiv.

7. Fuzzbox, "Bohemian Rhapsody," on the *What's the Point* 12" EP, WEA 1987.

   In an article in *Revue Philosophique* in 1939 ("La Mémoire collective chez les musiciens"), Maurice Halbwachs argues that for non-musicians—who can't remember music through the score—musical memory *has* to be attached to a "metamusical" experience: "The melody of a song is remembered because the words—a social product—are remembered." Cited in Alfred Schutz, "Making Music Together," in his *Collected Papers II: Studies in Social Theory*, ed. Arvid Broderson (The Hague: Martinus Nijhoff, 1964), p. 164.

8. Nicholas Tawa, *The Way to Tin Pan Alley* (New York: Schirmer Books, 1990), p. 166. And titles, as we've seen, are equally important for selling instrumental music.

9. K. Peter Etzkorn, "Social Context of Songwriting in the United States," *Ethnomusicology* VII(2) (1963): 103–104. And see J. G. Peatman, "Radio and Popular Music," in P. F. Lazersfeld and F. Stanton ed., *Radio Research* (New York: Duell, Sloan and Pearce, 1942–1943); Tawa, *The Way to Tin Pan Alley*, p. 84.

   Contemporary manuals remain clear that the "craft" of songwriting is to come up with formulaic variations—see, for example, Sheila Davis, *The Craft of Lyric Writing* (Cincinnati, Ohio: Writer's Digest Books, 1985), passim.

10. Tawa, *The Way to Tin Pan Alley,* pp. 84, 90.

11. Chase is quoted in Tawa, *The Way to Tin Pan Alley,* p. 87. And see B. Lee Cooper, *Popular Music Perspectives: Ideas, Themes, and Patterns in Contemporary Lyrics* (Bowling Green, Ohio: Bowling Green State University Popular Press, 1991), p. 4. Cooper is here less interested in love songs than in the expression of social attitudes. His analysis of the pop treatment of education, for example, reveals that "Public education is clearly not respected in contemporary songs. Worse than that, it is openly ridiculed and condemned" (p. 17).

   For attempts to trace changes in American sexual mores through pop song lyrics see, for example, H. F. Mooney, "Popular Music since the 1920s," *American Quarterly* 20 (1968); J. T. Carey, "Changing Courtship Patterns in the Popular Song," *American Journal of Sociology* 74 (1969); R. R. Cole, "Top Songs in the Sixties: A Content Analysis," *American Behavioral Scientist* 14 (1971).

12. Among lyricists themselves the argument has had much more to do with formal craft. America's theater songwriters of the 1920s and 1930s seem to have despised the Tin Pan Alley tunesmiths not for their romantic ideology but for their incompetence. Lorenz Hart, for example, accused the Alley hacks of "sloppy versification, sophomoric diction, clichés, maudlin sentiments, and hackneyed verbiage." Quoted in Rhoda Koenig, "Prowling with the Alley Cats," *Independent,* August 26, 1992, p. 13. And James T. Maher suggests that in terms of "plot, situation and characterization" there was no real difference between theater and pop songs in the 1930s: theater songs were no more sophisticated about love; theater audiences no more "discriminating or subtle." Theater songs were, nevertheless, more interesting because of the "ambience, tradition and discipline" of the theater itself, which had a tradition of encouraging innovation and an audience which expected a "special quality" in the music for a theater night out. See Maher's introduction to Alec Wilder, *American Popular Song: The Great Innovators 1900–1950* [1972] (New York: Oxford University Press, 1990), pp. xxxi–iv.

13. Lawrence W. Levine, *Black Culture and Black Consciousness* (New York: Oxford University Press, 1977), p. 273. And see S. I. Hayakawa, "Popular Songs *vs* the Facts of Life," *Etc* 12 (1955).

14. Levine, *Black Culture and Black Consciousness,* pp. 274–283.

15. For a similar point about expressive conventions in African-American literature see Richard Wright's classic essay, "The Literature of the Negro in the United States," in *White Man, Listen!* (Garden City, N.Y.: Doubleday, 1957).

16. *New Musical Express,* August 21, 1982, p. 10.

17. As I. A. Richards put it in a different debate, "It is evident that the bulk of poetry consists of statements which only the very foolish would think of attempting to verify . . . Even when they are, on examination, frankly false, this is no defect." Quoted in James Anderson Winn, *Unsuspected Eloquence: A History of the Relations between Poetry and Music* (New Haven: Yale University Press, 1981), p. 303.

18. See J. P. Robinson and P. M.Hirsch, "Teenage Responses to Rock and Roll Protest Songs," and R. S. Denisoff and M. Levine, "Brainwashing or Background Noise? The

Popular Protest Song," both in R. S. Denisoff and R. A. Peterson, eds., *The Sounds of Social Change* (Chicago: Rand McNally, 1972). Such research is replicated at regular intervals, and with similar results, in *Popular Music and Society*.

19. For this argument see Donald Horton, "The Dialogue of Courtship in Popular Song," *American Journal of Sociology* 62 (1957).

20. For this incident see Dave Marsh, *Glory Days: Bruce Springsteen in the 1980s* (New York: Pantheon, 1987), pp. 254–266.

21. Bruce Springsteen, "Born in the USA," on *Born in the USA* LP, CBS 1984. For further discussion of this issue see Simon Frith, "Representatives of the People: Voices of Authority in Popular Music," in *Mediterranean Music Cultures and Their Ramifications* (Madrid: Sociedad Espanola de Musicologia, 1994).

22. Tawa, *The Way to Tin Pan Alley*, p. 95.

23. Peter Trudgill, "Acts of Conflicting Identity," in his *On Dialect: Social and Geographical Perspectives* (Oxford: Basil Blackwell, 1983), pp. 141–144.

24. Ibid., pp. 154–155. And see pp. 145, 148–150.

25. Ibid., p. 159. And see also p. 157.

26. Ibid., p. 159.

27. Levine notes that "every study of black urban communities and oral culture" shows ability with words to be as highly valued as physical strength—see *Black Culture and Black Consciousness*, p. 349.

28. See Roland Barthes, "Music, Voice, Language" [1977] in *The Responsibility of Forms* (Berkeley and Los Angeles: University of California Press, 1991), pp. 279–285.

29. I discuss Gracie Fields' vocal technique in more detail in "Northern Soul—Gracie Fields" in *Music for Pleasure*.

30. Most rappers would agree, I think, with Henri Lefebvre: "Language endows a thing with value, but in the process it devalues itself. Simultaneously it makes everyday life, is everyday life, eludes it, disguises and conceals it, hiding it behind the ornaments of rhetoric and make-believe, so that, in the course of everyday life, language and linguistic relations become *denials* of everyday life." Henri Lefebvre, *Everyday Life in the Modern World* [1968] (London: Allen Lane, 1971), pp. 120–121.

31. Public Enemy, "Don't Believe the Hype," on *It Takes a Nation of Millions to Hold Us Back*, Def Jam, 1988.

32. Leon Rosselson, "More Than Meets the Ear," *Poetry Review* 82(4) (1992/3): 8–9.

33. Ned Rorem, "The More Things Change: Notes on French Popular Song," *Settling the Score* (New York: Harcourt Brace, 1988), p. 251.

34. Ibid., p. 253.

35. The argument here is taken from Ginette Vincendeau, "The *Mise-en-Scène* of Suffering—French *Chanteuses Réalistes*," *New Formations* 4 (1987). And see Adrian Rifkin, *Street Noises: Parisian Pleasure 1900–1940* (Manchester: Manchester University Press, 1993), chap. 2.

36. On African-American uses of English see, for example, Geneva Smitherman, *Talkin and Testifyin: The Language of Black America* (Boston: Houghton Mifflin, 1977).

37. *Les Parapluies de Cherbourg* (Jacques Demy, France, 1964); *Les Demoiselles de Rochefort* (Jacques Demy, France, 1967).

38. Ruth Finnegan makes the point that such "framing" or "italicizing" also distinguishes

an oral poetic performance from ordinary speech, and in oral societies "ordinary" people are presumably equally embarrassed to "perform" poetry in public. See Ruth Finnegan, *Oral Poetry* (Cambridge: Cambridge University Press, 1977), pp. 25–26.

39. Quoted in Winn, *Unsuspected Eloquence*, p. 242. Compare the eighteenth-century view of *The Spectator:* "That nothing is capable of being well set to Musick, that is not Nonsens." (The reference here is to Italian opera.) Quoted in John Hollander, *The Untuning of the Sky: Ideas of Music in English Poetry, 1500–1700* [1961] (New York: W. W. Norton, 1970), pp. 382–383.

Winn notes that Dryden followed Renaissance humanism in distinguishing between poetry as masculine (and reasonable) and music as feminine (and sensual). He believed, in short, "that music is foreign, effeminate, destructive of sense, and successful only when imitating the passions" (p. 244). This was to echo a long-standing ecclesiastical argument. St. Augustine, as Winn points out, had distrusted music (and rhetoric) as pagan virtuosity which drew attention to itself (rather than obediently following formal rules of expression) (p. 50), and Wayne Koestenbaum adds that in feeling "guilty" when he was "more moved with the voice than with the ditty," Augustine was clear that music meant "languor and effeminacy," that words should be "master." As it was, music was "turning them in the wrong way," and Koestenbaum puts his own gloss on the sexual politics involved here: "music reverses, inverts, and sodomizes language." See Koestenbaum, *The Queen's Throat*, pp. 183–184, 188; and, for the medieval belief that music is a "distraction, as the irresistible Siren song that lures the helpless conscience to its wreck," Hollander, *The Untuning of the Sky*, p. 110. Hollander also traces the sixteenth- and seventeenth-century imagery of music as "effeminate" (pp. 257–258) and anti-reason (pp. 382–383).

It is interesting to note, in this context, that Alec Wilder assumes in his classic study of twentieth-century popular song the opposite proposition, that music brings good order to unruly words. Writing on Jerome Kern, he reflects that "it would have shocked him to see the world he had helped to create turn into a littered carnival ground for the untutored, undisciplined, insensitive young player-performer-writer. The ominous cloud of anarchy moving over the musical landscape would certainly have troubled such an orderly mind, such a gentle, lyric, controlled talent." Wilder, *American Popular Song*, p. 86.

40. Karlheinz Stockhausen, "Music and Speech," in Herbert Eimert and Karlheinz Stockhausen, eds., *Die Reihe—Speech and Music* [1960] (Bryn Mawr, Pa.: Theodore Presser, 1964), p. 58. For Hugo Ball and the problems of "pure verbal music" see Winn, *Unsuspected Eloquence*, pp. 320–321.

41. "Bewitched," words and music by Lorenz Hart and Richard Rodgers, 1946. In this song Hart deliberately breaks the rule formulated by Oscar Hammerstein II: "a rhyme should be unassertive, never standing out too noticeably," for "if a listener is made rhyme-conscious, his interest may be diverted from the story of the song." Quoted in Philip Furia, *The Poets of Tin Pan Alley: A History of America's Great Lyricists* (New York and Oxford: Oxford University Press, 1990), p. 185.

42. Levine, *Black Culture and Black Consciousness*, pp. 206–207.

43. Ibid., p. 238.

44. For the history of "the dozens" as verbal ritual (this term dates back to at least the

1890s), see John Dollard, "The Dozens: Dialectic of Insult," *American Imago* 1 (1939); and Roger D. Abrahams, "Playing the Dozens," *Journal of American Folklore* 75 (1962). Later discussions can be found in Smitherman, *Talkin and Testifyin*, pp. 118–128, and Levine, "The Ritual of Insult," *Black Culture and Black Consciousness*, pp. 344–358. While the origins of the particular tradition of insult ritual out of which rap emerges are almost certainly African, similar rituals, such as the Scottish "flytting," can be found in European cultures too. See Ken Simpson, "The Legacy of Flytting," *Studies in Scottish Literature* XXVI (1992). David Toop's *Rap Attack 2: African Rap to Global Hip Hop* (London: Serpent's Tail, 1991) remains the best study of rap in its historical context.

45. Ulf Hannerz, *Soulside: Inquiries into Ghetto Culture and Communication* (New York: Columbia University Press, 1969), pp. 129–135.

46. Kitagawa Junko notes that Kuwata, singer/writer for the Japanese rock band Southern All Stars, "first composes melodies with nonsense syllables that sound like English words, and finishes up with lyrics in Japanese after completing the melody." See "Some Aspects of Japanese Popular Music," *Popular Music* 10(3) (1991): 306.

47. Barbara Ferris Graves and Donald J. McBain, *Lyrical Voices: Approaches to the Poetry of Contemporary Song* (New York: John Wiley, 1972), p. vii. The most represented poet in this collection, with eight songs, is Donovan, followed by Leonard Cohen with seven; Dylan and Lennon/McCartney have three each.

48. David R. Pichashe, *Beowulf to Beatles and Beyond: The Varieties of Poetry* (New York: Macmillan, 1981), p. xiii (from the introduction to the first, 1972, edition).

49. Bob Sarlin: *Turn It Up! I Can't Hear the Words* (New York: Simon and Schuster, 1973). The quotes are taken from the Coronet edition (London, 1975), introduction and pp. 163, 176–177. See also Pichashe, *Beowulf to Beatles*, p. 275. And for a later version of the genre, see Matt Damsker, ed., *Rock Voices: The Best Lyrics of an Era* (New York: St. Martins Press, 1980) (which includes "American Pie"). Damsker has four songs each from Dylan, Joni Mitchell and Bruce Springsteen, three from John Prine, and two each from the Beatles and Leonard Cohen.

50. See Craig S. Abbott, "Modern American Poetry: Anthologies, Classrooms and Canons," *College Literature* 17(2/3) (1990).

51. Quoted in Tawa, *The Way to Tin Pan Alley*, p. 98.

52. Michael Gray, *The Art of Bob Dylan* (London: Hamlyn, 1981), p. 143. (This is the second edition of *Song and Dance Man*, London: Hart-Davis, MacGibbon, 1972.) Aidan Day, *Jokerman* (Oxford: Blackwell, 1988), p. 1.

53. Day, *Jokerman*, pp. 3–7.

54. Derek Attridge, "Rhythm in English Poetry," *New Literary History* 21 (1990): 1035. For a literary study of Dylan's words which does take account of their performance, see Betsy Bowden, *Performed Literature: Words and Music by Bob Dylan* (Bloomington: Indiana University Press, 1982).

55. Edward T. Cone, "Words into Music: The Composer's Approach to the Text," in Northrop Frye, ed., *Sound and Poetry* (New York: Columbia University Press, 1956), pp. 8–9, 15. And see Mark W. Booth, *The Experience of Songs* (New Haven: Yale University Press, 1981). See also Pierre Boulez, *Orientations* (Cambridge, Mass.: Harvard University Press, 1986), pp. 180–198.

56. Ned Rorem, "Poetry and Music," in *Settling the Score*, pp. 294–295. Rorem's emphases.
57. There's obviously an analogy here with the adaptation of books for film and television: the screened reading often seems wrong to us; the filmed version seems to deprive us of interpretive freedom (while adding "intensity," just like the musical adaptation of a poem).
58. Rorem, "Poetry and Music," p. 294. And see Jonathan Rée, "Funny Voices: Stories, Punctuation and Personal Identity," *New Literary History* 21 (1990). Rée notes that novelists have few resources to determine how a character's speech will be read/performed compared with those of a composer, who can determine pitch, voice type, metronome setting, and so forth (p. 1047), but, nonetheless, writers do use language, sentence structure, and punctuation to make a reading a reading aloud (p. 1049), and if, in Barbara Herrnstein Smith's words, "poems are pictures of utterances," then, Rée suggests, novels may be thought of as "pictures of oral storytelling" (p. 1056).
59. Quoted in Furia, *The Poets of Tin Pan Alley*, p. 39.
60. Or as Daniel Webb put it in 1769: "Strong passions, the warm effusions of the soul, were never destined to creep through monotonous parallels; they call for a more liberal rhythmus; for movements, not balanced by rule, but measured by sentiment, and flowing in ever new yet musical proportions." Quoted in Winn, *Unsuspected Eloquence*, p. 256. And see Frye, *Sound and Poetry*, p. xiii; and, for many illuminating thoughts on music, poetry, meter, and rhythm, C. Day Lewis, *The Lyric Impulse* (London: Chatto and Windus, 1965), and Charles O. Hartman, *Jazz Text: Voice and Improvisation in Poetry, Jazz and Song* (Princeton, N.J.: Princeton University Press, 1991).

    Winn points out that poets have consistently misunderstood what it means to be "musical." For example: "The Romantic poets loosened their syntax in the name of a more 'musical' poetry, a stylistic change which made their poetry *less*, not more, like the music of their contemporaries, the Viennese classical composers, arguably the most syntactical music in Western history" (pp. 269–270).
61. Quoted in Hartman, *Jazz Text*, p. 169. My emphasis. Robert Pring-Mill shows how Spanish-American "committed poetry" (which is, given its political ends, "unequivocally univocal in its purpose—with even its intentional ambiguities and ironies contributing to an 'intended meaning' aimed at an 'intended audience'") depends for its political effects on popular song *forms*, which give its arguments the force of aesthetic necessity. See *"Gracias a la Vida": The Power and Poetry of Song* (London: Queen Mary and Westfield College), The Kate Elder Lecture, 1990. Quote taken from p. 12.
62. Attridge, "Rhythm in English Poetry," pp. 1022–23. And note Claud Brown's comment (with reference to the specific rhythmic qualities of African-American English) that "spoken soul has a way of coming out metered without the intention of the speaker to invoke it." "The Language of Soul," in Richard Resh, ed., *Black America* (Lexington, Mass.: D. C. Heath, 1969), p. 244.
63. Finnegan, *Oral Poetry*, p. 126. And for the problems of this for the literary history of the lyric, see María Rosa Menocal's richly suggestive *Shards of Love: Exile and the Origins of the Lyric* (Durham, N.C., and London: Duke University Press, 1994), especially chapter 11, a lucid discussion of, among other things, Eric Clapton's "Layla."

9. The Voice

1. Roland Barthes, *Roland Barthes by Roland Barthes* [1975] (New York: Farrar, Straus and Giroux, 1977), p. 141. His emphases.

2. Quoted in Ellie M. Hisama, "Postcolonialism on the Make: The Music of John Mellancamp, David Bowie and John Zorn," *Popular Music* 12(2) (1993): 99. Her emphasis.

3. Quoted in Robert O'Meally, *Lady Day: The Many Faces of Billie Holiday* (New York: Arcade, 1991), p. 52.

4. The song line is from Bob Dylan's "Positively 4th Street," 7" single, CBS, 1965. For the use of shifters see Alan Durant, *Conditions of Music* (London: Macmillan, 1984), pp. 201–206.

5. I could add a further complication here: what is going on when a composer writes *in someone else's voice?* Elgar's *Enigma Variations*, for instance, originated in "a domestic evening" when the composer was messing around with a piece, "playing it in the different ways his friends might have done had they thought of it." As Elgar later explained: "I've written the variations each one to represent the mood of the 'party'— I've liked to imagine the 'party' writing the var[iation] him (or her) self and have written what I think they wd have written—if they were asses enough to compose—it's a quaint idea and the result is amusing to those behind the scene and won't affect the hearer who 'nose nuffin.'" Elgar was here using music not exactly to describe his friends but, in a sense, to be them—and this act of *impersonation* suggests that he, like Cone, did in the end think of music as being the composer's voice. See Francis Sparshott, "Portraits in Music—a Case Study: Elgar's 'Enigma' Variations," in Michael Krausz, *The Interpretation of Music* (Oxford: Clarendon Press, 1993), p. 234.

6. Edward T. Cone, *The Composer's Voice* (Berkeley: University of California Press, 1972), chap.1. But see also Carolyn Abbate, *Unsung Voices: Opera and Musical Narrative in the Nineteenth Century* (Princeton, N.J.: Princeton University Press, 1991): "To Cone's monologic and controlling 'composer's voice,' I prefer an aural vision of music animated by multiple, decentered voices localized in several invisible bodies" (p. 13). For Abbate, the "voices" in music "manifest themselves . . . as different *kinds* or modes of music that inhabit a single work. They are not uncovered by analyses that assume all music in a given work is stylistically or technically identical, originating from a single source in 'the Composer'" (p. 12; her emphasis). I return to this argument later in the chapter.

7. Anthony Storr, *Music and the Mind* (London: HarperCollins, 1993), p. 117. Storr also tells us that "Wagner's personality was charismatic and so is his music" (p. 120).

8. O'Meally, *Lady Day,* p. 97.

9. As David Brackett notes, "It is difficult to determine whether our response [to her voice] is based on what we know about Holiday's life, or on a socially mediated construction of affect conveyed by certain musical gestures." Either way, to repeat O'Meally's point, few entries on her "in even the most scholarly jazz history books" fail to refer to "her struggles with drugs and personal relationships." See David Brackett, *Interpreting Popular Music* (Cambridge: Cambridge University Press, 1995), p. 62.

10. Gregory Sandow, "Tough Love," *Village Voice,* January 13, 1987, p. 71.

11. Quoted in John Moore, "'The Hieroglyphics of Love': The Torch Singers and Interpretation," *Popular Music* 8(1) (1989): 39.

12. Umberto Fiore, "New Music, Popular Music, and Opera in Italy," unpublished paper, n.d., p. 4. His emphasis.

An opera buff like Wayne Koestenbaum might challenge this distinction. He has no doubts, for example, about Callas's individuality: "No note she sings remains the same; she changes voice *inside* the note, as if to say: 'Try to catch me, to name me, to confine me in your brutal classifications'" (his emphasis). But even for Koestenbaum the opera singer's "self" only emerges at moments of musical crisis: "at the moment of vulnerability and breakdown, the diva proves that the seamless singing has been masquerade, and now her cracked and decayed, raucous and undisguised self is coming out." Koestenbaum, *The Queen's Throat* (London: GMP, 1993), pp. 146, 127. In pop, "cracked and decayed" voices are always available.

It could also be argued that as Maria Callas became more obviously "personally expressive," so she became more of a pop than an opera singer (an effect of her marketing as a recording star). See Réal La Rochelle's illuminating *Callas: La Diva et le Vinyle* (Montréal: Les éditions Triptyque, 1987).

The problem of "how emotional expressivity is induced in song performance" when "the pitch parameter is restricted by the score" has interested psychologists too. How do we hear one performance as more "expressive" than another when the same notes have been sung? The point here seems to be that the singer's skill is "the ability to portray by acoustical means the particular emotional ambience embedded by the composer in the song," and not to bring their own, personal means of emotional expression to it (thus "dressing a song in an inappropriate ambience"). If classical singers do nevertheless use familiar rhetorical gestures ("expressive" singing is, in acoustic terms, more "agitated" than "unexpressive" singing), these are, in a sense, personally empty: the emotional meaning is in the music itself. We don't hear the singer as angry, anguished, and so forth, but the music. For an interesting discussion of these issues see Johan Sundberg, Jenny Iwarsson, and Håkon Hagegård, "A Singer's Expression of Emotions," paper presented to the Vocal Fold Physiology Conference, Korume, Japan, April 1994.

13. I'm describing here the use of voices in rock's mainstream gospel-derived tradition. Ray Charles and the Raelettes were undoubtedly the key influence (listen, for example, to "I'm Moving On" on *The Genius Sings the Blues*, London-Atlantic, 1961); Van Morrison is probably the best rock exponent (live, at least), taking advantage of his consequent "freedom from utterance" to use his voice as if it were a saxophone.

14. As was parodied by Lou Reed in "Walk on the Wild Side." There are male backup traditions too: not just the male voice choir used by the Pet Shop Boys, but also in black and white gospel—Elvis Presley used the Jordonnaires throughout his career, and even the vocally democratic doo-wop increasingly featured lead/backup male voices as it reached the pop charts (Dion and the Belmonts, for example; Frankie Lyman and the Teenagers). Gladys Knight's Pips, on the other hand, always came across as a simple gender role reversal. In country music the dominant gender convention is of the star male lead voice being tracked by an anonymous female backing voice, with the man all the way, but always just off center, a sweetener and a restraint—listen, for example, to how Emmylou Harris traces the desire behind Gram

Parsons' voice on his "solo" LPs, *GP* (Reprise, 1973) and *Grievous Angel* (Reprise, 1974).

15. O'Meally, *Lady Day*, pp. 31–32.

16. For the BBC see my "Art *vs* Technology: The Strange Case of Popular Music," *Media Culture and Society* 8(3) (1986): 263. For advertising see Roland Marchand, *Advertising the American Dream: Making Way for Modernity, 1920–1940* (Berkeley: University of California Press, 1985), p. 109.

17. "Significantly enough," as Bernard Gendron writes, "Crosby's singing style actually evoked the ire of spokespersons for moral purity, with Boston's Cardinal O'Connell referring to it as 'immoral and imbecile slush,' 'a degenerate low-down sort of inter-pretation of love,' and 'a sensuous effeminate luxurious sort of paganism.'" See Gen-dron's "Rock and Roll Mythology: Race and Sex in 'Whole Lotta Shakin' Going On,'" Working Paper 7 (Milwaukee: University of Wisconsin, Center for Twentieth Century Studies, 1985), p. 4.

18. John Rockwell, *Sinatra* (New York: Random House, 1984), pp. 51–52.

19. This generalization is perhaps too sweeping (Glenn Gould, for example, compares Barbra Streisand to Elizabeth Schwarzkopf in this respect), and there are clearly styles of classical singing—coloratura, for example—in which the performer draws attention to her vocal technique (and to not much else). But then that is probably the reason why Cecilia Bartoli is the only classical soprano I adore.

20. One of the most obvious distinctions between pre- and post-microphone singing relates to this: in the original big bands the voice is featured as just a (minor) instrument, the words sung briefly, after one long instrumental workout and before another. By the end of the big band era, the instrumental break had become the punctuation, a fill between the second vocal chorus and the third vocal verse.

21. Sandow, "Tough Love," pp. 71, 73.

22. Aidan Day, *Jokerman* (Oxford: Blackwell, 1988), p. 2.

23. Glenn Gould, "Streisand as Schwarzkopf," in *The Glenn Gould Reader*, pp. 309–310. Compare Gary Giddins on Ella Fitzgerald: "even when she recorded Tin Pan Alley muck, she could empower certain notes with a shivery reflex, *disassociating* the singer from the song yet giving the song a kick all the same." "Joy of Ella," *Village Voice*, April 27, 1993, p. 90. My emphasis.

24. Cone, *The Composer's Voice*, p. 78.

25. See Jane M. Gaines, "Bette Midler and the Piracy of Identity," in Simon Frith, ed., *Music and Copyright* (Edinburgh: Edinburgh University Press, 1993).

26. Quotes from Barthes, "The Grain of the Voice," in *The Responsibility of Forms* (Berkeley: University of California Press, 1991), pp. 276, 270, 271.

27. Koestenbaum, *The Queen's Throat*, p. 43. Barthes's essay does, in fact, read more like a heartfelt and elaborate defense of his taste (for Panzéra; against Fischer-Dieskau) than as a particularly convincing account of different vocal techniques as such.

28. This relates, I suppose, to a Lacanian psychoanalytic view of musical pleasure, though I do not find Lacan's own words on music particularly illuminating. See, for example, his "De l'objet musical dans le champ de la psychoanalyse" [1974], *scilicet* 617 (1976). From the perspective of a kind of Lacanian socio-linguistics, Barbara Bradby and Brian Torode argue that: "the lyrics of the modern popular song permit a man to fantasise addressing a woman as love-object in terms of rocking a crying baby to hush

it. This use of lullaby language exploits the words of the absent mother in order to silence the present lover." "Song-Work," paper presented at the British Sociological Association Conference, Manchester, 1982. And see their "Pity Peggy Sue," *Popular Music* 4 (1984), and, in the same issue, Sean Cubitt, "'Maybelline': Meaning and the Listening Subject"—"the real object of desire flees before us like Maybelline's Cadillac" (p. 222).

29. Jonathan Swift, "A Discourse Concerning the Mechanical Operation of the Spirit" [1704], in *A Tale of the Tub and Other Satires* (London: J. M. Dent [Everyman], 1909), pp. 180–181.

30. Aaron Neville's "Tell It Like It Is" was originally released as a single in 1966. A live version (recorded at Tipitina's, New Orleans, in 1982) is included on the Neville Brothers' *Neville-ization,* Black Top/Demon Records, 1984.

31. For Otis Redding, listen to *Live in Europe,* Atlantic LP, 1972. Elvis Presley's pleasure in his own voice is best captured on *Elvis: The First Live Recordings* (RCA, 1984), live recordings from the Lousiana Hayride in 1955–56, and *Essential Elvis Presley,* vols. 1–3 (RCA, 1986, 1989, 1990), studio ðuttakes from his early RCA and Hollywood days. It is here (singers responding to themselves) rather than with backup singers (responding to a leader) that we get, paradoxically, the musical version of Erving Goffman's "response cries," the noises people make in conversation in response to someone else. Goffman suggests that such cries "do not mark a flooding of emotion outward, but a flooding of relevance in," but in musical terms the voice suggests both such movements simultaneously. See Erving Goffman, *Forms of Talk* (Oxford: Basil Blackwell, 1981), p. 121.

32. We don't always get a singer's sex "right," though in my experience this is *not* usually an effect of pitch (the Laurie Anderson effect)—women's low voices and men's high voices are still heard as women's and men's voices; see the discussion of falsetto that follows in this chapter. The misjudgment seems, rather, to relate to genre expectation—the only singer I've known people systematically to misread is Jimmy Scott, and this seems to have more to do with his (torch singing) style than with his (not particularly high) pitch—listen, for example, to *Dream* (Sire, 1994).

33. Crash Test Dummies, "Mmm Mmm Mmm Mmm" (RCA, 1993).

34. Koestenbaum, *The Queen's Throat,* p. 165. He also suggests that "cultural folklore convinces us that we can tell someone is gay by voice alone" (p. 14).

35. Giddins, "Joy of Ella," p. 90.

36. Deborah Cameron has pointed out to me that there is actually a dispute among phoneticians concerning the "female falsetto"—how else would we describe what Minnie Riperton does with her voice on her 1974 Epic hit, "Lovin' You," for instance? And for a stimulating discussion of the special erotic appeal of the *low* female voice see Terry Castle, "In Praise of Brigitte Fassbaender (A Musical Emanation)" in her *The Apparitional Lesbian: Female Homosexuality and Modern Culture* (New York: Columbia University Press, 1993).

37. Ian Matthews, "Da Doo Ron Ron," Philips 7" single, 1972; Mathilde Santing, "I've Grown Accustomed to Her Face," on *Mathilde Santing* 10" LP, Idiot, 1982.

38. X-Ray Spex, "Oh Bondage Up Yours!", Virgin single, 1977.

39. Sean Cubitt, "Note on the Popular Song," unpublished, 1983. Koestenbaum suggests that film musical ghosts (Marni Nixon singing for Audrey Hepburn in *My Fair Lady*

and for Deborah Kerr in *The King and I*) are further examples of "singing without a body, singing from an erased place in the universe." *The Queen's Throat*, p. 11. And Wendy Wolf reminds me that part of the appeal of the pop video is that it re-embodies the pop voice.

40. Record references: Cocteau Twins, "Aikea Guinea," 12" EP, 4AD 1985; Ennio Morricone, *Once Upon a Time in the West*, Soundtrack LP, RCA 1969; Kraftwerk, "The Robots," on *The Man Machine* LP, Capitol 1978; the Stanley Brothers and the Clinch Mountain Boys, *The Columbia Sessions, 1949–50*, Rounder LP, 1980.

41. See Brackett, *Interpreting Popular Music*, chap. 2, for a detailed discussion of Crosby's and Holiday's contrasting "musical codes," and for critical responses to them. And compare Bernard Gendron's account of the white pop "dilution" of black rock 'n' roll songs in the 1950s: Gendron, "Rock and Roll Mythology," pp. 6–7.

   I am reminded in this context of the wonderful moment when Martin Hatch, who had till then, as a good ethnomusicologist, sat equably through all the music I'd played during a course at Cornell on the "good and bad in popular culture," leapt out of his seat on hearing Bryan Ferry's version of "These Foolish Things" (one of my favorite ever tracks) and exclaimed: "*Now* I believe in bad music!"

42. Gendron, "Rock and Roll Mythology," p. 7. Gendron suggests that we can also hear black performers like Chuck Berry, Little Richard, and Ray Charles caricaturing their own styles: "According to rock and roll mythology, they went from singing less black (like Nat King Cole or the Mills Brothers) to singing more black. In my judgement, it would be better to say that they adopted a more caricaturized version of singing black wildly, thus paving the way for soul music and the British invasion" (p. 10).

   For a more general discussion of race and musical caricature, see Eric Lott, *Love and Theft: Blackface Minstrelsy and the American Working Class* (New York and Oxford: Oxford University Press, 1993). Record references here are Jerry Lee Lewis, "Whole Lotta Shakin' Goin' On" (Sun, 1957), and the Rolling Stones, "I'm a King Bee," on *The Rolling Stones* (Decca, 1964). There's no doubt too that white rock 'n' roll fans enjoyed the danger of sounding "black" in the safety of their own heads. The (much less obvious) phenomenon of black singers sounding "white" has hardly been studied.

43. Jonathan Rée, "Funny Voices: Stories, Punctuation and Personal Identity," *New Literary History* 21 (1990): 1053.

44. Record references are to Dory Previn, "Lady with the Braid," on *Mythical Kings and Iguanas* (UA, 1971); Frank Sinatra, "One for My Baby," on *Frank Sinatra Sings for Only the Lonely* (Capitol, 1958); Patti Smith, "Land," on *Horses*, Arista LP, 1975; the Chi-Lites, "Have You Seen Her" (Brunswick, 1971); Meat Loaf, "Objects in the Rear View Mirror May Appear Closer Than They Are," on *Bat out of Hell II* (Virgin, 1993).

45. Dai Griffiths, "Talking About Popular Song: in Praise of 'Anchorage,'" in Rossana Dalmonte and Mario Baroni, eds., *Secondo Convegno Europeo di Analisi Musicale* (Trento: Universita degli Studi di Trento, 1992), p. 356. Record references: Randy Newman, "Lonely at the Top," on *Randy Newman/Live* (Reprise, 1971), and Michelle Shocked, "Anchorage," on *Short Sharp Shocked* (Cooking Vinyl, 1988).

46. Carolyn Abbate suggests that in classical music "narrative" should be taken to describe a specific musical *act*, "a unique moment of performing narrative within a surrounding music" (*Unsung Voices*, p. 19). I've been suggesting here that in pop the voice always does this act, but that is not necessarily the case, and Abbate's argument could

certainly be applied to pop's instrumental-narrative moments, whether they're performed by an improvising player like, say, Keith Richards, or by a calculating producer, like, say, Phil Spector.

47. Is it better, for example, for an opera to be sung in the language in which it was composed, which "sounds" right but may not be linguistically comprehensible to either singers or audience; or to translate the libretto into, say, English, which means that Anglophones now know what is being sung but the vocal *sounds* are no longer those in which the opera was originally composed? I would always opt for the first approach, but then words have always been the least of my musical pleasures.

48. Cone, *The Composer's Voice*, p. 119–121. For further consideration of this issue, with reference to instrumental interpretation, see Jerrold Levinson, "Performative *vs* Critical Interpretation in Music," in Krausz, *The Interpretation of Music*.

49. See John Moore, "'The Hieroglyphics of Love.'" I take the concept of "verbal space" from Griffiths, "Talking About Popular Song," p. 353. For technical discussion of interpretive singing see Will Friedwald, *Jazz Singing: America's Great Voices from Bessie Smith to Bebop and Beyond* (New York: Scribners, 1990). For the torch singer's art listen to Chris Connor's "All About Ronnie" (1954), on *Out of this World* (Affinity, 1984), or Jerry Southern's "I Thought of You Last Night" (1952), on *When I Fall in Love* (MCA, 1984).

50. O'Meally, *Lady Day*, p. 198. His emphasis. Martin Williams is quoted on p. 43.

51. Cone, *The Composer's Voice*, p. 53. Record references: Billie Holiday, "These Foolish Things" (1936), on *The Billie Holiday Story Volume 1* (CBS, n.d.); Bryan Ferry, "These Foolish Things," on *These Foolish Things* (Island, 1973).

52. Keightley's discussion concerns the Beach Boys—see "The History and Exegesis of Pop," p. 128.

53. The Shangri-Las, "Leader of the Pack," Red Bird single, 1964; the Angels, "My Boyfriend's Back," Smash single, 1963; the Shirelles, "I Met Him on a Sunday," Tiara/Decca single, 1958; Salt-n-Pepa, "Let's Talk About Sex," Next Plateau single, 1991.

54. Record references: Loretta Lynn and Conway Twitty, *Lead Me On* (MCA, 1971); Marvin Gaye and Tammi Terrell, *Greatest Hits* (Motown, 1970).

55. Records cited: Sinead O'Connor and M. C. Lyte, "I Want (Your Hands On Me)," Ensign 12" single, 1988; Willie Nelson, "Don't Give Up," on *Across the Borderline*, Columbia LP, 1993. For discussion of the former see Katrina Irving, "'I Want Your Hands On Me': Building Equivalences Through Rap Music," *Popular Music* 12(2) (1993): 117–120.

10. Performance

1. Greil Marcus, "Days Between Stations," *Interview*, October 1993.

2. Erving Goffman, *The Presentation of Self in Everyday Life* [1959] (Harmondsworth: Penguin, 1971), p. 28.

3. For the distinction between "textual" and "contextual" performance theories see Graham F. Thompson's very useful "Approaches to 'Performance,'" *Screen* 26(5) (1985): 81.

4. Nick Kaye, *Postmodernism and Performance* (London: Macmillan, 1994), p. 144.

5. See Thompson, "Approaches to 'Performance,'" p. 88. I'm also obviously indebted in

what follows to the work of Erving Goffman—for an exemplary study see his lecture on "The Lecture" in *Forms of Talk*.

6. Noël Carroll, "Performance," *Formations* 3 (1986).

7. As Erving Goffman famously put it, "All the world is not, of course, a stage, but the crucial ways in which it isn't are not easy to specify." *The Presentation of Self*, pp. 77–78.

8. John Kassan, for example, suggests that embarrassment (or its avoidance) became the key to public behavior in the nineteenth-century American city, because of the unstable context of honor, shame, and reputation. See John F. Kassan, *Rudeness and Civility: Manners in Nineteenth Century Urban America* (New York: Hill and Wang, 1990), pp. 114–115.

9. See Sally Banes's excellent study of this period, *Greenwich Village 1963: Avant-Garde Performance and the Effervescent Body* (Durham, N.C.: Duke University Press, 1993).

10. See Richard Bauman, "Verbal Art as Performance," *American Anthropologist* 77 (1975).

11. Which makes it different from a literary text. It may be true, as I discuss in Chapter 12, that books too only come into being when read, but they can and are studied as if they were always already structured, so to speak.

12. George Beiswanger, "Doing and Viewing Dances: A Perspective for the Study of Criticism," in George Beiswanger, Wilfried A. Hofman, and David Michael Levin, "Three Essays in Dance Aesthetics," *Dance Perspectives* 55 (Autumn 1973): 8.

13. Björk, "There's More To Life Than This," on *Debut*, Bapsi/One Little Indian LP, 1993.

14. Anne Lederman argues persuasively that folk musicians' use of a "deliberately dramatic, *staged* presentation" of their music on tour or in the recording studio enables them to assume that their "ordinary" (though equally rule-bound) performances in "informal" settings, or in their own communities, just come naturally. See "'Barrett's Privateers': Performance and Participation in the Folk Revival," in Neil V. Rosenberg, ed., *Transforming Tradition* (Urbana and Chicago: University of Illinois Press, 1993). Charles Keil makes a similar point about polka bands' performing norms in "People's Music Comparatively," *Dialectical Anthropology* 10 (1985).

15. Peter Bailey, "Conspiracies of Meaning: Music Hall and the Knowingness of Popular Culture," *Past and Present* 144 (1994).

16. Bailey relates the music hall use of linguistic humor to the nineteenth-century disciplining of working-class talk in general, by factory, office, and school, and to the legal policing of music hall speech, in particular.

17. Within street conversation Abrahams thus distinguishes the casual *running it down* from the "aggressive, witty performance talk" of *signifying*. Within signifying one can distinguish *talking smart* ("serious, clever, conflict talk") from *talking shit* (nonserious, all-join-in contest talk). Talking smart (which can be further divided into the "overtly aggressive" *putting down* and the "covertly aggressive" *putting on*) "arises within conversational context yet is judged in performance (stylistic) terms." Talking shit (which can be further divided into "nondirective" *playing* and "directive" *sounding*) is "performance interaction, yet built on a model of conversational back-and-forth." And we can further add to this picture the variations of women's talk *talking tough* and *talking sweet*. See Roger D. Abrahams, *Talking Black* (Rowley, Mass.: Newbury House, 1976), Figure 1, p. 46, and, for the general argument here, pp. 5–89. Zora Neale Hurston, who long ago observed that "drama" defined the "Negro expressive

self," described Negro boys and girls walking past each other on the street as "little plays by strolling players." See "Characteristics of Negro Expression," in Nancy Cunard, ed., *Negro* (London, 1934), p. 39.

18. For further discussion of this argument, in terms of the nineteenth-century appeal of minstrelsy, see Eric Lott, *Love and Theft* (New York and Oxford: Oxford University Press, 1993).

19. See Donald Horton, "The Dialogue of Courtship in Popular Song," *American Journal of Sociology* 62 (1957) for one account of this process.

20. For this point see Mark W. Booth, *The Experience of Songs* (New Haven: Yale University Press, 1981), chap. 11.

21. Alfred Schutz suggests that all musical experiences, however "mediated," whatever the variations of "intensity, intimacy and anonymity," refer to the "vivid present" that performers and listeners share in face-to-face relations. "Making Music Together," p. 174.

22. In the early 1970s the British folk scene became an unexpected source of stand-up comics—Billy Connolly, Mike Harding, Jaspar Carrott.

23. Even in the most "respectable" of the performing arts—classical theater, the ballet—female performers (like artists' models) were taken in the nineteenth century to be akin to prostitutes, while one could argue that an important strand of performance in the low arts, such as vaudeville and music hall, blues and jazz, has been the continuing, deliberate emphasis on the performer's off-stage *propriety*.

24. In this respect, female stage performers have an advantage over women with the everyday problem of walking down the street. See Susan McClary, *Feminine Endings* (Minneapolis: University of Minnesota Press, 1991), chap. 6. David Schiff suggests that McClary doesn't push her argument far enough here: "Opera is performance art, and one in which female performers do not merely 'enact' a male drama but essentially rewrite it in performance . . . If performers were given their rightful place in the history of music, it could easily be shown that Callas exerted a far greater influence on the course of opera in the past forty years than any composer did. Might not feminist musicology profitably shift the focus away from a male-controlled cultural product to a female-centered cultural process and celebrate these issues of feminine dominance? Our notion of music would be appropriately challenged and enriched." (David Schiff, "The Bounds of Music," *New Republic*, February 3, 1992, pp. 35–36.)

    Or, as Wayne Koestenbaum puts it, "Since the most electrifying singers were often women and castrati, the emphasis on performance undid opera's masculinity" (*The Queen's Throat* [London: GMP, 1933], p. 182).

25. The most entertaining collection of Madonna essays is Lisa Frank and Paul Smith, eds., *Madonnarama* (Pittsburgh: Cleis Press, 1993).

26. Listen, for instance, to Dolly Parton, *Best of Dolly Parton*, RCA LP, 1970.

27. Listen, for example, to Gracie Fields, *Stage and Screen*, EMI/World Record Club, n.d., which includes a live recording of her show at the Holborn Empire, October 11, 1933.

28. Listen, for example, to Millie Jackson, *Live and Uncensored*, Spring/Polydor, 1979.

29. Roland Barthes, *Roland Barthes by Roland Barthes* [1975] (New York: Farrar, Straus, and Giroux, 1977), pp. 177–178.

30. And as J. O. Urmson points out, in paying to see a performance we also expect that the star (Madonna, say) will, in good faith, continue to *be herself* (whatever the new

theme or costume). See his "The Ethics of Musical Performance," in Krausz, *The Interpretation of Music*.

31. Koestenbaum, *The Queen's Throat*, p. 168.

32. Which is not to say that the respondent isn't just as embarrassed by the misjudgment as the performer.

33. To be excluded from this excitement (the rock critic's common condition) is, oddly, to be embarrassed not for oneself but for everyone else. The point here is that intense or abandoned listening involves a loss of physical control—think of the ugliness of the audience in concert photos—and it is this which embarrasses: to be the only person to clap at the end of the first movement, the only person to leap to one's feet screaming. It is not embarrassing (well, I was never embarrassed) to be the only person taking notes.

34. See Susan Sontag, "Notes on 'Camp'" [1964] in her *Against Interpretation* (New York: Delta, 1966), p. 277.

   Camp strategy has been a useful solution to the male performing dilemma: how to make oneself an object of adoring—feminizing—attention while signaling clearly that *I'm still in charge!* For an interesting analysis of the camp basis of Mick Jagger's performance style, for example, see Sheila Whitely, "Mick Jagger: An Analysis of Sexuality, Style and Image," in Sheila Whitely and Stan Hawkins, eds., *Sexing the Groove: Representations and Identity in Popular Music*, forthcoming. For a general survey of the influence of camp sensibility on pop history see Jon Savage, "Tainted Love: The Influence of Male Homosexuality and Sexual Deviance on Pop Music and Culture since the War," in Alan Tomlinson, ed., *Consumption, Identity and Style* (London: Routledge, 1990).

   As Gary Jardim notes in his account of the Newark/New York 1970s and 1980s dance clubs, the same sort of "fascination with illusion and theater" and "grand sense of playfulness" fed into the *audience* performance that defined disco: "The elegant flow motion, the shuffle beat, the love spirit—they were all elements of style pioneered in the pre-disco gay club scene." See "Al Murphy and the Club Music Aesthetic in Newark," in Gary Jardim, ed., *Blue: Newark Culture, Volume Two* (Orange, N.J.: De Sousa Press, 1993), p. 145.

35. Guy Scarpetta, *L'Impureté* (Paris: Bernard Grasset, 1985), pp. 207–208. In Britain gossip about each successful new teenybop band is always the same: X or Y used to be *a rent boy!*

36. For graphic accounts of such calling forth see Fred Vermorel and Judy Vermorel, *Starlust* (London: W. H. Allen, 1985), and, for further discussion of what they mean, my "Afterthoughts" in Simon Frith and Andrew Goodwin, eds., *On Record* (New York: Pantheon, 1990).

37. See Paul Eckman, "Biological and Cultural Contributions to Body and Facial Movement," in John Blacking, ed., *The Anthropology of the Body* (London: Academic Press, 1977).

38. John Blacking, "Towards an Anthropology of the Body," in Blacking, *The Anthropology of the Body*, p. 7.

39. Sally Banes notes that the young break dancer in New York in the early 1980s, in attempting to be as "intricate, witty, insulting or obscene as possible," would "perhaps present his ass to his opponent in a gesture of contempt. Through pantomime, he

might extend the scatological insult even more graphically, pretending to befoul his opponent." Sally Banes, "Breaking," in Nelson George et al., *Fresh* (New York: Random House, 1985), p. 94.

40. As Erving Goffman notes, in judging whether someone else's performance is sincere or phony we pay special attention "to features of performance that cannot be readily manipulated." If they are, then we feel particularly deceived. *The Presentation of the Self*, p. 66.

41. Though what the truth is here is a difficult question to answer—see, for example, Jennie Livingstone's film about New York's transvestite balls, *Paris Is Burning*. "Driving the mechanism of these performed identities," as Peggy Phelan puts it, "is a notion of 'the real.'" These men-performing-as-women express real erotic desires (and invoke real erotic response): "Underneath the image of these visible women is a man, but it is extremely difficult to say what a man is. Underneath the film there is a performance but it is extremely difficult to say what the performance 'means.'" (Peggy Phelan, *Unmarked: The Politics of Performance*, London and New York: Routledge, 1993, pp. 96, 102.) And see Marjorie Garber, *Vested Interests: Cross-Dressing and Cultural Anxiety* (New York and London: Routledge, 1992), pp. 158–159.

42. Anne Hollander, *Seeing Through Clothes* (New York: Viking, 1978).

43. Quoted in Greg Tate, *Flyboy in the Buttermilk* (New York: Simon and Schuster, 1992), p. 115.

44. See John Baily, "Movement Patterns in Playing the Herati *dutr*," in Blacking, ed., *The Anthropology of the Body*.

45. "Stage dancer" is a specific band role in Britain, and has been at least since the days of Madness.

46. Francis Sparshott, *Off the Ground: First Steps to a Philosophical Consideration of the Dance* (Princeton, N.J.: Princeton University Press, 1988), p. 206.

47. See Adrian Stokes, *Invitation to the Dance* (London: Faber and Faber, 1942), p. 13.

48. As Sparshott points out, Adam Smith long ago noted that the type of movement valued in dance would be frowned on as "ostentatious" in ordinary life. See *Off the Ground*, p. 277. For a subtly choreographed move from walking to dancing see also the opening scene of *West Side Story* (thanks to Wendy Wolf for this example).

49. Like Francis Sparshott, I can't resist quoting here a 1588 account of what the function of dançe might be: "Dancing is practised to make manifest whether lovers are in good health and sound in all their limbs, after which it is permitted to them to kiss their mistress, whereby they may perceive if either has an unpleasant breath or exhales a disagreeable odour as of bad meat; so that in addition to divers other merits attendant on dancing, it has become essential for the wellbeing of society." ("Thoinot Arbeau" or Father Jean Tabourot, quoted in *Off the Ground*, p. 22.)

50. See Roderyk Lange, "Some Notes on the Anthropology of Dance," in Blacking, ed., *The Anthropology of the Body*, p. 243. Sarah Jeanne Cohen notes another distinction here between dance and sport: "For dance, both performer and audience shift into a special time-space dimension. This is not the case with sport." *Next Week, Swan Lake: Reflections on Dance and Dancers* (Hanover, N.H.: Wesleyan University Press, 1982), p. 66.

51. Cohen, *Next Week, Swan Lake*, p. 54. My emphasis.

52. It could be argued, I think, that the emphasis on effort (as against grace) is gendered—

in classic ballet, at least, men show the work that goes into their routines while women conceal it. Cohen suggests, though, that virtuosity, at least, should be seen as a personal rather than a gender quality, its "exuberance" reflecting the sense that the dancer is "rebelling" against "restrictions of form," so that our attention is drawn to the "tension" between dancer and music rather than, as is more usual, to their unity. See *Next Week, Swan Lake*, p. 75.

53. Banes, "Breaking," p. 83.

54. For discussion of these issues see Sparshott, *Off the Ground*, pp. 207–214.

55. See Banes, "Breaking," p. 87.

56. "To say that music is one of the essentials of dance is not to say that every dance must have a musical accompaniment. It is rather that some music is expected, even it be only a drum, and if there is no music, the dance is danced *in the absence* of music." (Sparshott, *Off the Ground*, p. 173. His emphasis.)

57. Edward T. Cone, *The Composer's Voice* (Berkeley: University of California Press, 1972), pp. 140–144. For the use of imitative or symbolic body movements in break dancing see Banes, "Breaking," p. 97.

58. For the most lucid and intelligent discussion of music video see Andrew Goodwin, *Dancing in the Distraction Factory: Music Television and Popular Music* (Minneapolis: University of Minnesota Press, 1992).

59. See Mark Fenster, "Genre and Form: The Development of the Country Music Video," and Robert Walser, "Forging Masculinity: Heavy-Metal Sounds and Images of Gender," in Simon Frith, Andrew Goodwin, and Lawrence Grossberg, eds., *Sound and Vision: The Music Video Reader* (London: Routledge, 1993).

60. It could be argued, in fact, that live audiences long ago learned how to respond to music from television—American programs like *American Bandstand* and *Soul Train* and British programs like *Ready Steady Go* and *Top of the Pops* were as significant in showing audiences as musicians at work. And the effect of such programs as the British music hall show *The Good Old Days* or the American country show *Hee-Haw* was undoubtedly to define (and mythologize) what it meant to enjoy live music hall or country shows.

61. For this argument see Lisa A. Lewis, "Being Discovered: The Emergence of Female Address on MTV," in Frith et al., *Sound and Vision*. Barbara Bradby has suggested that video allows male directors to "fragment" the female body just as record producers once fragmented female voices. My argument is that the viewer (and listener) still takes the (female) performer rather than the (male) director to be the source of musical meaning. See Bradby's "Sampling Sexuality: Gender, Technology and the Body in Dance Music," *Popular Music* 12(2) (1993).

11. Technology and Authority

1. Eduard Hanslick, *On the Musically Beautiful* [1854] (Indianapolis: Hackett, 1986), p. 72.

2. Evan Eisenberg, *The Recording Angel* (New York: McGraw-Hill, 1987), p. 158.

3. Quoted in Harry Allen, "Invisible Band," *Village Voice Electromag*, October 1988, p. 11.

4. As Shuhei Hosokawa has argued most eloquently, music can thus be treated as a form of information; the technologies at issue are information technologies—oral trans-

mission was supplemented by written information (the score), which was then supplemented by writing "sound with sound" (in the grooves), which was then supplemented by writing digitally (electronic instructions stored in hyperspace). See Hosokawa, *The Aesthetics of Recorded Sound* (Tokyo: Keisó Shobó, 1990), English summary, p. 2.

5. Glenn Gould, "The Prospects of Recording," *High Fidelity Magazine,* vol. 16, April 1966, p. 53.

6. Elizabeth Schwarzkopf, *On and Off the Record: A Memoir of Walter Legge* (London: Faber and Faber, 1982), p. 16. Legge mostly worked for EMI; his views were echoed by his colleague in Britain's other major classical music recording company from the 1930s to the 1960s, John Culshaw. See Culshaw's *Putting the Record Straight,* and David Hamilton, "Electronic Maestros," *New York Review of Books,* May 13, 1982.

7. Hamilton, "Electronic Maestros," p. 38.

8. For the record/book analogy see John McClure in Gould, "Prospects of Recording," p. 52.

9. Quoted in Gould, "Prospects of Recording," p. 47. This comment has often been reiterated—equally in vain—by rock musicians and critics, particularly since the rise of stadium rock concerts in which large sections of the audience hear a distorted or distant sound and can't see anything at all.

10. Theodor W. Adorno, "Opera and the Long-Playing Record" [1969], *October* 55 (1990): 64–66. Adorno is partly contrasting long-playing to "short-playing" records in this piece; he relates the latter to their epoch, "the desire for highbrow diversion" (see, for example, Thomas Mann's *The Magic Mountain*) and suggests that "this sphere of music is finished: there is now only music of the highest standards and obvious kitsch, with nothing in between. The LP expresses this historical change rather precisely."

11. Quoted in Gould, "Prospects of Recording," p. 49. And see p. 52.

12. Mohr quoted in Gould, "Prospects of Recording," p. 49; Arrau quoted on p. 52.

13. D. L. LeMahieu, *A Culture for Democracy* (Oxford: Clarendon Press, 1988), p. 85.

14. Philip Brophy, "The Architecsonic Object: Stereo Sound, Cinema and *Colors,*" in Philip Hayward, ed., *Culture, Technology and Creativity in the Late Twentieth Century* (London: John Libbey, 1991), pp. 107–108.

15. Gould, "Prospects of Recording," p. 54. There's no doubt that in rock too live recordings are "dated"—sound like archive recordings—in ways not necessarily true of studio recordings of the same music. It's as if they don't offer the same acoustic possibilities to changing ears; as if they do, in Gould's terms, capture just one, historically specific, spatio-temporal idea.

16. See Gould, "Prospects of Recording," p. 59. Scholes is quoted in LeMahieu, *A Culture for Democracy,* p. 87. I've always suspected that the CD's remote control was more significant for CD sales than its sound qualities, though it's not yet clear whether Personics ("You Pick the Songs! We Make the Tape!") will be a long-term commercial success. (The Personic catalogue for spring 1991 featured suggestions of tracks to include on tapes put together for loved ones in the Gulf War: "Sounds of Home," "Persian Gulf Blues," "Americana Songs." Personal choice, in other words, came prepackaged.)

17. Quoted in Gould, "Prospects of Recording," p. 59. In fact, the potential for active consumption is rarely matched by the practice: people are more likely to frequency-

hop than make up their own radio programs; to line up their CDs rather than to re-record tracks in a new order; to leave their hi-fi dials in much the same positions whatever music is playing.

18. Eisenberg, *The Recording Angel*, p. 144. And see Charles Keil, "People's Music Comparatively: Style and Stereotype, Class and Hegemony," *Dialectical Anthropology* 10 (1985): 124. The significance of records as resource and inspiration for both jazz and blues musicians is routinely noted in their biographies. For example, "Like many jazz artists of the twentieth century, including Lester Young and Charlie Parker, [Billie] Holiday received an important part of her musical education from records. By the time she was twelve, she had never left Baltimore but she had heard and studied closely the leading jazz artists of the world" (Robert O'Meally, *Lady Day* [New York: Arcade, 1991], p. 67).

19. Keil, "People's Music Comparatively," p. 125. For the simultaneous emergence of rock 'n' roll, examined from a similar perspective, see Richard A. Peterson, "Why 1955? Explaining the Advent of Rock Music," *Popular Music* 9(4) (1990). For a more general discussion of how recording technology determined popular concepts of the musically "authentic," see my "Art *vs* Technology: The Strange Case of Popular Music," *Media Culture and Society* 8(3) (1986).

20. Keil, "People's Music Comparatively," pp. 128–129.

21. Kenneth S. Goldstein, "A Future Folklorist in the Record Business," in Rosenberg, *Transforming Tradition*, pp. 118–121. Goldstein takes up another implication of the notion of good form here: "My experience has been that most people want to present themselves to the world formally, not informally." For folk singers, then, recorded "truth" was not something that made them sound "natural" but something that made them sound as they would most like to be heard. Goldstein saw his role in this respect as akin to that of the high street studio photographer, not snapping candid shots, but going to whatever technological trouble it took to capture people's *sense of themselves*.

22. Keil, "People's Music Comparatively," p. 129.

23. Alan Durant, "A New Day for Music? Digital Technologies in Contemporary Music-Making," in Hayward, ed., *Culture, Technology and Creativity*, p. 177.

24. Durant, "A New Day for Music?", p. 178.

25. For a useful summary of the ways in which early gramophones were sold in these terms domestically—"The mission of the Victrola is purely one of transmission"—see Holly Kruse, "Early Audio Technology and Domestic Space," *Stanford Humanities Review* 3(2) (1993). But even in these sales pitches, as Kruse notes, records were defined as "truthful" and "correct" in ideological as well as technical terms. Parents were told that these records would educate and uplift their children, keep them from becoming accustomed to "poor" music.

26. LeMahieu, *A Culture for Democracy*, p. 89.

27. Gary Giddins, "Computer Wars," *Village Voice*, December 8, 1992, p. 84.

28. Quoted in Harry Allen, "It Just Ain't Steak," *Voice Electromag*, October 1989, p. 7. Johnson also talks about digital recording giving the listener "a violin *sound* or a voice *sound*. It is, in fact, the sound of those instruments, but you can't reach in and pick out the individual instruments." See also David Schiff, "The Bounds of Music" (*The New Republic*, February 3, 1992), p. 32.

29. Aesthetic arguments about the results—what the music "should" sound like—are, in

practice, quickly overlaid here by accusations of remix engineers' sheer incompetence and of record companies' routine cheapness. There are too many CD "versions" of jazz and rock classics which have simply cut out crucial bits from the vinyl versions (Louis Armstrong's trumpet missing from his own recordings!) or completely misunderstood songs' acoustic dynamics (George Martin had to be called in to supervise a revised digital remix of the Beatles' *oeuvre*, while Jimmy Page made sure he took control of Led Zeppelin's digital reworkings himself).

For a useful round-up of jazz argument on this issue see Peter Pullman, "Digital Doldrums: Do CD Reissues Honor Jazz History or Mangle It?" *Voice Rock & Roll Quarterly*, March 1991.

30. Joseph Horowitz, *Understanding Toscanini* (New York: Alfred A. Knopf, 1987), p. 230.
31. Gould, "Prospects of Recording," p. 62.
32. The common feature of all the various record-based pursuits of "authentic" musical culture in this century (whether we look at blues or folk, jazz or "world music") is the constitutive role of the collector. "A dialectical energy of acquisitiveness and fantasy fuelled the [blues] revival," writes Jeff Titon, and the same point could be made about any of the other folk movements. Titon, "Reconstructing the Blues," in Rosenberg, *Transforming Traditions*, p. 226.

For an early account of the pleasures (and fetishism) of record collecting in the jazz world, see Stephen W. Smith, "Hot Collecting," in Fredric Ramsey and Charles Edward Smith, eds., *Jazzmen* (New York: Harcourt Brace, 1939).
33. Eisenberg, *The Recording Angel*, p. 162. And see Koestenbaum, *The Queen's Throat*, pp. 49–55.
34. Theodor W. Adorno, "The Curves of the Needle" [1928], *October* 55 (1990): 54. And see Dave Laing, "A Voice without a Face: Popular Music and the Phonograph," *Popular Music* 10(1) (1991). Adorno is referring implicitly here to the origins of the phonograph (in Edison's concept) as a *voice* preserving machine—for use in dictation, for example. The question becomes why it didn't develop (like the camera) as a tool for domestic records—baby's first words, alongside baby's first photo. Certainly in its early days the idea that one's voice could be preserved—and therefore possessed—apart from the body, as it were, intrigued writers. A. E. W.Mason, for example, tied the denouement of one of his detective stories (*The House of the Arrow*) around the victim's ability to speak, on phonograph record, after his death.
35. Adorno, "The Curves of the Needle," p. 54. Given that manufacturers have to make general choices about what sounds best, it is worth noting that radios and record players are usually designed to reproduce well the male rather than the female voice (just as film stock was developed to deal with white rather than black skin tones).
36. John Corbett, "Free, Single and Disengaged: Listening Pleasure and the Popular Music Object," *October* 54 (1990): 84–85.
37. Philip Brophy, "You Are There: Notes on 'Live' Music," unpublished paper, 1987, pp. 2–3.
38. Ibid., pp. 4, 5, 7.
39. Katherine Preston notes the very early selling of coin-operated phonographs in these terms: "These instruments will prove a great attraction in hotels, depots, church fairs, and all places where many people congregate." (Quoted in Preston, *Music for Hire*, pp. 236–237.) And it is arguable that the juke-box saved the record industry from the

effects of the depression in the 1930s. For the history of the use of records as public entertainment in Britain, see Thornton, *Club Cultures.*

40. Eisenberg notes that "when a number of people (a number greater than two) assemble in someone's home for the sole purpose of listening to records, they are much less likely to be family than friends, drawn together by an elective affinity." (*The Recording Angel,* p. 72.) The implication, I think, is that the *individual* identity that records define within the home needs public confirmation from outside it.

41. Quoted in LeMahieu, *A Culture for Democracy,* p. 84.

42. Brophy, "The Architecsonic Object," pp. 109–110. And see Frith, "Art *vs* Technology," for other examples of technology *expanding* our sense of music.

43. Michel Chion notes the implications of this distinction for how we read sound in film: "Take one image and compare the effect of a music cue played on a well-tuned piano with the effect of a cue played on a slightly out of tune piano with a few bad keys. We tend to read the first cue more readily as 'pit music,' while with the second, even if the instrument isn't identified or shown in the image, we will sense its concrete presence in the setting." *Audio-Vision,* p. 116.

44. Quoted in Horowitz, *Understanding Toscanini,* p. 415.

45. Jonathan Tankel, for example, describes the difference between the original Bob Clearmountain mix of Bruce Springsteen's "Dancing in the Dark," "coded for radio and home stereo," and the Arthur Baker remix, "recoded for the dance floor and the boom box." Jonathan David Tankel, "The Practice of Recording Music: Remixing as Recoding," *Journal of Communication* 40(3) (1990): 42–43.

46. For a subtle exploration of the issues here, relating them to the question of how we are placed by a film in cinematic space, see Philip Brophy, "The Architecsonic Object." The Keightley quote is from "The History and Exegesis of Pop" (M.A. thesis, Communications, McGill University, 1991), p. 78. Eisenberg notes how the introduction of stereo complicated listeners' understanding of "the phenomenology of the phonograph," "by adding a spatial, and hence a visual, aspect that at once clarified and confused . . . The exaggerated stereo effects used by rock producers serve not to project musicians in exterior space, but to direct listeners' attention to different zones of interior space." *The Recording Angel,* pp. 64–65.

47. John Corbett argues that one CD effect is to de-spatialize sound, to "conceal" music. A CD is an object with no material or visual presence, no posited spatial metaphor—digital music is music as time only. We could perhaps relate this to arguments about computer information generally—music too is now stored in hyperspace, as virtual sound. On the other hand, it could also be argued that music is used in computer games (as in animated films and pop videos) as a way of rooting sensations that might otherwise float spatially free. See Corbett, "Free, Single and Disengaged."

48. Tankel, "The Practice of Recording," p. 44.

49. Michael Ondaatje, *Coming Through Slaughter* (Toronto: General Publishing Co., 1976), pp. 93–94.

50. Steve Jones, "Critical Legal Studies and Popular Music Studies," *Stanford Humanities Review* 3(2) (1993): 88. His emphasis. And see Hosokawa, *The Aesthetics of Recorded Sound,* English summary, p. 8; Kramer, *The Time of Music,* pp. 45, 50, 69–70.

51. Quoted in Gould, "Prospects of Recording," p. 58. Babbitt interestingly echoes here a prediction made by Donald Tovey in the early days of recording: "There is nothing

to prevent the individual production of music directly in terms of the phonographic needle. That is to say, the composer, untrammelled by the technique of instruments, will prescribe all producible timbre in whatever pitches and rhythms he pleases, and will have no more direct cooperation with the craftsman who models the phonographic wave-lines, than the violinist may with Stradivarius." Quoted in Schutz, "Making Music Together," p. 165.

And see Alan Durant, "A New Age for Music?", p. 185: "At face value then, what this aspect [MIDI] of the technology leads to is extension and enrichment of traditional compositional processes, by offering solutions to problems of inaccurate, incomplete, or technically impossible performance, and by allowing for intensive scrutiny, manipulation and repair of anything entered into the machine."

52. For a useful account of current digital recording practices see Jeremy J. Beadle, *Will Pop Eat Itself? Pop Music in the Soundbite Era* (London: Faber and Faber, 1993), chap. 6. For general discussion of the issues here see Steve Jones, *Rock Formation: Music, Technology and Mass Communication* (Newbury Park, Calif.: Sage, 1992).

53. The best discussions of the issues here are Andrew Goodwin, "Sample and Hold: Pop Music in the Digital Age of Reproduction" [1988], in Frith and Goodwin, *On Record*; and Paul Théberge, "The 'Sound' of Music: Technological Rationalization and the Production of Popular Music," *New Formations* 8 (1989).

Now that the performance information embodied in a disc can be stored as MIDI data and used to drive other computers, music makers can also in effect compose new works *without knowing*. It would be possible, for example, as James Wyman suggests, to take a recorded performance (by Vladimir Horowitz, say, on a MIDI'd Yamaha grand piano), and use the resulting information "to play some sound other than a piano." See James Wyman, "It's MIDI Time," *Village Voice Electromag*, March 1989, p. 16. Sound can also be used in terms of "hypermedia" or a "hypertext," to drive images and written texts too.

54. One of the more ironic effects of such updating is the pursuit of the "authentic" performance: period instruments played in period settings and acoustics, brought to you by the magic of digital recording. (Thanks to Deborah Cameron for this point.)

55. There are aspects of this that I am too old to understand. How, for example, do people listen to CD singles, with their four or five versions of the same track? All through? Different mixes chosen on different occasions, in different moods? One version the favorite and programmed to repeat? The industry assumes this last habit; the other mixes are there for radio and/or club use. In practice I suspect that consumers "choose" the version familiar from club or radio play anyway. I remain a 7" single fetishist who never even played the B-side.

56. See Chris Cutler, "Necessity and Choice in Musical Forms, Concerning Musical and Technical Means and Political Needs" [1982], in his *File Under Popular* (London: RR Megacorp, 1991).

12. The Meaning of Music

1. Quoted (from a 1934 issue of *Modern Music*) in Joseph Horowitz, *Understanding Toscanini* (New York: Alfred A. Knopf, 1987), p. 267n.

2. Robert Cantwell, "When We Were Good: Class and Culture in the Folk Revival," in

Neil V. Rosenberg, ed., *Transforming Tradition* (Urbana and Chicago: University of Illinois Press, 1993), p. 38.

3. Quoted (from *Human, All-too-human*) in Julian Young, *Nietzsche's Philosophy of Art* (Cambridge: Cambridge University Press, 1992), p. 76.

4. Danto is quoted in Joseph Margolis, "Music as Ordered Sound: Some Complications Affecting Description and Interpretation," in Michael Krausz, ed., *The Interpretation of Music* (Oxford: Clarendon Press, 1993), p. 150. (Danto's article, "The Artworld," was published in *Journal of Philosophy* in 1964.) Compare Alfred Schutz's earlier sociological argument that musicians' ability to perceive the music in a score is founded not "on the conventional character of the visual signs," but rather on the "musical culture against the background of which the reader's or performer's interpretation of these signs takes place." See Schutz, "Making Music Together," p. 167.

5. My argument here is taken from Derrick F. Wright, "Musical Meaning and Its Social Determinants," *Sociology* 9(3) (1975): 424, 428.

6. Lucy Green, *Music on Deaf Ears* (Manchester: Manchester University Press, 1988), pp. 141, 143.

7. Quoted in Jonathan D. Kramer, *The Time of Music* (New York: Schirmer Books, 1988), p. 384.

8. Ola Stockfelt, "Adequate Modes of Listening," *Stanford Humanities Review* 3(2) (1993): 158.

9. Ibid., p. 159. For further discussion of how music "defines its own space but does so by moving through this space in its own unique manner," how "musical space, then, is a space of relationships," and how this relates to the "actual physical space in which music is performed," see Robert P. Morgan, "Musical Time/Musical Space" (*Critical Inquiry* 6 [1980]). Morgan observes that while people do read scores for pleasure, they don't read them like books (unless actually performing or preparing a performance) but skip back and forth "in the score's space" (p. 537).

10. Rose Rosengard Subotnik, *Developing Variations: Style and Ideology in Western Music* (Minneapolis: University of Minnesota Press, 1991), pp. 239, 249.

In her discussion of the relationship between the "musical" and "extra-musical" meanings of musical pieces, Lydia Goehr suggests that the "aesthetic character of a work" might be "derived or extrapolated, without derogatory connotation, from its historical character." In other words, what we hear as music's aesthetic value is not a quality *in* the music, but describes how we understand it in the framework of a historically specific interpretive musical culture. See Lydia Goehr, "Writing Music History," *History and Theory* 31(2) (1992): 194.

11. Kyle Gann, "What Normal People Hear," *Village Voice*, July 28, 1992, p. 86.

12. John Blacking, *"A Common-Sense View of All Music"* (Cambridge: Cambridge University Press, 1987), p. 146.

13. Alec Wilder, *American Popular Song* (New York: Oxford University Press, 1990), p. 289.

14. Keir Keightley, "The History and Exegesis of Pop," M.A. thesis, McGill University, 1991, p. 146.

15. I take this phrase from Goehr, "Writing Music History," p. 191.

16. Anthony Storr, *Music and the Mind* (London: HarperCollins, 1993), pp. 63, 76, 179.

17. Roger Scruton, "Notes on the Meaning of Music," in Krausz, *The Interpretation of Music*, p. 197.

18. Nicholas Cook, *Music, Imagination and Culture* (Oxford: Clarendon Press, 1990), pp. 1–2.

19. Robert Kraut, "Perceiving the Music Correctly," in Krausz, *The Interpretation of Music,* p. 113.

20. See Peter Kivy, *Music Alone* (Ithaca, N.Y.: Cornell University Press, 1990), p. 97.

21. Adam Smith, "Of the Nature of that Imitation which takes place in what are called the Imitative Arts" [1777?], in *Essays on Philosophical Subjects,* ed. W. P. D. Wightman and J. C. Boyne (Oxford: Clarendon Press, 1980), pp. 206–207.

22. See Carl Dahlhaus, *Esthetics of Music* [1967] (Cambridge: Cambridge University Press, 1982), p. 24.

23. See James A. Winn, *Unsuspected Eloquence* (New Haven: Yale University Press, 1981): "Renaissance thinkers had considered music inferior to poetry because its meaning was vague; later thinkers preferred music for that very vagueness" (p. 198).

24. Quoted in Dahlhaus, *Esthetics of Music,* p. 28.

25. Compare John Norris's 1678 "Letter Concerning Love and Music." Norris argued that music was an intellectual rather than a sensual pleasure because of "the Harmony and Proportion of Sounds." Music is "an Abstract and Intelligible Thing, and the Pleasure of it arises not from any Bodily Movement . . . but from the Soul itself contemplating the Beauty and Agreement of it." (Quoted in John Hollander, *The Untuning of the Sky* [New York: W. W. Norton, 1970], pp. 296–297.)

   Norris and Smith anticipate Peter Kivy—the expressiveness of music is explained by "the congruence of musical 'contour' with the structure of expressive features and behavior." See Peter Kivy, *The Corded Shell* (Princeton, N.J.: Princeton University Press, 1980), pp. 22–30, 50–52, 77. Music thus offers us the cognition of feelings rather than the feelings themselves (I take the latter position to be that of Susanne K. Langer and her followers).

26. Smith, "Of the Nature of that Imitation," p. 198.

27. Kevin Barry, *Language, Music and the Sign* (Cambridge: Cambridge University Press, 1987), pp. 60–61.

28. Smith, "Of the Nature of that Imitation," p. 185.

29. Ibid., p. 204.

30. Friedrich von Schlegel, "Fragments from *Das Athenaum*" [1798–1800], reprinted in P. Le Huray and J. Day, eds., *Music and Aesthetics in the Eighteenth and Early Nineteenth Centuries* (Cambridge: Cambridge University Press, 1981), p. 247; Jules Combarieu, "Music, Its Laws and Evolution" [1907], reprinted in Bojan Bujic, *Music in European Thought 1851–1912* (Cambridge: Cambridge University Press, 1988), p. 211.

31. Lydia Goehr, *The Imaginary Museum of Musical Works* (Oxford: Clarendon Press, 1992), p. 154.

32. Quoted in John F. Kassan, *Rudeness and Civility* (New York: Hill and Wang, 1990), p. 243. For the best account of the shift from music as rhetoric to music as object, see Mark Evan Bonds, *Wordless Rhetoric: Musical Form and the Metaphor of the Orator* (Cambridge, Mass.: Harvard University Press, 1991), and, for a more general discussion of what was involved here, Donald M. Lowe, *History of Bourgeois Perception* (Chicago: University of Chicago Press, 1982).

33. Cook, *Music, Imagination and Culture,* p. 15.

34. Eduard Hanslick, *On the Musically Beautiful* [1854; 1891] (Indianopolis: Hackett, 1986), p. 4.

35. Rose Rosengard Subotnik, "Towards a Deconstruction of Structural Listening: A Critique of Schoenberg, Adorno and Stravinsky," in E. Narmour and R. A. Solie, eds., *Explorations in Music, the Arts and Ideas* (Stuyvesant, N.Y.: Pendragon Press, 1988), p. 120.

36. Bonds, *Wordless Rhetoric*, p. 145, and see pp. 54, 68, 95, 133. The identification of music with rhetoric was, of course, another reason for the empirical philosophers' suspicion of it. For them, music was one of those arts of persuasion which, in Locke's words, "are for nothing else but to insinuate wrong ideas, move the passions, and thereby mislead the judgement, and so indeed are perfect cheats." (See Hollander, *The Untuning of the Sky*, p. 176.)

37. Goehr, *Imaginary Museum*, pp. 121, 178.

38. Hanslick, *On the Musically Beautiful*, p. 59. As a brooding, swaying pop fan, one of my pleasures in reading contemporary musicology has been to note the recurrent hostility of these professionals to the "amateur" listener—an interesting concept in itself. For musicians' resistance to the Hanslick line see Robert Francès, *The Perception of Music* [1958] (Hillsdale, N.J.: Lawrence Erlbaum Associates, 1988), p. 227.

39. Kant quoted in Le Huray and Day, *Music and Aesthetics*, p. 163; Adorno in Subotnik, "Towards a Deconstruction," pp. 104–105; Ives in Goehr, *Imaginary Museum*, p. 229.

40. Quoted in Goehr, *Imaginary Museum*, p. 210.

41. Quoted in Cook, *Music, Imagination and Culture*, p. 182.

42. Heinrich Adolf Kostlin, *Die Tonkunst* [1879], reprinted in Bujic, *Music in European Thought*, p. 154.

43. Robin Maconie, *The Concept of Music* (Oxford: Clarendon Press, 1990), pp. 116–117.

44. Roman Ingarden, *The Work of Music and the Problem of Its Identity* (London: Macmillan, 1986), pp. 117 and 151–152, and see the introduction by the translator, Adam Czerniawski, p. xii.

45. For this term see Patricia Carpenter, "The Musical Object," *Current Musicology* 5 (1967): 68; and Goehr, *The Imaginary Museum*, p. 173.

    Joseph Horowitz's *Understanding Toscanini* shows why the conductor consequently became the object of adulation. (He suggests that American orchestras had "consolidated a museum identity as showcases for dead masters" by 1870; pp. 134–135.)

46. For an ingenious attempt to transcribe—and so analyze—a studio track see Stan Hawkins, "Prince: Harmonic Analysis of Anna Stesia," *Popular Music* 11(3) (1992). The Coleman story is cited in Cook, *Music, Imagination and Culture*, pp. 158–159.

47. Hanslick, *On the Musically Beautiful*, p. 51.

48. John A. Sloboda, *The Musical Mind. The Cognitive Psychology of Music* (Oxford: Clarendon Press, 1985), p. 153.

49. Lenin is cited by Maxim Gorky in *Lenin on Literature and Art* (London: Lawrence and Wishart, 1967), p. 270; Freud is quoted in Pinchas Noy, "The Psychodynamic of Music, Part 1," *Journal of Music Therapy* 3(4) (1966): 127.

50. Laurence Kramer, *Music as Cultural Practice, 1800–1900* (Berkeley: University of California Press, 1990), p. 4.

51. G. Revesz quoted in Pinchas Noy, "The Psychodynamic Meaning of Music, Part II," *Journal of Music Therapy* 4(1) (1967): 11. My emphasis.

52. Richard Sterba, "Toward the Problem of the Musical Process," *The Psychoanalytic Review* 33 (1946): 41.

53. Smith, "Of the Nature of that Imitation," p. 201.

54. Deryk Cooke, *The Language of Music* (Oxford: Oxford University Press, 1959), p. 272. And see Roger Scruton, *The Politics of Culture and Other Essays* (Manchester: Carcenet Press, 1981), pp. 69, 87; and Nelson Goodman, *Languages of Art* (Oxford: Oxford University Press, 1969), pp. 255–265.

55. Cooke, *The Language of Music*, p. 205.

56. Sir William James, "Essays on the Poetry of Eastern Nations" [1772] and James Beattie, "An Essay on Music and Poetry as they affect the Mind" [1776], both reprinted in Le Huray and Day, *Music and Aesthetics*, pp. 145, 151.

57. Archibald Alison, *Essays on the Nature and Principles of Taste* [1790], reprinted in Le Huray and Day, *Music and Aesthetics*, p. 151.

58. Hanslick, *On the Musically Beautiful*, p. 23, and see pp. 20, 29.

59. Eduard von Hartmann, *The Philosophy of the Beautiful* [1887], reprinted in Bujic, *Music in European Thought*, p. 174.

60. Max Dessoir, "Aesthetics and General Theory of Art" [1906], in Bujic, *Music in European Thought*, p. 383. The best account of these issues remains Kivy, *The Corded Shell*.

61. Winn, *Unsuspected Eloquence*, p. 274. Winn notes that Berlioz, Lizst, and other mid-nineteenth-century composers accepted that "such programmatic hearing was inevitable," and provided their own program notes. In his study of a brass band contest in Yorkshire more than a hundred years later, Brian Jackson observed that the test piece was given a story in the program notes by the contest organizers—the composer had refused to supply one. See *Working Class Community* (London: Routledge and Kegan Paul, 1968), pp. 30–36.

62. As Kingsbury also notes, Leonard Meyer, writing from quite a different theoretical perspective, suggested that "in following and responding to the sound gestures made by the composer, the listener may become oblivious of his own ego, which has literally become one with that of the music." (A description that echoes Adam Smith.) See Henry Kingsbury, *Music, Talent and Performance* (Philadelphia: Temple University Press, 1988), pp. 171–177.

63. Frank Sibley, "Making Music Our Own," in Krausz, *The Interpretation of Music*, p. 165.

64. Sibley, "Making Music Our Own," p. 169. As he adds, the use of figurative description to characterize experience is not confined to music—such adjectives are a way in which we make sense of all aesthetic and, indeed, "natural" objects.

65. Ibid., pp. 175, 172.

66. Quoted in Cook, *Music, Imagination and Culture*, p. 160. Note also Roger Scruton's comment: "Surely it is this relation which most needs explaining: the relation between a listener, a piece of music, and a state of mind or character, which obtains whenever the listener *hears* the state of mind *in* the piece." ("Notes on the Meaning of Music," p. 197.)

67. See Kivy, *Music Alone*, p. 66.

68. Quoted (from *The Critic as Artist*) in Jan Mukarovsky, *Aesthetic Function, Norm and Value as Social Facts* (Ann Arbor, Mich.: University of Michigan, Department of Slavic Languages and Literature, 1970), pp. 76–77.

69. Ingarden, *The Work of Music*, p. 46.

70. Scruton, "Notes on the Meaning of Music," p. 199.

71. Storr, *Music and the Mind*, pp. 78, 149; Scruton, "Notes on the Meaning of Music," p. 200. And see David Lidov, "Mind and Body in Music," *Semiotica* 66(1/3) (1987): "Music is significant only if we identify perceived sonorous motion with somatic experience." If in graphic arts the basic reference point is "similarity" (and theories of representation), in music it is "causation," an interaction with the body (p. 70). Carolyn Abbate (drawing on Gustav Mahler) notes that deafness, "as a metaphor for loss of understanding," describes "the experience of observing moving forms with a sense of their emptiness." In Mahler's own words, "life becomes horrible to you, like the motion of dancing figures in a brightly-lit ballroom, into which you are peering from the outside, in the dark night—from such a distance that you can't hear the music they dance to!" (See Abbate, *Unsung Voices*, pp. 124–125.)

72. Storr, *Music and the Mind*, p. 183.

73. Scruton, "Notes on the Meaning of Music," p. 201.

74. "What makes a musician is not that he knows how to play one instrument or another, or that he knows how to read music: it is that he is able to grasp musical structure in a manner appropriate for musical production—the most obvious (though of course by no means the only) example of such production being performance." (Cook, *Music, Imagination and Culture*, p. 85.)

75. Ibid., p. 40.

76. Ned Rorem, *Settling the Score* (New York: Harcourt Brace, 1988), p. 228.

77. "A musical culture is a tradition of imagining sound as music. Its basic identity lies in its mechanism for constituting sounds as intentional objects, from the level of a single note to that of a complete work. This means that the ubiquitous discrepancies between the manner in which musicians conceive music and that in which listeners experience it are endemic to musical culture. Indeed, they define it." (Cook, *Music, Imagination and Culture*, p. 223.)

78. Roland Barthes, *Roland Barthes by Roland Barthes* [1975] (New York: Farrar, Straus and Giroux, 1977), pp. 55–56.

13. Toward a Popular Aesthetic

1. Aaron Copland, *Music and Imagination* (Cambridge, Mass.: Harvard University Press, 1952/1980), p. 111.

2. Carol Dix, *Say I'm Sorry to Mother: The True Story of Four Women Growing Up in the Sixties* (London: Pan, 1978), p. 40.

3. Theo van Leeuwen, "Music and Ideology: Notes Towards a Socio-semiotics of Mass Media Music," in Terry Threadgold, ed., *Sydney Association for Studies in Society and Culture Working Papers* 2(1) (1988): 29–30. Van Leeuwen is drawing here on John Shepherd and his colleagues' pioneering *Whose Music? A Sociology of Musical Languages* (New York: Transaction Books, 1977).

4. As Bruce Johnson remarks, what sounds "right" musically is therefore not just a matter

of music. A performer can be true to the sociability of an event while getting her notes quite wrong—in most popular genres we expect musicians to take risks, to make "mistakes." See Bruce Johnson, "Klactoveesedstene Music, Soundscape and Me," in Helmi Järviluoma, ed., *Soundscapes* (Tampere: Department of Folk Tradition, 1994), pp. 42–43.

5. Frank Kogan, "Spoonie Gee," *Reasons for Living* 2 (1986). "Spoonin' Rap" by Spoonie Gee (Sound Around Town, 1979); "Love Rap" by Spoonie Gee (Bobby Robinson Music, 1980).

6. Which inevitably means performance as narrative: "Someone once said that while Coleman Hawkins gave the jazz saxophone a voice, Lester Young taught it how to tell a story. That is, the art of personal confession is one jazz musicians must master before they can do justice by their tradition. I couldn't relate to Cecil's music until I learned to hear the story he was shaping out of both black tradition and his complex 'life as an American Negro.'" Greg Tate, *Flyboy in the Buttermilk: Essays on Contemporary America* (New York: Simon and Schuster, 1992), p. 25.

7. John Miller Chernoff, *African Rhythm and African Sensibility* (Chicago and London: University of Chicago Press, 1979), p. 36 (his emphasis). Compare Christopher Waterman on *Jùjú*: "Jùjú history suggests that the role of musical style in the enactment of identity makes it not merely a reflexive but also a potentially *constitutive* factor in the patterning of cultural values and social interaction. Yoruba musicians, responding creatively to changes in the Nigerian political economy, fashioned a mode of expression that enacted, in music, language, and behaviour, a syncretic metaphoric image of an ideal social order, cosmopolitan yet firmly rooted in autochthonous tradition. This dynamic style configuration, consonant with Yoruba ideologies of the 'open hierarchy' as an ideal pattern of aesthetic and social organization, allowed jùjú performance to play a role in the stereotypic reproduction of 'deep' Yoruba values during a period of pervasive economic and political change." Christopher A. Waterman, "*Jùjú* History: Toward a Theory of Sociomusical Practice," in Stephen Blum, Philip V. Bohlman, and Daniel M. Neuman, eds., *Ethnomusicology and Modern Music History* (Urbana and Chicago: University of Illinois Press, 1991), pp. 66–67.

8. See Paul Gilroy, "It Ain't Where You're From, It's Where You're At . . .," *Third Text* 13 (1990–91), and "Sounds Authentic: Black Music, Ethnicity, and the Challenge of a Changing Same," *Black Music Research Journal* 10(2) (1990).

9. Philip V. Bohlman, "Of *Yekkes* and Chamber Music in Israel: Ethnomusicological Meaning in Western Music History," in Blum, Bohlman, and Neuman, eds., *Ethnomusicology and Modern Music History*, pp. 259–260. For the practices of amateur music making in American academic communities, see Robert A. Stebbins, "Music Among Friends: The Social Networks of Amateur Musicians," *International Review of Sociology* 12 (1976).

10. Gina Arnold, *Route 666: On the Road to Nirvana* (New York: St. Martin's Press, 1993), p. 227.

11. John Blacking, *"A Commonsense View of All Music"* (Cambridge: Cambridge University Press, 1987), p. 129.

12. For another example of this process see Donna Gaines's graphic study of young people's use of music in American suburbia, *Teenage Wasteland* (New York: Pantheon, 1991).

13. Gilroy, "Sounds Authentic," p. 134.

14. Jonathan Rée, "Funny Voices: Stories, 'Punctuation' and Personal Identity," *New Literary History* 21 (1990): 1055.

15. Ibid., p. 1058. This is to echo Nietzsche's argument in *The Gay Science* that "the process of creating the self is an *artistic* process, a task of ordering the events in one's life that in some respects is analogous to the writing of a *Bildungsroman,* a story of the growth of personality from naivety to maturity, and in other respects is analogous to the task of constructing a character that will engage the esteem and attention of the reader." (Julian Young's summary in *Nietzsche's Philosophy of Art* [Cambridge: Cambridge University Press, 1992], p. 107.)

16. Kwame Anthony Appiah, *In My Father's House* (London: Methuen, 1992), p. 283.

17. Mark Slobin, *Subcultural Sounds* (Hanover and London: Wesleyan University Press, 1993), p. 55. In Nazi Germany, for example, music was used to differentiate youth groups in relation to the German state: against the Hitler youth were placed both the "Edelweiss Pirates," who used German pop music in a consciously working-class gesture against National Socialism and *volk* sounds, and the "swingers," who used English language jazz and a sense of international modernism. (See Detlev J. K. Peukert, "Young People: For or Against the Nazis?", *History Today,* October 1985.)

18. Simon Frith, *Literary Studies as Cultural Studies: Whose Literature? Whose Culture?* (Glasgow: University of Strathclyde, 1991), p. 21.

19. I take this point from Veronica Doubleday's review of Martin Stokes's *The Arabesk Debate* in *Popular Music,* 13(2) (1994).

20. Gilroy, "Sounds Authentic," p. 127.

21. Helen Myers quotes Channu, a village singer in Felicity, Trinidad: "Indian music sounds much sweeter. Whatever the Indian sing and whatever music they play, they don't do it of a joke. It's a serious thing for whoever understand it. It brings such serious feelings to you. Calypso they only sing. You might hear calypso. You will just feel happy to jump up. But if you hear a real technical piece of Indian music, you might sit down stiff and still, and you might be contrasting so much that you mightn't know when it start or when it finish." ("Indian Music in Felicity," in Blum, Bohlman, and Newman, eds., *Ethnomusicology and Modern Music History,* p. 236.)

   Myers notes (p. 240) that "in the past, villagers have tended to select Indian models for their temple repertory and for other religious contexts. They have selected Western models, including calypso, soca and disco, for dance and other entertainment music." For these Trinidadians, "Indianized pieces, borrowed from a twentieth-century urban Hindi culture," are therefore heard as "more authentic than the local Westernized repertory, a reflection of their New World heritage."

   And see Sara Cohen's current research on ethnic communities in Liverpool for further anthropological insight into how musical identities work.

22. Chernoff, *African Rhythm and African Sensibility,* pp. 125, 140.

23. As Appiah puts it: "The problem of who I really am is raised by the facts of what I appear to be: and though it is essential to the mythology of authenticity that this fact should be obscured by its prophets, what I appear to be is fundamentally how I appear to others and only derivatively how I appear to myself." (*In My Father's House,* p. 121.)

24. Ruth Finnegan, *The Hidden Musicians* (Cambridge: Cambridge University Press,

1989). And see Robert A. Stebbins, *Amateurs: On the Margin between Work and Leisure* (Beverly Hills and London: Sage, 1979).

25. Portishead, *Dummy*, Go-Beat, 1994.

26. Blacking, "*A Commonsense View of All Music*," p. 60.

Index